D A N U B E   C A N A L

Schottenring and Alsergrund
Pages 108–113

Stephansdom Quarter
Pages 70–89

Hofburg Quarter
Pages 90–107

Belvedere Quarter
Pages 144–159

STEPHANSDOM
QUARTER

HOFBURG
QUARTER

BELVEDERE
QUARTER

VIENNA

EYEWITNESS TRAVEL

VIENNA

Main Contributor **Stephen Brook**

LONDON, NEW YORK,
MELBOURNE, MUNICH AND DELHI
www.dk.com

Project Editor Carolyn Pyrah
Art Editor Sally Ann Hibbard
Editors Marcus Hardy, Kim Inglis
Designers Vanessa Hamilton, Andy Wilkinson
Design Assistant Elly King
Production Hilary Stephens
Picture Research Ellen Root
DTP Designer Adam Moore

Contributors
Gretel Beer, Rosemary Bircz, Caroline Bugler, Deirdre Coffey, Fred Mawer

Photographer
Peter Wilson

Illustrators
Richard Draper, Stephen Gyapay, Chris Orr, Robbie Polley, Ann Winterbotham

Printed and bound by L. Rex Printing Company Limited, China

First Published in Great Britain in 1994 by
Dorling Kindersley Limited
80 Strand, London WC2R 0RL

14 15 16 17 10 9 8 7 6 5 4 3 2

Reprinted with revisions 1994, 1995, 1996, 1997, 1998, 1999, 2000, 2001,
2002, 2003, 2004, 2006, 2008, 2010, 2012, 2014

Copyright © 1994, 2014 Dorling Kindersley Limited, London
A Penguin Random House Company

A CIP catalogue record is available from the British Library.

ISBN 978 1 40932 916 9

Floors are referred to throughout in accordance with British usage;
ie the "first floor" is the floor above ground level.

MIX
Paper from
responsible sources
FSC
www.fsc.org   FSC™ C018179

Front cover main image: Karlskirche, Vienna

◀ Interior of the Vienna Opera House

Contents

How to
Use this Guide **6**

Karl V, Holy Roman Emperor from
1519 to 1556 *(see p26)*

Introducing
Vienna

Great Days in
Vienna **10**

The History of
Vienna **18**

Vienna at a Glance **42**

Vienna Through the
Year **64**

Bronze and copper Anker Clock in Hoher
Markt *(see p86)*

Façade of Schönbrunn Palace *(see pp174–7)*

Vienna Area by Area

Grinzing restaurant *(see pp188–9)*

Travellers' Needs

Dobostorte *(see p206)*

Survival Guide

The Vienna Boys' Choir *(see p41)*

Karlskirche in the Belvedere
Quarter *(see pp148–49)*

HOW TO USE THIS GUIDE

This Eyewitness Travel Guide helps you get the most from your stay in Vienna with the minimum of difficulty. The opening section, *Introducing Vienna*, locates the city geographically, sets modern Vienna in its historical context and describes events through the entire year. *Vienna at a Glance* is an overview of the city's main attractions. *Vienna Area by Area* starts on page 68. This is the main sightseeing section, which covers all the important sights, with photographs, maps and illustrations. It also includes day trips from Vienna, a river trip and four walks around the city. Carefully researched tips for hotels, restaurants, cafés and bars, markets and shops, entertainment and sports are found in *Travellers' Needs*. The *Survival Guide* contains practical advice, from how to make a telephone call to using the transport system and its ticket machines.

Finding your Way around the Sightseeing Section

Each of the six sightseeing areas in the city is colour-coded for easy reference. Every chapter opens with an introduction to the part of Vienna it covers, describing its history and character, followed by a Street-by-Street map illustrating a typical part of the area. Finding your way around each chapter is made simple by the numbering system used throughout. The most important sights are covered in detail in two or more full pages.

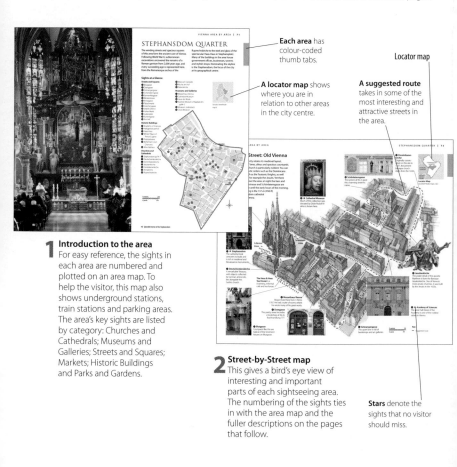

Each area has colour-coded thumb tabs.

A locator map shows where you are in relation to other areas in the city centre.

Locator map

A suggested route takes in some of the most interesting and attractive streets in the area.

1 Introduction to the area
For easy reference, the sights in each area are numbered and plotted on an area map. To help the visitor, this map also shows underground stations, train stations and parking areas. The area's key sights are listed by category: Churches and Cathedrals; Museums and Galleries; Streets and Squares; Markets; Historic Buildings and Parks and Gardens.

2 Street-by-Street map
This gives a bird's eye view of interesting and important parts of each sightseeing area. The numbering of the sights ties in with the area map and the fuller descriptions on the pages that follow.

Stars denote the sights that no visitor should miss.

Vienna Area Map

The coloured areas shown on this map *(see inside front cover)* are the six main sightseeing areas used in this guide. Each is covered in a full chapter in *Vienna Area by Area (pp68–181)*. They are highlighted on other maps throughout the book. In *Vienna at a Glance (pp42–63)*, for example, they help you locate the top sights. They are also used to help you find the location of the three guided walks *(pp182–9)*.

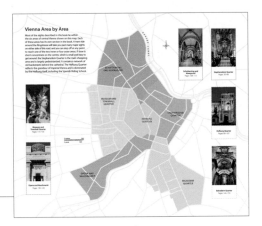

Numbers refer to each sight's position on the area map and its place in the chapter.

Practical information provides all the information you need to visit every sight. Map references pinpoint each sight's location on the *Street Finder* map *(pp262–7)*.

The visitors' checklist provides all the practical information needed to plan your visit.

3 Detailed information on each sight
All the important sights in Vienna are described individually. They are listed in order, following the numbering on the area map at the start of the section. Practical information includes a map reference, opening hours, telephone numbers, admission charges and facilities available for each sight. The key to the symbols used is on the back flap.

Stars indicate the features no visitor should miss.

4 Vienna's major sights
Historic buildings are dissected to reveal their interiors; museums and galleries have colour-coded floorplans to help you find important exhibits.

A timeline charts the key events in the history of the building.

INTRODUCING VIENNA

GREAT DAYS IN VIENNA

Whether you are a history buff, an art lover, an outdoors' enthusiast or a fan of thrill rides, in Vienna you will be sure to find something that appeals to you. From imperial palaces and art galleries to parks and a funfair, Vienna has attractions for everyone. Listed here are some ideas for themed days out and suggested itineraries for 2-, 3- and 5-day short breaks to get the most from the city. Prices include all travel, food and admission costs. Family pricing allows for two adults and two children.

Schönbrunn Palace, whose formal gardens contain a palm house and zoo

Vienna of the Habsburgs

Two adults allow at least €110

- Visit the vast Hofburg Complex
- Dine on Emperor's Pancakes
- Take a tour of Schönbrunn Palace and Gardens

Morning
Start the day early with a visit to the huge **Hofburg Complex** (see pp98–99), which includes the former Habsburg winter residence, a church, chapel, the **Spanish Riding School** (see pp100–101), museums and the Austrian National Library. Take a tour of the former **Habsburg State Apartments** (see pp102–3), the **Sisi Museum** (dedicated to Empress Elisabeth of Austria) and the Silberkammer, which houses the Imperial Silver Collection. For lunch, dine in the complex at the **Café Hofburg** (see p212), where traditional specialities such as *Kaiserschmarren* (Emperor's Pancakes) and *Rindsgulasch* (beef goulash) are served.

Afternoon
After lunch, take a trip out to **Schönbrunn Palace and Gardens** (see pp174–7), the former summer residence of the Habsburgs. Take the "Imperial Tour" of the palace, which will guide you through 22 of the palace's state rooms, aided by a free explanatory audio guide. You will be impressed by the palace's grandeur. If you still have time after the tour, wander out into the park and visit the garden's **maze** (see p174) and labyrinth for a unique outdoor adventure as well as some picturesque scenery.

The Mozart monument in the Burggarten, made by Viktor Tilgner in 1896

Green Vienna

Two adults allow at least €100

- Tour a Butterfly House
- Dine in a 1794 café
- Take a stroll on a man-made island
- Climb a 252-m (827-ft) tower

Morning
Start the day with a trip to **Burggarten** (see p104), a park in central Vienna that was created by the Habsburgs on land around the Hofburg. Here you can wander among the trees and view statues of Goethe, Mozart and Emperor Franz I. The park is also well known for its greenhouses, designed by the Jugendstil architect Friedrich Ohmann. Among them is the Butterfly House (*Schmetterlinghaus*), home to over 150 different species which fly around in a recreated rainforest environment. Next, take a lunch break at the nearby **Café Mozart** (see p213), on Albertinaplatz. In this historic and elegant café, which has been in existence since 1794, you can dine on gourmet vegetarian or traditional Austrian dishes and enjoy some pastries for dessert.

Afternoon
After lunch, pay a visit to **Donaupark** (see p163), which was created in 1964 and is one of Vienna's largest parks. Here you can go for a leisurely stroll or jog, or a ride along the cycle paths. For a relaxing moment, sit down by Lake Iris, which is an artificial lake in the centre. A must-see while in the park is the **Donauturm** (see p163),

Gustav Klimt's Beethoven Frieze on display in the Secession Building

which is 252 m (827 ft) high and has a revolving restaurant, a café and an observation deck. A lift will take you to the top of the tower where you can view the whole Vienna metropolitan area. On a clear day, the view stretches to beyond the city.

The elegant exterior of the historic and popular Café Mozart

Art and Architecture

Two adults allow at least €100

- Tour an art museum designed in Jugendstil
- Dine on classic Greek food
- View an imperial art history museum

Morning

Begin your day with a visit to the **Secession Building** *(see p142)*, which was designed in Jugendstil style and is now used as an exhibition hall for displays of contemporary art. Exhibitions have included Oswald Oberhuber and Maja Vukoje. The building is also home to Gustav Klimt's famous *Beethoven Frieze*. After viewing the art, try nearby **Kostas** *(see p216)* for a classic Greek lunch of moussaka.

Afternoon

Having eaten, head for the **MuseumsQuartier** *(see pp120–23)* and, for an unforgettable experience, visit the **Kunsthistorisches Museum** (Museum of the History of Art) *(see pp124–7)*. Here you easily can spend a whole afternoon viewing magnificent works of art and antiquities, many of which are from imperial Habsburg collections. The Picture Gallery on the first floor is especially impressive and features paintings from the artists Giovanni Bellini, Titian, Pieter Bruegel and Diego Velázquez among others. After a day of browsing, stop off at the restaurant-café-bar **Lux** *(see p215)*, just west of the MuseumsQuartier, for a glass of wine or some juice.

A Family Day

Family of 4 allow at least €200

- Explore the Volksprater Funfair in the Prater
- Lunch at the Prater's Schweizerhaus restaurant
- Ride a rickshaw along the Hauptallee

Morning

This day starts with a trip to the **Volksprater Funfair** *(see p164)*, the oldest amusement park in the world. Take a spin on the famous Ferris wheel built in 1897. Older kids might then like to ride on the daring Volare roller coaster, while parents with smaller children might enjoy the carousel, or the 4-km (2.5-mile) miniature railway. For lunch, visit the **Schweizerhaus restaurant** inside the park and sample some hearty fare, such as beef stew and fried chicken.

Afternoon

After lunch, families can rent a rickshaw (or, perhaps, a mountain bike, tandem or children's bike) from the Bicycle Rental Hochschaubahn stand, near the Hochschaubahn roller coaster. Go for a two-hour ride down the **Hauptallee** *(see p165)* in the Prater's green area, which is a boulevard famous for jogging and cycling, or just enjoying a pleasant stroll. Return to one of the funfair's fast-food stands for an ice-cream cone or soft drink.

One of the many attractions at Volksprater Funfair

2 Days in Vienna

- Take a stroll around the streets of Old Vienna
- Watch the elegant horses of the Spanish Riding School
- Enjoy the panorama from Vienna's famous Ferris wheel

Day 1
Morning Start at the landmark **Stephansdom** cathedral *(see pp74–7)*, then wander around the pedestrianised medieval streets of **Old Vienna** *(see pp72–3)*. Take a stroll along **Kärntnerstrasse** *(see p107)*, the city's main shopping street to the **Opera House** *(see pp140–41)* for a tour and perhaps tickets to the evening show.

Afternoon Pick up a **Ring Tram** *(see p254)* for a bargain 30-minute ride around **Ringstrasse** *(see pp34–5)*, Vienna's grandest boulevard. Then head to the **Wien Museum Karlsplatz** *(see p150)*, to learn about the city's history, or the **Belvedere** *(see pp154–9)*, for some fine Austrian art and attractive gardens.

Day 2
Morning Head to the **Hofburg** *(see pp98–99)*, the imperial palace of the Habsburgs, where the main draws are the sumptuous **State Apartments and Treasuries** *(see pp102–3)*. But first, see whether there are any tickets available for a performance of the **Spanish Riding School** *(see pp100–101)*, held frequently at 11am.

Afternoon Walk a city block from the Hofburg to the **MuseumsQuartier** *(see pp120–23)*, a superb cultural complex next to the **Kunsthistorisches Museum** *(see pp124–7)*. Choose carefully between the various museums here; it's all too easy to attempt to see too much. Afterwards, get some fresh air in the **Prater** park *(see pp164–5)*, and take a spin on the famous giant Ferris wheel.

A traditional horse-drawn carriage, or Fiaker, a fun way of getting around Vienna

3 Days in Vienna

- Explore the imperial marvels of the Hofburg palace complex
- Tour Vienna's grand opera house
- Take a ride in an old-fashioned carriage around Old Vienna

Day 1
Morning Visit the vast imperial palace of the Habsburgs, the **Hofburg** *(see pp98–99)*. Most visitors head straight to the lavish **State Apartments and Treasuries** *(see pp102–3)*, but be sure to leave time to visit the **Neue Burg** *(see p97)*, part of the palace complex and home to three interesting museum

The Kunsthistorisches Museum, housing Habsburg imperial art and treasures

collections. Get tickets for a show of the **Spanish Riding School** *(see pp100–101)*, held frequently at 11am.

Afternoon Take the **Ring Tram** *(see p254)* for the 30-minute loop around the elegant **Ringstrasse** *(see pp34–5)*, before getting off at the **Opera House** *(see pp140–41)* for a tour and perhaps tickets to a show. Wander up **Kärntnerstrasse** *(see p107)*, Vienna's main shopping street, en route to the **Stephansdom** *(see pp74–7)* cathedral. End the day with a ride in an open horse-drawn **Fiaker** *(see p251)* around **Old Vienna** *(see pp72–3)*.

Day 2
Morning Choose from several interesting art and culture museums at the **Museums-Quartier** *(see pp120–23)* and the adjacent **Kunsthistorisches Museum** *(see pp124–9)*. Afterwards, stroll over to the **Naschmarkt** *(see p138)* for an alfresco lunch from one of the food stalls here.

Afternoon Leave central Vienna, with a stop at the playful, fairy-tale-like **Hundertwasserhaus** *(see pp166–7)*, to explore **Prater** park *(see pp164–5)*. Be sure to take a ride on the Ferris wheel.

Day 3
Morning Head southwest of the city centre to verse yourself in Vienna's history at the fascinating **Wien Museum**

Karlsplatz *(see p150)*, and visit the beautifully ornate **Karlskirche** *(see pp148–9)* nearby.

Afternoon Leave the city centre for a peaceful walk around the **Belvedere** *(see pp154–9)*, with its lovely gardens and impressive art collection.

5 Days in Vienna

- Take a tour of Vienna's musical history
- See the work of Austria's finest artists at the Belvedere
- Wander the beautiful Schönbrunn palace and gardens

Day 1

Morning Start at the **Stephans-dom** *(see pp74–7)*, Vienna's great centrepiece cathedral, before wandering the pedestrianised medieval streets of **Old Vienna** *(see pp72–3)*, packed with shops, cafés and restaurants. Consider a pricey but fun introduction to the city by horse-drawn **Fiaker** *(see p251)*, from in front of the Stephansdom.

Afternoon Drop in on Mozart's old home at the **Mozarthaus Vienna** *(see p78)*, and continue the musical theme at the **Haus der Musik** *(see p82)*. Then, admire the musical monuments in the pretty **Stadtpark** *(see p184)*, or take in decorative art at the **Austrian Museum of Applied Arts** *(see pp84–5)*.

Day 2

Morning The old Habsburg imperial palace, the **Hofburg** *(see pp98–103)*, can easily occupy a whole morning, so be sure to prioritise seeing the **State Apartments and Treasuries** *(see pp102–3)* here. But before you do that, check to see whether there are tickets available for a performance of the **Spanish Riding School** *(see pp100–101)*, held frequently at 11am.

Afternoon The Hofburg has several excellent museums and galleries, particularly in the

The distinctive Secession building, built in Jugendstil style

Neue Burg *(see p97)*. Once you have had your fill of art, stroll down **Ringstrasse** *(see pp34–5)*, Vienna's historic boulevard, or see it from the **Ring Tram** *(see p254)* for a quicker ride to the flamboyant **Opera House** *(see pp140–41)*.

Day 3

Morning Begin the day with a lesson in Vienna's history at the magnificent **Wien Museum Karlplatz** *(see p150)*. Look in on the elegant **Karlskirche** *(see pp148–9)* on your way to the **Naschmarkt** *(see p254)* for lunch from one of its many street food stalls.

Afternoon The unusual **Secession Building** *(see p142)* is worth a closer look; but save some energy for the superb **MuseumsQuartier**

(see pp120–23) and the world-class art of the **Kunsthistorisches Museum** *(see pp124–9)*.

Day 4

Morning Start at the **Belvedere** *(see pp154–9)* to see works by some of Austria's finest artists: Gustav Klimt, Egon Schiele and Oskar Kokoschka. Head a little further out of town and visit the **Central Cemetery** *(see pp170–71)*, an elaborate resting place for many famous Austrians with a fascinating funerary museum.

Evening Lighten the mood with a look at the unusual municipal apartment block **Hundertwasserhaus** *(see pp166–7)* en route to the **Prater** park *(see pp164–5)*, where you can take a spin on the city's famous Ferris wheel.

Day 5

Morning Leave Vienna for the Rococo masterpiece **Schönbrunn** *(see pp174–7)*, the Habsburg's former summer residence. Spend some time exploring the beautiful palace gardens, which include a zoo, a maze, and some "Roman ruins", actually constructed in 1778.

Afternoon It's easy to spend a whole day at Schönbrunn, but to explore more widely, take a walk around the attractive adjacent neighbourhood of **Hietzing** *(see pp186–7)*. The quiet streets are filled with interesting architecture.

Schönbrunn Palace and Gardens, the former summer residence of the Habsburgs

Putting Vienna on the Map

Vienna has a population of about 1.75 million and covers an area of 415 sq km (160 sq miles). The River Danube flows through it and the Danube Canal flows through the city centre. It is the capital of the Republic of Austria, of which it is also a federal state, and is the country's political, economic, cultural and administrative centre. At the heart of Central Europe, it makes a good base from which to explore cities such as Bratislava, Prague, Budapest, Zagreb, Salzburg and Munich, as well as many Austrian towns.

Vienna and Environs

Floridsdorf
Nussdorf
Kagran
Raasdorf
Döbling
Brigittenau
Donaustadt
Ottakring
Leopoldstadt
Gross-
Enzersdorf
VIENNA
Donau
Hietzing
Simmering
Meidling
Favoriten
Mauer
Kaiserebersdorf
Mannswörth
Perchtoldsdorf
Zwölfaxing
Schwechat
Maria
Lanzendorf
Maria
Enzersdorf

KEY

☐ Urban Area

▬ Motorway

▬ Major road

Railway

Country boundary

Minor Road

Prague
Hradec
Kralove
EPUBLIC
Havlíčkův Brod
Tábor
Jihlava
Třebíč
České Budějovice
Znojmo
Gmünd
Horn
Mistelbach
Hollabrunn
SLOVAKIA
Zvolen
Freistadt
Rastenfeld
Krems
Stockerau
Trnava
Nitra
Melk
Tulln
St. Pölten
VIENNA
See inset
map above
Bratislava
Haag
Donau
Amstetten
Bruck an der Leitha
Steyr
Waidhofen
Eisenstadt
Neusiedler
See
Győr
Vác
Mitterbach
Wiener Neustadt
Neuenkirchen
Bromberg
Budapest
Windischgarsten
Hieflau
Oberpullendorf
Enns
Leoben
Bruck an der Mur
Szombathely
Székesfenérvár
Judenburg
Veszprém
HUNGARY
Friesach
Graz
Zalaegerszeg
Wolfsberg
Balaton
Lake
Dunaföldvár
Leibnitz
Klagenfurt
Drau
Maribor
Nagykanizsa
Szekszárd
Ptuj
Čakovec
Kaposvár
Celje
Varaždin
Pécs
Ljubljana
Koprivnica
SLOVENIA
Novo Mesto
Vrbovec
Drau
Rijeka
Zagreb
CROATIA
Nova
Gradiška
Oločac
BOSNIA AND
HERZEGOVINA
Bihać
Banja Luka

0 kilometres   100
0 miles   50

Central Vienna

This book divides Vienna into six areas in the centre of
town, and has further sections for sights on the outskirts
of the city, suggested walks and day trips, as well as
practical information. Each of the six main areas has its
own chapter, and contains a selection of sights that convey
some of that area's history and distinctive character, such
as the Stephansdom in the Stephansdom Quarter and the
imperial buildings in the Hofburg Quarter. Most of the
city's famous sights are in or close to the city centre and
are easy to reach on foot or by public transport.

Bars in Sterngasse
Sterngasse, in the Jewish Quarter *(see p86)*, is packed
with lively bars like these spilling out into the street.
This district is the oldest part of the city.

0 metres   500

0 yards   500

View over the Rooftops from Am Hof
Am Hof, the largest enclosed square in Vienna, is circled by a number of interesting houses, some with statuary on their roofs and pediments (see p89).

Rathauskeller Façade
The city has plenty of wine cellars – many associated with old vineyards – where wine, beer and simple food is served. This one is located beneath the city hall (see p132).

Pallas Athene Fountain
The figure of Pallas Athene by Carl Kundmann was placed on the fountain in front of the Parliament building in 1902 (see p123).

THE HISTORY OF VIENNA

Vienna was originally a Celtic settlement on the site of the present-day city. Under the Romans it became the garrison of Vindobona, supporting the nearby town of Carnuntum. Its location on the edge of the Hungarian plains, however, made it vulnerable to attack, and Barbarian invasions reduced the town to ruins by the early 5th century. In the 10th century, the German Babenberg dynasty acquired Vienna, and during their reign of almost three centuries the city became a major trading centre. Later, in the 13th century, Vienna came under the control of the Habsburgs. In the 16th century, Turkish invasions threatened Vienna and devastated its outskirts. Only in 1683 were the Turks finally defeated, allowing Vienna to flourish. Immense palaces were built around the court within the city, and in the liberated outskirts, and by the 18th century Vienna was a major imperial and cultural centre. Napoleon's occupation of Vienna in 1809 shook the Habsburgs' confidence, as did the revolution of 1848 – the year Franz Joseph came to the throne. By 1914, Vienna's population had expanded to two million, as people from all over the Habsburg Empire flocked to this vibrant centre. After World War I, the Habsburg Empire collapsed and Vienna's role as the Imperial capital ended. In the following years a strong municipal government – "Red Vienna"– tried to solve the social problems of the city. Austria was annexed by Nazi Germany in the Anschluss of 1938 and then, following Hitler's defeat in 1945, came under Allied control. Vienna regained its independence in 1955, when Austria became a sovereign state.

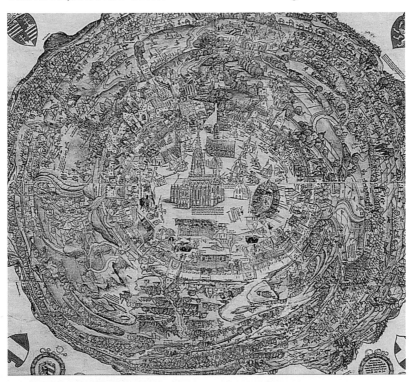

Circular plan of Turkish siege, from 1529

◀ Detail from *The Marriage of Joseph II to Isabella of Parma* (1760) by the Martin van Meytens School

Vienna's Rulers

Vienna emerged from the Dark Ages as a German outpost controlled by Babenberg dukes, who brought great prosperity to the city by the 12th century. There followed a period of social disorder, and intermittent Bohemian rule known as the Interregnum. Vienna fell into Habsburg hands in the 13th century and remained the cornerstone of their domains until the dynasty's downfall in 1918. From 1452 until 1806, Habsburg rulers were almost invariably elected as Holy Roman Emperor, enabling Vienna to develop as an Imperial capital on the grandest scale.

Duke Friedrich II with falconer

1278–82 Rudolf I of Germany is regent of Austria

1246–50 Interregnum under Margrave Hermann of Baden after death of Duke Friedrich II

900	1000	1100	1200	1300	1400
BABENBERG RULERS				**HABSBURG RULERS**	
900	1000	1100	1200	1300	1400

976 Leopold of Babenberg

1198–1230 Duke Leopold VI

1177–1194 Duke Leopold V

1358–65 Duke Rudolf IV

1141–77 Duke Heinrich II Jasomirgott

1251–76 Interregnum under Przemysl Ottakar II

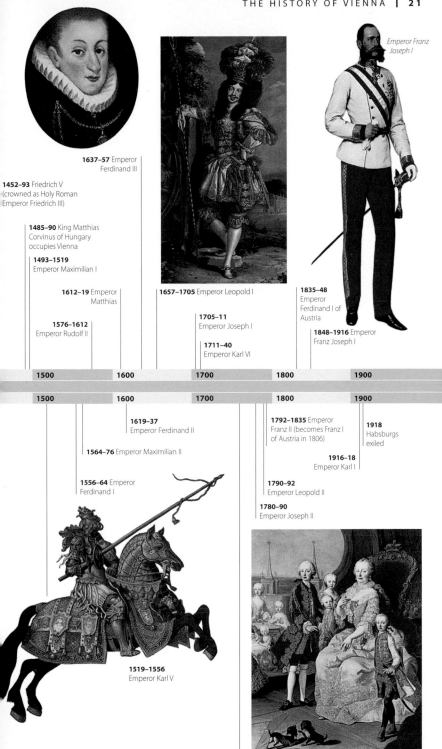

1637–57 Emperor Ferdinand III

1452–93 Friedrich V (crowned as Holy Roman Emperor Friedrich III)

1485–90 King Matthias Corvinus of Hungary occupies Vienna

1493–1519 Emperor Maximilian I

1612–19 Emperor Matthias

1576–1612 Emperor Rudolf II

1657–1705 Emperor Leopold I

1705–11 Emperor Joseph I

1711–40 Emperor Karl VI

Emperor Franz Joseph I

1835–48 Emperor Ferdinand I of Austria

1848–1916 Emperor Franz Joseph I

| 1500 | 1600 | 1700 | 1800 | 1900 |

| 1500 | 1600 | 1700 | 1800 | 1900 |

1619–37 Emperor Ferdinand II

1564–76 Emperor Maximilian II

1556–64 Emperor Ferdinand I

1519–1556 Emperor Karl V

1792–1835 Emperor Franz II (becomes Franz I of Austria in 1806)

1916–18 Emperor Karl I

1790–92 Emperor Leopold II

1780–90 Emperor Joseph II

1918 Habsburgs exiled

1740–80 Empress Maria Theresa

Early Vienna

The region around Vienna was first inhabited in the late Stone Age, and Vienna itself was founded as a Bronze Age settlement in about 800 BC. Settled by Celts from about 400 BC, the Romans incorporated it into the province of Pannonia in 15 BC, establishing the garrison of Vindobona by the 1st century AD. Later overrun by Barbarian tribes, Vindobona diminished in importance until the 8th century, when the Frankish Emperor Charlemagne made it part of his Eastern March and part of the Holy Roman Empire.

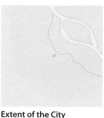

Extent of the City
▨ 150 AD　▢ Today

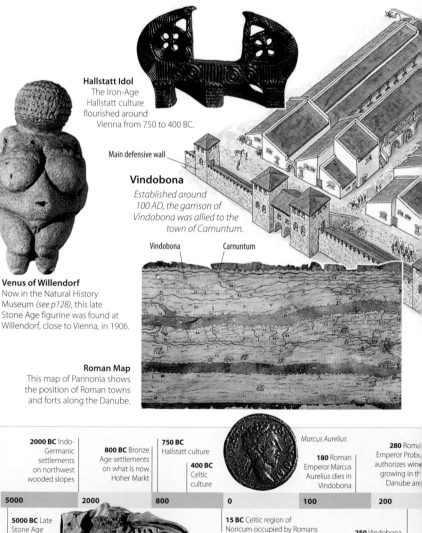

Hallstatt Idol
The Iron-Age Hallstatt culture flourished around Vienna from 750 to 400 BC.

Main defensive wall

Vindobona
Established around 100 AD, the garrison of Vindobona was allied to the town of Carnuntum.

Vindobona　　Carnuntum

Venus of Willendorf
Now in the Natural History Museum (see p128), this late Stone Age figurine was found at Willendorf, close to Vienna, in 1906.

Roman Map
This map of Pannonia shows the position of Roman towns and forts along the Danube.

2000 BC Indo-Germanic settlements on northwest wooded slopes

800 BC Bronze Age settlements on what is now Hoher Markt

750 BC Hallstatt culture

400 BC Celtic culture

Marcus Aurelius

180 Roman Emperor Marcus Aurelius dies in Vindobona

280 Roma Emperor Probu authorizes wine growing in th Danube are

| 5000 | 2000 | 800 | 0 | 100 | 200 |

5000 BC Late Stone Age culture

Preserved shoe from the Hallstatt culture

15 BC Celtic region of Noricum occupied by Romans

250 Vindobona, developed as a garrison town, has a population of 20,000

Marcus Aurelius
This great Roman emperor and philosopher came to Carnuntum to fight the Germanic tribes; he died in Vindobona in 180 AD.

Gold Jewellery
The Romans were first attracted to the region around Vindobona for its valuable resources, among them gold.

Stables

Soldiers' quarters

Soldier's Tomb
This tomb, excavated at Carnuntum, dates from around the 1st century AD.

Where to See Early Vienna

Many of the Roman walls and ditches have left their mark on the layout of Vienna, but excavations have not been numerous. The most impressive are at Hoher Markt (see p86), at No. 10 Am Hof (p89), and in the Michaelerplatz (p94). The most extensive remains are not in Vienna itself but at Carnuntum, about 25 miles (40 km) east of Vienna, where two amphitheatres and other ruins survive.

The Hoher Markt, in the very heart of Vienna, is the site of excavations of the Roman garrison of Vindobona.

This Gorgon's Head, a large Roman relief of the mythical Medusa, is from Hoher Markt.

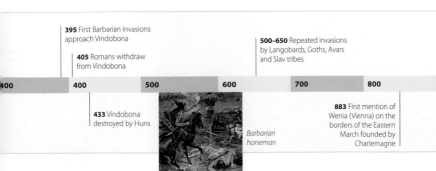

395 First Barbarian invasions approach Vindobona

405 Romans withdraw from Vindobona

433 Vindobona destroyed by Huns

500–650 Repeated invasions by Langobards, Goths, Avars and Slav tribes

400 | 400 | 500 | 600 | 700 | 800

Barbarian horseman

883 First mention of Wenia (Vienna) on the borders of the Eastern March founded by Charlemagne

Medieval Vienna

In 955 the Holy Roman Emperor Otto I expelled Hungarian tribes from the Eastern March *(see p22)*. In 976 he made a gift of Vienna to the German Babenbergs, who, despite further incursions by the Hungarians, restored the city's importance as a centre of trade and culture. Following Friedrich II's death in 1246 and the ensuing Interregnum *(see p20)*, the Habsburgs began centuries of rule over Austria. Vienna became a major European city and hub of the Holy Roman Empire.

Extent of the City

☐ 1400   ☐ Today

St Ruprecht
St Ruprecht was the patron saint of salt merchants, who brought this precious commodity along the Danube from salt mines in western Austria. Today his statue overlooks the Danube canal.

Death of Friedrich II
Duke Friedrich II was the last of the Babenbergs to rule Vienna. He died in battle against invading Hungarian forces in 1246.

Stephansdom ⟍

The Nobility
Often elected as Holy Roman Emperors, the Habsburgs attracted nobility from all over their huge empire.

Duke ⟍
Friedrich II

Coronation Robe
This magnificent medieval robe (1133), originally from Palermo, formed part of the Habsburg's imperial regalia.

---

955 Otto I of Germany defeats the Hungarians, restoring Christianity and re-establishing the Eastern March ("Ostmark", later renamed Ostarrichi)

1030 The Hungarians besiege Vienna

1147 Stephansdom consecrated

1136 Death of Margave Leopold III

900

1000

1100

909 Eastern March invaded by Hungarian forces

976 Otto I makes Leopold of Babenberg Margrave of the Eastern March, initiating Babenberg rule

1137 Vienna becomes a fortified city

1156 Heinrich II Jasomirgott moves his court to Vienna; builds Am Hof *(see p89)*

Richard the Lionheart
In 1192, Richard I of England, returning from the crusades in the Holy Land, was captured and held to ransom by Duke Leopold V.

Tributary of the River Danube

Medieval city wall

Where to See Medieval Vienna

Gothic churches include the Stephansdom (see pp74–7, Maria am Gestade (p87), the Burgkapelle, Minoritenkirche (p105), Ruprechtskirche (p83) and Augustinerkirche (p104). The Michaelerkirche (p94) includes some Gothic sculptures and the Schottenkirche medieval art (p112). Surviving medieval houses include the Basiliskenhaus in Schönlaterngasse (p80).

Verduner Altar
This masterpiece forms part of the treasury of the huge abbey at Klosterneuburg (see p163). Its 51 panels were completed in 1181 by Nikolaus of Verdun. The abbey itself was consecrated in 1136.

Stained glass (about 1340) in the Cathedral Museum (p80).

Hungarian encampment

University
Vienna's University was founded in 1365 by Duke Rudolf IV. This miniature (about 1400) shows the medieval university building and some of the tutors and their students.

1278–82 Rudolf I becomes ruler of Austria after defeating Ottakar II; 640 years of Habsburg rule follow	**1359** Rudolf IV lays foundation stone of the Stephansdom tower	**1477** Friedrich III's son Maximilian I marries Mary of Burgundy, heiress to the Low Countries
1288 Viennese uprising against Habsburgs crushed	**1365** University founded	

1200 **1300** **1400**

Seal of Przemysl Ottakar II

1 Vienna granted a charter

1246 Death of Friedrich II followed by Interregnum, during which Przemysl Ottakar II rules Vienna

1273 Count Rudolf of Habsburg crowned Rudolf I of Germany

1330 First Gothic section of Maria am Gestade built

1438 Albrecht V elected Holy Roman Emperor; Vienna made seat of Empire

1452 Friedrich V crowned as Holy Roman Emperor Friedrich III

1485 Vienna occupied by King Matthias Corvinus of Hungary

Renaissance Vienna

Under Maximilian I, Vienna was transformed into a centre for the arts. The Habsburgs were invariably elected Holy Roman Emperor, and by the 16th century their mighty empire had expanded into Spain, Holland, Burgundy, Bohemia and Hungary. But it was under constant threat: from Turkish attacks, the plague, and disputes between Protestants and Catholics that destabilized the city until 1576, when the Jesuits spearheaded the Counter-Reformation.

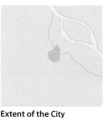

Extent of the City
◻ 1600   ◻ Today

Book Illustration
This Renaissance war wagon (1512) is from Maximilian I's collection of books of engravings and illustrations.

Maximilian I married Mary of Burgundy in 1477 and acquired the Burgundian domains.

Viennese Enamel Casket
This ornate enamel and crystal casket is typical of the skilful craftsmanship practised in Vienna in the 16th century.

Imperial Crown
This beautiful crown was made by Bohemian craftsmen in 1610 for Rudolf II and can now be seen in the Hofburg Treasuries *(see pp102–3.*

Ferdinand I married Anna of Bohemia and Hungary, and inherited Bohemia in 1526. It was a Habsburg domain until 1918.

1516 Maximilian's grandson, Karl V, inherits Spain

1519 Karl V inherits Burgundy titles and is elected Holy Roman Emperor; his brother Ferdinand I becomes Austria's archduke

1533 Ferdinand I moves his court to the Hofburg in Vienna

1556 Karl V's son, Philip II, inherits Spain; Ferdinand I takes Bohemia, Austria, Hungary, and imperial title

1571 Protestant Maximilian II allows religious freedom; 80% of city is Protestant

| 1500 | 1520 | 1540 | 1560 | 158 |

1498 Emperor Maximilian I founds Vienna Boys' Choir

Suleiman the Magnificent

1541 Plague

1572 Spanish Riding School founded

1490 Hungarians expelled from Vienna

1529 Graf Niklas Salm vanquishes Turkish army besieging Vienna

1551 Jesuits start Counter-Reformation

1577 Protestant services forbidden by Rudolf II

Triumphal Arch of Maximilian I
The German artist Albrecht Dürer (1471–1528) paid homage to Maximilian I in a famous volume of engravings, which included this design for a triumphal arch.

Philip I married Juana of Castile and Aragon in 1496 and acquired Spain.

Where to See Renaissance Vienna

The Schweizertor *(see p99)* in the Hofburg is the most colourful surviving remnant of Renaissance Vienna, though the Salvatorkapelle portal *(p87)* surpasses it in elegance. Also in the Hofburg is the Renaissance Stallburg *(p95)*. Some courtyards, such as those at No. 7 Bäckerstrasse *(p81)* and the Mollard-Clary Palace *(p96)*, preserve a few Renaissance features.

The Family of Maximilian I

Painted by Bernhard Strigel (around 1520), this portrait can be read as a document of how, by marrying into prominent European families, the Habsburg family was able to gain control of almost half of Europe.

Karl V inherited Spain from his mother, Juana of Castile and Aragon, in 1516.

Mary of Burgundy was married to Maximilian I and was Duchess of the Burgundian domains.

The Schweizertor, built in the 16th century, forms the entrance to the Schweizerhof of the Hofburg *(p99)*.

Alte Burg
The medieval core of the Hofburg was constantly being rebuilt. This engraving shows its appearance in the late 15th century, before Ferdinand I had it rebuilt in the 1550s.

...dallion ...mmem-orating ...ximilian II

1618 Bohemian rebellion starts Thirty Year's War

1629 Plague claims 30,000 lives

1643 Swedish forces threaten Vienna

1673–9 War with France over the Low Countries

1600 | **1620** | **1640** | **1660**

1598–1618 Protestantism is banned

1620 Ferdinand II defeats Protestant Bohemian aristocracy; Counter-Reformation spreads throughout Habsburg domains

1621 Jews expelled from Inner City

17th-century French infantry

Baroque Vienna

The Turkish threat to Vienna ended in 1683 when Kara Mustapha's forces were repelled. Under Karl VI the city expanded and the Karlskirche and the Belvedere palaces were constructed. Around the Hofburg, mansions for noble families sprang up, built by architects such as Johann Bernhard Fischer von Erlach *(see p149)* and Johann Lukas von Hildebrandt *(see p154)*. Vienna was transformed into a resplendent Imperial capital.

Extent of the City

1700   Today

Winter Palace of Prince Eugene
J B Fischer von Erlach and Johann Lukas von Hildebrandt designed the Winter Palace (see p82) for Prince Eugene, hero of the Turkish campaign.

Plague
This lithograph depicts the plague of 1679, which killed around 30,000 Viennese.

Turkish Bed
Ornamented with martial emblems, this bed was designed for Prince Eugene in 1707.

Coffee Houses
The first coffee houses opened in Vienna in the mid-17th century and they have been a prized institution ever since.

Baroque Architecture
Baroque architecture was at its most prolific in Vienna in the early 18th century.

Trautson Palace *(see p119)*

1683 Turkish siege of Vienna by 200,000 soldiers, under Kara Mustapha, from 14 July to 12 September

1700–14 The war of the Spanish Succession

1680

1690

1700

1679 Plague in Vienna

1683–1736 Prince Eugene of Savoy wins more victories over Turks and French, restoring Austria's fortunes

Kara Mustapha

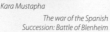

The war of the Spanish Succession: Battle of Blenheim

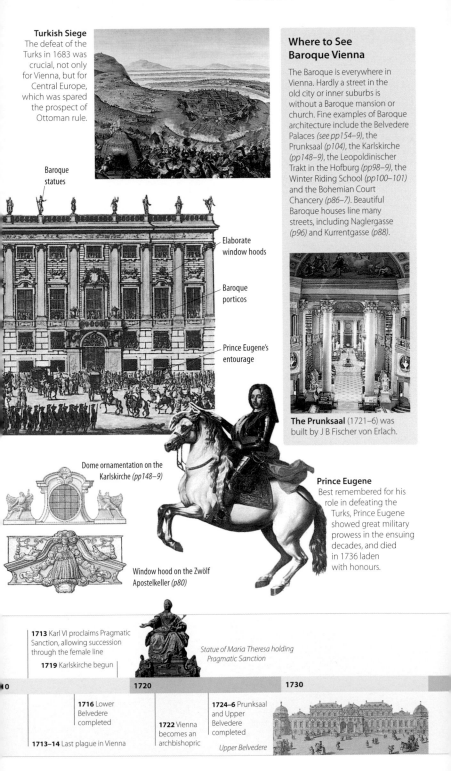

Turkish Siege
The defeat of the Turks in 1683 was crucial, not only for Vienna, but for Central Europe, which was spared the prospect of Ottoman rule.

Baroque statues

Where to See Baroque Vienna

The Baroque is everywhere in Vienna. Hardly a street in the old city or inner suburbs is without a Baroque mansion or church. Fine examples of Baroque architecture include the Belvedere Palaces (see pp154–9), the Prunksaal (p104), the Karlskirche (pp148–9), the Leopoldinischer Trakt in the Hofburg (pp98–9), the Winter Riding School (pp100–101) and the Bohemian Court Chancery (p86–7). Beautiful Baroque houses line many streets, including Naglergasse (p96) and Kurrentgasse (p88).

Elaborate window hoods

Baroque porticos

Prince Eugene's entourage

The Prunksaal (1721–6) was built by J B Fischer von Erlach.

Dome ornamentation on the Karlskirche (pp148–9)

Prince Eugene
Best remembered for his role in defeating the Turks, Prince Eugene showed great military prowess in the ensuing decades, and died in 1736 laden with honours.

Window hood on the Zwölf Apostelkeller (p80)

1713 Karl VI proclaims Pragmatic Sanction, allowing succession through the female line

1719 Karlskirche begun

Statue of Maria Theresa holding Pragmatic Sanction

1720

1730

1716 Lower Belvedere completed

1722 Vienna becomes an archbishopric

1724–6 Prunksaal and Upper Belvedere completed

Upper Belvedere

1713–14 Last plague in Vienna

Vienna under Maria Theresa

The long reign of Maria Theresa was a time of serenity, wealth and sensible administration, despite a background of frequent wars. The vast palace of Schönbrunn was completed by the Empress, who also presided over Vienna's development as the musical capital of Europe. She was succeeded by Joseph II, who introduced many reforms, including religious freedom and public health measures. However, these reforms made him unpopular with his subjects, including the nobility who were angered by the way he handed out titles to bankers and industrialists.

Extent of the City
1775   Today

Rococo Table
Wilhelm Martitz designed this Rococo table in 1769 for Maria Theresa, who employed artists committed to the elaborate Rococo style.

Karlskirche   Stephansdom

Young Mozart
Mozart often performed for the Habsburgs, who were highly receptive to his genius.

Burgtheater Programme
This programme was printed for the first performance of Mozart's *The Marriage of Figaro* in 1786, which took place in the original Burgtheater on Michaelerplatz.

Christoph von Gluck

1744–9 Schönbrunn Palace is extensively altered by Maria Theresa's court architect, Nikolaus Pacassi

1754 Vienna's first census records a population of 175,000

1740   **1750**   **1760**

1740 Maria Theresa comes to the throne; war of the Austrian Succession

1762 First performance of Christoph von Gluck's *(see p40) Orpheus and Eurydice* in the Burgtheater

1766 Prater, formerly an imperial game reserve, opened to the public by Joseph II

Schönbrunn Palace

Damenkarussell

This painting by Martin van Meytens depicts the Damenkarussell (1743), which was held at the Winter Riding School (see pp100–101) to celebrate the defeat of the French army at Prague.

Where to See Maria Theresa's Vienna

Schönbrunn Palace (see pp174–7) and the Theresianum (p153) date from the reign of Maria Theresa. Joseph II later commissioned the Josephinum (p113) and the Narrenturm (p113), and opened the Augarten (p166) and Prater (pp164–5) to the public. A Rococo organ is in the Michaelerkirche (p94), and some of Maria Theresa's tableware is in the Hofburg Treasuries (pp102–3).

Schönbrunn Palace is filled with Rococo interiors commissioned by Maria Theresa.

View from the Belvedere

Under Maria Theresa, the Viennese were able to enjoy a prosperous city. This townscape by Bernardo Bellotto (1759–61) shows them sauntering through the gardens of the Belvedere, with the palaces and churches of the city in the distance.

Belvedere Gardens

The Rococo high altar which is in the Michaelerkirche dates from around 1750.

The Pope

In 1782 Pope Pius VI came to Vienna in an attempt to undo the religious reforms of Joseph II.

1775 Augarten opened to the public by Joseph II

1781 Joseph II's Edict of Toleration

Allgemeine Krankenhaus

1784 Joseph II founds the Allgemeine Krankenhaus and Narrenturm (see p113)

70

1780

1790

1782 Pope Pius VI in Vienna

1786 First performance of Mozart's *The Marriage of Figaro* in the Burgtheater

1790–2 Emperor Leopold II

1791 First performance of Mozart's *The Magic Flute*

Biedermeier Vienna

Napoleon's defeat of Austria was a humiliation for Emperor Franz I. The French conqueror briefly occupied Schönbrunn Palace, demolished part of the city walls, and married Franz I's daughter. After the Congress of Vienna, Franz I and his minister, Prince Metternich, imposed autocratic rule in Austria. The middle classes, excluded from political life, retreated into the artistic and domestic pursuits that characterized the Biedermeier age. Revolution in 1848 drove Metternich from power but led to a new period of conservative rule under Franz Joseph.

Extent of the City

1830　　Today

Prince Metternich
The architect of the Congress of Vienna, Metternich gained political supremacy of Austria over four decades. In 1848 revolutionary mobs drove him from Vienna.

Assembly of statesmen at the Congress of Vienna, 1814–15 by Engelbert Seibertz

The Congress of Vienna

After the defeat of Napoleon in 1814, the victorious European powers gathered in Vienna to restore the established order that had been severely disrupted by the French emperor. The crowned heads and elected rulers of Europe spent a year in the city, where the court and nobility entertained them with a succession of balls and other diversions. The outcome was the restoration of reactionary rule across Europe that, although repressive in many countries, managed to maintain the peace until a series of revolutions swept across Europe in 1848.

The singer Michael Vogl

Franz Schubert playing the piano

1800 Vienna's population 232,000

1806 The Holy Roman Empire ends after Franz II abdicates and becomes Emperor Franz I of Austria

1811 Austria suffers economic collapse and state bankruptcy

1812–14 Napoleon defeated by Russia, Prussia, England and Austria

Franz Grillparzer

1800　　**1810**　　**1820**

1805 First performance of Beethoven's Eroica Symphony and *Fidelio* in Theater an der Wien. Napoleon wins victory at Austerlitz

1809 Napoleon moves into Schönbrunn Palace and marries Franz I's daughter Maria-Louisa

Napoleon Bonaparte

1815–48 Period of political suppression known as the Vormärz

1814–15 Congress of Vienna held under Presidency of Metternich; Austria loses Belgium but gains parts of Northern Italy

1825 Johann Strauss the Elder leads his first waltz orchestra

The 1848 Revolution
This painting from 1848 by Anton Ziegler shows the revolution in Vienna, when the middle classes and workers fought together against Metternich.

Biedermeier Chair
This style of furniture characterized the domestic aspirations of Vienna's middle classes in the 1820s.

Where to See Biedermeier Vienna

Napoleon's partial demolition of the city walls led to the creation of the Burggarten (p104) and the Volksgarten (p106). Domestic architecture flourished – Biedermeier houses include the Geymüllerschlössel (p162) and the Dreimäderlhaus (p133) – as did the applied arts (pp84–5).

The Geymüllerschlössel, dating from 1802, is home to Vienna's Biedermeier museum.

Schubertiade

Franz Schubert (see p40) wrote over 600 songs. These were often performed at musical evenings such as the one shown in this painting, An Evening at Baron von Spaun's, by Moritz von Schwind (1804–71).

The Grand Gallop
Waltzes, popularized by Johann Strauss I (the Elder) (see p40), were extremely popular in the 1820s.

1827 Death of Beethoven	**1830** Vienna's population reaches 318,000	**1837** First railway constructed	**1846** Johann Strauss the Younger becomes music director of the court balls until 1870	**1850** City population reaches 431,000
	1831–2 Cholera epidemic			
	1830		**1840**	
1828 Death of Schubert			**1845** Gas lighting introduced	
1831 The dramatist Franz Grillparzer completes *Des Meeres und der Liebe Wellen*			**1848** Revolution in Vienna; Metternich forced from office, and Emperor Ferdinand I abdicates to be replaced by Franz Joseph	

Ringstrasse Vienna

The Emperor Franz Joseph ushered in a new age of grandeur, despite the dwindling power of the Habsburgs. The city's defences were demolished and a circular boulevard, the Ringstrasse, was built, linking new cultural and political institutions. Vienna attracted gifted men and women from all over the empire, as well as traders from Eastern Europe. However, the resulting ethnic brew often resulted in overcrowding and social tension.

Extent of the City

☐ 1885   ☐ Today

Votivkirche (1856–79) *p113*
Heinrich Ferstel

Neues Rathaus (1872–83) *p132*
Friedrich von Schmidt

Parliament (1874–84)
p123 Theophil Hansen

The Natural History Museum
(1871–1890) *pp130–31*
Gottfried Semper

Kunsthistorisches Museum
(1871–1890) *pp124–9*
Gottfried Semper

The Suicide of Archduke Rudolf at Mayerling

In 1889 the 30-year-old heir to the throne was found dead with his mistress Mary Vetsera. The Archduke's suicide was more than a social scandal. It was a blow to the Habsburg regime, since he was a progressive and intelligent man. His despair may have been aggravated by court protocol that offered no outlet for his ideas.

Theophil Hansen
This Danish-born architect (1813–91) studied in Athens before settling in Vienna. The Greek influence is most evident in his Parliament building on the Ringstrasse.

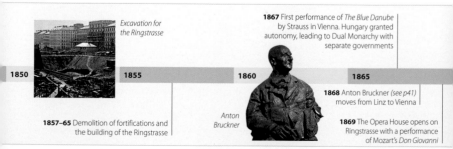

Excavation for the Ringstrasse

1867 First performance of *The Blue Danube* by Strauss in Vienna. Hungary granted autonomy, leading to Dual Monarchy with separate governments

1850

1855

1860

1865

1857–65 Demolition of fortifications and the building of the Ringstrasse

Anton Bruckner

1868 Anton Bruckner *(see p41)* moves from Linz to Vienna

1869 The Opera House opens on Ringstrasse with a performance of Mozart's *Don Giovanni*

The Danube
The River Danube often flooded its banks, so its course was altered and regulated in the 1890s by a system of canals and locks.

Vienna Café Society
In the 19th century, Vienna's cafés became the haunts of literary and political cliques.

Museum of Applied Arts
(1867–71) *pp84–5*
Heinrich Ferstel

Horse-drawn Trams
Trams appeared on the Ringstrasse in the 1860s. Horseless trams ran along it by the end of the 19th century.

Stadtpark

Opera House (1861–69) *pp140–41*
Eduard van der Nüll and August Siccardsburg

The Opening of the Stadtpark
Laid out on either side of the River Wien, the Stadtpark was inaugurated in 1862.

Ringstrasse

This great boulevard, built on the orders of Franz Joseph, separates the Stephansdom and Hofburg Quarters from the suburbs. Completed in the 1880s, the Ringstrasse is as grand now as it was then.

1874 First performance of Strauss's *Die Fledermaus* at the Theater an der Wien. Opening of Central Cemetery

1889 Suicide of Archduke Rudolf at Mayerling

70 — 1875 — 1880 — 1885

1873 Stock market crash

1872 Johannes Brahms settles in Vienna as director of the Gesellschaft der Musikfreunde. Death of Austrian poet and dramatist Franz Grillparzer

1879 Lavish historical parade along the Ringstrasse celebrates Franz Joseph's silver wedding

1890 Vienna expands as the outer suburbs are incorporated into the city

Vienna in the 1900s

The turn of the century was a time of intellectual ferment in Vienna. This was the age of Freud, of the writers Karl Kraus and Arthur Schnitzler, and of the Secession and Jugendstil *(see pp56–9)*. At this time artists such as Gustav Klimt and the architects Otto Wagner and Adolf Loos *(see p94)* created revolutionary new styles. This was all set against a decaying Habsburg empire, which Karl I's abdication in 1918 brought to an end. After World War I Austria became a republic.

Extent of the City
◻ 1912　　◻ Today

Wiener Werkstätte
Josef Hoffmann *(see p58)*, designer of this chair, was the principal artist and founder of this Viennese arts workshop *(see p85)*.

Kirche Am Steinhof
This stupendous church was designed by Otto Wagner and decorated by Kolo Moser (see p59).

Looshaus
The restrained elegance of this former tailoring firm is typical of Loos's style *(see p94)*.

The Secession
This poster by Kolo Moser *(see p59)* was used to publicize the Secession's exhibitions.

Angels by Othmar Schimkowitz

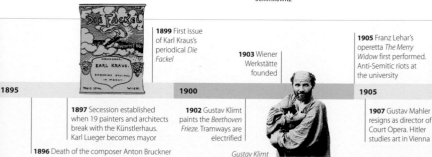

1899 First issue of Karl Kraus's periodical *Die Fackel*

1903 Wiener Werkstätte founded

1905 Franz Lehar's operetta *The Merry Widow* first performed. Anti-Semitic riots at the university

1895

1900

1905

1897 Secession established when 19 painters and architects break with the Künstlerhaus. Karl Lueger becomes mayor

1902 Gustav Klimt paints the *Beethoven Frieze*. Tramways are electrified

1907 Gustav Mahler resigns as director of Court Opera. Hitler studies art in Vienna

1896 Death of the composer Anton Bruckner

Gustav Klimt

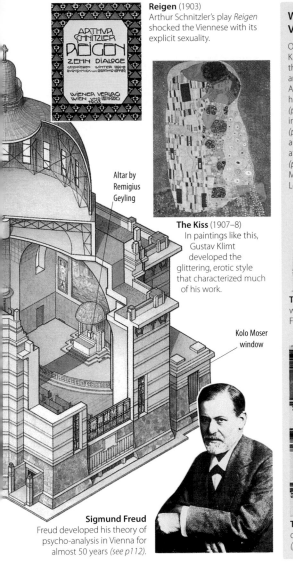

Reigen (1903)
Arthur Schnitzler's play *Reigen* shocked the Viennese with its explicit sexuality.

The Kiss (1907–8)
In paintings like this, Gustav Klimt developed the glittering, erotic style that characterized much of his work.

Altar by Remigius Geyling

Kolo Moser window

Sigmund Freud
Freud developed his theory of psycho-analysis in Vienna for almost 50 years *(see p112)*.

Where to See 1900s Vienna

Otto Wagner designed the Karlsplatz Pavilions *(see p150)*, the Wagner Apartments *(p143)* and the Kirche am Steinhof *(p162)*. Adolf Loos designed the Looshaus *(p94)* and the American Bar *(p107)*. Suburban architecture includes the Wagner Villas *(p162)*. Works by Klimt, Schiele and Kokoschka are displayed at the Upper Belvedere *(pp156–7)*, the Museum of Modern Art *(p122)* and the Leopold Museum *(p122)*.

The Secession Building is where Gustav Klimt's Beethoven Frieze is exhibited *(p57)*.

The Wagner Apartments are decorated with Jugendstil motifs *(p58)* by Kolo Moser *(p59)*.

1911 Death of Gustav Mahler

1914 Archduke Ferdinand assassinated in Sarajevo; international crisis follows resulting in World War I

1910

1915

1910 Death of Karl Lueger

1913 Arnold Schönberg's *Chamber Symphony* and works by Anton von Webern and Alban Berg performed at the Musikverein, provoking a riot

1916 Death of Franz Joseph

1908 *The Kiss* by Klimt is first exhibited

1918 Declaration of Austrian Republic after abdication of Emperor Karl I. Austria shrinks from an empire of 50 million to a state of 6.5 million

Modern Vienna

Two decades of struggle between the left and right political parties followed World War I, ending with the union of Austria with Germany – the Anschluss – in 1938. After World War II Vienna was split among the Allies until 1955, when Austria regained its independence.

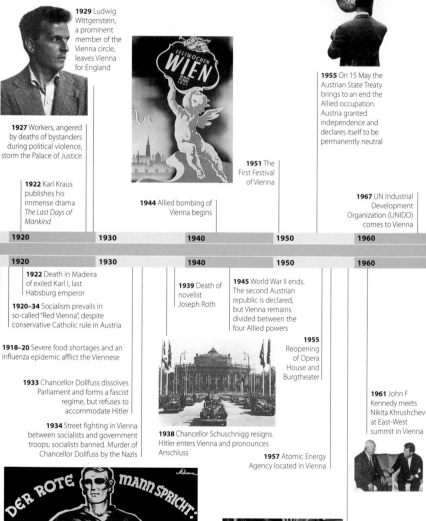

1929 Ludwig Wittgenstein, a prominent member of the Vienna circle, leaves Vienna for England

1927 Workers, angered by deaths of bystanders during political violence, storm the Palace of Justice

1922 Karl Kraus publishes his immense drama *The Last Days of Mankind*

1951 The First Festival of Vienna

1944 Allied bombing of Vienna begins

1955 On 15 May the Austrian State Treaty brings to an end the Allied occupation. Austria granted independence and declares itself to be permanently neutral

1967 UN Industrial Development Organization (UNIDO) comes to Vienna

1920	1930	1940	1950	1960

1920	1930	1940	1950	1960

1922 Death in Madeira of exiled Karl I, last Habsburg emperor

1920–34 Socialism prevails in so-called "Red Vienna", despite conservative Catholic rule in Austria

1918–20 Severe food shortages and an influenza epidemic afflict the Viennese

1933 Chancellor Dollfuss dissolves Parliament and forms a fascist regime, but refuses to accommodate Hitler

1934 Street fighting in Vienna between socialists and government troops; socialists banned. Murder of Chancellor Dollfuss by the Nazis

1939 Death of novelist Joseph Roth

1938 Chancellor Schuschnigg resigns. Hitler enters Vienna and pronounces Anschluss

1945 World War II ends. The second Austrian republic is declared, but Vienna remains divided between the four Allied powers

1955 Reopening of Opera House and Burgtheater

1957 Atomic Energy Agency located in Vienna

1961 John F Kennedy meets Nikita Khrushchev at East-West summit in Vienna

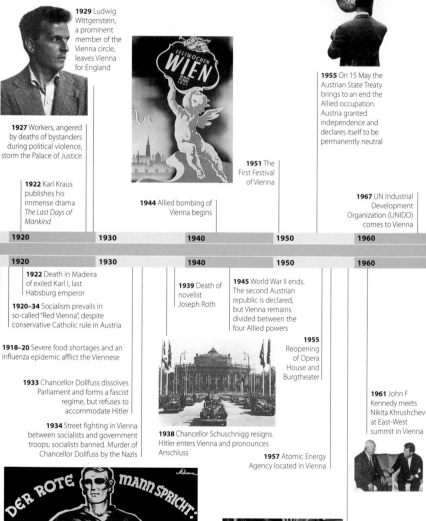

1959 Ernst Fuchs and Arik Brauer establish the school of fantastic realism

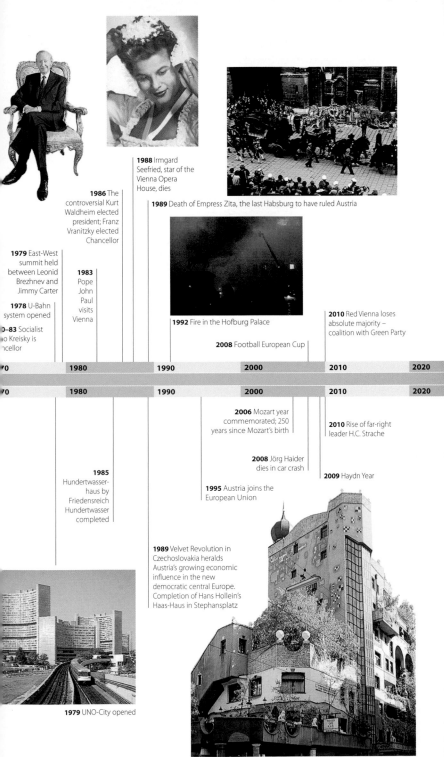

1988 Irmgard Seefried, star of the Vienna Opera House, dies

1986 The controversial Kurt Waldheim elected president; Franz Vranitzky elected Chancellor

1989 Death of Empress Zita, the last Habsburg to have ruled Austria

1979 East-West summit held between Leonid Brezhnev and Jimmy Carter

1983 Pope John Paul visits Vienna

1978 U-Bahn system opened

0–83 Socialist o Kreisky is ncellor

1992 Fire in the Hofburg Palace

2010 Red Vienna loses absolute majority – coalition with Green Party

2008 Football European Cup

| | 1980 | 1990 | 2000 | 2010 | 2020 |

70

| | 1980 | 1990 | 2000 | 2010 | 2020 |

70

2006 Mozart year commemorated; 250 years since Mozart's birth

2010 Rise of far-right leader H.C. Strache

2008 Jörg Haider dies in car crash

2009 Haydn Year

1985 Hundertwasser-haus by Friedensreich Hundertwasser completed

1995 Austria joins the European Union

1989 Velvet Revolution in Czechoslovakia heralds Austria's growing economic influence in the new democratic central Europe. Completion of Hans Hollein's Haas-Haus in Stephansplatz

1979 UNO-City opened

Music in Vienna

From the late 18th to the mid 19th centuries Vienna was the music capital of Europe, and its musical heritage and magnificent venues remain one of the city's chief attractions. At first the Habsburg family and the aristocracy were the city's musical paymasters, but with the rise of the middle classes during the Biedermeier period *(see pp32–3)* music became an important part of bourgeois life. Popular music also flourished as migration from all parts of the Habsburg Empire brought in richly diverse styles of music and dance.

Classicism

In the 18th century, Vienna's musical life was dominated by the Imperial Court. The composer Christoph Willibald Gluck (1714–87) was Court *Kapellmeister* (in charge of the court orchestra) to Maria Theresa until 1770, and wrote 10 operas specially for Vienna, including *Orpheus and Eurydice* (1762). His contemporary Wolfgang Amadeus Mozart (1756–91) later built on these foundations.

Joseph Haydn (1732–1809) moved to Vienna in the 1790s from Prince Paul Esterházy's palace in Eisenstadt, where his house is now a museum *(see pp178–9)*, and wrote masterpieces such as his great oratorio *The Creation*.

Performance of *The Creation* (1808) on Haydn's birthday

Romanticism

With the arrival of Ludwig van Beethoven (1770–1827) in Vienna in the mid-1790s, the age of the composer as romantic hero was born. Beethoven was a controversial figure in his time, and many of his most innovative works were only successful outside Vienna. His funeral, however, was a state occasion, and was attended by more than 10,000 people.

Performance of *The Magic Flute* (1791) by Mozart

The music of Franz Schubert (1797–1828) was little known in his short lifetime. He mostly performed chamber works, piano music and songs at Biedermeier *Schubertiaden* – evenings of music with friends. His music became more popular following his death. After this, "serious" music went through a fallow period in Vienna, but Johann Strauss I (1804–49) and Joseph Lanner (1801–43) began creating dance music, centred on the waltz.

The waltz was a sensation, not least because it was the first ballroom dance in

Biedermeier *Schubertiade* evening

which couples danced clasped closely together. The ladies of Vienna gained renown throughout Europe for the grace and tireless energy of their waltzing.

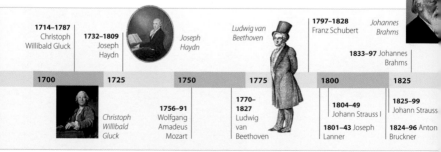

1714–1787 Christoph Willibald Gluck	**1732–1809** Joseph Haydn	*Joseph Haydn*	*Ludwig van Beethoven*		**1797–1828** Franz Schubert	*Johannes Brahms*
					1833–97 Johannes Brahms	
1700	**1725**	**1750**	**1775**	**1800**	**1825**	
		1756–91 Christoph Willibald Gluck · Wolfgang Amadeus Mozart	**1770– 1827** Ludwig van Beethoven	**1804–49** Johann Strauss I · **1801–43** Joseph Lanner	**1825–99** Johann Strauss · **1824–96** Anton Bruckner	

Age of Franz Joseph

A new era of high musical art began in the 1860s. Johannes Brahms (1833–97) came to Vienna in 1862, and incorporated popular musical styles into works such as his Liebeslieder waltzes and Hungarian Dances. The Romantic composer Anton Bruckner (1824–96) came to the city from Upper Austria in 1868. Johann Strauss II (1825– 99) rose to the status of civic hero, composing nearly 400 waltzes, including his famous operetta *Die Fledermaus*. One popular offshoot of the period was *Schrammel* music, named after Joseph Schrammel (1852–95) and characterized by an

Jugendstil poster (1901) for the Waltz depicting Johann Strauss II

ensemble of guitars, violins and accordion. Popular music also influenced Gustav Mahler (1860–1911), director of the Vienna Opera for 10 years.

The Moderns

The early years of the 20th century saw the rise of the Second Viennese School: Alban Berg (1885–1935), Arnold Schönberg (1874–1951) and Anton von Webern (1883–1945). These composers were not well received in Vienna, and Schönberg found he had to start his own society to get his works, and those of his colleagues, heard. In 1933 he emigrated to the USA.

Since World War II no composers of comparable stature have arisen, though Kurt Schwertsik (born 1935) and H K Gruber (born 1943) now attract international attention. However, the Vienna Philharmonic, established in 1842, is still one of the finest orchestras in the world. The State Opera continues to enjoy a strong reputation, and Vienna has an abundance of fine orchestras, opera and operetta venues, chamber ensembles and choirs, including the Vienna Boys' Choir.

The Johann Strauss II orchestra at a Court ball

Concert poster (1913) for Arnold Schönberg

1860–1911 Gustav Mahler	1874–1951 Arnold Schönberg	
	1875	
1883–1945 Anton von Webern	1885–1935 Alban Berg	
852–95 Joseph Schrammel		

Vienna Boys' Choir

The world-famous Vienna Boys' Choir, the Wiener Sängerknaben, was founded in 1498 by that great patron of the arts, Maximilian Today the boys perform masses by Mozart, Schubert or Haydn on Sundays and church holidays at the Burgkapelle *(see p105)*. To obtain a seat you need to book at least eight weeks in advance.

VIENNA AT A GLANCE

Vienna is a compact city and most of its sights are contained within a small area. However, the city boasts an astonishing array of monuments, palaces, parks and museums, which themselves house an impressive array of art and artefacts from all over the world and from all periods of history. Nearly 150 sights are listed in the *Area by Area* section of this book, but to help make the most of your stay, the next 20 pages offer a guide to the very best that Vienna has to offer. As well as churches, palaces, museums and galleries, there are sections on Jugendstil art and coffee houses. Many of the sights listed have a cross-reference to their own full entry. To start with, some of Vienna's top tourist attractions are listed below.

Vienna's Top Tourist Attractions

Opera House
See pp140–41.

Burgtheater
See pp134–5.

Prater
See pp164–5.

Karlskirche
See pp148–49.

Schönbrunn *See pp174–7.*

Spanish Riding School
See pp100–101.

Kunsthistorisches Museum
See pp124–9.

Stephansdom *See pp74–7.*

Belvedere
See pp154–9.

Café Central
See p63.

MuseumsQuartier
See p120–23.

◄ Close-up of the decorative roof tiles on the Stephansdom

Vienna's Best: Historic Houses and Palaces

Baroque mansions dominate the streets of the Stephansdom Quarter, while outside the centre of Vienna are the grand summer palaces where the Habsburg emperors and aristocracy lived during warm Middle European summers. The interiors of several of the houses can be visited, while others can only be admired from the outside or from their inner courtyards and staircases. Further details can be found on pages 46–7.

Sigmund Freud's House
This waiting room in the house on Berggasse, where Sigmund Freud lived from 1891 to 1938, has been lovingly restored.

Kinsky Palace
This mansion (1713–16) by Johann Lukas von Hildebrandt *(see p154)*, was built for the Daun family, and is sometimes called the Daun Kinsky Palace. Wirich Philipp Daun was commander of the city garrison, and his son Leopold Joseph Daun was Maria Theresa's field marshal.

Schottenring and Alsergrund

Museum and Townhall Quarter

Hofburg Quarter

Hofburg
The apartments here are made up of over 20 rooms; among them are ceremonial halls and living quarters which were once occupied by Franz Joseph *(see pp34–5)* and the Empress Elisabeth.

Opera and Naschmarkt

Schönbrunn Palace

0 kilometres 2
0 miles 1

Schönbrunn Palace
This palace, by J B Fischer von Erlach, was built on a scale to rival the palace of Versailles outside Paris. Parts of it were later redesigned by Maria Theresa's architect Nikolaus Pacassi *(see p174)*.

Neidhart Fresco House
Frescoes dating from 1400, depicting the songs of the medieval minnesinger Neidhart van Reuenthal, decorate the dining room of this former house of a wealthy clockmaker.

0 metres	500
0 yards	500

Mozarthaus Vienna
Mozart lived in this Baroque building for three years between 1784 and 1787, and composed one of his most famous works, *The Marriage of Figaro*, here.

Stephansdom Quarter

DANUBE CANAL

Winter Palace of Prince Eugene
J B Fischer von Erlach and Johann Lukas von Hildebrandt designed this Baroque palace, with its spectacular staircase, for the war hero Prince Eugene *(see pp28–9)*.

Belvedere Quarter

Zum Blauen Karpfen
A stucco relief of a blue carp and a frieze of *putti* adorn the façade of this 17th-century house on Annagasse.

Belvedere
Designed by Johann Lukas von Hildebrandt, Prince Eugene's summer palaces were built on what were originally the southern outskirts of Vienna. The Upper Belvedere now houses the Museum of Austrian Art.

Exploring Vienna's Historic Houses and Palaces

A stroll around Vienna's streets offers the visitor an unparalleled choice of beautifully preserved historic buildings, from former imperial residences to humbler burgher's dwellings. The majority date from the 17th and 18th centuries, and illustrate the various phases of Baroque architecture. In most cases their original function as residences of the rich and famous has been superseded; a number have now been turned into museums, and their interiors are open to the public.

Façade of the Schönborn-Batthyány Palace

Town Palaces

The most extensive town palace is the **Hofburg**, with its museums and imperial apartments. The staircase of the magnificent **Winter Palace of Prince Eugene** is on view to the public, as is the **Liechtenstein Palace** (1694– 1706), the winter home of the Liechtenstein family. The Neo-Gothic **Ferstel Palace** (1860) houses the Café Central (see p60). The **Obizzi Palace** is home to the Clock Museum (see p88) and the **Lobkowitz Palace** to a theatre museum (see p106). Town palaces which can be admired from the outside only are the **Kinsky Palace** (1713– 16), **Trautson Palace** and **Schönborn-Batthyány Palace**.

Garden Palaces

Although it seems strange that palaces within the city limits should be termed garden palaces, when they were built they were outside the city boundaries, and offered a cool refuge during the hot summer months for the inhabitants. The most famous example is **Schönbrunn Palace**, where the state apartments can be seen as part of a guided tour. The **Belvedere**, to the south of the city, houses the Museum of Austrian Art, and many rooms retain their original splendid decoration. The **Hermesvilla** (1884), a cross between a hunting lodge and a Viennese villa, was commissioned by Franz Joseph for his wife Elisabeth. The interior of the Neo-Classical **Rasumofsky Palace** (1806–7), can sometimes be seen on special occasions. The **Liechtenstein Garden Palace** houses the private art collection of the Liechtenstein family (see p113). The pieces include Renaissance sculpture and Baroque paintings.

Frescoed ceiling of the Liechtenstein Garden Palace

Suburban Villas

The Döbling district museum is housed in the Biedermeier **Villa Wertheimstein** (1834–5), where the interior is furnished in its original flamboyant and overcrowded manner. By contrast, the **Geymüller-schlössel**, containing the Sobek Collection of clocks and watches, is a model of taste and restraint. In Hietzing, the **Villa Primavesi** (1913–15) is a small Jugendstil masterpiece designed by Josef Hoffmann (see p58) for the banker Robert Primavesi.

Burghers' Houses

On Tuchlauben, the **Neidhart Fresco House** is decorated with secular frescoes from around 1400. Charming Baroque houses of modest dimensions can be seen on **Naglergasse** and **Kurrentgasse** and in inner districts such as **Spittelberg** and **Josefstadt**. A particularly fine example of external decoration can be seen on the Baroque inn **Zum Blauen Karpfen** in Annagasse (see p82). The **Dreimäderlhaus** in Schreyvogelgasse, built in an intermediate style between Rococo and Neo-Classicism, is also worth visiting.

Façade and gardens of the Hermesvilla

Memorial Houses

Vienna abounds in the former residences of famous composers. They are not all of great architectural merit, and their interest resides mainly in the exhibits they contain. The **Pasqualatihaus** was one of Beethoven's many Viennese residences – it was here that he composed the opera *Fidelio* – and it now houses portraits and other mementoes of the great composer. The **Heiligenstadt Testament House** (at No. 6 Probusgasse, Heiligenstadt), where Beethoven stayed in an attempt to cure his deafness, is now a memorial. The first-floor apartment of the **Haydn Museum** in Haydngasse is pleasantly furnished and

Courtyard of the Heiligenstadt Testament House

filled with letters, manuscripts, personal possessions and the composer's two pianos. Mozart and his family lived from 1784–7 in the **Mozarthaus Vienna**. This is where Mozart wrote *The Marriage of Figaro.*

The **Freud Museum** houses furnishings, documents and photographs, and the waiting room is as it looked when Sigmund Freud used to see his patients. It is also used as a study centre.

Decorative Details

Many of the historic houses and palaces of Vienna were built during a period corresponding to the Baroque and late Baroque styles of architecture. Details such as window hoods and pediments over doorways were often extremely ornate.

Caryatid on the doorway of the Liechtenstein Palace

Decorative window hood on the façade of the Trautson Palace

Decorative urns on the Lobkowitz Palace

Decorative pediment with shield on the Schönborn-Batthyány Palace.

Stucco *putti* on the façade of Zum Blauen Karpfen

Finding the Palaces and Houses

Vienna's Best: Museums and Galleries

Vienna boasts an astonishing number of museums, and many of the collections are housed in elegant former palaces or handsome buildings specially commissioned for the purpose. Some of the museums are of international importance, while others are of more local or specialist interest. Further details can be found on pages 50–51.

Sacred and Secular Treasuries
The Ainkurn sword (around 1450) can be seen in the Imperial Treasuries in the former imperial palace of the Hofburg.

Natural History Museum
This museum has displays of fossils, ethnography, mineralogy and a much-visited dinosaur hall.

Schottenring and Alsergrund

Museum and Townhall Quarter

Kunsthistorisches Museum
Hans Holbein's portrait of Jane Seymour (1536) is one of hundreds of Old Master paintings displayed in this fine art museum.

Hofbur Quarter

Opera and Naschmarkt

MuseumsQuartier
This vast cultural centre contains the largest Egon Schiele collection in the world, including this *Self-portrait with Lowered Head* (1912).

Albertina
This museum houses temporary exhibitions, mainly based on the Albertina's celebrated collection of prints and drawings (here, Albrecht Dürer's *The Hare* dated 1502).

Wien Museum Karlsplatz
Stained-glass windows from the Stephansdom (around 1390) are among the many items here documenting Vienna's history.

Cathedral Museum
This St Andrew's cross reliquary (about 1440) is one of many medieval religious treasures held by the cathedral.

Austrian Museum of Applied Arts
The applied arts of Vienna, such as this early 19th-century beaker and Wiener Werkstätte furniture *(see pp56–7)*, are among the varied artefacts on display in this museum.

DANUBE CANAL

Stephansdom Quarter

The Belvedere
The Upper Belvedere displays art from the Middle Ages onwards, including medieval painting and sculpture and Renaissance and Baroque works. Ferdinand Waldmüller's *Roses in the Window*, shown here, is part of this collection, as is Gustav Klimt's *The Kiss*. The Lower Belvedere and Orangery house temporary exhibitions.

Belvedere Quarter

Heeresgeschichtliches Museum
Paintings of battles and military commanders, such as Sigmund L'Allemand's portrait of Field Marshal Gideon-Ernst Freiherr von Laudon (1878), are part of this museum's collection.

0 kilometres 0.5
0 miles 0.25

Exploring Vienna's Museums and Galleries

Vienna's museums exhibit an amazing variety of fine, decorative and ethnic art from all periods of history and from different regions of the world. The visitor can see artifacts from all over the ancient world as well as more recent collections, from medieval religious art to 19th- and 20th-century paintings. Silverware is displayed in the city's imperial collections, and Vienna is also unrivalled for its turn-of-the-century exhibits.

Interior of Friedensreich Hundertwasser's Kunsthaus Wien

Ancient and Medieval Art

Vienna has marvellous collections of medieval art. The **Neidhart Fresco House** contains medieval secular frescoes, while a number of superb Gothic altarpieces can be seen in the historic Palace Stables at the **Belvedere**. Displayed in the **Cathedral Museum** are outstanding Gothic sculptures as well as masterpieces of applied art; the highlight is a 9th-century Carolingian Gospel. The **Sacred and Secular Treasuries** in the Hofburg are awash with precious medieval objects, including the insignia and crown of the Holy Roman Empire, and a unique collection of medieval objects and Gothic paintings is on display in the treasury of the **Deutschordenskirche**. The splendours of the Verduner Altar at **Klosterneuburg** await those

prepared to make a short journey out of the centre of Vienna. The **Ephesos Museum** of the Hofburg houses ancient Roman and Greek antiquities unearthed at the turn of the century.

Old Masters

The picture gallery in the **Kunsthistorisches Museum** has one of the best collections of Old Masters in the world, reflecting the tastes of the many generations of Habsburg collectors who formed it. There are works by Flemish and Venetian artists, and the best collection of Bruegels on display in any art gallery, as well as Giuseppe Arcimboldo's (1527–93) curious portraits composed of fruit and vegetables. The **Academy of Fine Arts** houses some fine examples of Dutch and Flemish works, its prize exhibit being Hieronymus Bosch's triptych of the *Last*

Judgement, which contains some of the most horrifying images in Christan art. There are also paintings by Johannes Vermeer (1632–75) and Peter Paul Rubens (1577–1640). The ground floor of the **Upper Belvedere** focuses on Austrian paintings and sculptures from the 17th and 18th centuries. The Belvedere itself is a masterpiece of Baroque architecture.

19th- and 20th-Century Art

A permanent display of 19th- and 20th-century Austrian art is housed in the **Upper Belvedere**. The most famous exhibits are by Gustav Klimt. *Beethoven Frieze* is regarded as one of the masterpieces of Viennese Art Nouveau and can be seen in the **Secession Building**.
   The Museum of Modern Art, which is located in the MuseumsQuartier (*see p122*), contains exhibits by 20th-century European artists. They include works by the Viennese avant-garde.
   The **Leopold Museum** has an enormous Egon Schiele collection, as well as Expressionist and Austrian inter-war paintings. The work of Friedensreich Hundertwasser, perhaps Vienna's best-known modern artist, is on show at the **Kunsthaus Wien**. Prints, drawings and photographs are housed in the **Albertina**.

Parthian monument (around AD 170) in the Ephesos Museum

The Applied Arts and Interiors

On display in the **Austrian Museum of Applied Arts** is a rich collection of the decorative arts, including Oriental carpets, medieval ecclesiastical garments, Biedermeier and Jugendstil furniture, and the archives of the Wiener Werkstätte. The **Wien Museum Karlsplatz** houses a reconstructed version of the poet Franz Grillparzer's apartment as well as Adolf Loos's (see p94) drawing room. In the **Silberkammer** of the Hofburg is a dazzling array of dinner services collected by the Habsburgs. The **Lobmeyr Museum** exhibits glassware designed by Josef Hoffmann.

Glass by Josef Hoffmann in the Lobmeyr Museum

Picture clock in the Clock Museum

Specialist Museums

Clock enthusiasts can visit the **Clock Museum** and the Sobek Clock and Watch Collection at the **Geymüllerschlössel**. Music is celebrated at the **Sammlung Alter Musikinstrumente**, while the darker side of life can be seen at the **Kriminalmuseum**, and at the **Bestattungsmuseum**, which houses exhibits to do with Viennese funeral rites. The **Heeresgeschichtliches Museum** houses reminders of Austria's military past. The **Hofjagd und Rüstkammer** exhibits historical weaponry. Other specialist museums include the **Österreichisches Filmmuseum** and the **Haus der Musik**.

Natural History and Science

Still occupying the building constructed for it in the 19th century is the **Natural History Museum**, which has displays of mineralogy, dinosaur skeletons and zoology. The **Josephinum** houses a range of wax anatomical models, while the **Technical Museum** documents the contribution Austria has made to developments in technology, ranging from home-made items such as an amateur wooden typewriter, to the invention of the car.

Ethnology and Folklore

Vienna's Museum of Ethnology in the Hofburg, the **Weltmuseum Wien**, contains objects from all over the world. There are artifacts from Mexico and a collection of musical instruments, masks and textiles from the Far East. The Benin collection from Africa is also on display in the museum (see p97). There is also a section on Eskimo culture. The **Museum für Volkskunde** in Josefstadt houses fascinating exhibits on Austrian folklore and rural life over the centuries.

Benin carving in the Weltmuseum Wien

Finding the Museums

Vienna's Best: Churches

Vienna's most potent symbol is its cathedral – the Stephansdom – a masterpiece of Gothic architecture which stands out in a city where the overwhelming emphasis is on the Baroque. After the defeat of the Turks in 1683 *(see pp28–9)*, many churches were built or remodelled in the Baroque style, although it is often possible to detect the vestiges of older buildings beneath later additions. Many church interiors are lavishly furnished, and several have fine frescoes. Churches are generally open during the day except when mass is being held. Stage concerts or organ recitals are given in the evenings in some churches. A more detailed overview of Vienna's churches is on pages 54–5.

Peterskirche
The tall dome of this late Baroque church dominates the view as you approach from the Graben.

Schottenring
and Alsergrund

Maria am Gestade

Hofburg
Quarter

Museum and
Townhall Quarter

Opera and
Naschmarkt

Michaelerkirche
This church has one of the most impressive medieval interiors in Vienna. The Neo-Classical façade and this cascade of Baroque stucco angels over the high altar were later additions.

Maria-Treu-Kirche
A statue of Mary Immaculate graces the square in front of this Baroque church (1716). Its façade dates from 1860.

0 kilometres   0.5
0 miles   0.25

Augustinerkirche
Antonio Canova's (1753–1822) tomb for Archduchess Maria Christina is in the Gothic Augustinerkirche, which once served as the Habsburgs' parish church.

Maria am Gestade
Dating from the 14th century, this church was restored in the 19th century. This 15th-century Gothic panel shows *The Annunciation*.

Ruprechtskirche
Vienna's oldest church has a Romanesque nave and bell tower, a Gothic aisle and choir, and stained-glass windows which date back to the turn of the 14th century.

Stephansdom
The richly carved Wiener Neustädter Altar from 1447 was a gift from Friedrich III *(see p21)*.

Jesuitenkirche
A series of twisted columns rise up to support the vault of the Jesuitenkirche (1623–31), which also features a *trompe l'oeil* dome.

Belvedere Quarter

ephansdom Quarter

ube Canal

Karlskirche
J B Fischer von Erlach's eclectic Baroque masterpiece (1714 –39) boasts a dome, minarets and two Chinese-inspired lateral pavilions.

Franziskanerkirche
The dramatic high altar (1707) by Andrea Pozzo features a Bohemian statue of the Virgin Mary as its centrepiece.

Exploring Vienna's Churches

Many of Vienna's churches have undergone modifications over the centuries, and they often present a fascinating mixture of styles, ranging from Romanesque to Baroque. The great era for church building in the city was in the 17th and 18th centuries, when the triumphant Catholic church, in a spate of Counter-Reformation fervour, remodelled several early churches and built new ones. A number of churches were also constructed after the Turks were defeated in 1683 *(see pp28–9)*, and the city as a whole was able to spread out beyond its earlier confines.

Medieval Churches

At the heart of the city is the **Stephansdom**. Parts date from Romanesque times but most of the cathedral is Gothic; it contains a collection of Gothic sculpture, including a pulpit by Anton Pilgram *(see p76)*. Vienna's oldest church is the **Ruprechtskirche**, which stands in its own square in the Bermuda Triangle *(see p86)*; its plain façade contrasts with the delicate Gothic tracery of **Maria am Gestade**, which has a filigree spire and a lofty, vaulted interior. The early interior of the **Deutschordenskirche** contains a number of heraldic blazons. A late Romanesque basilica with Gothic modifications lurks behind the façade of the **Michaelerkirche**. The 14th-century

Madonna and Child in the Minoritenkirche

Augustinerkirche contains the hearts of the Habsburg families *(see pp26–7)* down the centuries as well as Antonio Canova's tomb for Maria Christina *(see p104)*. The façade of the **Minoritenkirche** is built in French Gothic style with an ornate interior; the same is true of the **Burgkapelle**.

17th-Century Churches

There is little Renaissance architecture in Vienna, but a number of churches built before the Turkish siege survive. The **Franziskanerkirche**, with its gabled façade and theatrical high altar, and the **Jesuitenkirche** are fine examples of the architecture inspired by the Counter-Reformation *(see p26)*. The **Ursulinenkirche**, built between 1665 and 1675, has a high-galleried interior and **Annakirche** is notable for its beautiful Baroque tower. The **Dominikanerkirche** has a majestic early Baroque façade, built in the 1630s by Antonio Caneval. Although it dates back

to Romanesque times, the bulk of the rather squat **Schottenkirche** was built between 1638 and 1648. In the middle of the Baroque square of Am Hof is the impressive façade of the **Kirche am Hof**. It was founded by the Carmelites and is also known as "Church of the Nine Choir Angels".

Carving of St Anne (about 1505) in Annakirche, attributed to Veit Stoss

Late Baroque and Neo-Classical Churches

After the Turkish defeat *(see pp28–9)*, a number of Viennese High Baroque churches were built. The most exotic is the **Karlskirche**, and just off the Graben is the great **Peterskirche**. The tiny, ornate **Stanislaus-Kostka Chapel** was once the home of a Polish saint. Two graceful 18th-century churches are to be found on the edge of the inner city: the majestic **Maria-Treu-Kirche** and the **Ulrichskirche**. Joseph Kornhäusel's **Stadttempel** has a Neo-Classical interior.

Towers, Domes and Spires

Vienna's skyline is punctuated by the domes, spires and towers of its fine churches. Topping **Maria am Gestade** is a delicate openwork lantern, while the **Ruprechtskirche** tower is characteristically squat. The towers of the **Jesuitenkirche** are Baroque and bulbous, and **Karlskirche** has freestanding columns. **Peterskirche** has an oval dome and small towers.

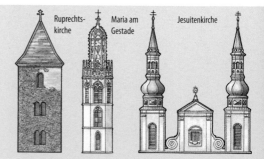

Ruprechtskirche   Maria am Gestade   Jesuitenkirche

The frescoed interior of the late Baroque Stanislaus-Kostka Chapel

19th-Century Churches

During the 19th century the prevailing mood of Viennese architecture was one of Romantic historicism. Elements of past styles were adopted and re-created, for churches and for many other municipal buildings, specifically on the Ringstrasse *(see pp34–5)*. The **Griechische Kirche** on Fleischmarkt, took its inspiration from Byzantine architecture, and the inside is replete with iconostases and frescoes. The **Votivkirche**, built just off the Ringstrasse as an

expression of gratitude for Franz Joseph's escape from assassination, is based on French Gothic architecture; its richly-coloured interior contains the marble tomb of Count Niklas Salm, who defended Vienna from the Turks during the siege of 1529 *(see p26)*. On Lerchenfelder Strasse the red-brick **Altlerchenfelder Kirche** is a 19th-century architectural hodge-podge of Gothic and Italian Renaissance styles.

20th-Century Churches

A masterpiece of early 20th-century church architecture is Otto Wagner's *(see p59)* massive **Kirche am Steinhof**, built to serve a psychiatric hospital. The interior has a slightly clinical air, since it is tiled in white, but the austerity is relieved by Kolo Moser's *(see p59)* stained-glass windows and mosaics. The **Luegerkirche**, which is located in the Central

The haphazard, sculpted blocks of the modern Wotruba-Kirche

Cemetery, was built by a protégé of Otto Wagner, Max Hegele, and has the same monumental feel about it. For true devotees of the modern, there is the **Wotruba-Kirche** on Georgsgasse in the suburb of Mauer, designed by the sculptor Fritz Wotruba. Not universally liked, this looks as if it is a haphazard assembly of concrete blocks.

19th-century interior of the Altlerchenfelder Kirche

Peterskirche

Karlskirche

Vienna's Best: Jugendstil

A stroll around Vienna's streets will reveal the
richness of the city's turn-of-the-century architecture.
Some of the buildings are well known and instantly
recognizable, and a few of the public ones, such as
the Secession building, can be seen inside. However, it
can be just as rewarding to discover the lesser-known
buildings and monuments of the period and to savour
the variety of finely-crafted architectural details.
Further details can be found on pages 58–9.

Strudelhof Steps
The setting for a famous novel of
the same name by Heimato von
Doderer (1896–1966), these
magnificent steps were built
by Theodore Jäger in 1910.

| 0 metres | 800 |
| 0 yards | 800 |

Schotten
and Alserg

Museum an
Townhall
Quarter

Wagner Apartments
Otto Wagner's two apartment blocks
(1899) overlook the River Wien. No. 40, the
Majolikahaus, is covered with ceramic
decoration. No. 38 has gold Jugendstil motifs.

Opera and
Naschmarkt

Kirche am Steinhof
Commissioned for the grounds of a lunatic asylum
on the outskirts of the city, this church with its grand
copper dome was designed by Otto Wagner in 1905.
The stained-glass windows are by Kolo Moser.

| 0 kilometres | 2 |
| 0 miles | 1 |

Otto-Wagner-Hofpavillon
Otto Wagner's imperial station
pavilion (1899) was built as a
showcase for his work.

Anker Clock
This clock, created by the artist Franz Matsch in 1911, sits on a bridge spanning two buildings on the Hoher Markt. Every hour, on the hour, moving figures parade across the clock face.

Postsparkasse
One of Otto Wagner's masterpieces, this post office savings bank exhibits the finest workmanship outside, and inside. Even the interior ventilator shafts are by Wagner.

Stadtpark Portals
The city's municipal park is adorned with magnificent portals (1903–7), designed by Friedrich Ohmann as part of a project to regulate the flow of the River Wien.

Karlsplatz Pavilions
Two pavilions standing in Karlsplatz were built as part of Otto Wagner's scheme for Vienna's turn-of-the-century underground system.

Secession Building
Nicknamed the Golden Cabbage because of its golden filigree dome, the Secession Building was designed at the turn of the century by Joseph Maria Olbrich for exhibitions of avant-garde art. In the basement is Gustav Klimt's *Beethoven Frieze*.

Danube Canal

Stephansdom Quarter

Hofburg Quarter

Belvedere Quarter

Exploring Viennese Jugendstil

The turn of the century saw a flowering of the visual arts in Vienna. A new generation of avant-garde artists formed the Secession in 1896 and, together with architects and designers, forged close ties between the fine and decorative arts, and created new architectural styles.

Hoffman tea service (1903) in the Austrian Museum of Applied Arts

Painting and Drawing

Viennese art at the turn of the century did not conform to one particular style, but there were common elements. These included an obsession with line and rich surface pattern, as well as themes such as the *femme fatale*, love, sex and death.

The finest collection of paintings from this period is in the **Belvedere** where pictures by Gustav Klimt (1862–1918) and Egon Schiele (1890–1918) feature prominently. Paintings by both artists and their contemporaries also form part of the permanent display at the **Wien Museum Karlsplatz**. Further examples are at the **Museum of Modern Art** in the MuseumsQuartier. The **Albertina** sometimes shows Schiele drawings. Klimt's *Beethoven Frieze* is in the **Secession Building**, and the decorative schemes he produced for the **Burgtheater** and **Kunsthistorisches Museum** are still in situ.

Decoration (1891) by Gustav Klimt in the Kunsthistorisches Museum

Applied Arts

The Wiener Werkstätte – an arts and crafts studio – was founded by Josef Hoffmann (1870–1956) and others in 1903, and produced jewellery, fabrics, ceramics, metalwork, cutlery, bookbinding and fashion accessories with the same artistic consideration normally given to painting or sculpture. An outstanding collection is in the **Austrian Museum of Applied Arts**, which also houses a document archive open to researchers. Glass designed by Hoffmann for the Viennese firm of Lobmeyr is displayed in the **Lobmeyr Museum**.

Favourite Jugendstil Motifs

Jugendstil motifs were similar to those employed by the French Art Nouveau movement, but were generally made up of a more rigorous, geometric framework. Decorations based on organic plant forms such as sunflowers were very popular, as were female figures, heads and masks. Abstract designs made up of squares and triangles were also used to great effect.

Sunflower motif from the Karlsplatz Pavilions by Otto Wagner

Postcard designed by Joseph Maria Olbrich from *Ver Sacrum*

Furniture

The leading Secession designers, such as Hoffmann and Kolo Moser (1868–1918), wanted interior design to return to the simple lines of Biedermeier style *(see pp32–3)* after the excesses of the Ringstrasse era. The **Austrian Museum of Applied Arts** has several interesting displays of their work, as well as that of the Thonet firm, which made the bentwood furniture admired by the Wiener Werkstätte. Furniture was often conceived as just one element of interior design. Unfortunately, many interiors have disappeared or are not open to the public, but the **Wien Museum Karlsplatz**, which also has some pieces of Jugendstil furniture, has a recreation of Adolf Loos's *(see p94)* living room. This is a rare example of a progressive Viennese interior from the turn of the century, created before the architect finally broke with the Secession.

Writing desk and chair by Kolo Moser (1903) in the Austrian Museum of Applied Arts

Altar in the Kirche am Steinhof (1905–7)

Architecture

Anyone walking around Vienna will notice several buildings with charming Jugendstil details. By the 1890s young architects were beginning to react against buildings of the Ringstrasse era, many of which were pastiches of earlier historical styles. The leading architects at this time were Otto Wagner (1841–1918) and Joseph Maria Olbrich (1867–1908), who collaborated on a number of projects, notably the design and installation of a new city railway and its stations, the most famous examples of which are the **Otto-Wagner-Hofpavillon** at Hietzing and the **Karlsplatz Pavilions**, as well as the **Wagner Apartments** on the Linke Wienzeile. Working independently, Wagner produced the extraordinary **Kirche am Steinhof** as well as the **Postsparkasse**, while Olbrich designed the **Secession Building** as an exhibition space

for radical artists and designers. Hoffmann created a number of houses for Secession artists in **Steinfeldgasse**. There are also some Jugendstil houses in **Hietzing**, while the **Anker Clock** by Franz Matsch (1861–1942) is an example of the late flowering of the style. Other examples of street architecture are the **Strudelhof Steps** (1910) by Theodore Jäger and the **Stadtpark Portals** by Friedrich Ohmann (1858–1927) and Joseph Hackhofer (1863–1917).

Postcard design by Joseph Maria Olbrich from *Ver Sacrum*

Gold leaf detail from the Wagner Apartments

Lettering by Alfred Roller from *Ver Sacrum*

Abstract fabric design by Josef Hoffmann

Vienna's Best: Coffee Houses

Coffee houses have been an essential part of Viennese life for centuries. More than just a place to drink coffee, they are meeting places, somewhere to linger over a snack or a light lunch, and refuges from city life. Each attracts its own clientele and has its own atmosphere. Most also serve alcohol. Further details of what coffee houses have to offer can be found on pages 62–3.

Landtmann
This comfortable and formal coffee house used to be frequented by Sigmund Freud. Today it is visited by theatregoers and actors from the nearby Burgtheater, and by journalists and politicians.

Schottenring and Alsergrund

Central
Once the meeting place of writers and free thinkers, the most splendid of all the coffee houses in Vienna has now been restored to its former grandeur.

Eiles
Its location near various government offices has made the Eiles a favourite haunt of officials and lawyers.

Museum and Townhall Quarter

Hofburg Quarter

Sperl
Just outside the city centre, the Sperl has a faithful clientele, including many young people who come here for the billiard tables and hot strudels.

Opera and Naschmarkt

Café Museum
The Café Museum was built in 1899 with an interior by Adolf Loos (see p94), but was remodelled in the 1930s to designs by Josef Zotti that replaced Loos's stylish but spartan seating with comfortable banquettes.

Hawelka
This famous coffee house has long cultivated its bohemian image. The atmosphere is warm and theatrical, and no visit to Vienna is complete without a late-night cup of coffee or a drink here.

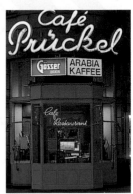

0 kilometres 0.5

0 miles 0.25

Prückel
The Prückel may not have the chic elegance of establishments like the Central, but it has become a mecca for bridge players and locals who crowd into its back room.

Danube Canal

Stephansdom Quarter

Belvedere Quarter

Kleines
One of the smallest, quaintest coffee houses in Vienna, the Kleines still attracts a loyal clientele of actors.

Frauenhuber
The oldest coffee house in Vienna, this is where Mozart once performed. Its location off Kärntner Strasse makes it handy for shoppers and for tourists visiting the nearby Stephansdom.

Exploring Vienna's Coffee Houses

The Viennese coffee house serves many functions and to make the best of the institution it helps to understand the many roles it plays in the lives of local people. In a coffee house you can read the newspapers, share a simple lunch with a friend, or in some play a game of bridge or billiards. Most places serve wines, beers and spirits as well as coffee. The coffee house is a priceless urban resource and, though no longer unique to Vienna, it is here that it has flourished in its most satisfying form. Vienna also has many *Café-Konditoreien (see p202)*.

Waiter at the Dommayer café

The History of the Coffee House

Legend maintains that the first coffee house opened its doors after the defeat of the Turks in 1683 *(see p28)*. However, historians insist that coffee was known in the city long before this date. Coffee houses took the form we know today in the late 18th century. They reached their heyday in the late 19th century, when they were patronized by cliques of like-minded politicians, artists, writers, composers, doctors or civil servants. In 1890, for instance, the controversial literary group Jung Wien met regularly at the **Griensteidl**, while the essayist Peter Altenberg was reputed to have never been seen outside his favourite café, the **Central**.

Today, as in the past, the **Ministerium**, **Museum**, **Frauenhuber**, **Raimund**, **Eiles**, **Schwarzenberg** and **Zartl** continue to attract their own specific clientele.

18th-century Viennese girl holding a coffee grinder

Coffee House Etiquette

There is a simple but formal etiquette attached to a coffee house. A waiter, almost certainly dressed in a tuxedo, however shabby the coffee house, will take your order, which will often be served with a plain glass of water. Once you have ordered you are free to occupy your table for as long as you like. A cup of coffee is not cheap, but entitles you to linger for an hour or two and to read the newspapers which are freely available. The grander coffee houses, such as the **Landtmann** and **Central**, will also have a selection of foreign newspapers and periodicals.

What Coffee Houses have to Offer

Coffee houses often function as local clubhouses. At the **Sperl** you can play billiards, at the **Prückel** there are bridge tables, and at the **Dommayer** you can

Types of Coffee

Just as the coffee house is a Viennese institution, so too are the extraordinary varieties of coffee that are available. Just asking for a cup of coffee in Vienna will not always guarantee a result, as the Viennese are exceedingly particular about how they take their coffee; over the centuries they have devised their own specific vocabulary to convey to the waiter precisely how they like their beverage served. The list that follows will cover most variations of the Viennese cup of coffee, although you may well find local ones.

Brauner: coffee with milk (small or large).
Melange: a blend of coffee and hot milk.
Kurz: extra strong.
Obers: with cream.
Mokka: strong black coffee.
Kapuziner: double Mokka with a hood of cream and a dusting of cocoa powder.
Schwarzer: black coffee (small or large).
Konsul: double Mokka with a dash of cream.
Koffeinfreier Kaffee: decaffeinated coffee.

Türkischer: plain, strong black Turkish coffee served in the traditional manner.

Espresso: strong black coffee made by machine. Ask for it *gestreckt* for a weak one.

attend literary readings. The **Central** and **Bräunerhof** both offer live piano music with your coffee. The **Kleines** is, as its name suggests, too tiny to offer entertainment, but still draws a regular crowd. The **Imperial** is part of the hotel of the same name. Coffee houses outside the city centre include the excellent **Westend**.

Coffee house sign

What to Eat

Most coffee houses offer snack foods throughout the day, simple lunches and occasional specialities, such as pastries, which are served at particular times. The **Hawelka** serves hot jam-filled buns *(Buchteln)* late at night, and the **Sperl** often has fresh strudel late morning. Larger coffee houses, such as **Diglas, Landtmann** and Bräunerhof, offer extensive lunchtime menus as well as a range of excellent pastries made on site.

Coffee Plain and Simple

There are times when you quite simply just want a good cup of coffee – when newspapers or a table of your own are luxuries you can dispense with. On such occasions you should keep an eye out for an Espresso bar, where you can lean informally against a counter and order coffee at a half or a third of the price you would normally expect to pay at a coffee house. The *Café-Konditoreien* belonging to the Aida chain, apart from serving delicious cakes and pastries, also function as Espresso bars.

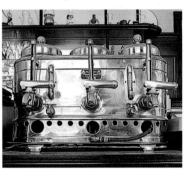

Old Viennese coffee machine in Diglas

Pharisäer: strong black, with whipped cream on top, served with a small liqueur glass of rum.

Schlagobers: strong black coffee served with either plain or whipped cream.

Einspänner: large glass of coffee with whipped cream on top.

Kaisermelange: black coffee with an egg yolk and brandy.

VIENNA THROUGH THE YEAR

Spring often arrives unexpectedly, with a few days of sunshine and warmth. The climax of spring is the Wiener Festwochen in May–June. Summers are long and hot, and ideal for swimming and for river trips on the Danube *(see pp180–81)* during July and August, when some venues officially close. Vienna comes alive again in September when the most important theatres reopen. More often than not, there is an Indian summer at this time, and it is still warm enough to sit in the Stadtpark. As autumn turns to winter, the streets fill with stalls selling chestnuts and by the feast of St Nicholas on 6 December, snow has often fallen. Christmas is a family occasion, but the New Year is celebrated in style as it heralds the start of the carnival season. The Wiener Tourismusverband *(see p239)* has details of important events.

Spring

Vienna is beautiful in spring and is the time for the **Wiener Festwochen** *(see May)*. It is also a season that brings a few days of balmy weather, and when beautiful colours appear in the parks and the Prater woods *(see pp164–5)*. This is the best time of the year to visit the Stadtpark *(see p100)* with its open-air bandstand and much-photographed resident peacock. The Volksgarten, Burggarten and the great parks of the Belvedere and Schönbrunn also come into their own and there are some splendid views of the city from the Stephansdom tower.

A collection of life-sized dolls on display during the Wiener Festwochen

March

Easter Market *(two weeks before Easter)*, held at the Freyung. Items on sale include arts, crafts and traditional food.
Schönbrunner Schlosskonzerte *(until end Oct)*, at the Orangery, Schönbrunn Palace *(see p174)*. Performances of popular melodies of Johann Strauss.

Runners taking part in the annual City Marathon

April

Volksprater Funfair *(1 Apr–31 Oct)*, held in the Prater woods *(pp162–63)*.
City Marathon starts from UNO-City by Donaupark *(see p163)*, passing Schönbrunn Palace, goes around the inner city and ends at Heldenpaltz at the Hofburg.
Frühlingsfestival *(2nd week Apr to mid-May)*. Classical music festival alternating between the Musikverein *(p150)* and the Konzerthaus *(p229)*.
Spanish Riding School *(until Jun)*. Lipizzaner horses' performances in the Winter Riding School *(pp100–101)*.
Hofburg Orchestra *(until Oct)*. Concerts at Musikverein *(p150)* and Hofburg *(pp98–9)*.
Kursalon *(until end Oct)*. Open-air concerts *(p229)*. Indoor concerts all year.

May

Tag der Arbeit *(1 May)*. Public holiday. Every year, Labour Day is celebrated with parades on Rathausplatz and Ringstrasse.
Maifest *(1 May)*, in the Prater *(pp164–5)* with music and children's programmes.
Vienna Music Festival *(6 May–21 Jun)*, part of the Wiener Festwochen programme, which begins a few days earlier at the Wiener Konzerthaus *(p229)* and MuseumsQuartier *(p122)*.
Dancing on the *Vindobona* *(15 May to end Sep)*. Board the boat at Schwedenplatz for a cruise on the Danube.
Wiener Festwochen *(mid-May to mid-Jun)*. Vienna's greatest festival features operas, plays and performing arts.

Average Daily Hours of Sunshine

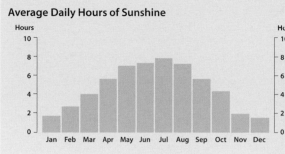

Sunshine Chart
June, July and August are the hottest months in Vienna, with between six and eight hours of sunshine each day, but summer can also be quite damp and humid. Although the city cools down in September, Indian summers are quite common.

Summer

Summer can be both the busiest and most relaxing time in Vienna. The great theatres may be officially closed, but the Jazz Festival is on at the Opera House and the Volkstheater in July. The Danube beaches are ideal for sunbathing, swimming and other watersports on sunny days. In the evenings, people relax at the Heuriger wine taverns on the outskirts of the city.

Summer outside the Votivkirche

June

Corpus Christi (late May–Jun). Public holiday. Catholic festival held in honour of the Eucharist.
Vienna Pride and Regenbogen-parade (mid-Jun). Lesbian and gay parade on the Ringstrasse.

The Concordia Ball (2nd Fri in Jun) takes place at the Neues Rathaus (p132).
Ball der Universität (18 Jun). Popular ball held at the University (p132).
Donauinselfest (last weekend in Jun), three-day pop concert on Danube island.

July

Outdoor films, operas and concerts (until Sep) shown on a giant screen in Rathausplatz. Seating is provided free.
Oper Klosterneuburg (Jul). Performances are in the Kaiserhof courtyard of the palatial religious foundation, Klosterneuburg, a short way north of Vienna (see p131).
Jazzfest (1st two weeks Jul). Well-known artists perform at many venues, including the Opera House (pp140–41), Porgy & Bess Jazz and Music Club (p229) and the arcaded courtyard of the Neues Rathaus (p132).
Piber Meets Vienna (Jul–Aug). Mares with their foals and young horses in training from the Piber Lipizzaner Stud come to the Spanish Riding School (see pp100–101) for summer shows that are less formal than the usual displays.

Bathing beside the Danube

Music in churches (Jul–Aug). Many churches stage summer concerts while the big cultural venues take a summer break.
Impulstanz (International Dance Festival) (end Jul–mid-Aug) at the Volkstheater (p230) and Universitäts Sportzentrum at Schmelz.
Seefestspiele Mörbisch (Thu–Sun mid-Jul to end Aug). An operetta festival, which takes place in Mörbisch, some 40 km (25 miles) away.

August

Maria Himmelfahrt (15 Aug). Public holiday. A Catholic festival, which celebrates the assumption of the Madonna.

Seefestspiele Mörbisch, an annual operetta festival performed against the backdrop of Lake Neusiedl

Average Monthly Rainfall

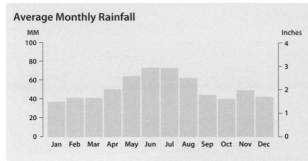

Rainfall Chart
The summer months are not only the hottest but also the wettest, helping to keep the city cool. During spring and autumn, days can be mild, with some drizzle, until November, which can be very wet. Around 600 mm (23 inches) of rain falls annually.

Autumn

In Vienna, autumn means a new start. The theatres, and particularly Vienna's great opera houses, reopen once again. Shops get ready to tempt buyers with their range of autumn fashions. Then, almost overnight, all the shop windows seem to be filled with figures of St Nicholas and his wicked companion Krampus. This cute little furry devil appears everywhere. It is only after 6 December that the shop windows are finally cleared for Christmas displays.

September

Spanish Riding School performances *(until end Oct)* and training sessions of the Lipizzaner horses *(pp100–101)*.
Vienna Boys' Choir *(mid-Sep to Dec)* perform at Mass at the Burgkapelle *(p105)* on Sunday mornings.
Trotting in the Krieau *(until Jun)*. Trotting races at the Prater *(pp164–5)*.

October

National Holiday *(26 Oct)*. Celebrations to mark the passing of the Neutrality Act in

The Vienna Boys' Choir performing at the Konzerthaus

Krampus, the wicked furry devil who accompanies St Nicholas

1955, which was followed by the withdrawal of the Allied troops stationed in Austria since 1945.
Viennale *(end Oct)*. Film festival at Gartenbau, Parkring 12; Metro, Johannesgasse 4; Künstlerhaus, Akademiestrasse 13; and Stadtkino, Schwarzenbergplatz 7–8.
Wien Modern *(until end Nov)*. Modern music festival at the Konzerthaus *(p229)*.

November

Allerheiligen *(1 Nov)*. Public holiday. Catholic festival celebrating All Saints' Day.
KlezMore Festival Vienna *(2nd week Nov)*. Traditional Klezmer music at various city locations.
Vienna Art Week *(3rd week Nov)*. Contemporary art festival hosted by numerous galleries, studios and museums with guided tours, lectures and performances.
Krippenschau *(until mid-Dec)*. Display of historic mangers at Peterskirche *(p89)*.
Christkindlmarkt *(2nd Sat Nov to end Dec)*. Christmas market and children's workshop by the Rathaus *(p132)*.
Christmas markets *(from last Sat Nov)* held at the Freyung, Heiligenkreuzerhof, Schönbrunn, Karlsplatz, Spittelberg and Maria-Theresien-Platz.

Average Monthly Temperature

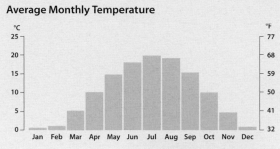

Temperature Chart
The chart shows the average temperatures each month. Top temperatures in July and August can reach 30° C (77° F) although May and September are also quite warm. Winters are icy, and temperatures can be as low as -1.4° C (29.5° F) in January.

Winter

Roasting chestnuts over hot coals is a regular winter sight on Vienna's streets. As Christmas draws near, stalls offer mulled wine and hot snacks and shops enter into the festive spirit putting up lights and decorations.

The Viennese celebrate Christmas Eve with a traditional meal consisting of *Fischbeuschel-suppe*, a creamy fish soup, followed by fresh fried carp. The usual dish eaten on Christmas Day is goose, although turkey is becoming more popular.

New Year also marks the start of Fasching, Vienna's famous Carnival season.

December

Christmas markets *(continue from November)*.
Maria Empfängnis *(8 Dec)*. Public holiday. Catholic festival

Public Holidays

New Year's Day (1 Jan)
Epiphany (6 Jan)
Easter Sunday
Easter Monday
Tag der Arbeit (1 May)
Ascension Day (6th Thu after Easter)
Whit Monday (6th Mon after Easter)
Corpus Christi (2 Jun)
Maria Himmelfahrt (15 Aug)
National Holiday (26 Oct)
Allerheiligen (1 Nov)
Maria Empfängnis (8 Dec)
Christmas Day (25 Dec)
Stefanitag (26 Dec)

Chestnut-roasting in winter

celebrating the Immaculate Conception.
Midnight Mass *(Christmas Eve)* held in the Stephansdom *(pp74–5)*. No tickets needed but arrive early for seats.
Stefanitag *(26 Dec)*. Public holiday for Boxing Day.
New Year's Eve performance of *Die Fledermaus* *(31 Dec)* at the Opera House *(pp140–41)* and Volksoper *(p229)*. It is also shown on a large screen in Stephansplatz *(p72)*.
New Year's Eve concerts at the Konzerthaus *(p229)* and Musikvereinsaal *(p150)*.
Kaiserball *(31 Dec)* at the Hofburg *(pp98–9)*.
New Year's Eve in the city centre: a street party with snacks and drink. Marquees provide music and cabaret.

January

New Year's Concert *(31 Dec & 1 Jan)* by the great Vienna Philharmonic at the Musikverein *(p150)*. Requests for tickets for the next year's concert must arrive on 2 Jan *(p228)*.
Beethoven's Ninth Symphony *(31 Dec & 1 Jan)* is performed at

the Konzerthaus *(p229)*.
Fasching *(6 Jan to Ash Wed)*, the Vienna Carnival includes the **Heringsschmaus** *(Ash Wed)*, a hot and cold buffet.
Holiday on Ice *(mid- to end Jan)*. This is held at the Stadthalle, Vogelweidplatz.
Resonanzen *(2nd to 3rd week Jan)*. Festival of ancient music at the Konzerthaus *(p229)*.
Vienna Ice Dream *(mid-Jan to end Feb)*. Ice-skating in front of City Hall *(p132)*.

February

Opera Ball *(last Thu before Shrove Tue)*, one of the grandest balls of Fasching *(p141)*.
Johann Strauss Ball *(mid-Feb)*. The ball season waltzes on at the Kursalon *(see pp184–5)*.
Szene Bunte Wähne *(end Feb)*. International dance festival, featuring performances for a young audience at the MuseumsQuartier *(pp122–3)* and the WUK cultural centre, Währinger Strasse 59.
Accordion Festival *(end Feb)*. Concerts at various venues.

The Christkindlmarkt, in front of the Neues Rathaus

VIENNA AREA BY AREA

STEPHANSDOM QUARTER

The winding streets and spacious squares of this area form the ancient core of Vienna. Following World War II, subterranean excavations uncovered the remains of a Roman garrison from 2,000 years ago, and every succeeding age is represented here, from the Romanesque arches of the Ruprechtskirche to the steel and glass of the spectacular Haas-Haus in Stephansplatz. Many of the buildings in the area house government offices, businesses, taverns and stylish shops. Dominating the skyline is the Stephansdom, the focus of the city at its geographical centre.

Sights at a Glance

Streets and Squares
3 Blutgasse
4 Domgasse
6 Grünangergasse
10 Schönlaterngasse
12 Sonnenfelsgasse
14 Bäckerstrasse
18 Annagasse
23 Fleischmarkt
24 Griechengasse
26 Jewish District
27 Hoher Markt
31 Judenplatz
33 Kurrentgasse
35 Am Hof

Historic Buildings
9 Academy of Sciences
13 Heiligenkreuzerhof
15 Haas-Haus
17 Winter Palace of Prince Eugene
22 Postsparkasse
28 Bohemian Court Chancery
29 Altes Rathaus

Churches and Cathedrals
1 *Stephansdom pp74–7*
2 Deutschordenskirche
7 Dominikanerkirche
8 Jesuitenkirche
16 Franziskanerkirche
19 Annakirche
25 Ruprechtskirche

30 Maria am Gestade
34 Kirche am Hof
36 Peterskirche

Museums and Galleries
5 Mozarthaus Vienna
11 Cathedral Museum
20 Haus der Musik
21 *Austrian Museum of Applied Arts pp84–5*
31 Museum Judenplatz
32 Clock Museum

See also Streetfinder map 6

◀ Splendid interior of the Stephansdom

For map symbols *see back flap*

Street-by-Street: Old Vienna

This part of the inner city retains its medieval layout,
offering a complex of lanes, alleys and spacious courtyards.
The influence of the church is particularly evident. You can
find remains of monastic orders such as the Dominicans
and feudal orders such as the Teutonic Knights, as well
as ideological orders, for example the Jesuits. Yet there
is nothing ossified about the area: at night the bars and
restaurants on Bäckerstrasse and Schönlaterngasse are
thronged with people until the early hours of the morning.
Dominating everything is the 137-m (450-ft)
spire of the Stephansdom cathedral
in the very heart of Vienna.

⓫ ★ Cathedral Museum
Much of this collection was
donated by Duke Rudolf IV
who is shown here.

To Rotenturm-
strasse

To Kärntner
Strasse

STEPHANS-
PLATZ

STOBELGASSE

BLUTGASSE

SINGERSTRASSE

GRÜN

❶ ★ Stephansdom
The cathedral took
centuries to build and
is rich in medieval and
Renaissance monuments.

❷ Deutschordenskirche
A remarkable Treasury,
with objects collected
by German aristocrats,
lies alongside this
Gothic church.

**The Haas & Haas
Tea House** is a
charming, informal
café and tea house.

❺ Mozarthaus Vienna
Mozart lived here from 1784 to
1787. He had a suite of rooms where
he wrote many of his great works.

❹ Domgasse
This pretty street includes
a bookshop at No. 8,
Buchhandlung 777.

❸ Blutgasse
Courtyards like this are
typical of the tenement
houses on Blutgasse.

⑦ Dominikaner-kirche
Originally consecrated on this site in 1237, the present Baroque church dates from the 1630s.

Locator Map
See Street Finder, maps 2 & 6

⑩ Schönlaterngasse
The lantern at No. 6 gave this charming street its name.

⑧ Jesuitenkirche
This pulpit detail of the apostle Matthew is from the Baroque Jesuitenkirche. One of Vienna's most ornate churches, it was built by the Jesuits in the 1620s.

⑨ ★ Academy of Sciences
The great hall (Aula) of the Academy is one of the noblest salons in Vienna.

⑥ Grünangergasse
This quiet lane is full of bookshops and art galleries.

0 metres	50
0 yards	50

Key

— Suggested route

● Stephansdom

Situated in the centre of Vienna, the Stephansdom is the soul of the city itself; it is no mere coincidence that the urns containing the entrails of some of the Habsburgs lie in a vault beneath its main altar. A church has stood on the site for over 800 years, but all that remains of the original 13th-century Romanesque church are the Giants' Doorway and Heathen Towers. The Gothic nave, choir and side chapels are the result of a rebuilding programme in the 14th and 15th centuries, while some of the outbuildings, such as the Lower Vestry, are Baroque additions.

★ Giants' Doorway and Heathen Towers
The entrance and twin towers apparently stand on the site of an earlier heathen shrine.

KEY

① **Lower Vestry**

② **The symbolic number "05"** of the Austrian Resistance Movement was carved here in 1945.

③ **Main entrance**

④ **Pilgram's Pulpit** (see p76)

⑤ **Entrance to the catacombs**

⑥ **The North Tower**, according to legend, was never completed because its master builder, Hans Puchsbaum, broke a pact he had made with the devil by pronouncing a holy name. The devil then caused him to fall to his death.

⑦ **South-eastern entrance**

★ Singer Gate
This was once the entrance for male visitors. A sculpted relief above the door depicts scenes from the life of St Paul.

★ Steffl or Spire
The 137-m high (450-ft) Gothic spire is a famous landmark. From the Sexton's Lodge *(see p77)*, visitors can climb the stairs as far as a viewing platform.

★ Tiled Roof
Almost a quarter of a million glazed tiles cover the roof; they were meticulously restored after the damage caused in the last days of World War II.

Johannes Capistranus

On the exterior north-eastern wall of the choir is a pulpit built after the victory over the Turks at Belgrade in 1456. It was from here that the Italian Franciscan, Giovanni da Capestrano (1386–1456), is said to have preached against the Turkish invasion in 1451. The 18th-century Baroque statue above it depicts the triumphant saint – known in Austria as Johannes Capistranus – trampling on a defeated Turkish invader.

1147 The first Romanesque building on the site consecrated by the Bishop of Passau		**1304** Duke Rudolf IV initiates work on High Gothic Albertine Choir		**1515** Anton Pilgram carves his pulpit		**1711** Pummerin bell cast from remains of guns left by Turks on their retreat from Vienna		**1948** Reconstruction and restoration carried out	
1100	**1200**	**1300**	**1400**	**1500**	**1600**	**1700**	**1800**	**1900**	**2000**
	1230 Second Romanesque building erected on the same ground	**1359–1440** Main aisle, southern arches and southern tower built	**1515** Double wedding of grandchildren of Maximilian with children of the King of Hungary takes place	**1556** North Tower is roofed over — **1783** Stephansdom churchyard closed after plague			**1916** Emperor Franz Joseph's funeral	**1945** Cathedral catches fire during bombing	

Inside the Stephansdom

The lofty vaulted interior of the Stephansdom contains an impressive collection of works of art spanning several centuries. Masterpieces of Gothic sculpture include the fabulously intricate pulpit, several of the figures of saints adorning the piers, and the canopies or baldachins over many of the side altars. To the left of the High Altar is the early 15th-century winged Wiener Neustädter Altar bearing the painted images of 72 saints. The altar panels open out to reveal delicate sculpture groups. The most spectacular Renaissance work is the tomb of Friedrich III, while the High Altar adds a flamboyant Baroque note.

The Catacombs
A flight of steps leads down to the catacombs, which extend under the cathedral square.

Portrait of Pilgram
Master craftsman Anton Pilgram left a portrait of himself, holding a square and compass, below the corbel of the original organ.

★ Pilgram's Pulpit
Pilgram's intricate Gothic pulpit is decorated with portraits of the Four Fathers of the Church (theologians representing four physiognomic temperaments), while Pilgram himself looks out from a "window" below.

Organ Gallery and Case
In 1960 this modern organ was installed in the loft above the entrance. A more recent organ is in the south choir area.

The Pummerin Bell

The bell that hangs in the North Tower, known as the *Pummerin* or "Boomer", is a potent symbol for the city reflecting Vienna's turbulent past. The original bell was made from melted-down cannons abandoned when the Turks fled Vienna in 1683. The bell crashed down through the roof in 1945 when fire swept through the Stephansdom, so a new and even larger bell was cast using the remains of the old.

★ **Wiener Neustädter Altar**
Friedrich III commissioned the elaborate altarpiece in 1447. Painted panels open out to reveal an earlier carved interior showing scenes from the life of the Virgin Mary and Christ. This panel portrays the *Adoration of the Magi* (1420).

★ **High Altar**
Tobias Pock's altarpiece shows the martyrdom of St Stephen. The sculptures were fashioned by Johann Jakob Pock in 1647.

KEY

① **The Canopy with the Pötsch Madonna** is a 16th-century canopy that shelters a 1697 icon of the Madonna, to which Prince Eugene's victory over the Turks at Zenta was attributed. It comes from Pócs, a village in Hungary.

② **Main entrance**

③ **The Statue of Crucified Christ** above the altar has, according to legend, a beard of human hair that is still growing.

④ **The Tirna Chapel** houses

the grave of the military hero Prince Eugene.

⑤ **Bishop's Gate**

⑥ **Lift to the Pummerin Bell**

⑦ **Christ with Toothache** (1420) is the irreverent name of this figure; legend has it that Christ afflicts mockers with toothache.

⑧ **Exit from crypt**

⑨ **Albertine Choir**

⑩ **Emperor Friedrich III's tomb** is made from ornate red marble

and has a lid bearing a life-like carved portrait of the Emperor. It dates from the 15th century.

⑪ **The Sexton's Lodge** houses the stairs that lead up the steeple.

⑫ **Chapel of St Catherine**

⑬ **The Madonna of the Servants**

⑭ **The Füchsel Baldachin** is a fine Gothic canopy.

⑮ **The Trinity Altar** probably dates from around 1740.

❷ Deutschordens-kirche

Singerstrasse 7. **Map** 2 E5 & 6 D3.
Tel 5121065. Ⓤ Stephansplatz.
Church: **Open** 7am–6pm daily.
Treasury: **Open** 10am–noon Tue, Thu
& Sat, 3–5pm Wed & Fri. **Closed** Sun,
Mon & public hols.

This church belongs to the Order
of Teutonic Knights, a chivalric
order, which was established in
the 12th century. It is 14th-
century Gothic, but was
restored in the 1720s in Baroque
style by Anton Erhard **Martinelli**.
It retains Gothic style elements
such as pointed arched windows.
Numerous coats of arms of
teutonic knights and memorial
slabs are displayed on the walls.
The altarpiece from 1520 is
Flemish and incorporates panel
paintings and carvings of scenes
from the Passion beneath some
very delicate traceried canopies.
  The Order's Treasury is
situated off the church's
courtyard and now serves as
a museum, displaying various
collections acquired by its
Grand Masters over the
centuries. The starting point is
a room, which houses a large
collection of coins, medals and
a 13th-century enthronement
ring. This leads into the second
room containing chalices and
Mass vessels worked with silver
filigree. Following this is a
display of maces, daggers and
ceremonial garb. The final
exhibits show some Gothic

Inner courtyard of No. 9 Blutgasse, the Fähnrichshof

paintings and a Carinthian
carving of *St George and the
Dragon* (1457).

❸ Blutgasse

Map 2 E5 & 6 D3. Ⓤ Stephansplatz.

A local legend relates that this
street acquired its gruesome
name – Blood Lane – after a
massacre in 1312 of the Knights
Templar (a military and religious
order) in a skirmish so violent
that the streets flowed with
blood. But there is no evidence
to support this story and the
street's charm belies its name.
  Its tall apartment buildings
date mostly from the 18th
century. Walk into No. 3 and
see how the city's restorers
have linked up the buildings
and their courtyards. No. 9,
the Fähnrichshof, is
particularly impressive.

Winged altarpiece in
the Deutschordens-
kirche (1520)

❹ Domgasse

Map 2 E5 & 6 D3. Ⓤ Stephansplatz.

In addition to the Figarohaus,
Domgasse boasts some
interesting buildings, including
the Trienter Hof, with its airy
courtyard. No. 6 is a house of
medieval origin called the
Kleiner Bischofshof or small
bishop's house: it has a 1761
Matthias Gerl façade. Next door
is the site of the house where
Georg Franz Kolschitzky lived
and, in 1694, died. It is said
that he claimed some Turkish
coffee beans as a reward for
his bravery in the 1683 Turkish
siege, and later opened
Vienna's first coffee house.
The truth of this story,
however, is doubtful.

❺ Mozarthaus Vienna

Domgasse 5. **Map** 2 E5 & 6 D3.
Tel 5121791. Ⓤ Stephansplatz.
Open 10am–7pm daily. 🖼
Ⓦ mozarthausvienna.at

Mozart and his family occupied
a flat on the first floor of this
building from 1784 to 1787. Of
Mozart's 11 Viennese residences,
this is the one where he is said
to have been happiest. It is
also where he composed a
significant number of his
masterworks: the exquisite
Haydn quartets, a handful
of piano concerti, and *The
Marriage of Figaro*. Restored
for the anniversary year 2006,
the Mozarthaus now has
exhibitions on two upper floors
as well as the first-floor flat.

Elaborate nave of the Dominikanerkirche

❻ Grünangergasse

Map 6 D3 & D4. Ⓤ Stephansplatz.

This quiet lane takes its name from the creperie Zum Grünen Anker at No. 10, a tavern that was frequented by Franz Schubert in the 19th century.

No. 8's portal has crude carvings of rolls, croissants and pretzels. It is known as the Kipferlhaus after a Viennese crescent-shaped roll. The former Fürstenberg Palace, from 1720, has a Baroque portal with carved hounds racing to the top of the keystone.

❼ Dominikaner-kirche

Postgasse 4. **Map** 2 E5 & 6 E3. **Tel** 5129174. Ⓤ Stephansplatz, Schwedenplatz. **Open** 7am–7pm Mon–Sat, 7am–9pm Sun.

The Dominican order of monks came to Vienna in 1226, and by 1237 they had consecrated a church here. In the 1630s

Antonio Canevale designed their present church, which boasts a majestic and really rather handsome Baroque façade. The interior is equally imposing. The central chapel on the right has swirling Rococo grilles and candelabra, and there is a very beautiful gilt organ above the west door. Its casing dates from the mid-18th century. The frescoes by Tencalla and Rauchmiller are especially noteworthy, as is the high altar.

❽ Jesuitenkirche

Dr-Ignaz-Seipel-Platz 1. **Map** 2 E5 & 6 E3. **Tel** 512 523 20. Ⓤ Stubentor, Stephans-platz, Schwedenplatz. **Open** 7am–7pm Mon–Sat, 8am–7pm Sun & hols.

Andrea Pozzo, an Italian architect, redesigned the Jesuitenkirche between 1703 and 1705 and its broad, high façade dominates the Dr-Ignaz-Seipel-Platz. In the 1620s the Jesuits decided to move their headquarters here in order to be

near the Old University, which they controlled. The Jesuit order was the dominant force behind the Counter-Reformation. The Jesuits were not afraid of making a statement, and the church's grand design and high façade reflects this dominance.

The interior is gaudy, with plump marble columns screening the side chapels. Pozzo's ceiling frescoes are cleverly executed using a *trompe l'oeil* effect and the pews are richly carved.

❾ Academy of Sciences

Dr-Ignaz-Seipel-Platz 2. **Map** 2 E5 & 6 E3. Ⓤ Schwedenplatz, Stubentor. **Tel** 515810. **Open** 8am–5pm Mon–Fri.

Once the centrepiece of the Old University, the Akademie der Wissenschaften has an impressive Baroque façade. Designed in 1753 by Jean Nicolas Jadot de Ville-Issey as the *Aula*, or great hall, it has since been restored. A double staircase leads up to a huge salon that, despite being reconstructed after a fire in 1961, is still one of the great rooms of Vienna.

Elaborate frescoes adorn the ceilings of the Ceremonial Hall and the walls are composed of marble embellished with Rococo plasterwork. Haydn's *Creation* was performed here in 1808 in the presence of the composer: it was the eve of his 76th birthday and his last public appearance.

Fountain by Franz Joseph Lenzbauer on the Academy of Sciences (about 1755)

The Baroque Bernhardskapelle *(left)*, seen from Schönlaterngasse

❿ Schönlaterngasse

Map 2 E5 & 6 E3. ⓤ Stephansplatz, Schwedenplatz. Alte Schmiede: **Tel** 5128329. **Open** 9am–5pm Mon–Fri.

The attractive curving lane derives its name (Pretty Lantern Lane) from the handsome wrought-iron lantern which is clamped to No. 6. This is a copy of the 1610 original which is now in the Wien Museum Karlsplatz *(see p150)*. At No. 4, a solid early 17th-century house guards the curve of the street. No. 7, the Basiliskenhaus, which is of medieval origin, displays on its façade an artist's impression of a mythical serpent, dating from 1740. A serpent is reputed to have been discovered in 1212 in a well by the house.

The composer Robert Schumann lived at No. 7a from 1838 to 1839. No. 9 is the Alte Schmiede – the large smithy from which it takes its name has

been reassembled in the basement. This complex also contains an art gallery and a hall used for poetry readings and musical workshops.

⓫ Cathedral Museum

Stephansplatz 6. **Map** 2 E5 & 6 D3. **Tel** 515 52 33 00. ⓤ Stephansplatz. **Open** Reopens 2015: see www.dommuseum.at for times. 📷 ♿

The Cathedral Museum, known in German as the Dom und Diözesan-museum, reopens in 2015 following renovations; meanwhile some of its treasures can be seen in the western gallery of the cathedral itself. Its collection includes 18th-century religious paintings by important Austrian artists such as

Franz Anton Maulbertsch, and both medieval and 16th- and 17th-century rustic carvings. There are also works by the Dutch painter Jan van Hemessen and, in the Treasury, many items that were the personal gift of Duke Rudolf IV to the Cathedral. His shroud is housed here as well as a famous portrait of him by a Bohemian master dating from the 1360s *(see p72)*. Other items include the St Leopold reliquary from 1592, encrusted with figures of saints and coats of arms, and some outstanding enamels from the 12th-century.

⓬ Sonnenfelsgasse

Map 2 E5 & 6 E3. ⓤ Stephansplatz, Schwedenplatz.

Fine houses line this pleasant street. Though by no means uniform in style, most of the dwellings on the north side of the street are solid merchant and patrician houses dating from the late 16th century. No. 19, which was built in 1628 and renovated in 1721, was once part of the Old University *(see p79)*. No. 11 has an impressive courtyard. Many of the balconies overlooking the courtyard have been glassed in to their full height so as to provide extra living space. No. 3 has the most elaborate façade, and contains a *Stadtheuriger* called the Zwölf Apostelkeller. This is an urban equivalent of the *Heurige*, the wine growers' inns found in the villages outside Vienna *(see pp200–201)*.

The street was named after a soldier called Joseph von Sonnenfels. He became Maria Theresa's legal adviser and under his guidance, she totally reformed the penal code and abolished torture.

Gothic Madonna (1325) in the Cathedral Museum

⓭ Heiligen-kreuzerhof

Schönlaterngasse 5. **Map** 2 E5 & 6 E3.
Tel 5125896. Ⓤ Schwedenplatz.
Open 6am–9pm Mon–Sat. **Closed**
Sun. Ⓖ Bernhardskapelle: **Open** on request

In the Middle Ages, the rural monasteries expanded by establishing a presence in the cities. Secularization in the 1780s diminished such holdings, but this one, belonging to the abbey of Heiligenkreuz *(see p178)*, survived.

The buildings around the courtyard housing the city's Applied Arts College present a serene 18th-century face. On the south side of the courtyard is the Bernhardskapelle. Dating from 1662, but altered in the 1730s, the chapel is a Baroque gem. Across from the chapel a patch of wall from Babenberg times *(see pp24–5)* has been exposed to remind you that, as so often in Vienna, the building is much older in origin than it at first appears.

Fresco at No. 12 Bäckerstrasse

⓮ Bäckerstrasse

Map 2 E5 & 6 D3. Ⓤ Stephansplatz.

Nowadays people visit this street, which used to house the city's bakers in medieval times, to sample its nightlife rather than its bread. The architecture here is also of considerable interest: No. 2 sits beneath a 17th-century tower, and has a pretty courtyard. Opposite, at No. 1, is the site of the Alte Regensburgerhof, the outpost of Bavarian merchants who were given incentives to work in Vienna in the 15th century. No. 8 is the former palace of Count Seilern, dating from 1722, and No. 7 is famous for its arcaded Renaissance courtyard and stables, the

only surviving example in Vienna. Two other houses of Renaissance origin are located at Nos. 12 and 14.

⓯ Haas-Haus

Stephansplatz 12. **Map** 2 E5 & 6 D3.
Tel 5356083. Ⓤ Stephansplatz.
Open 8am–2am daily. Ⓖ

Commissioning a modern building directly opposite the Stephansdom was a sensitive task, and the city entrusted its design to one of Austria's leading architects, Hans Hollein. The result is the 1990 Haas-Haus, a shining structure of glass and blue-green marble that curves elegantly round right into the Graben. The building has a very pleasing asymmetrical appearance, with decorative elements such as lopsided cubes of marble attached to the façade, a protruding structure high up resembling a diving board and a Japanese bridge inside. The atrium within is surrounded by cafés, shops, a restaurant, DO & CO *(see p212)* and offices.

⓰ Franziskaner-kirche

Franziskanerplatz 4. **Map** 4 E1 & 6 D4.
Tel 5124578. Ⓤ Stephansplatz.
Open 6:30am–noon & 2–5:30pm
Mon–Sat, 7am–5:30pm Sun. Ⓖ

The Franciscans were fairly late arrivals in Vienna and one of their first tasks was to build a church on the site of a former medieval convent. Dating from 1603, the church totally dominates the Franziskanerplatz.

The façade is in South German Renaissance style, and is topped by an elaborate scrolled gable with obelisks. The Moses Fountain in front of the church was designed by

Detail from Andrea Pozzo's altar (1707) in the Franziskanerkirche

the Neo-Classicist Johann Martin Fischer in 1798. The interior is in full-blown Baroque style and includes a finely modelled pulpit dating from 1726, and richly-carved pews. A dramatic high altar by Andrea Pozzo rises to the full height of the church. Only the front part of the structure is three-dimensional – the rest is *trompe l'oeil*. Look out for a 1725 *Crucifixion* by Carlo Carlone among the paintings in the side altars.

You usually have to ask a passing monk for permission to see the church organ. It is worth being persistent, as this is the oldest organ in Vienna (1642), designed by Johann Wöckerl. It has statues of angel musicians and beautifully painted doors on religious themes.

Gleaming façade of
Haas-Haus (1990)

Statuary in the hall of the Winter Palace of Prince Eugene

⑰ Winter Palace of Prince Eugene

Himmelpfortgasse 4–8. **Map** 4 E1 & 6 D4. **Tel** 795 57 134. ⓤ Stephansplatz. Vestibule: **Open** 10am–6pm daily.

The Winter Palace was commissioned in 1694 by Prince Eugene of Savoy (see p29), hero of the 1683 Turkish siege. It was begun by Johann Bernhard Fischer von Erlach (see p149) and taken over by Johann Lukas von Hildebrandt (see p154) in 1702. The result is an imposing town mansion, one of the most magnificent Baroque edifices in Vienna. Maria Theresa bought it for the state in 1752. It is now an exhibition venue for the Belvedere (see pp154–9), devoted to the interaction between contemporary art and the Baroque setting of the palace.

⑱ Annagasse

Map 4 E1 & 6 D4. ⓤ Stephansplatz. Zum Blauen Karpfen: **Closed** to the public.

Now splendidly Baroque, Annagasse dates from medieval times. It is pedestrianized and a pleasant place to browse in the bookshops.

Of note are the luxurious Mailberger Hof and the stucco-decorated Römischer Kaiser hotels (see p198). No. 14's lintel has a Baroque carving of babes making merry, while above this is a relief of the blue carp that gives the house, once a pub, its name: Zum Blauen Karpfen. No. 2 is the 17th-century Esterházy Palace, which is now a casino. It used to be possible to see the Countess Esterházy sweeping her front doorstep!

⑲ Annakirche

Annagasse 3b. **Map** 4 E1 & 6 D4. **Tel** 5124797. ⓤ Stephansplatz. **Open** 7am–7pm daily.

There has been a chapel in Annagasse since 1320, but the present Annakirche dates from 1629 to 1634, and it was renovated by the Jesuits during the early 18th century. Devotion to St Anne has deep roots in Vienna and this very intimate church is often full of quiet worshippers.

The finest exterior feature of the church is the moulded copper cupola over the tower. Daniel Gran's ceiling frescoes are now fading and his richly-coloured painting glorifying St Anne on the High Altar is more striking. Gran, together with Franz Anton Maulbertsch, was a leading painter of the Austrian Baroque period. The first chapel on the left houses a copy of a carving of St Anne from about 1505 – the original is in the cathedral museum (see p80). St Anne is portrayed as a powerfully maternal figure and shown with her daughter, the Virgin Mary, who in turn has the baby Jesus on her knee. The carving is attributed to the sculptor Veit Stoss.

⑳ Haus der Musik

Seilerstätte 30. **Map** 4 E1. **Tel** 513 48 50. ⓤ Stephansplatz, Stubenring. **Open** 10am–10pm daily. ⬛ 🅿 on request. ⬛ 📷 ⓦ hdm.at

The House of Music makes the most of the latest audio-visual and interactive technologies to explain and demonstrate all aspects of music. Visitors move through "experience zones" such as the Instrumentarium, with its giant instruments, and the Polyphonium, which is a collection of different sounds.

Moulded copper cupola over the tower of the Annakirche

Detail on the façade of the Griechische Kirche on Griechengasse

㉑ Austrian Museum of Applied Arts

See pp84–5.

㉒ Postsparkasse

Georg-Coch-Platz 2. **Map** 2 F5 & 6 F3. **Tel** 059905. Ⓤ Schwedenplatz. **Open** 8am–3pm Mon–Wed & Fri, 8am–5:30pm Thu.

This building is the Austrian Post Office Savings Bank and is a wonderful example of Secession architecture *(see pp56–9)*. Designed between 1904 and 1906 by Otto Wagner, it still looks unashamedly modern. The building features the architect's characteristic overhanging eaves, spindly aluminium columns supporting a canopy, heroic sculptures of angels and ornament-like nailheads protruding from the surface of the building.

Wagner was a pioneer in incorporating many functional elements into his decorative schemes. Inside the banking hall the metal columns are clad in aluminium, and tubular heating ducts encircle the hall.

㉓ Fleischmarkt

Map 2 E5 & 6 D2–E3. Ⓤ Schwedenplatz. Griechische Kirche: **Tel** 5333889. **Open** 9am–4pm Mon–Fri.

Fleischmarkt, the former meat market, dates from 1220. The small cosy inn called the

Griechenbeisl *(see p210)* is its best-known landmark. On its façade is a woodcarving of a bagpiper known as *Der liebe Augustin* (Dear old Augustin). Rumour has it that during the 1679 plague, this bagpiper slumped drunk into the gutter one night and, taken for dead, was put in the plague pit. He woke, attracted attention by playing his pipes and was rescued. Miraculously, he did not catch the plague.

Next to the Griechenbeisl is the beautiful Neo-Byzantine Griechische Kirche (Greek church of the Holy Trinity). The versatile architect Theophil Hansen *(see p34)* created its rich, gilt appearance in the 1850s. A passage links the Griechenbeisl to Griechengasse.

㉔ Griechengasse

Map 2 E5 & 6 E2. Ⓤ Schwedenplatz. Griechenkirche St Georg: **Tel** 5357882. **Open** by appt, 9am–4pm Mon–Fri, 10am–1pm for mass only Sat & Sun.

This street name refers to the Greek merchants who settled here in the 18th century and it leads up from Rotenturmstrasse. The house on the right dates from 1611 but has since been altered. Opposite is the Greek Orthodox Griechenkirche St Georg, not to be confused with the Griechische Kirche in Fleischmarkt. This one was built in 1803 but the gable was added later, in 1898. No. 7 is a 17th-century house. The façade was rebuilt in the late 18th century.

Ivy-clad façade of Ruprechtskirche

㉕ Ruprechtskirche

Ruprechtsplatz. **Map** 2 E5 & 6 D2. **Tel** 5356003. Ⓤ Schwedenplatz. **Open** 10am–noon Mon–Fri, 3–5pm Mon, Wed, Fri; for mass 5pm Sat (6pm Jul & Aug). ♿ Donation expected.

St Ruprecht *(see p24)* was the patron saint of Vienna's salt merchants and the church that takes his name overlooks the merchants' landing stage on the Danube canal. There is a statue of the saint holding a tub of salt at the foot of the Romanesque tower. Salt was a valuable commodity in the Middle Ages, and evidence suggests that the church dates back to the 11th century, making it the oldest church in Vienna. The interior is less interesting, having been restored at various times, but the chancel has two panes of Romanesque stained glass. The choir is 13th century, the vaulted south aisle 15th century.

Carving of the bagpiper on the façade of the Griechenbeisl, Fleischmarkt

㉑ Austrian Museum of Applied Arts

The MAK (Museum für angewandte Kunst) acts both as a showcase for Austrian decorative arts and as a repository for fine objects from around the world. Originally founded in 1864 as a museum for art and industry, it expanded and diversified over the years to include objects representing new movements and contemporary design. The museum has a fine collection of furniture, including some classical works of the German cabinet-maker David Roentgen, textiles, glass, Islamic and East Asian art and fine Renaissance jewellery. In 1993 the museum was completely renovated and each room was redesigned by a different leading artist. The result is a series of displays that lend the exhibits a unique, unusual flavour.

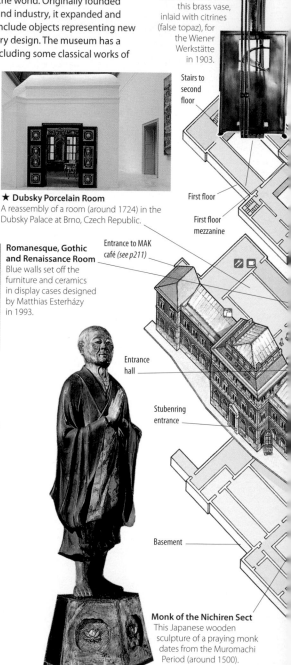

★ **Wiener Werk-stätte Collection**
Kolo Moser created this brass vase, inlaid with citrines (false topaz), for the Wiener Werkstätte in 1903.

Stairs to second floor

First floor

First floor mezzanine

Entrance to MAK café *(see p211)*

Entrance hall

Stubenring entrance

Basement

★ **Dubsky Porcelain Room**
A reassembly of a room (around 1724) in the Dubsky Palace at Brno, Czech Republic.

Romanesque, Gothic and Renaissance Room
Blue walls set off the furniture and ceramics in display cases designed by Matthias Esterházy in 1993.

Monk of the Nichiren Sect
This Japanese wooden sculpture of a praying monk dates from the Muromachi Period (around 1500).

Museum Guide

The basement houses the individual collections, and the extension is used for special exhibitions. Most of the permanent collection is displayed in the ground-floor galleries, although the Wiener Werkstätte collection plus 20th- and 21st-century architecture is on the first floor. Stairs in the west wing lead to the contemporary design rooms.

Key

- Romanesque, Gothic, Renaissance
- Baroque, Rococo
- Wiener Werkstätte
- Art Nouveau, Art Deco
- Islamic Art
- Biedermeier
- 20th-century design
- Individual collections
- Temporary exhibition space
- Non-exhibition space

The Wiener Werkstätte

In 1903 Josef Hoffman (pictured) and Kolo Moser founded a co-operative arts and crafts workshop, the Wiener Werkstätte. This promoted all aspects of design from postage stamps and book illustrations to fabric, furniture, jewellery and interiors. The museum houses its archives, which include sketches, fabric patterns and fine pieces.

VISITORS' CHECKLIST

Practical Information
Stubenring 5. **Map** 2 F5 & 6 F3.
Tel 711360. **Open** 10am–10pm
Tue, 10am–6pm Wed–Sun.
Closed Mon, 1 Jan, 25 Dec. 🖉
🖲 🗟 🗟 🖳 🖰 🖰 **W** mak.at

Transport
🆄 Stubentor. 🚌 3A, 74A. 🚋 2.
🆂 Landstrasse.

Lecture Hall

Mundus Chair
Bentwood furniture was made popular by the 19th-century designer, Michael Thonet (1796–1871), who pioneered bentwood furniture techniques in the 1830s. This example was manufactured by Mundus in 1910.

Library

Ground floor

Knotted Mameluke Carpet
This 16th-century Egyptian silk rug is the only known surviving example of its kind.

★ Biedermeier Room
This cherrywood sofa (1825–30), designed and manufactured by Danhauser'sche Möbelfabrik, is an outstanding example of Viennese Empire-style Biedermeier design (see pp32–3). The original upholstery has been reproduced.

㉖ Jewish District

Map 2 F5 & 6 D2. Ⓤ Schwedenplatz.
Stadttempel: **Tel** 531040. **Open** Mon–
Thu for tours at 11:30am and 2pm
(take identification).

Vienna's Jewish District is more
famous today for its area of bars
and discos called the Bermuda
Triangle than for its Jewish
community. Judengasse is now
a bustling lane lined with
clothes shops and bars. There
are some solid Biedermeier
apartment blocks and on
Ruprechtsplatz, in the former
town hall, a kosher restaurant,
the Arche Noah. Behind it is a
jutting tower, the Kornhäusel-
turm. Named after Josef
Kornhäusel, an architect from
the Biedermeier period *(see
pp32–3)*, it was apparently built
as a refuge from his wife.

Close to Arche Noah is
Sterngasse. This street has an
English-language bookshop
called Shakespeare & Co. *(see
p225)* and the Neustädter-Hof, a
Baroque palace built by Anton
Ospel in 1734. A Turkish
cannonball, fired in 1683, is
embedded in its façade.

Vienna's oldest surviving
synagogue, the Stadttempel,
designed by Kornhäusel in the
1820s, is on Seitenstettengasse.
On the same street is the
headquarters of Vienna's Jewish

The Anker Clock in Hoher Markt

community. It used to house
the Jewish museum, which
is now located in Dorotheergasse *(see p95)*.

㉗ Hoher Markt

Map 2 E5 & 6 D2. Ⓤ Stephansplatz,
Schwedenplatz. Roman Museum:
Tel 5355606. **Open** 9am–6pm Tue–
Sun & hols. **Closed** 1 Jan, 1 May,
25 Dec 🅿

Hoher Markt is the oldest
square in Vienna. In medieval
times fish and cloth markets
were held here, and so were
executions. Today it is possible

to view the subterranean ruins
of a former Roman garrison
beneath it *(see p23)*. Discovered
after World War II, the ancient
foundations show groups of
houses bisected by straight
roads leading to the town
gates. It seems probable that
they were 2nd- and 3rd-
century officers' houses. The
excavations are well laid out
and exhibits of pottery, reliefs
and tiles supplement the ruins.

In the centre of the square
is the Vermählungsbrunnen
(Nuptial Fountain), also
known as the Josefsbrunnen.
Emperor Leopold I vowed
to commemorate the safe
return of his son Joseph
from the Siege of Landau
and commissioned Johann
Bernhard Fischer von Erlach
to design this monument,
which was built by von Erlach's
son Joseph Emanuel between
1729 and 1732. The fountain
celebrates the betrothal of
Joseph and Mary and bears
figures of the high priest and
the couple, with gilt urns,
statues of angels and fluted
columns supporting an
elaborate canopy.

Linking two office buildings
on the square is the bronze
and copper sculptural Anker
Clock. Commissioned by the
Anker Insurance Company, and
designed by Franz Matsch, it
was completed in 1914. Every
hour a procession of cut-out
historical figures, ranging from
the Emperor Marcus Aurelius
and Duke Rudolf IV to Joseph
Haydn, glide from one side of
the clock to the other to the
sound of organ music. Noon is
the best time to see it, as all the
figures are on display then.

㉘ Bohemian Court Chancery

Judenplatz 11. **Map** 2 D5 & 5 C2.
Tel 531110. Ⓤ Stephansplatz.
Open 8am–3:30pm Mon–Fri.

Habsburg rulers were also
kings of Bohemia, which was
governed from this magnificent
palace (1709–14). Its architect
was the finest of the day:
Johann Bernhard Fischer von

Vienna's Jews – Past and Present

A Jewish community has thrived in Vienna since at least the 12th
century, with Judenplatz and, later, the Stadttempel at its core.
Unfortunately, the Jews' commercial success caused envy and in
1421, after a charge of ritual murder, almost the entire Jewish
population was burnt to death, forcibly baptised or expelled.
Thereafter Jewish fortunes fluctuated, with periods of prosperity
alternating with expulsions. The 1781 Edict of Tolerance lifted legal
constraints that had applied to Jews and by the late 19th century
the city's cultural and intellectual life was dominated by Jews. Anti-
Semitism spread in the early 20th century and burgeoning Nazism
forced many Jews to leave. Of those who remained, 65,000 were
murdered. In 1938, 170,000 Jews lived in the city; 50 years later

there were 7,000.
Now Eastern
European Jews are
adding to the
number.

The interior of the
Stadttempel

Erlach *(see p148)*. Matthias Gerl enlarged the Chancery between 1751 and 1754 to accommodate the Ministry of the Interior. Its glory is the huge Baroque portals, yet the building is as subtle as it is powerful. The elegantly-curved window frames on the first floor are particularly noteworthy.

The building's interior, now a courthouse, and its two courtyards, are less impressive, partly due to reconstruction undertaken after serious bomb damage in World War II.

Ironwork at the Rathaus entrance

㉙ Altes Rathaus

Wipplinger Strasse 8. **Map** 2 D5 & 6 D2. Ⓤ Schwedenplatz. Salvatorkapelle: **Tel** 3178394. **Open** 9am–5pm Mon–Thu, or by appointment. Austrian Resistance Archive: **Tel** 2289469 319. **Open** 9am–5pm Mon–Wed, Fri; 9am–7pm Thu. 🅦 doew.at

After the German brothers Otto and Haymo of Neuburg conspired to overthrow the Habsburgs *(see p24)* in 1309, their property was confiscated and donated to the city. Over the centuries the site was expanded to form the complex of buildings that until 1883 served as the city hall or *Rathaus*.

The entrance of the Altes Rathaus is festooned with ornamental ironwork. The building is now occupied by offices and shops. The District Museum, which deals with the first municipal district of Vienna (roughly covering the area within the Ring), is also here. Of much greater interest is the

Portal figure by Lorenzo Mattielli in the Bohemian Court Chancery

Austrian Resistance Archive on the first floor, where Austrian Resistance to Nazism is documented. Although many Austrians welcomed Hitler's takeover in 1938, a distinguished minority fiercely resisted it, and this exhibition pays tribute to them.

In one corner of the Altes Rathaus is the Andromeda Fountain. Located in the main courtyard, it was the last work by sculptor Georg Raphael Donner who designed it in 1741. The relief shows Perseus rescuing Andromeda.

At No. 5 Salvatorgasse is a late 13th-century chapel, the Salvatorkapelle, the only surviving building of the original medieval town house. It has since been enlarged and renovated, but retains its fine Gothic vaults. The walls are lined with old marble tomb slabs, some from the 15th century. Its pretty organ dates from around 1740 and is sometimes used for recitals in the chapel. On the outside wall on Salvatorgasse is an exquisite Renaissance portal dating from 1520 to 1530 – a rare example of Italianate Renaissance style.

㉚ Maria am Gestade

Salvatorgasse 12. **Map** 2 D5 & 5 C2. **Tel** 53395940. Ⓤ Schwedenplatz, Stephansplatz. **Open** 7am–7pm daily & inside at rear by appointment only.

One of the city's oldest sights is this lofty, Gothic church with its 56-m high (180-ft) steeple and immense choir windows. Mentioned as early as 1158, the present building dates from the late 14th century. It was restored in the 19th century. The church has had a chequered history and during the occupation of Vienna by Napoleon in 1809 his troops used it as an arsenal.

Inside, the nave piers are enlivened with Gothic canopies sheltering statues from various periods: medieval, Baroque and modern. The choir contains two High Gothic panels (1460): they depict the Annunciation, the Crucifixion and the Coronation of the Virgin.

Behind the high altar the windows contain medieval stained glass, which is patched with surviving fragments. Tucked away on the north side of the choir is a chapel with a beautiful painted stone altar from 1520. The main parts of the interior are visible from the front entrance, but to walk around inside you need to make an appointment.

Gothic canopies in the Maria am Gestade church

Holocaust memorial in Judenplatz

memorial, the Museum Judenplatz at No. 8 and the excavated remains of the medieval synagogue that lie beneath the square. The museum celebrates the vibrant Jewish quarter that was centred on the square until the expulsion of the Jews in 1421, an event gleefully recorded in an inscription, *Zum Grossen Jordan*, on the façade of No. 2. The museum also houses a public database of the 65,000 Austrian Jews killed by the Nazis and, in the basement, the excavated synagogue.

❸ Judenplatz

Map 2 D5 & 5 C2. Ⓤ Stephansplatz, Herrengasse. Museum Judenplatz: **Tel** 535 04 31. **Open** 10am–6pm Sun–Thu, 10am–2pm Fri. **Closed** on main Jewish holidays. 🅿 ♿ except to synagogue. 🎦 free, 2pm & 5pm Thu & Sun (take identification). 🆆 jmw.at

Judenplatz was the site of the Jewish ghetto in medieval times. In the centre of the square stands a statue of the German playwright and critic Ephraim Lessing by Siegfried Charoux. The Nazis did not like a tribute to a writer whose works plead for toleration towards Jews, and they destroyed it in 1939. It was later redesigned by the same sculptor and reinstated in the square in 1982.

In 1996 British artist Rachel Whiteread was the controversial winner of a competition to design a monument for the Jewish victims of the Nazi regime, to be unveiled in the square on 9 November 1999, the anniversary of Kristal Nacht. A heated public debate ensued and, following many changes, including the repositioning of the monument by one metre, Judenplatz was reopened on 25 October 2000 as a place of remembrance. It now contains Whiteread's Holocaust

❸ Clock Museum

Schulhof 2. **Map** 2 D5 & 5 C2. **Tel** 5332265. Ⓤ Stephansplatz. **Open** 10am–6pm Tue–Sun. **Closed** 1 Jan, 1 May, 25 Dec. 🆆 wienmuseum.at

You don't have to be a clock fanatic to enjoy a visit to this wonderful and fascinating museum. Located in the beautiful former Obizzi Palace (1690), the museum contains a fine collection of clocks, some of which were accumulated by an earlier curator, Rudolf Kaftan. Others belonged to the novelist Marie von Ebner-Eschenbach.

Lavish specimen in the Clock Museum

On the first floor are displayed the mechanisms of tower clocks from the 16th century onwards, with painted clocks, grandfather clocks and pocket watches. On the other floors are huge astronomical clocks and a wide range of novelty timepieces.

There are more than 3,000 exhibits. A major highlight is the astronomical clock by David Cajetano, dating from the 18th century. It has over 30 readings and dials that show, among other things, the dates of solar and lunar eclipses. Many other exhibits date from the Biedermeier and *belle époque* periods.

At every full hour the three floors of the museum resound to the incredible sound of numerous clocks striking, chiming and playing. All are carefully maintained to keep the correct time.

The museum gives its visitors a comprehensive account of the history of chronometry through the ages, and of clock technology through the 15th century through to the present day.

❸ Kurrentgasse

Map 2 D5 & 5 C2. Ⓤ Stephansplatz. Grimm bakery: **Open** 7am–6:30pm Mon–Fri, 7am–1pm Sat.

This narrow street is shaded by elegant tall Baroque houses, their lower floors filled with cosy bars and pricey Italian restaurants. It's a pleasant place to while away an afternoon. The Grimm bakery at No. 10 is one of the best in Vienna and offers an astonishing variety of breads. No. 12, a house dating from 1730, has an attractive pink cobbled courtyard filled with numerous plants and trees.

One of the many fascinating showrooms in the Clock Museum

Statue on top of No. 10 Am Hof

🚳 Kirche am Hof

Schulhof 1. **Map** 2 D5 & 5 C2.
Tel 5338394. Ⓤ Herrengasse.
Open 7am–noon, 4–6pm daily. ♿

This Catholic church, which is
picturesquely dedicated to the
Nine Choirs of Angels, was
founded by Carmelite friars in
the late 14th century. The
façade, at present being
renovated, was redesigned
by the Italian architect Carlo
Carlone in 1662 to provide
space for a large balustraded
balcony. The church is now
used for services by Vienna's
large Croatian community.
    It is also worth taking a
walk behind the church into
Schulhofplatz to look at the
tiny restored shops which
snuggle happily between the
buttresses of the Gothic choir.

🚴 Am Hof

Map 2 D5 & 5 C2. Ⓤ
Stephansplatz, Schottentor.

This is the largest enclosed
square in Vienna. The Romans
established a garrison here
and, later, the Babenberg
ruler Duke Heinrich II
Jasomirgott built his castle
close to where No. 2 Am Hof
stands. In the centre of the
square is the Mariensäule
(Column of Our Lady),
a monument that
commemorates the end
of the threat of Swedish

invasion during the Thirty Years
War (see p27). Dating from
1667, it was designed by Carlo
Carlone and Carlo Canevale.
    There are a number of
interesting houses around the
square. Opposite the church is
the palatial Märkleinisches Haus
which was designed by Johann
Lukas von Hildebrandt (see
p154) in 1727. Its elegant façade
was wrecked by the insertion of
a fire station on the ground
floor in 1935 (it now houses the
Vienna Fire Brigade Museum).
The 16th-century red house
next door is the headquarters
of Johann Kattus, a producer
of sparkling wine. No. 10,
designed by Anton Ospel, is
the Bürgerliche Zeughaus, the
citizens' armoury, where the
city's fire services are now
permanently based. The façade
is dominated by the Habsburg
coat of arms and military
emblems. The allegorical statues
above are by Lorenzo Mattielli.
    At No. 12 the bay-windowed
Urbanihaus dates from the 1730s,
and its iron inn sign dates from
the same period. Next door is
the Collalto Palace – it was here,
in 1762, that Mozart made his
first public appearance aged
just six (see p40).

🚶 Peterskirche

Petersplatz 6. **Map** 2 D5 & 5 C3.
Tel 53364330. Ⓤ Stephansplatz.
Open 7am–6pm daily.

A church has stood here since
the 12th century, but the oval
structure you see today dates
from the early 18th century.
It was modelled on St Peter's
in Rome and a number of
architects collaborated on the
design, notably Gabriele
Montani. The interior is
amazingly lavish, and there's
an exuberant, eye-catching
pulpit (1716) by the sculptor
Matthias Steindl. The richly
clothed skeletons on the right
and beneath the altar are the
remains of early Christian
martyrs originally deposited in
the catacombs in Rome. The
frescoes inside the huge dome,
depicting the Assumption of
the Virgin, are by J M Rottmayr.
    In 1729 Lorenzo Mattielli
designed the sculpture of
St John Nepomuk to the right
of the choir. This priest earned
his sainthood by being thrown
into the River Vltava in Prague in
1393 after he refused to
reveal the secrets of the
confessional to King
Wenceslas IV; his
martyrdom by
drowning later
became a
favourite
subject of
artists.

18th-century engraving of
Peterskirche

HOFBURG QUARTER

What began as a modest city fortress has grown over the centuries into a vast palace, the Hofburg. The palace was still expanding up until a few years before the Habsburgs fell from power in 1918. The presence of the court had a profound effect on the surrounding area. The former gardens of the palace are now the Volksgarten and

Burggarten, and some of the buildings are now splendid museums. Streets such as Herrengasse and Bankgasse are lined with the palaces that the nobility built in their eagerness to be as close as possible to the centre of imperial power. This area is bustling with tourists by day, but at night it is almost deserted.

Sights at a Glance

Streets and Squares
1 Michaelerplatz
6 Josefsplatz
7 Dorotheergasse
8 Graben
10 Kohlmarkt
12 Naglergasse
13 Herrengasse
29 Minoritenplatz
31 Bankgasse
35 Neuer Markt
36 Kärntner Strasse
38 Stock-im-Eisen-Platz

Historic Buildings
2 Looshaus
3 Grosses und Kleines Michaelerhaus
5 Stallburg
11 Demel Konditorei
14 Mollard-Clary Palace
15 *Hofburg Complex pp98–9*
24 Prunksaal
26 *Spanish Riding School pp100–101*
28 Bundeskanzleramt
33 Lobkowitz Palace
37 American Bar

Churches and Cathedrals
4 Michaelerkirche
23 Augustinerkirche
25 Burgkapelle
30 Minoritenkirche
34 Kapuzinerkirche und Kaisergruft

Museums and Galleries
16 Neue Burg
17 Ephesos Museum
18 Sammlung Alter Musikinstrumente
19 Hofjagd und Rüstkammer
20 Weltmuseum Wien
22 Albertina
27 *State Apartments and Treasuries pp102–3*

Parks and Gardens
21 Burggarten
32 Volksgarten

Monuments
9 Pestsäule

See also Street Finder maps 5 and 6

Street-by-Street: Imperial Vienna

The streets around the Hofburg are no longer filled with the carriages of the nobility. Most of the palaces have become offices, embassies or apartments. Yet this district remains the most fashionable in Vienna, crammed with elegant shops, art galleries and coffee houses, which offer enjoyable interludes between visits to the many museums and churches in the area.

⑭ Mollard-Clary Palace
This mansion, built at the end of the 17th-century, has a façade designed by J L Hildebrandt.

⑬ Herrengasse
This was a prime site for the palaces of the nobility.

Herrengasse U-Bahn

⑪ Demel Konditorei
This Café-Konditorei offers delightful decor and exquisite pastries.

⑧ Grosses und Kleines Michaelerhaus
Joseph Haydn *(see p40)* once lived in rooms overlooking the handsome courtyard of the Grosses Michaelerhaus.

② ★ Looshaus
Built in 1912, this unadorned design outraged the conservative sensibilities of the ornament-loving Archduke Franz Ferdinand *(see p168)*.

① Michaelerplatz
Roman remains have been excavated here.

④ ★ Michaelerkirche
The crypt of this church contains well-preserved corpses from the late 18th century.

Key

— Suggested route

0 metres	50
0 yards	50

⑥ Josefsplatz
An equestrian statue of Joseph II stands at the centre of this elegant square.

⑫ Naglergasse
This lane has some of the finest Baroque façades in the city.

⑧ Graben
The Spar-Casse Bank, with its gilt bee on the pediment, is just one of many fine buildings on the pedestrianized Graben.

Locator Map
See Street Finder, maps 2 & 5

⑩ Kohlmarkt
This street has a number of shops by Hans Hollein, one of Austria's finest architects.

⑨ ★ Pestsäule
Built after the plague of 1679, this is the most imposing of the Baroque plague columns.

⑦ Dorotheergasse
Lining this narrow lane are art galleries and auction houses, and the much-loved Café Hawelka *(see pp60–63)*.

⑤ Stallburg
Once a royal residence, the Stallburg now houses the Spanish Riding School stables and the Lipizzaner Museum.

The Palffy Palace
Built in the 16th century, this was a venue for a performance of Mozart's *The Marriage of Figaro.*

The Pallavicini Palace is a late 18th-century aristocrats' palace, strategically located opposite the Hofburg.

❶ Michaelerplatz

Map 5 C3. Ⓤ Herrengasse.

Michaelerplatz faces the grandiose entrance into the Hofburg, the Michaelertor. Opposite are the Michaelerkirche and Looshaus. On one side of Michaelerplatz is the Michaelertrakt, commissioned by Franz Joseph in 1888 when the new Burgtheater *(see pp134–5)* on the Ringstrasse opened, and the original theatre dating from 1751, which occupied this site, was demolished. An old design by Joseph Emanuel Fischer von Erlach *(see p149)* was used as the basis for a new design by Ferdinand Kirschner (1821–96). It was finished in 1893, complete with gilt-tasselled cupolas and statuary representing Austria's land and sea power.

At the centre is an excavation site that reveals remains of a Roman encampment, as well as some medieval foundations.

❷ Looshaus

Michaelerplatz 3. **Map** 2 D5 & 5 C3. **Tel** 211365000. Ⓤ Herrengasse. **Open** 8am–3pm Mon–Wed & Fri, 8am–5:30pm Thu. ♿

Erected opposite the Michaelertor in 1910–12, and designed by Adolf Loos, this building so outraged Franz Ferdinand *(see p168)* that he declared he would never use the Michaelertor

Michaelerplatz fountain

again. Today it's hard to understand why: the outside is unexceptional but the inside is a lesson in stylish elegance.

Adolf Loos

Unlike his contemporary Otto Wagner *(see p59)*, Adolf Loos (1870–1933) loathed ornament for its own sake. Instead, he used smooth lines and exquisite interior decoration; his buildings' lack of "eyebrows" (the window hoods on many of Vienna's buildings) scandalized Viennese society. Surviving interiors include Knize *(see p95)*, the American Bar *(see p107)* and the Café Museum *(see p139)*.

❸ Grosses und Kleines Michaelerhaus

Kohlmarkt 11 & Michaelerplatz 6. **Map** 2 D5 & 5 C3. Ⓤ Herrengasse. **Closed** to the public.

At No. 6 Michaelerplatz a footpath leads to the Baroque Kleines Michaelerhaus (1735). Look out for a vivid painted relief of Christ on the Mount of Olives with a crucifixion in the background (1494) on the side of the Michaelerkirche. The Baroque façade of the Grosses Michaelerhaus is at No. 11 Kohlmarkt. It has a handsome courtyard and coach house. From here there is a fine view of the older parts of the Michaelerkirche. The buildings around the courtyard were erected in about 1720, and the composer Joseph Haydn *(see p40)* is said to have lived in an unheated attic here in 1749.

❹ Michaelerkirche

Michaelerplatz 1. **Map** 2 D5 & 5 C3. **Tel** 5338000. Ⓤ Herrengasse/ Stephansplatz. **Open** 7am–10pm daily. 🔊 ♿ 📷 Tours of the crypt: 11am & 1pm Mon–Sat.

The Michaelerkirche was once the parish church of the court. Its earliest parts were built in the 13th century, and the choir dates from 1327–40. The Neo-Classical façade is from 1792. Its porch is topped by Baroque statues (1724–25) by Lorenzo Mattielli depicting the Fall of the Angels. Inside are Renaissance and 14th-century frescoes, and a glorious, vividly carved organ from 1714 by Johann David Sieber. The main choir (1782), replete with tumbling cherubs and sunbursts, is by Karl Georg Merville. The altarpiece of the north choir (1755) is by Franz Anton Maulbertsch.

Off the north choir is the crypt entrance. In the 17th and 18th centuries parishioners were frequently buried beneath their church. Corpses clothed in their burial finery, well-preserved due to the constant temperature, can still be seen in open coffins.

Baroque organ (1714) in the Michaelerkirche

❺ Stallburg

Reitschulgasse 2. **Map** 4 D1 & 5 C3.
Ⓤ Stephansplatz, Herrengasse.

The Stallburg was built in the
mid-16th century for Archduke
Maximilian. This former royal
residence was later converted
to stables for the Hofburg.
These are ranged around a
large courtyard with arcades
on three storeys. The Stallburg
houses the Spanish Riding
School stables (see pp100–101).
For much of the 18th century,
the Stallburg was the home
of the Imperial art collection.
In 1776, the collection was
transferred to the Belvedere so
that it would be accessible to
the public, and in 1891 it was
moved to its present home, the
Kunsthistoriches Museum.

❻ Josefsplatz

Augustinerstrasse. **Map** 4 D1 & 5 C4.
Ⓤ Stephansplatz, Herrengasse.

In the centre of the Josefsplatz
is an equestrian statue (1807)
of Joseph II by Franz Anton von
Zauner. Despite his reforms,
Joseph II was a true monarchist,
and during the 1848 revolution
(see p33) loyalists used the
square as a gathering place.
Facing the Hofburg are
two palaces. No. 5 is the
Pallavicini Palace (1783–4),
a blend of Baroque
and Neo-Classical styles
by Ferdinand von
Hohenberg. No. 6 is

the 16th-century Palffy Palace.
On the right of the Prunksaal
(see p104) is the Redoutensaal.
It was built from 1750–60 and
was the venue for masked balls
in imperial times. To the left is
an extension to the library
which was built a few years
later. Both are by Nikolaus von
Pacassi, a favourite architect
of Maria Theresa.

❼ Dorotheergasse

Map 4 D1 & 5 C4. Ⓤ Stephansplatz.
Jewish Museum: **Tel** 5350431.
Open 10am–6pm Sun–Fri. 🅦 jmw.at

At No. 11 of this street is the
Eskeles Palace, now home to
the Jewish Museum (Jüdisches
Museum) which, along with its
extension in Judenplatz (see
p88), chronicles the city's rich
Jewish heritage. At No. 17 is the
Dorotheum (see pp224–5), from
the 17th century. A pawnbrokers
and, more importantly, an
auction house, it has branches
all over Vienna. Halfway along
the street is the Evangelical
church (1783–4), originally by
Gottlieb Nigelli. Towards the top
end, close to Graben, are two
immensely popular Viennese
gathering places, Café Hawelka
at No. 6 (see pp60–3), and
Trzesniewski sandwich buffet at
No. 1 (see p213). There are
many art and antique
dealers in this area.

Baroque plague column (Pestsäule)

❽ Graben

Map 2 D5 & 5 C3. Ⓤ Stephansplatz.
Neidhart Fresco House: **Open** 10am–
1pm & 2–6pm Tue–Sun & hols.

Facing No. 16 of this
pedestrianized street is the
Joseph Fountain by Johann
Martin Fischer. Further along
is his identical Leopold Fountain
(both 1804). No. 13, the clothing
shop Knize (see p223), is by
Adolf Loos. No. 10, the Anker-
haus by Otto Wagner, is topped
by a studio used by Wagner
himself and, in the 1980s, by
Friedensreich Hundertwasser
(see p166). No. 21 is Alois Pichl's
Spar-Casse Bank from the 1830s.
Just off the Graben at No. 19
Tuchlauben is the Neidhart
Fresco House, containing
medieval frescoes (see pp56–9).

❾ Pestsäule

Graben. **Map** 2 D5 & 5 C3.
Ⓤ Stephansplatz.

During the plague of 1679,
Emperor Leopold I vowed to
commemorate Vienna's
eventual deliverance. The
plague over, he commissioned
Matthias Rauchmiller, Lodovico
Burnacini and the young Johann
Bernhard Fischer von Erlach
(see p149) to build this Baroque
plague column. Devised by the
Jesuits, its most striking image
shows a saintly figure and an
angel supervising the destruction
of a hag representing the
plague, while above the
bewigged Emperor prays.

Statue in Josefsplatz of Joseph II by Franz Anton von Zauner (1746–1822)

Exterior of Schullin shop *(see p223)*

❿ Kohlmarkt

Map 2 D5 & 5 C3. Ⓤ Herrengasse.

Leading directly up to the Imperial Palace, the Kohlmarkt is pedestrianized and lined with some of Vienna's most exclusive shops and remarkable shopfronts. No. 9, the Jugendstil Artaria Haus (1901), was the work of Max Fabiani (1865–1962), a protégé of Otto Wagner *(see p59)*. No.16, the bookshop and publishers Manz, boasts a characteristic portal from 1912 by Adolf Loos *(see p94)*. The striking abstract shopfront of jewellers Schullin (1982) was designed by the architect Hans Hollein *(see p93)*.

⓫ Demel Konditorei

Kohlmarkt 14. **Map** 2 D5 & 5 C3.
Tel 53517170. Ⓤ Stephansplatz.
Open 9am–7pm daily. ♿

This famous pastry shop at No. 14 Kohlmarkt still bears its imperial patent – K.u.k. Hof-Zuckerbäcker – proudly lettered above the shopfront. The pastry shop was founded in Michaelerplatz in 1785 and acquired by the pâtissier Christoph Demel in 1857, before moving to its present site on Kohlmarkt in 1888. Its many small rooms are in an ornate late 19th-century style.

⓬ Naglergasse

Map 2 D5 & 5 C2. Ⓤ Herrengasse.

During the Middle Ages needle-makers had their shops here, which is how the street acquired its name. This narrow lane also follows the line of a wall that used to stand here in Roman times. Today Naglergasse is lined with a succession of gorgeous Baroque houses. The delightful Renaissance bay window of No. 19 is ornamented with carved cherubs. No. 13 dates from the 16th century but has been considerably altered since. No. 21 (1720) is now an inn with a particularly snug and cosy interior.

⓭ Herrengasse

Map 2 D5 & 5 B2. Ⓤ Herrengasse.

Flanking the Hofburg, this street was the prime location for the palaces of the Habsburg nobility. In 1843 a visiting writer, J G Kohl, wrote of the street's "silent palaces", and today little has changed.

The base of the provincial government of Lower Austria, the Landhaus, is at No. 13; the façade of the present building dates from the 1830s.

In the courtyard a tablet from 1571 warns visitors not to carry weapons or to fight here. The injunction was famously ignored when the 1848 Revolution *(see p33)* was ignited on this very spot.

The long, low Neo-Classical façade of No. / received its present appearance from Ludwig Pichl and Giacomo Quarenghi in 1811. At No. 5 Anton Ospel (1677–1756) gave the Wilczek Palace (built before 1737) an original façade, with angled pilasters lending the central bays an illusion of perspective.

Coat of arms in the courtyard of the Mollard-Clary Palace

⓮ Mollard-Clary Palace

Herrengasse 9. **Map** 2 D5 & 5 B3.
Tel 53410710. Ⓤ Herrengasse. Globe Museum **Open** 10am–6pm Tue–Sun (to 9pm Thu).

At No. 9 Herrengasse is the former Mollard-Clary Palace, a mansion constructed by Domenico Martinelli in 1698. The façade was the first commission for Johann Lukas von Hildebrandt *(see p154)*.

From 1923 until 1997 the palace housed the Lower Austrian Provincial Museum, or Landesmuseum. Today the building houses offices and the Globe Museum.

In the courtyard is a 16th-century elaborate wrought-iron well cover and a carved stone coat of arms (1454).

⓯ Hofburg Complex

See pp98–103.

Inside the ornately-decorated Demel Konditorei

⓰ Neue Burg

Heldenplatz. **Map** 1 D1 & 5 B4.
Tel 52524484. Ⓤ Volkstheater,
Herrengasse. 🚃 1, 2, D.
Open 10am–6pm Wed–Sun.
📷 🌐 hofburg.vienna.info

The Neue Burg, a massive
curved building situated on
Heldenplatz, was added to the
Hofburg Complex in 1881–1913.
It embodies the last gasp of
the Habsburg Empire as it
strained under aspirations of
independence from its domains,
when the personal prestige of
Emperor Franz Joseph was all that
seemed able to keep it intact. It
was not the perfect moment to
embark on an extension to the
Hofburg, but the work was
undertaken nevertheless, and the
Neue Burg was built to designs
by the Ringstrasse architects Karl
von Hasenauer (1833–94) and
Gottfried Semper (1803–79). Five
years after its completion, the
Habsburg empire ended.

In 1938, Adolf Hitler stood on
the terraced central bay to
proclaim the Anschluss – the
union of Austria and Germany –
to tens of thousands of
Viennese *(see p38)*.

Today the Neue Burg is home
to the reading room of the
National Library, as well as a
number of museums *(see
following entries)*.

⓱ Ephesos Museum

As Neue Burg. **Tel** 525244902.
Open 10am–6pm Wed–Sun.
🌐 khm.at

For decades Austrian
archaeologists
have been
excavating the
Greek and
Roman site of
Ephesus in
Turkey. Since 1978 their
discoveries have been on
display in the main block of the
Neue Burg. Also on show are
finds from the Greek island of
Samothrace, excavated in the
1870s. The main exhibits include
a colossal frieze commemorating
Lucius Verus's victory over the
Parthians in AD 165, and many
architectural fragments.

Armour at Hofjagd und Rüstkammer

⓲ Sammlung Alter Musikinstrumente

As Neue Burg. **Tel** 525244602.

Pianos that belonged to
Beethoven, Schubert and
Haydn, among countless other
items, are housed in the musical
instrument museum. More
important, however, is the
collection of Renaissance
instruments, widely believed to
be the finest in the world. The
claviorgan (1596), the oldest
surviving example of this
instrument, is particularly
fascinating, and features stops
used to create special effects
such as birdsong.

Renaissance cittern from the
Sammlung Alter Musikinstrumente

⓳ Hofjagd und Rüstkammer

As Neue Burg. **Tel** 525244502.

The Hofburg's weapons
collection is impressive both for
its size and for the workmanship
of its finest items: ivory and
filigree inlay on weapons,
medieval ceremonial saddles
and jewelled Turkish and Syrian
maces. Particularly resplendent
are the 16th-century ceremonial
suits worn by the Habsburgs for
tournaments and military
parades, and the decorative
fighting and hunting weapons.

The museum was based on
the personal armouries of the
Habsburg emperors and, not
surprisingly, houses one of the
finest collections in Europe.

⓴ Weltmuseum Wien

As Neue Burg. **Tel** 534305052.
Open 10am–6pm Mon, Wed–Sun.
🌐 weltmuseumwien.at

Ranged around an arcaded
Italian Renaissance-style
courtyard, at the west end of
the Neue Burg, is the ethnological
museum. To one side are the
Oriental collections: lacquer
screens, clothes, furniture,
weapons, ceramics, farm tools,
masks and musical instruments.
In a neighbouring room are
African figurines and masks. The
artifacts from Benin are the
highlight of the African collection.
Australasia and Polynesia
dominate the displays upstairs,
with fabrics from Bali, weapons
from Borneo and many musical
instruments from the Far East.

The large pre-Columbian
collection from Mexico includes
an Aztec feather headdress,
while the permanent collection
features a section on
Eskimo culture.

⓯ The Hofburg Complex

The vast Hofburg Complex contains the former imperial apartments, several museums, a chapel, a church, the Austrian National Library, the Spanish Riding School and the President of Austria's offices. It was the seat of Austrian power for over six centuries, and successive rulers were all anxious to leave their mark. Seven centuries of architectural development can be seen in the 10 or so buildings, ranging from Gothic to late 19th-century historicism.

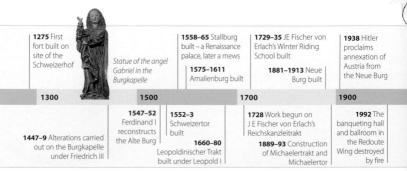

★ **Prunksaal**
The showpiece of the Austrian National Library (1722–35) is the flamboyant, wood-panelled Prunksaal, or Hall of Honour.

★ **Michaelertrakt** (1893)
The curved façade of the Michaelertrakt is surmounted by an imposing dome.

1275 First fort built on site of the Schweizerhof	*Statue of the angel Gabriel in the Burgkapelle*	**1558–65** Stallburg built – a Renaissance palace, later a mews	**1729–35** JE Fischer von Erlach's Winter Riding School built	**1938** Hitler proclaims annexation of Austria from the Neue Burg
		1575–1611 Amalienburg built	**1881–1913** Neue Burg built	
1300	**1500**	**1700**		**1900**
	1547–52 Ferdinand I reconstructs the Alte Burg	**1552–3** Schweizertor built	**1728** Work begun on J E Fischer von Erlach's Reichskanzleitrakt	**1992** The banqueting hall and ballroom in the Redoute Wing destroyed by fire
1447–9 Alterations carried out on the Burgkapelle under Friedrich III		**1660–80** Leopoldinischer Trakt built under Leopold I	**1889–93** Construction of Michaelertrakt and Michaelertor	

Mozart Memorial (1896)
Viktor Tilgner's statue of
the composer stands
just inside the
Ringstrasse entrance.

★ Prince Eugene Statue
Anton Dominik von Fernkorn
designed this monument of
Prince Eugene (1865).
The pedestal is by
Eduard van der Nüll.

★ Schweizertor
This 16th-century
Renaissance
gateway leads to
the Schweizerhof,
the oldest part of
the Hofburg,
originally a
stronghold with
four towers.

KEY

① Reichkanzleitrakt
② Michaelertor
③ Spanish Riding School *(see pp100–101)*
④ Stallburg (Stables) *(see p95)*
⑤ Redoute Wing
⑥ Alte Burg
⑦ Burgkapelle *(see p105)*

⑧ Statue of Joseph II (1806) in Josefsplatz *(see p95)*
⑨ Augustinerkirche *(see p104)*
⑩ Albertina *(see p104)*
⑪ Burggarten *(see p104)*
⑫ Neue Burg *(see p97)*
⑬ **Burgtor** or outer gate was built to a design by Peter Nobile in 1821–4.

⑭ Heldenplatz
⑮ Leopoldinischer Trakt
⑯ **Amalienburg** is an oddly-shaped building constructed in 1575 for the emperor Maximilian's son Rudolf. It has a Renaissance façade and an attractive Baroque clock tower.

㉖ Spanish Riding School

The origins of the Spanish Riding School are obscure, but It Is believed to have been founded in 1572 to cultivate the classic skills of *haute école* horsemanship. By breeding and training horses from Spain, the Habsburgs formed the Spanische Reitschule. Today, 80-minute shows take place in the building known as the Winter Riding School. Commissioned by Karl VI, it was built from 1729 to 1735 to a design by Josef Emanuel Fischer von Erlach. There are two entrances to the building – one from door 2, Josefsplatz, the other from the Michaelerkuppel.

Specially-bred Lipizzaner stallions are trained from the age of three.

The black bicorn hat has a gold braid stripe from the upper left to the lower centre.

Jackets are coffee-coloured – waisted, double-breasted and with two rows of brass buttons.

Buckskin jodhpurs are worn.

Pale leather gloves are worn.

Long boots covering the knees are part of the uniform.

Tack
The elegant saddle with embroidered cloth differs from modern versions and complements the historical dress of the riders; the curb rein is generally used.

Stables
The three-storey-high Renaissance former palace of the Stallburg is across the road from the Winter Riding School. It now provides stabling for the horses.

The Horses' Steps

The steps made by the horses and riders are part of a carefully orchestrated ballet. Many derive from exercises that were developed during the Renaissance period by cavalrymen, who needed agile horses capable of special manoeuvres.

The Croupade: the horse leaps into the air with hind legs and forelegs bent under its belly.

Levade: the horse stands on its hind legs with hocks almost touching the ground.

VISITORS' CHECKLIST

Practical Information
Michaelerplatz 1, A-1010. **Map** 5
C3. **Tel** 5339031. **Open** 9am–4pm
Tue–Sun (visitor centre);
performances from 11am Sat &
Sun. **Closed** 1 Jan, 6 Jan, 1 May,
Ascension Day, Corpus Christi,
15 Aug, 26 Oct, 1 Nov, 8 Dec,
25–26 Dec (dates do vary). 🎧
📷 💿 ♿ some areas. 🌐 srs.at

Transport
Ⓤ Herrengasse. 🚍 1A, 2A to
Michaelerplatz.

Portrait of Karl VI
An equestrian portrait of Emperor
Karl VI who commissioned the
building, hangs in the royal box.
Whenever a rider enters the hall,
he must express his respect to the
founder of the school by raising
his bicorn hat to the portrait.

The Lipizzaner Horses

The stallions that perform their athletic feats on the sawdust of the
Winter Riding School take their name from the stud at Lipizza near
Trieste in Slovenia *(see below)*, which was founded by Archduke Karl in
1580. Today the horses are bred on the Austrian National Stud Farm at
Piber near Graz. The breed was originally produced by crossing Arab,
Berber and Spanish horses. The horses are renowned for their grace
and stamina. You may be able to obtain a ticket without a reservation
to see them at their morning training session.

nterior of the Winter
iding School

he gracious interior is lined with
5 columns and adorned with
aborate plasterwork, chandeliers
nd a coffered ceiling. At the head of
he arena is the court box. Spectators
t here or watch from upper galleries.

Capriole: this is a leap
into the air with a
simultaneous kick of
the hind legs.

The Piaffe: the horse
trots on the spot, often
between two pillars.

❷⁷ State Apartments and Treasuries

The state apartments in the Reichskanzleitrakt (1723–30) and the Amalienburg (1575) include rooms occupied by Franz Joseph from 1857 to 1916, Empress Elisabeth's apartments from 1854 to 1898 and the rooms where Tsar Alexander I lived during the Congress of Vienna in 1815. The Treasuries hold sacred and secular treasures amassed during centuries of Habsburg rule, They include relics of the Holy Roman Empire, the crown jewels and liturgical objects of the imperial court.

★ 10th-century Crown
The insignia of the Holy Roman Empire includes this crown set with enamel plaques and cabochons.

Emperor Maximilian I
(around 1500)
This portrait by Bernhard Strigel hangs in the room containing Burgundian treasure. Emperor Maximilian married Mary, Duchess of Burgundy in 1477.

Cradle of the King of Rome
Designed by the French painter Prud'hon, Maria Louisa gave this cradle to her son, the King of Rome *(see p177)*.

KEY

① **Entrance through the Michaelerkuppel to State Apartments and Silberkammer**

② **Entrance to Treasuries**

③ **Passage to Neue Burg and Heldenplatz**

④ **Sisi Museum**

⑤ **Ticket office**

⑥ **Entrance through the Kaisertor to State Apartments and Silberkammer**

⑦ **Exit from apartments**

Crucifix after Giambologna
(around 1590)
This type of crucifix, a Cristo Morto, can be traced back to a similar model by Giambologna which is in Florence.

Key

☐ Franz Joseph's State Apartments
☐ Elisabeth's State Apartments
☐ Alexander's State Apartments
☐ Sacred Treasury
☐ Secular Treasury
☐ Sisi Museum
☐ Non-exhibition space

The Silberkammer

On display in the ground-floor rooms of the court tableware and silver depot is a dazzling array of items – gold, silver and the finest porcelain – that were once used at the Habsburg state banquets. One of the highlights is a 33-m long (100-ft) gilded bronze centrepiece with accompanying candelabra from around 1800. Visitors can also admire the mid-18th- century Sèvres dinner service that was a diplomatic gift from Louis XV to Maria Theresa.

Goblet from the Laxenburg Service (around 1821)

VISITORS' CHECKLIST

Practical Information
Map 4 D1 & 5 B3. State Apartments (Kaiserapparte-ments), Sisi Museum & Silberkammer: Michaelerkuppel. **Tel** 5337570. **Open** 9am–5:30pm daily (to 6pm Jul & Aug). 🦽 📷 Sat & Sun. 🅦 hofburg-wien.at Treasuries (Schatzkammer): Schweizerhof. **Tel** 525240. **Open** 9:30am–5:30pm daily (to 6pm Jul & Aug); 24 Dec: to 3pm; 31 Dec: to 4pm. 🦽 🖥 🔲 📷 🅦 kaiserliche-schatzkammer.at

Elisabeth's Gymnastic Equipment
The Empress was a fitness enthusiast, and the bars at which she exercised are still in place in her dressing room.

★ **Imperial Dining Hall**
The table is laid as it used to be in Emperor Franz Joseph's day *(see p34–5),* in the room where the Imperial family used to dine.

Guide to Treasuries

Entering the Secular Treasury, Rooms 1–8 contain items from the Austrian Empire (with Room 5 commemorating Napoleon). Rooms 9–12 exhibit treasures from the Holy Roman Empire, while the Burgundian Inheritance is displayed in Rooms 13–16. Rooms I–V, furthest from the entrance, house the Sacred Treasury.

★ **Empress Elisabeth**
Winterhalter's portrait of the Empress (1865) with stars in her hair hangs in the Sisi Museum.

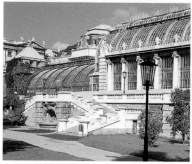

Greenhouses in the Burggarten by Friedrich Ohmann (1858–1927)

㉑ Burggarten

Burgring/Opernring. **Map** 4 D1 & 5 B4.
Ⓤ Karlsplatz. 🚋 1, 2, D. **Open** Apr–
Oct: 6am–10pm; Nov–Mar: 6:30am–
7pm daily.

Before leaving Vienna, Napoleon showed his contempt for the Viennese by razing part of the city walls which had proved so ineffective at preventing his entry. Some of the space left around the Hofburg was later transformed by the Habsburgs into a landscaped garden, planted with a variety of trees. It was opened to the public in 1918.

Overlooking the garden are greenhouses (1901–7) by the Jugendstil architect Friedrich Ohmann, and near the Hofburg entrance is a small equestrian statue (1780) of Emperor Franz I by the sculptor Balthasar Moll. Closer to the Ringstrasse is the Mozart Memorial (1896) by Viktor Tilgner.

㉒ Albertina

Augustinerstrasse 1. **Map** 4 D1 & 5 C4.
Tel 53483540. Ⓤ Karlsplatz,
Stephansplatz. **Open** 10am–6pm daily
(to 9pm Wed). 🖼 ♿ 🎧 🎬 ✏ 📷
Ⓦ albertina.at

Once hidden away at the Opera end of the Hofburg is the Albertina, now a distinctive landmark. Its raised entrance boasts a controversial freestanding diving-board roof by architect Hans Hollein (see p93). The palace once belonged to Maria Theresa's daughter, Maria Christina, and her husband Duke Albert of Sachsen-Teschen,

after whom the gallery is named. Today the Albertina houses a collection of one million prints, over 65,000 water colours and drawings, and some 70,000 photographs. The gems of the collections are by Dürer, with Michelangelo and Rubens also well represented. Picasso heads a fine 20th-century section.

Temporary exhibitions feature paintings on loan along with works from the Albertina. The Batliner Collection, which comprises over 500 works of art and is one of the most significant private collections in Europe, is on permanent loan.

The extension on the Burggarten side houses study facilities and the largest of the three exhibition halls. Renovation has restored a number of features of the Albertina to their former glory, including the façades and the central courtyard. Most notably, the Habsburg State Rooms are now open to the public. They represent a remarkable example of Neo-Classical architecture and interior decoration, inspired by the Archduchess Maria Christina herself.

㉓ Augustinerkirche

Augustinerstrasse 3. **Map** 4 D1 & 5 C4.
Tel 5337099. Ⓤ Stephansplatz.
Open 7am–6pm Mon–Fri, 8am–7pm
Sat & Sun.

The Augustinerkirche has one of the best-preserved 14th-century Gothic interiors in Vienna; only the modern chandeliers strike a jarring note. The church also houses the Loreto Chapel, dating back to 1724, containing the silver urns that preserve the hearts of the Habsburg family (see pp26–7). Here too is one of the most powerful works by the Italian Neo-Classical sculptor Antonio Canova, the tomb of

Maria Christina, favourite daughter of Maria Theresa. Like the tomb of Leopold II, which is also here, Maria Christina's tomb is empty; the royal remains lie in the Kaisergruft (see p106).

The church is also celebrated for its music, including masses by Schubert or Haydn held here on Sundays.

㉔ Prunksaal

Josefsplatz 1. **Map** 4 D1 & 5 C4.
Tel 53410394. Ⓤ Herrengasse.
Open 10am–6pm Tue–Sun,
10am–9pm Thu. 🖼 Ⓦ onb.ac.at

Commissioned as the court library by Karl VI, the main hall, or Prunksaal, of the National Library was designed by Johann Bernhard Fischer von Erlach (see p149) in 1719. After his death in 1723, the building was completed by his son. The collection consists of approximately 2.6 million books, and includes the personal library of Prince Eugene (see pp28–9), as well as books that were taken from monastic libraries closed during the religious reforms of Joseph II (see p31).

The Prunksaal is 77 m (252 ft) long and is the largest Baroque library in Europe. Paired marble columns frame the domed main room, and bookcases line the walls. Spanning the vaults are frescoes by the Baroque painter Daniel Gran (1730), which were restored by Franz Anton

Domed interior of the Prunksaal in the National Library building

Maulbertsch (1769). The many fine statues, including the likeness of Karl VI in the centre of the hall, are the work of Paul Strudel (1648–1708) and his brother Peter (1660–1714).

㉕ Burgkapelle

Hofburg, Schweizerhof. **Map** 4 D1 & 5 B4. **Tel** 5339927. Ⓤ Herrengasse. **Open** 11am–3pm Mon–Thu, 11am–1pm Fri for guided tours only. **Closed** Public holidays. 🎫 📷 📹 Vienna Boys' Choir: **Open** Jan–Jun & Sep–Dec: 9:15am Sun (book via website). 🎫 🌐 **hofburgkapelle.at**

From the Schweizerhof, steps lead up to the Burgkapelle, or Hofburg Chapel, originally constructed in 1296 but modified 150 years later. On Sundays, visitors can hear the Wiener Sängerknaben, the Vienna Boys' Choir *(see p43)*. The chapel interior has Gothic statuary in canopied niches and Gothic carvings, and boasts a bronze crucifix (1720) by Johann Känischbauer.

㉖ Spanish Riding School

See pp100–101.

㉗ State Apartments and Treasuries

See pp102–3.

㉘ Bundeskanzleramt

Ballhausplatz 2. **Map** 1 C5 & 5 B3. **Tel** 531150. Ⓤ Herrengasse. **Closed** to the public.

The Bundeskanzleramt (1717–19), the Austrian Chancery and Foreign Ministry, was designed by Johann Lukas von Hildebrandt *(see p154)*. It was expanded to its present size in 1766 by Nikolaus Pacassi. Major events that shaped Austria's history have taken place here, including meetings of the Congress of Vienna *(see p32)* in 1814–15, the final deliberations in 1914 that led to the outbreak of World War I, and the murder of Chancellor Dollfuss by Nazi terrorists in 1934 *(see p38)*.

No. 4 Minoritenplatz

㉙ Minoritenplatz

Map 2 D5 & 5 B3. Ⓤ Herrengasse.

At No. 1 Minoritenplatz is the Baroque-style State Archives building (the archives are no longer housed here), built on to the back of the Bundeskanzleramt in 1902. There are a number of palaces around the square. No. 3 is the former Dietrichstein Palace of 1755, an early building by Franz Hillebrand. It now contains the offices of the Federal Chancellor and the Foreign Office. No. 4 is the side of the Liechtenstein Palace *(see p106)*. The mid-17th-century Starhemberg Palace is at No. 5. Now housing ministry offices, it was the residence of Count Ernst Rüdiger von Starhemberg, a hero of the 1683 Turkish siege *(see p29)* when he led the Austrian forces within the city.

㉚ Minoritenkirche

Minoritenplatz 2. **Map** 1 C5 & 5 B3. **Tel** 676 6264113. Ⓤ Herrengasse. **Open** 9am–6pm daily.

This ancient church was established here by the Minor Friars in around 1224, although the present structure dates from 1339. The tower was given its odd pyramidal shape during the Turkish siege of 1529, when shells sliced the top off the steeple. In the 1780s the Minoritenkirche was restored to its original Gothic style, when Maria Theresa's son, Joseph II *(see p30)*, made a gift of the church to Vienna's Italian community. The church retains a fine west portal (1340) with statues beneath traceried canopies; the carvings above the doorway are modern.

The interior of the church is unexpectedly bright and large and contains a mosaic copy of Leonardo da Vinci's *Last Supper*. Napoleon Bonaparte commissioned Giacomo Raffaelli to execute this work as he proposed to substitute it for the original in Milan and remove the real painting to Paris. Following Napoleon's downfall at Waterloo in 1815, Raffaelli's version was bought by the Habsburgs. In the south aisle is a painted statue of the Madonna and Child (dating from around 1350), while at the same spot in the north aisle is a faded fragment of a 16th-century fresco of St Francis of Assisi.

Gothic statue (about 1400) of Leopold III in the Burgkapelle

❸❶ Bankgasse

Map 1 C5 & 5 B3. Ⓤ Herrengasse.

Few streets in Vienna are more crammed with the palaces of the nobility.

At Nos. 4–6 is the former Strattmann-Windischgrätz Palace (1692–1734), which was originally designed by Johann Bernhard Fischer von Erlach *(see p149)*. The present façade (1783–4) was the work of Franz Hillebrand, who considerably increased the size of the building by incorporating the palace next door. Today, it houses the Hungarian Embassy.

Nos. 5–7 are the back of the Starhemberg Palace. No. 9 is the Liechtenstein Palace, built as a town residence for the Liechtenstein family by Domenico Martinelli (1694–1706). No. 2 is the Schönborn-Batthyány Palace (1695).

❸❷ Volksgarten

Dr-Karl-Renner-Ring. **Map** 1 C5 & 5 A3. **Tel** 5339083. Ⓤ Herrengasse. **Open** Apr–Oct: 6am–10pm daily; Nov–Mar: 6:30am–7pm daily. ♿

Like the Burggarten landscaped garden *(see p104)*, the elegant Volksgarten was created after the destruction of the city walls

Statuary above the portal to the Lobkowitz Palace

by Napoleon, and opened up a space previously occupied by fortifications. Unlike the Burggarten, the Volksgarten was opened to the public soon after its completion in 1820. The formal plantations, especially the splendid rose gardens, are matched in grandeur by the garden's ornaments, notably the Temple of Theseus (1823) by Peter von Nobile. It was built to house Canova's statue of the Greek god, which now graces the staircase of the Kunsthistorisches Museum. Other compositions include Karl von Hasenauer's monument to the poet Franz Grillparzer *(see p35)* and the fountain memorial to the assassinated Empress Elisabeth (1907) by Friedrich Ohmann *(see p59)* and the sculptor Hans Bitterlich.

Formal rose garden in the Volksgarten

❸❸ Lobkowitz Palace

Lobkowitzplatz 2. **Map** 4 D1 & 5 C4. **Tel** 525243460. Ⓤ Karlsplatz, Stephansplatz. **Open** 10am–6pm Wed–Mon. ♿ ♿ Ⓦ khm.at

This large palace was built for Count Dietrichstein in 1685–7 by Giovanni Pietro Tencala and altered by Johann Bernhard Fischer von Erlach *(see p149)* in 1710. In 1753 it was acquired by the Lobkowitz family. Balls were held here during the Congress of Vienna *(see p32)*.

Since 1991 the palace has been the Austrian Theatre Museum, which houses a model of the first Hofburg theatre and the Eroica-Saal (1724–29) – where many first performances of Beethoven's work took place. The main exhibits chronicle Austrian theatre in the 1940s.

❸❹ Kapuzinerkirche und Kaisergruft

Tegetthoffstrasse 2. **Map** 4 D1 & 5 C4. **Tel** 5126853. Ⓤ Stephansplatz. Kaisergruft: **Open** 10am–6pm daily. Kapuzinerkirche: **Open** 6am–6pm daily. ♿ ♿ Ⓦ kaisergruft.at

Beneath the Kapuzinerkirche are the vaults of the Kaisergruft, the imperial crypt founded in 1619 by the Catholic Emperor Matthias. Here lie the remains of 138 Habsburgs, including Maria Theresa and her husband Franz Stephan in a large tomb by Balthasar Moll (1753). The most poignant tomb is that of Franz Joseph, flanked by his assassinated wife Elisabeth and their son Rudolf, who committed suicide *(see p34)*. The last reigning Habsburg, Empress

Tomb of Karl VI by Balthasar Moll

Zita, died in 1989 and her remains are also buried in the crypt.

㉟ Neuer Markt

Map 4 D1 & 5 C4. Ⓤ Stephansplatz.

Known as the Mehlmarkt or flour market until around 1210, the Neuer Markt was also used as a jousting area. Of these origins nothing is left, though a few 18th- century houses remain. In the middle of the Neuer Markt is a replica of the Donner Fountain (1737–9) by Georg Raphael Donner, a symbolic celebration of the role played by rivers in the economic life of the Habsburg Empire. The four figures denote tributaries of the Danube, while the central figure represents Providence. The original figures are in the Lower Belvedere (see p159).

㊱ Kärntner Strasse

Map 4 D1 & 5 C5. Ⓤ Stephansplatz.
Malteserkirche: **Open** 7am–7pm daily.
Lobmeyr Museum: **Open** 9am–5pm Mon–Fri, 10am–6pm Sat.

This pedestrianized street was the main highway to Carinthia in medieval times. Now it is the old city's principal shopping street. Day and night, it is packed with people shopping, buying fresh fruit juice from stands, pausing in cafés, or listening to the street musicians.

No. 37 is the Malteserkirche. This church was founded by the Knights of Malta who were invited to Vienna early in the 13th century by Leopold VI. The interior retains lofty Gothic windows and vaults.

At No. 1 is the Lobmeyr Museum, which houses glass designed by Josef Hoffmann (see p58), among others, for the Viennese firm of Lobmeyr.

Around the corner at No. 5 Johannesgasse is the superb Questenberg-Kaunitz Palace which dates from the early 18th century. Its design has been attributed to the architect Johann Lukas von Hildebrandt (see p154).

㊲ American Bar

Kärntner Strasse 10. **Map** 4 D1 & 6 D3. Ⓤ Stephansplatz.

Beneath a garish depiction of the Stars and Stripes is this bar designed by Adolf Loos (see p94) in 1908. The interior, restored in 1990, is a gem. The bar is tiny, with every detail worked out by Loos, such as the tables lit from below

The Donner Fountain in Neuer Markt

and the exquisite glass cabinets for storing glasses. One of his hallmarks is the use of mahogany panelling, and this bar is no exception. Mirrors give the impression that the interior is larger than it actually is, and onyx and marble panels reflect a soft light.

Façade of the American Bar

㊳ Stock-im-Eisen-Platz

Map 2 D5 & 5 C3. Ⓤ Stephansplatz.

This square is at the intersection of Stephansplatz, Kärntner Strasse and Graben. Opposite Haas-Haus (see p77) is the Equitable Palace (1891), once headquarters to the Equitable Life Insurance Company. There is also an old tree trunk with nails in it in the square. Passing locksmiths' apprentices would bang in a nail to ensure a safe passage home.

SCHOTTENRING AND ALSERGRUND

This part of the city is dotted with sites of interest, such as the ornate Ferstel Palace and the glass-roofed Freyung Passage that runs through it. The Schottenring and the Schottentor are named after the Benedictine monks who came here in Babenberg times to found the Schottenkirche Monastery. Later rulers of Austria were responsible for the area's other monuments: Joseph II

built a huge public hospital, now the Josephinum, and Franz Joseph founded the Votivkirche as a way of giving thanks after escaping assassination in 1853. To the east, nearer the Danube Canal, quiet residential streets are broken only by the imposing Liechtenstein Garden Palace, one of many summer palaces built beyond the city gates by Vienna's nobility.

Sights at a Glance

Streets and Squares
1 Freyung Passage
2 Freyung

Churches and Cathedrals
3 Schottenkirche
5 Servitenkirche
9 Votivkirche

Museums and Galleries
4 Freud Museum
6 Liechtenstein Garden Palace
7 Josephinum
8 Narrenturm

See also Street Finder maps 1, 2 and 5

Street-by-Street: Around the Freyung

At the core of this elegant part of the city is the former medieval complex of the Schottenkirche and its courtyards and school. On the other side of the Freyung square are some beautiful Baroque palaces, including Hildebrandt's Kinsky Palace (1713–16), and the Palais Ferstel. The Freyung Passage links the Freyung square with Herrengasse, which is lined with Baroque mansions as well as the city's first skyscraper. Backing onto the Schottenring is the Italianate Börse.

❸ ★ Schottenkirche
Founded in 1177 and redecorated in the Baroque period, this fine church has a museum and there is a famous school alongside it.

Passageway leading from No. 2 Helferstorferstrasse to the Freyung

HELFERSTORFERSTRASSE

SCHOTTENGASSE

FREYUNG

HERRENGASSE

❷ ★ Freyung
This square is overlooked by fine buildings, including the former Schottenkirche priory, originally founded in 1155, then rebuilt in 1744 and, due to its appearance, known by the Viennese as the "chest of drawers house".

❶ ★ Freyung Passage
The Freyung and Herrengasse are connected by a luxury shopping arcade.

The Café Central has a papier-mâché statue of the poet Peter Altenberg next to the main entrance. Altenberg spent a great deal of time in various coffee houses around the city (see pp60–63).

To Herrengasse
U-Bahn

A central courtyard lies hidden within the former stock exchange buildings.

Locator Map
See Street Finder, maps 2 & 5

SCHOTTENRING AND ALSERGRUND

MUSEUM AND TOWNHALL QUARTER

STEPHANS-DOM QUARTER

The Börse or stock exchange, was commissioned when the Ringstrasse was conceived *(see pp34–5)*. Designed by Theophil Hansen, it was completed in 1877 and today houses offices, a gardening centre and a restaurant.

The Hermann Gmeiner Park includes a playground with wendy houses and open spaces and commemorates the life and work of Hermann Gmeiner (1919–86). He founded SOS Children's Villages, a world-wide organization that cares for orphans.

The Schönborn-Batthyány Palace is a fine Baroque palace built from 1699 to 1706.

Key

— Suggested route

| 0 metres | 50 |
| 0 yards | 50 |

❶ Freyung Passage

Map 2 D5 & 5 B2. Ⓤ Herrengasse.

Facing the Freyung is the Italian-style *palazzo* known as the Palais Ferstel, dating from 1860 and taking its name from the architect, Heinrich von Ferstel. Wander in and you will find yourself in the glass-roofed Freyung Passage: lined with elegant shops, it converges on a small courtyard of which the centrepiece is a many-tiered statue portraying the lissom water-sprite of the Danube holding a fish. It then emerges on Herrengasse. As an example of civilized urban amenities, the passage is a great success. It also has an entrance into one of Vienna's grandest coffee houses, the Café Central *(see pp60–63)*.

Danube Mermaid's Fountain (1861) in Freyung Passage

❷ Freyung

Map 2 D5 & 5 B2. Ⓤ Herrengasse. Kinsky Palace: **Open** 10am–5pm Mon–Fri.

The Freyung is a curiously shaped "square". Its name derives from the right of sanct-uary granted to the monks of the Schottenkirche that lasted until Maria Theresa abolished it. Fugitives from persecution who entered the area were safe from arrest. No. 4 is the Kinsky Palace (1713–16), by Johann Lukas von Hildebrandt *(see p154)*. Next door is the Porcia Palace of 1546, one of the oldest in Vienna, though much altered. At No. 3 is the Harrach Palace; the

Façade of the Schottenkirche

interior has some fine Rococo doors. Opposite is the Austria Fountain: its four figures symbolize the major rivers of the Habsburgs' lands. Behind is the former Schottenkirche priory, unkindly known as the chest-of-drawers house.

❸ Schottenkirche

Schottenstift, Freyung 6. **Map** 2 D5 & 5 B2. **Tel** 53498600. Ⓤ Schottentor, Herrengasse. Museum: **Open** 11am–5pm Thu–Sat. **Closed** Sun & hols.

Despite its name (Scottish church) this 1177 monastic foundation was established by Irish Benedic-tines. The adjoining buildings have a fine medieval art collection that includes the famous Schotten altarpiece (1475).

The church has been altered repeatedly and has undergone extensive renovation. Today it presents a rather drab Neo-Classical façade, with a rich Baroque interior.

❹ Freud Museum

Berggasse 19. **Map** 1 C3. **Tel** 3191596. Ⓤ Schottentor. 🚍 40A. 🚋 D. **Open** 9am–6pm daily. Ⓦ freud-museum.at

No. 19 Berggasse differs little from any other 19th-century apartment in Vienna, yet it is now one of the city's most famous addresses. The father of psychoanalysis, Sigmund Freud, lived, worked and received patients here from 1891 until his departure from Vienna in 1938.

The flat housed Freud's family as well as his practice. The catalogue lists 420 items of memorabilia on display, including letters and books, furnishings, photographs documenting Freud's long life, and various antiquities.

Although quickly abandoned when the Nazis forced Freud to leave the city where he had lived almost all his life, the flat still preserves an intimate domestic atmosphere.

❺ Servitenkirche

Servitengasse 9. **Map** 1 C3. **Tel** 31761950. Ⓤ Rossauer Lände. **Open** 7–9am, 6–7pm Mon–Fri, 7–9am, 5–8pm Sat, 7am–noon, 5–8pm Sun.

Although off the beaten track, this Baroque church (1651–77) is well worth a visit. Inside, a riot of Baroque decoration includes elaborate stucco ornamentation, a fine wrought-iron screen near the entrance, and an exuberant pulpit (1739), partly by Balthasar Moll.

Freud's Theories

Sigmund Freud (1856–1939) was not only the founder of the techniques of psychoanalysis, but a theorist who wrote many essays and books expounding his contentious ideas. Modern concepts such as subconscious, ego, sublimation and Oedipus complex, evolved from Freudian theories. Freud posited different structural systems within the human psyche that, if seriously out of balance, result in emotional or mental disturbance.

❻ Liechtenstein Garden Palace

Fürstengasse 1. **Map** 1 C2.
Tel 3195767153. **U** Friedensbrücke.
🚌 40A. 🚊 D. **Open** for guided tours only, 3–4pm daily (in German; tours in English must be pre-arranged).
W palaisliechtenstein.com

Designed by Domenico Martinelli and completed in 1692, the summer palace of the Liechtenstein family now houses the art collection of Prince Hans-Adam II von und zu Liechtenstein. Behind the imposing Palladian exterior, notable features include the Neo-Classical library, and the Hercules Hall and grand staircase with their magnificent frescoes. The art collection centres on the Baroque, with a special focus on Rubens, and numerous paintings and sculptures by German, Dutch and Italian masters from the Renaissance through to the 19th century. The palace stands in an extensive English-style garden, designed in the 19th century.

❼ Josephinum

Währinger Strasse 25/1. **Map** 1 C4.
Tel 4016026007. **U** Schottentor.
🚊 37, 38, 40, 41, 42. **Open** 10am–6pm Fri & Sat. **Closed** public hols. 🚫 ♿

The ardent reformer Joseph II *(see p30)* established this military surgical institute. Designed by Isidor Canevale in 1785, it is now a medical museum. Some rooms contain memorabilia from the 19th century, when Vienna was a leading centre for medical research, but the main attraction is the unusual collection of wax anatomical models commissioned by the emperor from Tuscan artists.

❽ Narrenturm

Spitalgasse 2. **Map** 1 B3. **Tel** 52177606.
U Schottentor. 🚊 5, 33.
Open 10am–6pm Wed, 10am–1pm Sat. **Closed** public hols 🚫

What used to be the Allgemeines Krankenhaus, founded by Joseph II *(see p30)* in 1784, has been renovated and

Detail on the Votivkirche façade

now houses various faculties of the University of Vienna. At the far end of the complex is the Narrenturm Tower, a former lunatic asylum designed by Isidor Canevale. The tower now houses the Museum for Pathological Anatomy, which includes a reconstruction of an apothecary's shop and wax models. The few ground-floor rooms open to the public only show a small part of the collection, but serious students can enrol on a guided tour of the corridors upstairs.

❾ Votivkirche

Rooseveltplatz 8. **Map** 1 C4 & 5 A1.
Tel 4061192. **U** Schottentor.
Open 9am–1pm, 4–6pm Tue–Sat, 9am–1pm Sun. 🚫 ♿ side entrance.

After a deranged tailor tried but failed to assassinate Emperor Franz Joseph on 18 February 1853, a collection was made to pay for a new church to be built opposite the Mölker-Bastei, where the attempt had been made. The architect was Heinrich von Ferstel, who began the church in 1856 though it was not dedicated until 1879. The lacy steeples and spire are very attractive. Many of the church's chapels are dedicated to Austrian regiments and military heroes. The finest monument is the Renaissance sarcophagus tomb of Niklas Salm in the chapel just west of the north transept. Salm commanded Austria's forces during the 1529 Turkish siege.

Wooden pietà in Gothic style (1470) in the Servitenkirche

MUSEUM AND TOWNHALL QUARTER

The Emperor Franz Joseph commissioned the major institutional buildings of the Habsburg empire, and the city, along the Ringstrasse in the mid-19th century *(see pp34–5)*. Today these buildings remain a successful and imposing example of good urban planning. The districts that lie to the west of the Ringstrasse are untouched, including Josefstadt, which still retains an 18th-century atmosphere with its picturesque streets, modest palaces and Baroque churches. The area's cultural institutions are vibrant: the brilliant productions staged by the Burgtheater and the wide-ranging exhibits at the Natural History Museum and the Kunsthistorisches Museum are all popular today.

Sights at a Glance

Streets and Squares
- ❻ Sankt-Ulrichs-Platz
- ❼ Spittelberg Pedestrian Area
- ⑰ Mölker-Bastei

Historic Buildings
- ❷ Alte Backstube
- ❹ Theater in der Josefstadt
- ❺ Trautson Palace
- ❾ Parliament
- ⑫ Neues Rathaus
- ⑭ University
- ⑮ Café Landtmann
- ⑯ Dreimäderlhaus
- ⑱ Pasqualatihaus
- ⑲ *Burgtheater pp134–5*

Churches and Cathedrals
- ❸ Maria-Treu-Kirche
- ⑬ Dreifaltigkeitskirche

Museums and Galleries
- ❶ Museum für Volkskunde
- ❽ MuseumsQuartier
- ❿ *Kunsthistorisches Museum pp124–9*
- ⑪ *Natural History Museum pp130–31*

See also Street Finder maps 1, 3 and 5

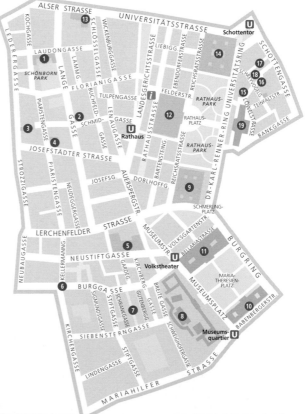

◀ Statue of Pallas Athene on the Parliament building fountain

For map symbols see back flap

Street-by-Street: Josefstadt

Tucked behind the grand museums of the Ringstrasse is the 18th-century district known as Josefstadt, named after Emperor Joseph II. Although outside the Inner City, Josefstadt has a vibrant cultural life of its own, with a popular theatre, many good restaurants, and handsome churches and museums. Students from the university and lawyers from the courthouses provide a constantly changing clientele for the district's varied establishments.

❸ ★ Maria-Treu-Kirche
Founded by the fathers of the Piarist order, this church was built from 1716.

The Plague Column here commemorates an epidemic that occurred in 1713.

❹ Theater in der Josefstadt
Founded in 1788, Vienna's oldest theatre has kept its doors open continuously since it was rebuilt by Josef Kornhäusel (see p86) in 1822.

No. 29 Lange Gasse
Originally built for servants and workers in the 18th century, the cottages lining this courtyard have changed little over the years.

To Lerchenfelder Strasse

PIARISTENGASSE

MARIA TRE

JOSEFSTÄDTER STRASSE

ZELTGASSE

❷ Alte Backstube
A working bakery from 1701 to 1963, since 1965 it has been a museum and restaurant.

Key

— Suggested route

Locator Map
See Street Finder, map 1

❶ ★ **Museum für Volkskunde**
The Schönborn Palace houses exhibits reflecting folklore and rural life in Austria.

Schönborn Park
is a secluded, leafy retreat. Among the sculptures is this bust (1974) of the composer Edmund Eysler by Leo Gruber.

No. 53 Lange Gasse has handsome statuary on its gates. It was built in the early 18th century when Vienna was expanding beyond the old city walls.

The Schnattl Restaurant, occupying the spacious ground floor and courtyard of an old house on Lange Gasse, is one of Vienna's finest *(see p215)*.

0 metres   50
0 yards   50

❶ Museum für Volkskunde

Laudongasse 15–19. **Map** 1 B4.
Tel 4068905. Ⓤ Rathaus. **Open** 10am–5pm Tue–Sun. **Closed** 1 Jan, Easter Mon, 1 May, 1 Nov, 25 Dec. 🅿
♿ 🖥 volkskundemuseum.at

The charming Museum of Austrian Folklore is a reminder that Vienna is not only full of imperial grandeur. Here you will find artifacts reflecting the culture of people in Austria and neighbouring countries. Exhibits include objects dating from the 17th to 19th centuries. The museum is housed in the 18th-century Schönborn Palace, designed by Johann Lukas von Hildebrandt as a homely two-storey mansion and altered in 1760 by Isidor Canevale. Today it has a rather imposing façade with statuary running along its top. There is a pleasant park behind the palace.

❷ Alte Backstube

Lange Gasse 34. **Map** 1 B5.
Ⓤ Rathaus. 🚌 13A. **Tel** 4061101.
Open 11am–midnight Mon–Fri, 5pm–midnight Sat, noon–11pm Sun.
Closed mid-Jul–mid-Aug and public hols. ♿

One of the finest middle-class houses in Vienna was built at No. 34 Lange Gasse in 1697 by the jeweller Hans Bernhard Leopold. The sandstone sculpture above the doorway symbolizes the Holy Trinity. Inside is an old bakery, the Alte Backstube, that was in continuous use from 1701 to 1963. The baking ovens were never removed, and the rooms have been sympathetically restored and incorporated into a traditional restaurant and café. They also contain a museum dedicated to the art of baking where 18th-century equipment is on display.

A few doors away, at No. 29, it's worth glancing into the courtyard to see the rows of single-storey houses facing each other – a rare example of working-class Vienna that is more than 200 years old.

❸ Maria-Treu-Kirche

Jodok-Fink-Platz. **Map** 1 B5. **Tel** 40504 25. Ⓤ Rathaus. 🚋 13A. 🚌 2. **Open** for services and by appointment.

Overlooking Jodok-Fink-Platz and flanked by monastic buildings stands the Church of Maria Treu. It was founded in 1698 by the fathers of the Piarist order.

This outstanding church was originally designed by Johann Lukas von Hildebrandt in 1716 and altered by Matthias Gerl in the 1750s. The elegant twin towers were not completed until 1854. Inside, there is a splendid Baroque frescoed ceiling in vibrant colours from 1752–3 by the great Austrian painter Franz Anton Maulbertsch. A chapel immediately to the left of the choir contains an altarpiece of the Crucifixion dating from about 1774, also painted by Maulbertsch.

Directly in front of the church and rising up from the square is a Baroque pillar topped with a statue of the Madonna, attended beneath by statues of saints and angels. Like many such columns in Vienna, it commemorates an outbreak of plague, in this case the epidemic of 1713.

Ceiling frescoes above the altar in the Maria-Treu-Kirche

❹ Theater in der Josefstadt

Josefstädter Strasse 26. **Map** 1 B5. **Tel** 427000. Ⓤ Rathaus. 🚋 13A. 🚌 2. **Open** for performances. 🖥 josefstadt.org

This intimate theatre *(see p230)*, one of the oldest still standing in Vienna, has enjoyed a

The façade of the glorious Theater in der Josefstadt

glorious history. Founded in 1788, it was rebuilt by Joseph Kornhäusel *(see p86)* in 1822, and has been in operation ever since, accommodating ballet, opera and theatre performances. Beethoven composed and conducted his overture *The Consecration of the House* for the reopening of the theatre in 1822 after its renovation. The director Max Reinhardt supervised the restoration of this attractive theatre in 1924. Today, it puts on mostly light plays and comedies.

❺ Trautson Palace

Museumstrasse 7. **Map** 3 B1. Ⓤ Volkstheater. **Closed** to the public.

Set back from the street next to the Volkstheater is this elegant Baroque palace, designed in 1710 by Johann Bernhard Fischer von Erlach *(see p149)*. Most Viennese palaces have flat fronts but on this one the central bays of the façade jut out with real panache. Nor is there anything restrained about the ornamentation: above the cornice and pediment is one of the largest collections of statuary atop any palace in the whole of Vienna. This includes a large statue of Apollo playing the lyre.

Passing beneath the tall portal you will see on the left an immense staircase, with carvings of bearded giants bearing its weight, by the Italian sculptor Giovanni Giuliani. This leads to the ceremonial hall.

Originally built for Count Johann Leopold Donat Trautson, who was in the service of Joseph I, the palace was acquired in 1760 by Maria Theresa *(see pp30–31)*. She donated it to the Royal Hungarian Bodyguard that she had founded. It has housed the Ministry of Justice since 1961, so there is no public access to the interior.

❻ Sankt-Ulrichs-Platz

Between Neustiftgasse and Burggasse. **Map** 3 B1. Ⓤ Volkstheater. Café Nepomuk: **Tel** 650 790 25 08. **Open** 9am–11pm Mon–Sat, 10am–8pm Sun. Ulrichskirche: **Tel** 5231246. **Open** on request or for services only.

This tiny sloping square is an exquisite survival of early Vienna. The dainty Baroque house at No. 27 is now the Café Nepomuk, and adjoining it is a Renaissance house that escaped destruction by the Turks during the sieges of the city, most probably because the Turkish commander Kara Mustafa pitched his own tent nearby.

The house partly obscures the façade of the Baroque Ulrichskirche, built by Josef Reymund from 1721–4. Handsome patrician houses encircle it, of which the prettiest is No. 2, the Schulhaus. Elaborately decorated, it dates from the mid-18th century. In the church the composer Gluck was married and Johann Strauss the Younger was christened.

❼ Spittelberg Pedestrian Area

Map 3 B1. **Ⓤ** Volkstheater. Amerlinghaus: **Open** 2–10pm Mon–Fri. Market: **Open** Apr–Jun & Sep–Nov:10am–6pm Sat; Jul & Aug: 2–9pm Sat. ♿

A group of streets – the pedestrianized Spittelberggasse, Gutenberggasse and Schrankgasse – has been well restored to present a pretty group of 18th- and 19th-century houses. Traditionally the area was lower class and very lively, home to the actors, artists and strolling players of the day. The houses were mostly tenements, without gardens or courtyards.

The charm of the district was rediscovered in the 1970s and the city authorities set about restoring the buildings. Today, it is a district of restaurants, cafés

Façade detail at No. 20 Spittelberggasse

and boutiques. It hosts a Christmas market, and a regular arts and crafts market from April to November. The Amerlinghaus theatre at No. 8 Stiftgasse is the area's cultural centre and provides a venue for exhibitions and events. The Spittelberg is a great success, and café life keeps the cobbled streets buzzing into the early hours.

The Amerlinghaus at No. 8 Stiftgasse was the birthplace of the painter Friedrich Amerling. Today it is a community centre, theatre and *Beisl (see p201)*.

No. 10 Stiftgasse has a handsome façade, decorated with statues.

Nos. 18 and 20 Spittelberggasse are fine examples of Baroque houses.

BURGGASSE

SCHRANKGASSE

SPITTELBERGGASSE

GUTENBERGGASSE

KIRCHBERGGASSE

No. 29 Gutenberggasse is a delightfully pretty Biedermeier building.

SIEBENSTERNGASSE

Spittelberggasse acts as the venue for an arts and crafts market that is held on every Saturday from April to November, and daily during Easter and Christmas.

The Witwe Bolte restaurant used to be an inn in the 18th century; legend has it that Emperor Joseph II was thrown out of here in 1778.

No. 9 Spittelberggasse is a beautifully-decorated house, with skilfully painted *trompe l'oeil* windows, dating from the 18th century.

❽ MuseumsQuartier Wien

Once home to the Imperial stables and carriage houses, the MuseumsQuartier Wien is one of the largest cultural centres in the world. It houses a diverse range of facilities from classical art museums to venues for film, theatre, architecture, dance, new media and a children's creativity centre, as well as a variety of shops, cafés and restaurants. Blending the Baroque architecture of the imperial stables with bold modern buildings, such as the white limestone façade of the Leopold Museum and the dark grey basalt of the Museum of Modern Art Ludwig Foundation Vienna, this impressive and diverse complex aims to provide an almost unprecedented experience.

★ **Leopold Museum**
Self-portrait with Chinese Lantern (1912) by Egon Schiele is part of the world's largest collection of Schiele's works, housed in this museum.

★ **ZOOM Kindermuseum**
Providing an exciting place to learn, children are encouraged to explore in the ZOOM Lab, play in ZOOM Ocean, be creative in ZOOM Atelier and have fun exploring the ZOOM exhibitions.

KEY

① Tanzquartier Wien

② math.space

③ Architekturzentrum Wien

④ quartier21 (alternate entrance)

⑤ Main entrance in the Fischer von Erlach Wing

quartier21
As Vienna's centre for contemporary applied art, quartier21 provides a range of frequently changing exhibitions for the public, as well as numerous fashion, design, book and music shops.

Halls E + G
This foyer leads to the former Winter Riding Hall, now Halls E + G showing a variety of concert, theatre and dance performances. The foyer is also the entrance to the Kunsthalle Wien which exhibits international modern art.

Main Courtyard
Often called the largest open-air festival hall in Vienna, from here the diverse architecture of the complex can be appreciated.

★ Museum of Modern Art Ludwig Foundation Vienna
Homme accroupi (1907) by Andre Derain is part of the collection of European contemporary and modern art in this museum, otherwise known as MUMOK.

Exploring the MuseumsQuartier Wien

Over 20 different cultural institutions are gathered together in the MuseumsQuartier Wien, together with a wide variety of restaurants, cafés and shops. The sight is an ideal starting point for any trip to Vienna, as many other attractions are nearby. It is advisable to begin your visit by going to the Visitor Centre in the Fischer von Erlach Wing, to obtain a programme detailing the events and the exhibitions happening in the complex.

Die Quelle (1923), Leopold Museum

Architekturzentrum Wien
Tel 5223115. **Open** 10am–7pm daily.
🖉 🆆 azw.at
The permanent exhibition at this venue is concerned with thematic and structural diversity in 20th-century architecture. Committed to providing access to architecture, the venue introduces new architectural work to the public. The four to six temporary exhibitions a year aim to complement this by linking modern architecture with architectural history.

Museum of Modern Art Ludwig Foundation Vienna (MUMOK)
Tel 52500. **Open** 2–7pm Mon, 10am–7pm Tue–Sun (to 9pm Thu).
🆆 mumok.at
This museum contains one of the largest European collections of modern and contemporary art, from American Pop Art, Photo Realism, Fluxus and Nouveau Réalism to Viennese Actionism, Arte Povera, Conceptual and Minimal Art, as well as other contemporary art from Central and Eastern Europe. The galleries are split historically and chronologically over five levels, two underground.

quartier21
Tel 52358810. **Open** 10am–8pm daily, except special events.
Over 40 different groups have turned quartier21 into Vienna's centre for contemporary applied art. The attractions for the public, which are on the ground floor, include fashion, design, book and music shops, an exhibition space for art schools, and large event halls.

Leopold Museum
Tel 525700. **Open** 10am–6pm daily (10am–9pm Thu).
🆆 leopoldmuseum.org
Home to over 5,000 works of art, the Leopold Collection of Austrian art was compiled over five decades by Rudolf Leopold. The exhibition space spans five floors. One of the museum's highlights is the world's largest Egon Schiele collection (on the second floor) along with Expressionist paintings and Austrian inter-war paintings.
Paintings after 1945 and works by Albin Egger-Lienz, including *Die Quelle*, are on the first floor, while an exhibition on Secessionism and Art Nouveau is on the ground level, with major works by Gustav Klimt, Richard

Gerstl and Oskar Kokoschka. The lower two levels include art from other 19th- and early 20th-century Austrian artists.

Tanzquartier Wien
Tel 5813591. 🆆 tqw.at
The Tanzquartier Wien offers facilities and training to dancers and presents dance and other performances to the public.

ZOOM Kindermuseum
Tel 5247908. **Open** 8:30am–4pm Tue–Fri, 10am–4pm Sat, Sun, school hols & public hols. 🆆 kindermuseum.at
This lively centre offers an unconventional approach to the world of the museum for children, from babies up to the age of 12. The aim is to encourage learning about exhibition subjects through play and exploration, such as the ZOOM Lab for older children, while younger ones can have a dip in the ZOOM Ocean with their parents.

KUNSTHALLE wien
Tel 5218933. **Open** 10am–7pm daily (to 10pm Thu). 🆆 kunsthallewien.at
This striking red brick building is a home for innovation and creativity, showing exhibitions of international and contemporary art. The exhibitions emphasize cross-genre and cross-border trends in the arts. Highlights range from experimental architecture, video, photography and film, to new media.

math.space
Tel 5235881/1730. **Open** varies, phone to check. 🆆 math.space.or.at
Linking maths to the arts, this centre for the popularization of maths is aimed at people of all ages, with interactive workshops for children and many programmes for adults.

The Red Horseman (1974) by Roy Lichtenstein in MUMOK

❾ Parliament

Dr-Karl-Renner-Ring 3. **Map** 1 C5 & 5
A3. **Tel** 401100. Ⓤ Volkstheater.
🚋 1, 2, D. **Open** for 🕐 except when
parliament is in session: mid-Sep–mid-
Jul: 11am, 2pm, 3pm, 4pm Mon–Thu;
11am, 1pm, 2pm, 3pm, 4pm Fri; 11am,
noon, 1pm, 2pm, 3pm, 4pm Sat; mid-
Jul–mid-Sep: 11am, noon, 1pm, 2pm,
3pm, 4pm Mon–Sat. ♿
Ⓦ **parlament.gv.at**

Façade of the Parliament building and the Athenebrunnen fountain

The architect Theophil Hansen
(see p34) chose a strict Neo-
Classical style when he
designed the Parliament
building (and the neighbouring
Palais Epstein). The building
was originally constructed as
part of the Ringstrasse
development to act as the
Reichsrat building (the
Parliament of the Austrian
part of the Habsburg empire).
Construction began in 1874
and finished in 1884.

The Parliament's entrance is
raised above street level and
approached up a broad ramp.
At the foot of the ramp are the
the bronze Horse Tamers (1901)
by sculptor Josef Lax; the ramp
itself is decorated with marble
figures of Greek and Roman
historians. On the roof there
are chariots and impressive
statues of ancient scholars
and statesmen.

In front of the central portico is
the Athenebrunnen, a fountain
dominated by the figure of Pallas
Athene, goddess of Wisdom. It
was designed by Carl Kundmann
and was placed here in 1902.
In this splendid, if chilly, setting
on 11 November 1918 after the
collapse of the Habsburg empire,
the parliamentary deputies
proclaimed the formation of the
republic of Deutsch-Österreich.
It was renamed the Republic of
Austria in 1919.

During World War II, half of
the Parliament building was
completely destroyed.
Reconstruction was eventually
completed by June 1956, but
the restoration of some of the
damaged artwork, only began
in the 1990s.

The Austrian Parliament

The Austrian parliament is composed of two houses –
the Lower House, or *Nationalrat*, and the Upper House,
or *Bundesrat*. The Lower House has 183 seats and its
members are elected for a four-year term by proportional
representation. It comprises the governing party and the
opposition. The Upper House is composed of elected
representatives from Austria's nine provinces, and its
function is to approve legislation
passed by the Lower House.
Bills may also be presented to
parliament by the general
public or by the Chambers of
Labour (representing consumers
and employees) and the
Chambers of the Economy
(representing employers and
industry). The federal President
is elected for a six-year term
and is largely a figurehead.
Theoretically, he or she has the
power to veto bills and dissolve
parliament, though this has
never occurred.

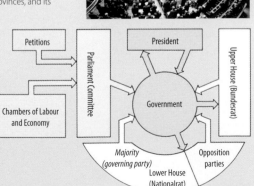

⑩ Kunsthistorisches Museum

More than one and a half million people visit the Museum of the History of Art every year. Its collections are based largely on those built up over the centuries by generations of Habsburg monarchs. Originally the works of art were housed in the Hofburg and the Belvedere, but when the Ringstrasse was built *(see pp34–5)* two magnificent buildings were erected to house the collections of imperial art and natural history. The former are on display in this museum where lavish internal decoration complements the exhibits.

Second floor

Coin collection

★ **Hunters in the Snow** (1565)
The last painting in Pieter Bruegel the Elder's series of the seasons shows hunters returning to the village on a winter's day.

First floor

★ **The Artist's Studio**
In this 1665 allegory of art, Johannes Vermeer shows an artist in decorative dress painting a model posing as Clio, the Muse of History.

★ **Salt Cellar** (1540–3)
Benvenuto Cellini's sumptuous gold *Saliera* shows the sea and earth united, represented by a female earth goddess and the sea god Neptune.

Key to Floorplan

- ☐ Egyptian and Near Eastern collection
- ☐ Collection of Greek and Roman antiquities
- ☐ Kunstkammer rooms: sculpture and decorative arts collections
- ☐ Picture gallery
- ☐ Coin cabinets
- ☐ Non-exhibition space

Portrait of the Infanta Margarita Teresa (1659)
Diego Velázquez captures the fragility of the eight-year-old Spanish princess in all her finery in this official portrait.

Gemma Augustea
The Emperor Augustus dressed as Jupiter sits next to Roma, the personification of Rome, in this Roman cameo carved from onyx.

Ground floor

Museum Guide

The museum displays range over three floors. On the ground floor are sculpture and decorative arts, and the Egyptian, Near Eastern and antiquities collections. The first floor holds the painting collections, and on the second floor – somewhat hidden – lies one of the largest and greatest coin collections in the world.

King Thutmosis III
Sculpted around 1460 BC, this royal portrait of Thutmosis III is a remnant of a standing or kneeling figure.

Main entrance from Maria-Theresien-Platz

Rotunda

The Apotheosis of the Renaissance

Many prominent artists were employed to decorate the museum's interior. As part of an extravagant decorative scheme, the Hungarian painter Michael Munkácsy contributed a fabulous *trompe l'oeil* ceiling painting for the main staircase depicting *The Apotheosis of the Renaissance* (1890). It features Leonardo, Raphael, Michelangelo, Veronese and Titian and their models, all presided over by Pope Julius II.

Exploring the Kunsthistorisches' Picture Collection

The collection focuses on Old Masters from the 15th to the 18th centuries, and largely reflects the personal tastes of its Habsburg founders. Venetian and 17th-century Flemish paintings are particularly well represented, and there is an excellent display of works by earlier Netherlandish and German artists. Broadly speaking, the pictures are hung following regional schools or styles of painting, although there is considerable overlap between the various categories.

The Fur (around 1635–40) by Peter Paul Rubens

Flemish Painting

Because of the historic links between the Habsburg monarchy and the Netherlands, there are several works from this part of Europe (present-day Belgium). The works of the early Flemish masters, who pioneered the development of oil painting, are characterized by their luminous colours and close attention to detail. This can be seen in the triptychs by Rogier van der Weyden and Hans Memling, and Jan van Eyck's *Cardinal Niccolo Albergati* (1435). The highlight for many is Room X, in which about half of all Pieter Bruegel the Elder's surviving works are displayed, including his *Tower of Babel* and most of the cycle of *The Seasons*, all from the mid-16th century. Three

rooms, XIII, XIV and XX, are devoted to Rubens and include large-scale religious works such as the *Ildefonso Altarpiece* (1630–32) and *The Fur*, an intimate portrait of his wife. Rubens' collaborator and pupil, Anthony Van Dyck, is also represented here by some outstanding works in which his sensitivity to human emotion is fully portrayed.

Dutch Painting

Protestant Holland's newly rich merchants of the 17th century delighted in pictures that reflected their own world rather than the hereafter. The Dutch genre scenes include works of great domestic charm such as Pieter de Hooch's lovely *Woman with Child at her Breast* (1663–5) and Gerard ter Borch's *Woman Peeling Apples* (1661) while Jacob van Ruisdael's *Great Forest* (1655–60) shows the advances made by Dutch painters in their observations of the natural world. All the Rembrandts on show in

Large Self-Portrait (1652) by Rembrandt van Rijn

Room XV are portraits; there is the picture of his mother as the prophetess Hannah (1639) and, in contrast to earlier works, the *Large Self-Portrait* shows the artist wearing a plain smock, with the emphasis on his face. The only painting by Johannes Vermeer is the enigmatic *The Artist's Studio* (Room 24). It is a complicated work with layers of symbolism; whether it is a self portrait or not has never been resolved.

Italian Painting

The Italian galleries have a strong collection of 16th-century paintings from Venice and the Veneto. In Room I the broad chronological and stylistic sweep of Titian's work, from his early *Gypsy Madonna* (1510) to the

Susanna and the Elders (1555) by Tintoretto

late *Nymph and Shepherd* (1570–5), can be seen. Other Venetian highlights include Giovanni Bellini's graceful *Young Woman at her Toilette* (1515) and Tintoretto's *Susanna and the Elders*. This is considered to be one of the major works of Venetian Mannerism. Giuseppe Arcimboldo's series of allegorical portrait heads representing the elements and the seasons are usually on show in Room 19, together with other works commissioned by Emperor Rudolf II. Italian Baroque painting includes works by Annibale Carracci and Michelangelo Merisi da Caravaggio, including the huge *Madonna of the Rosary*. Painted between 1606 and 1607, it depicts an intensely realistic Madonna advising St Dominic to distribute rosaries.

Summer (1563) by Giuseppe Arcimboldo

French Painting

Although the number of French paintings on show is relatively small, there are some minor masterpieces. The minutely detailed and highly original portrait of *The Court Jester Gonella* (1440–45), is thought to be the work of Jean Fouquet. It depicts a wily old man, seemingly squeezed into the picture, believed to be a famous court jester of the time. A more formal court portrait from 1569 is that of the youthful Charles IX of France by François Clouet. *The Destruction of the Temple in Jerusalem*, a monumental work painted by Nicolas Poussin in 1638, depicts the Emperor Titus watching the Old Testament prophecy of the destruction of the Temple of Solomon come true. It combines agitated movement with thorough archaeological research. Joseph Duplessis' *Christopher Willibald Ritter von Gluck at the Spinet* shows the famous composer gazing into the heavens for inspiration.

British and German Painting

There are few British works. Perhaps the most appealing is the *Landscape of Suffolk* (around 1750) by Thomas Gainsborough. There are also portraits by Gainsborough, Reynolds and Lawrence.

The German collection is rich in 16th-century paintings. There are several Albrecht Dürer works, including his *Madonna*

Stag Hunt of Elector Friedrich the Wise (1529), by Lucas Cranach the Elder, in the German Collection

with the Pear (1512). Other works include the *Stag Hunt of Elector Friedrich the Wise* (1529) by Lucas Cranach the Elder and seven portraits by Hans Holbein the Younger.

Spanish Painting

Room 10 houses several fine portraits of the Spanish royal family by the artist Diego Velázquez. He lived from 1599 to 1660 and was the court painter to Philip IV. His works include three portraits of Philip IV's daughter, the Infanta Margarita Teresa (in one aged three, another aged five and in a third aged eight), as well as a portrait of her sickly infant brother, Philip Prosper. Other Spanish works include paintings by Alonso Sánchez Coello and Antonio de Pereda.

Exploring the Kunsthistorisches' Other Collections

Apart from the picture gallery, the Kunsthistorisches Museum houses several distinct collections of three-dimensional art and objects. Most of the European sculpture and decorative art is from approximately the same period as the paintings (from the 15th to the 18th centuries), but there is also a fine display of medieval objects, while exhibits on show in the Egyptian, Greek and Roman rooms provide an intriguing record of the world's earliest civilizations.

sculptures on display were made to contain deceased souls. Other rooms house mummified animals, Egyptian scripts and artifacts such as pots, clothing and jewellery.

Also shown are a glazed brick relief of a lion from Babylon, and items from Arabia.

Oriental and Egyptian Antiquities

Five specially decorated rooms adorned with Egyptian friezes and motifs provide the perfect setting for the bulk of the museum's collection of Egyptian and Near Eastern antiquities. The nucleus of the collection was formed under the earlier Habsburg monarchs. Most of the items were either bought in the 19th century, after Napoleon's Egyptian expedition had increased interest in the area, or added early this century, when Austrian archaeologists excavated at Giza; an outstanding example is the so-called *Reserve Head* (around 26th century BC). The entire 5th-dynasty Tomb Chapel of Ka-Ni-Nisut, from the Pyramid district of Giza, and its well-preserved hieroglyphics (from around 2400BC) are on display in Room II.

Blue ceramic hippopotamus from Middle Kingdom Egypt (around 2000 BC)

The remarkable collection of objects and sculpture spans a wide chronological period from the Pre-Dynastic era until Roman times. There is a bust of King Thutmosis III *(see p125)* as well as portraits of Egyptian gods and goddesses. In Rooms I and V, where the decorative scheme incorporates Egyptian columns from Aswan, there are items associated with the mortuary cult in Ancient Egypt, including sarcophagi, canopic jars (which used to contain the entrails of mummified corpses), scarabs, mummy cases and papyrus books of the dead. In Room VIII there is a small blue ceramic statue of a hippopotamus. These were often found in Middle Kingdom tombs, as hippopotamus hunting was a royal privilege given to citizens who had won the king's favour. Many of the small-scale

Room I from the Egyptian galleries, with papyrus stalk columns from Aswan (around 1410 BC)

Greek and Roman Antiquities

Only part of the museum's Greek and Roman collection is housed in the main building; the finds from Ephesus and Samothrace are displayed in the Neue Burg *(see p97)* in the Hofburg.

If you approach the collection from the Egyptian galleries, the first room you come to (Room X) is devoted to early Greek sculpture. Rooms 6–7 house the Austria Romana collection which includes a statue of the *Youth from Magdalensberg*, a 16th-century cast of a lost Roman statue, found buried in an Austrian field. The main gallery (Room XI), decorated in the style of an imperial Roman villa, includes a mosaic of Theseus and the Minotaur, a Roman marble statue of Isis, Greek sculpture and a sarcophagus with fine relief decoration. Rooms XII and XIII house numerous portrait heads.

The collection also boasts figurines and bronzes from Greece and Rome, vases from Tanagra (a town in Ancient Greece) and a large collection of Roman cameos, jewellery, busts of Roman Emperors and Roman glass. Etruscan and Cypriot art are in rooms 1–3. Coptic, Byzantine and Germanic items are shown in the rest of the rooms, where pride of place goes to the Treasure of Nagyszentmiklós, a late 9th-century collection of golden vessels found in Romania in 1799.

Medal of Ulrich II Molitor (1581)

Sculpture and Decorative Arts

The collection consists of many treasures bought or commissioned by Habsburg connoisseurs, particularly Rudolf II and Archduke Leopold William, for their Kunstkammern. These were chambers of artifacts and natural wonders intended to represent the sum total of human knowledge of the day. In addition to sculpture, these princely treasuries contained precious items of high craftsmanship, exotic, highly unusual novelties, and scientific instruments. Among the most intriguing are some intricate automata, including a musical box in the form of a ship, and a moving clock. Some of the royal patrons worked in the studio themselves; on display is some glass blown by the Archduke Ferdinand II and also embroidery hand-sewn by Maria Theresa. As in the Picture Gallery, the main emphasis is on the Renaissance and Baroque, although there is a great display of medieval items. These include fine, late Gothic religious carved statues by

Virgin with Child (about 1495) by Tilman Riemenschneider

artists such as Tilman Riemenschneider, some medieval ivories, drinking horns and communion vessels. The highlights of the Italian Renaissance rooms are a marble bust of a laughing boy by Desiderio da Settignano, a marble relief of Bacchus and Ariadne and a fine bronze and gilt figurine called Venus Felix after an antique marble statue. Included in the large German Renaissance collection are early playing cards and a table centrepiece, incorporating "vipers' tongues" (in fact, fossilized sharks' teeth), said to ward off poison. Other gems include Benvenuto Cellini's Salt Cellar (*see p124*), made for the French king François I, and some statuettes by Giambologna.

Youth from Magdalensberg, 16th century, cast after a Roman original

Coins and Medals

Tucked away on the second floor is one of the most extensive coin and medal collections in the world. For those with a special interest in the area it is exceptional. Once again, the nucleus of the collection came from the former possessions of the Habsburgs, but it has been added to by modern curators and now includes many 20th-century items. Only a fraction of the museum's 500,000 pieces can be seen in the three exhibition rooms.

Room I gives an overview of the development of money. It includes coins from Ancient Greece and Rome, examples of Egyptian, Celtic and Byzantine money, and medieval, Renaissance and European coins, as well as the whole range of Austrian currency.

Also on display is a collection of primitive forms of money such as stone currency from Yap Island in Micronesia.

Rooms II and III house an extensive collection of 19th- and 20th-century medals. The portrait medallions are often miniature works of art in themselves. Particularly noteworthy are the unusual silver and gilt medals belonging to Ulrich Molitor, the Abbot of Heiligenkreuz, and the silver medallion which was engraved by Bertrand Andrieu and minted to commemorate the baptism of Napoleon's son. This shows the emperor as a proud father, lifting aloft his baby, the King of Rome (*see p177*).

⓫ Natural History Museum

Almost the mirror image of the Kunsthistorisches Museum, the Natural History Museum was designed by the same architects, and opened in 1889. Its carefully devised interior decoration reflects the nature of the collections. These are quite wide ranging and include archaeological, anthro-pological, mineralogical, zoological and geological displays. There are casts of dinosaur skeletons, the world's largest display of skulls illustrating the history of man, one of Europe's most comprehensive collections of gems, prehistoric sculpture, Bronze Age items, and extinct birds and mammals.

★ **Hallstatt Archaeological Finds**
This reconstructed chariot from the Bycis Kala cave in Moravia dates from the early Iron Age.

Children's centre

Aquarium

Lecture Hall

★ **Venus of Willendorf**
This ancient fertility figure *(see p22)* found in Lower Austria is around 24,000 years old.

Main entrance from Maria-Theresien-Platz

Key to Floorplan

- ☐ Mineralogy
- ☐ Geology, Palaeontology
- ☐ Archaeology
- ☐ Anthropology
- ☐ Zoology
- ☐ Temporary exhibition space
- ☐ Non-exhibition space

★ **Cast of Iguanodon bernissartensis**
This is just one of several dinosaur skeletons and casts displayed in the palaeontology department.

The central cupola
was designed by Johannes Benk around 1881. It is crowned by a bronze statue of the Greek god Helios.

Zigzag Herons
Part of the Birds of the World display, this pair came from Brazil over 150 years ago. They are now very rare.

First floor

Micro-theatre

Ground floor

Museum Guide

The museum displays range over two floors. To the right of the entrance on the ground floor are the rooms that are devoted to gemstones and mineralogy; to the left are the rooms housing the displays that chart the evolution of humans and also contain the prehistoric collections. On the first floor are the zoological rooms and temporary exhibitions.

Portrait of Kaiser Francis I (1773)
This portrait by Franz Messmer and Ludwig Kohl is of the Natural History Museum's founder and hangs on the stairs.

Caryatid Symbolizing Iron
This allegorical figure forms part of the decorative scheme of the mineralogy room. It represents the metal iron.

Maria-Theresien-Platz

This square separates the Kunsthistorisches Museum from the Natural History Museum and focuses around an 1888 statue of Maria Theresa *(see p31)* by Kaspar von Zumbusch. It shows the Empress clasping the Pragmatic Sanction of 1713, which made it possible for a woman to succeed to the throne. Below, her generals are portrayed setting forth on horseback from four spurs projecting from the base of the statue, while further back against the plinth stand her principal nobles and advisors, including her doctor van Swieten.

⓬ Neues Rathaus

Friedrich-Schmidt-Platz 1. **Map** 1 B5 &
5 A2. **Tel** 52550. Ⓤ Rathaus. 🚋 D, 1,
71. **Open** for 🕐 1pm Mon, Wed & Fri
& through phone bookings for groups.

The new town hall is the
seat of the Vienna City and
Provincial Assembly. Built from
1872 to 1883 to replace the
Altes Rathaus *(see p87)*, it is
unashamedly Neo-Gothic in
style. The architect, Friedrich
von Schmidt, was chosen by
the authorities in a competition
for the best design.

A huge central tower, 100 m
(325 ft) high and topped by
the 3-m (11-ft) statue of a
knight in armour with a lance,
dominates the front façade.
Known affectionately as the
Rathausmann, it was designed
by Franz Gastell and made by
the wrought-iron craftsman
Alexander Nehr. The most
attractive feature is the lofty
loggia with its delicate tracery
and curved balconies. The
building has seven courtyards
and concerts are held in the
Arkadenhof courtyard. At the
top of the first of two grand
staircases is the *Festsaal*, a
ceremonial hall that stretches
the length of the building. Round
all four sides are Neo-Gothic
arcades and statues of Austrian
worthies. In front of the building
is the wide Rathausplatz Park.

⓭ Dreifaltigkeits-kirche

Alser Strasse 17. **Map** 1 B4.
Tel 4057225. Ⓤ Rathaus.
Open 8–11:30am Mon–Sat, 8am–
noon Sun. ♿ entrance on
Schlösselgasse for services.

Built between 1685 and 1727,
the church of the Holy Trinity
contains an altarpiece (1708) in
the north aisle by the painter

16th-century crucifix by Veit Stoss, in the
Dreifaltigkeitskirche

Martino Altomonte, and a
graphic crucifix in the south
aisle from the workshop of Veit
Stoss. It was to this church that
Beethoven's body was brought
after he died in 1827. Following
the funeral service which was
attended by many of his
contemporaries, including
Schubert and the poet Franz
Grillparzer, the cortege bore his
coffin to the cemetery at
Währing on the city outskirts.

⓮ University

Universitätsring 1. **Map** 1 C4 & 5 A2.
Tel 42770. Ⓤ Schottentor.
Open 6:30am–8:30pm Mon–Fri,
8am–1pm Sat. ♿ 🕐 6pm Thu
(in German), 11:30am Sat (in English).

Founded in 1365 by Duke
Rudolf IV, the University of
Vienna now has over 90,000
students. The versatile architect
Heinrich Ferstel designed its
present home in 1883, adopting
an Italian Renaissance style.

From the entrance hall,
huge staircases lead up to the
university's ceremonial halls. In
1895 Gustav Klimt was commissioned to decorate the hall with
frescoes, but the degree of
nudity portrayed in some
panels proved unacceptable to
the authorities. Eventually, when
no agreement could be
reached, Klimt returned his fee
to the government and took
back the paintings; they were
destroyed during World War II.

Front elevation of the Neues Rathaus showing the Rathausmann on his tower some 98 m
(320 ft) above the ground

A spacious arcaded courtyard, lined with busts of the university's most distinguished professors, is located in the centre of the building. Among the figures on display include the founder of psychoanalysis, Sigmund Freud *(see p112)*, and the philosopher Franz Brentano. Nearby are the smoke-filled and poster-daubed corridors of today's university students.

⓯ Café Landtmann

Universitätsring 4. **Map** 1 C5 & 5 B2. **Tel** 24100100. Ⓤ Schottentor, Herrengasse. 🚊 1, D. **Open** 7:30am–midnight daily. ♿

If the Café Central *(see p60)* was, and perhaps still is, the coffee house of Vienna's intelligentsia, this café *(see p60)* is undoubtedly the coffee house of the affluent middle classes. With mirrors and elegant panelling, it is an exceedingly comfortable place. Established in 1873 by coffee-maker Franz Landtmann, it is still a popular café. It was Sigmund Freud's *(see p112)* favourite coffee house.

The attractive Dreimäderlhaus *(left)* on Schreyvogelgasse

⓰ Dreimäderlhaus

Schreyvogelgasse 10. **Map** 1 C5 & 5 B2. Ⓤ Schottentor.

A delightful remnant of Biedermeier Vienna is found in the houses on one side of the cobbled Schreyvogelgasse. The prettiest is the Dreimäderlhaus (1803). There is a legend that Schubert had three sweethearts *(drei Mäderl)* ensconced here, but it is more likely that the house was named after the 1920s' operetta, *Dreimäderlhaus*, which uses his melodies.

One of the arcades surrounding the University courtyard

⓱ Mölker-Bastei

Map 1 C5 & 5 B2. Ⓤ Schottentor.

A few paces away from the bustling Schottentor, a quiet street has been built on to a former bastion of the city walls. It boasts some beautiful late-18th-century houses. Beethoven lived here, and the Emperor Franz Joseph nearly met his death on the bastion in 1853 when a tailor attempted to assassinate him. No. 10 is the house where the Belgian Prince Charles de Ligne lived during the Congress of Vienna in 1815 *(see p32)*. De Ligne, an elderly aristocrat, wrote several cynical commentaries on the various activities of the crowned heads of Europe who came to Vienna at that time. A ladies' man, he caught a fatal chill while waiting for an assignation on the bastion.

Plaque on the front of the Pasqualatihaus

⓲ Pasqualatihaus

Mölker-Bastei 8. **Map** 1 C5 & 5 B2. **Tel** 5358905. Ⓤ Schottentor. Museum: **Open** 10am–1pm & 2–6pm Tue–Sun. **Closed** Mon, public hols. 📷

The Pasqualatihaus is no different in appearance from any of the other houses along this lane, but it is the most famous of more than 30 places where Ludwig van Beethoven resided in Vienna. Named after its original owner, Baron Johann von Pasqualati, it was Beethoven's home between 1804 and 1808, and 1810 and 1815. He composed many of his best-loved works here, including the Symphonies 4, 5, 7 and 8, the opera *Fidelio*, the Piano Concerto No. 4, and string quartets. Today, the rooms on the fourth floor which the composer occupied house a small museum. Various memorabilia, such as a lock of Beethoven's hair, a photograph of his grave at Währing cemetery, a deathbed engraving and early editions of his scores are on display. The museum also contains busts and paintings of Beethoven and his patron Prince Rasumofsky, the Russian ambassador to Vienna.

Liebenberg monument (1890) below the Mölker-Bastei

⑲ The Burgtheater

The Burgtheater is the most prestigious stage in the German-speaking world *(see also p230)*. The original theatre built in Maria Theresa's reign was replaced in 1888 by today's Italian Renaissance-style building by Karl von Hasenauer and Gottfried Semper. It closed for refurbishment in 1897 after the discovery that the auditorium had several seats with no view of the stage. Forty-eight years later a bomb devastated the building, leaving only the side wings containing the Grand Staircases intact. Subsequent restoration was so successful that today its extent is hard to assess.

JOHANN
NESTROY
1801 – 1862

Busts of playwrights
Lining the walls of the Grand Staircases are busts of playwrights whose works are still performed here, including this one of Johann Nestroy by Hans Knesl.

Entrance for tours

★ **Grand Staircases in North and South Wings**
Two imposing gala staircases lead up from the side entrances to the foyer. Each is a mirror image of the other.

Main entrance on Universitätsring

KEY

① **Candelabra lining the staircase**

② **Ceiling frescoes** by the Klimt brothers and Franz Matsch cover the north and south wings.

③ **Two statues of the Muses** of music and dramatic art adorn the roof.

④ **Sculpted cherubs on the balustrade** (1880–83)

Foyer
The 60-m long (200-ft) curving foyer serves as a waiting area during intervals. Portraits of famous actors and actresses line its walls.

Auditorium
The central part of the Burgtheater was rebuilt in 1952–5 after war damage, but the auditorium is still decorated in the imperial colours of cream, red and gold.

★ **Der Thespiskarren**
This ceiling fresco (1886–8) by Gustav Klimt, part of the series *The History of the Theatre*, depicts Thespis, the first performer of a Greek tragedy.

Front Façade
A statue of Apollo (about 1883) seated between Melpomene and Thalia presides over a frieze of Bacchus and Ariadne by Rudolf Weyr.

1741 Maria Theresa founds the Burgtheater in an empty ballroom at the Hofburg

1874 Work on the present building begins

1945 World War II fire destroys the auditorium

1897 The auditorium is adapted

1750

1850

1900

1950

1750–1776 Joseph II reorganizes the theatre and promotes it to the status of a national theatre

The Old Burgtheater in the mid-18th century

1888 The Burgtheater opens on 14 October in the presence of the Emperor Franz Joseph and his family

1955 Theatre reopens with Grillparzer's King Ottokar

OPERA AND NASCHMARKT

This is an area of huge contrasts, ranging from the stateliness of the Opera House and the opulence of the Opernring shops to the raucous modernity of Mariahilfer Strasse. This long street is lined with cinemas and department stores, drawing shoppers not just from Vienna but from much of eastern Europe. The other major thoroughfare in our area is the Linke Wienzeile, which runs parallel to the Rechte Wienzeile. Both roads stretch from just beyond the Ringstrasse to

the city outskirts, following the curving and sometimes subterranean River Wien. Between these roads is the bustling Naschmarkt, which is overlooked by Otto Wagner's Jugendstil apartments on the Linke Wienzeile. Visitors wanting to escape the crowds should visit the celebrated Café Museum, located near the three great cultural institutions of the area – the Academy of Fine Arts, the Opera House and the Secession Building.

Sights at a Glance

Streets and Squares
8 Mariahilfer Strasse

Historic Buildings
1 Opera House pp140–41
2 Hotel Sacher
5 Theater an der Wien
7 Wagner Apartments

Museums and Galleries
3 Academy of Fine Arts
4 Secession Building
9 Kaiserliches Hofmobiliendepot
10 Haydn Museum

Markets
6 Naschmarkt

See also Street Finder maps 3, 4 and 5

◀ Façade of the Secession Building

For map symbols see back flap

Street-by-Street: Opernring

Between the Opera House and the Karlskirche, two of the great landmarks of Vienna, lies an area that typifies the varied cultural vitality of the city as a whole. Here are an 18th-century theatre, a 19th-century art academy, and the Secession Building. Mixed In wIth these cultural monuments are emblems of the Viennese devotion to good living: the Hotel Sacher, as sumptuous today as it was a century ago; the Café Museum *(see p60)*, still as popular as it was in the 1900s; and the hurly-burly of the colourful Naschmarkt, where you can buy everything from oysters and exotic fruits to second-hand clothes.

❸ ★ **Academy of Fine Arts**
This Italianate building is home to one of the best collections of old masters in Vienna.

The Goethe Statue was designed by Edmund Hellmer in 1890.

The Schiller Statue dominates the park in front of the Academy of Fine Arts.

EL

SCHILLERPLATZ

NIBE

❹ ★ **Secession Building**
This delightful structure, built in 1898 as a showroom for the Secession artists, houses the *Beethoven Frieze* by Gustav Klimt *(see p58)*.

MAKARTGASSE

❺ **Theater an der Wien**
Today this 18th-century theatre is used as an opera house. It has been the venue for many premieres, among them Beethoven's *Fidelio*.

GETREIDEMARKT

MILLÖCKERGASSE

LINKE WIENZEILE

❻ **Naschmarkt**
This market sells everything from fresh farm produce to bric-a-brac. It is liveliest on Saturday mornings.

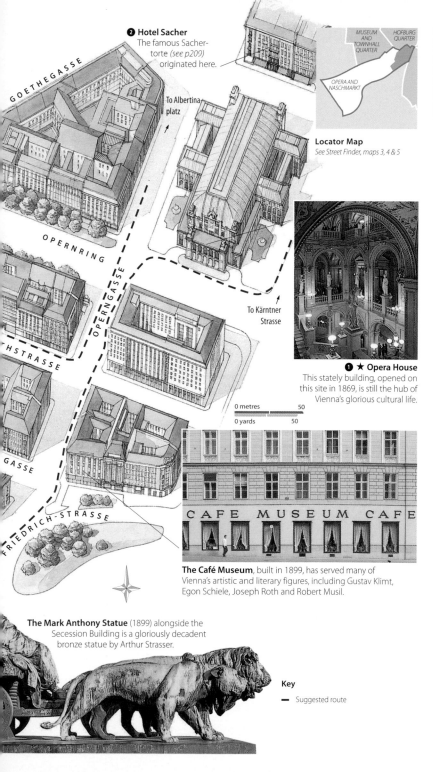

② Hotel Sacher
The famous Sacher-torte *(see p209)* originated here.

To Albertina platz

GOETHEGASSE

OPERNRING

OPERNGASSE

...HSTRASSE

...GASSE

FRIEDRICH-STRASSE

To Kärntner Strasse

Locator Map
See Street Finder, maps 3, 4 & 5

MUSEUM AND TOWNHALL QUARTER

HOFBURG QUARTER

OPERA AND NASCHMARKT

① ★ Opera House
This stately building, opened on this site in 1869, is still the hub of Vienna's glorious cultural life.

0 metres   50
0 yards   50

CAFE MUSEUM CAFE

The Café Museum, built in 1899, has served many of Vienna's artistic and literary figures, including Gustav Klimt, Egon Schiele, Joseph Roth and Robert Musil.

The Mark Anthony Statue (1899) alongside the Secession Building is a gloriously decadent bronze statue by Arthur Strasser.

Key

— Suggested route

❶ The Opera House

Vienna's state Opera House, or Staatsoper, was the first of the grand Ringstrasse buildings to be completed *(see pp34–5)*; it opened on 25 May 1869 to the strains of Mozart's *Don Giovanni*. Built in Neo-Renaissance style, it initially failed to impress the Viennese. Yet when it was hit by a bomb in 1945 and largely destroyed, the event was seen as a symbolic blow to the city. With a brand new auditorium and stage incorporating the latest technology, the Opera House reopened on 5 November 1955 with a performance of Beethoven's *Fidelio*.

Reliefs of Opera and Ballet (1861–9)
Painted allegorical lunettes by Johann Preleuthner represent ballet, tragic opera and comic opera. The one here depicts comic opera.

★ **Grand Staircase**
A superb marble staircase sweeps up from the main entrance to the first floor. It is embellished with statues by Josef Gasser of the seven liberal arts (such as Music and Dancing) and reliefs of opera and ballet.

★ **Schwind Foyer**
The foyer is decorated with scenes from operas painted by Moritz von Schwind. Among the busts of famous composers and conductors is Rodin's bronze bust of Mahler (1909).

Main entrance

KEY

① **One of the five bronze statues** by Ernst Julius Hähnel, depicting Heroism, Drama, Fantasy, Humour and Love, stands under the arches of the loggia.

② **The Auditorium**

★ **Tea Room**
Franz Joseph and his entourage used to spend the intervals in this graceful room, which is decorated with silk hangings bearing the Emperor's initials.

The Vienna Opera Ball

On the last Thursday of the Vienna Carnival *(see p67)* the stage is extended to cover the seats in the auditorium to create space for the Opera Ball *(see p231)*. This is an expensive society event which opens when the cream of the *jeunesse dorée* – well-to-do girls clad in white and their escorts – take to the floor.

VISITORS' CHECKLIST

Practical Information
Opernring 2, A-1010. **Map** 4 D1 & 5 C5. **Tel** 514442250.
Open for performances.
📅 call 514442606/ 2421 for details. 🚫 ♿ 📷
🌐 wiener-staatsoper.at

Transport
Ⓤ Karlsplatz. 🚊 D, 1, 2, 71.

The Architects
The architects of the Opera House, August Siccard von Siccardsburg (right) and Eduard van der Null (left).

Fountain
On either side of the Opera House stand two graceful fountains. Designed by Hans Gasser, this one depicts the legendary siren Lorelei supported by figures representing Grief, Love and Vengeance.

The Magic Flute Tapestries
One of the two side salons, the Gustav Mahler Saal, is hung with modern tapestries by Rudolf Eisenmenger illustrating scenes from *The Magic Flute*.

❷ Hotel Sacher

Philharmonikerstrasse 4. **Map** 4 D1 & 5 C5. **Tel** 514560. Ⓤ Karlsplatz. **Open** 8am–1am daily. ♿ Ⓦ **sacher.com**

Founded by the son of Franz Sacher, who, according to some, was the creator of the *Sachertorte* in 1840 *(see p209)*, this hotel *(see p199)* came into its own under Anna Sacher. The cigar-smoking daughter-in-law of the founder ran the hotel from 1892 until her death in 1930. During her time the Sacher became a venue for the extra-marital affairs of the rich and noble. It is still a discreetly sumptuous hotel.

❸ Academy of Fine Arts

Schillerplatz 3. **Map** 4 D2 & 5 B5. **Tel** 588161818. Ⓤ Karlsplatz. 🚋 D, 1, 2, 71. **Open** 10am–6pm Tue–Sun & public hols. 📷 ♿ Ⓦ **akademiegalerie.at**

Theophil Hansen built the Academy of Fine Arts in Italian Renaissance style from 1872 to 1876. In 1907 Adolf Hitler was barred from entrance on the grounds that he lacked talent. Today the Academy acts as an arts college and has a gallery showing changing exhibitions. These include late Gothic and

Façade of the Secession Building

early Renaissance works, some Rubens' pieces, 17th-century Dutch and Flemish landscapes, as well as a 19th-century Austrian collection.

❹ Secession Building

Friedrichstrasse 12. **Map** 4 D2. **Tel** 5875307. Ⓤ Karlsplatz. **Open** 10am–6pm Tue–Sun. **Closed** 1 May, 1 Nov, 25 Dec. 📷 ♿ Ⓦ **secession.at**

Joseph Maria Olbrich designed the unusual Secession Building in Jugendstil style *(see pp56–9)* as a showcase for the Secession movement's artists *(see p36)*. The almost windowless building, with its filigree globe of entwined laurel leaves on the roof, is a squat cube with four towers. The motto of the founders, emblazoned in gold on the façade, states, *"Der Zeit ihre Kunst, der Kunst ihre Freiheit"*, which translates as: "To every Age its Art, to Art its Freedom". Alongside the building stands the marvellous statue of Mark Anthony in his chariot being drawn by lions (1899), by Arthur Strasser. Gustav Klimt's *Beethoven Frieze* is the Secession's

best-known exhibit. Designed in 1902 as a decorative painting, it covers three walls and is 34 m (110 ft) long. It shows interrelated groups of figures and is thought to be a commentary on Beethoven's Ninth Symphony *(see also p37)*.

❺ Theater an der Wien

Linke Wienzeile 6. **Map** 3 C2. **Tel** 58830200. Ⓤ Karlsplatz. 🚌 59A. **Open** for performances. Ⓦ **theater-wien.at**

Emanuel Schikaneder founded this theatre *(see p226)* in 1801; a statue above the entrance shows him playing Papageno in Mozart's *The Magic Flute*. The premiere of Beethoven's *Fidelio* was staged here in 1805. Today it hosts popular opera performances.

Typical stall at the Naschmarkt

❻ Naschmarkt

Map 3 C2–C3. Ⓤ Kettenbrücken-gasse. Market: **Open** 6am–6:30pm Mon–Fri, 6am–6pm Sat. Schubert Museum: **Tel** 5816730. **Open** 10am–1pm, 2–6pm Wed & Thu.

The Naschmarkt is Vienna's liveliest market. It has many well-established shops and some of the best snack bars in Vienna *(see p216)*. As you walk west it gradually becomes less formal, with flower vendors', wine producers' and farmers' stalls spilling out onto the street and offering meats, breads and so on. This area in turn leads into the flea market – a chaos of makeshift stalls.

It's also worth going to No. 6 Kettenbrückengasse, by the U-Bahn, to see the simple flat where Franz Schubert died in 1828. It displays facsimiles, prints and a family piano.

Columned entrance to the Theater an der Wien

The Majolikahaus, one of the Wagner Apartments

❼ Wagner Apartments

Linke Wienzeile 38 & 40. **Map** 3 C2.
Ⓤ Kettenbrückengasse.

Looking onto the Naschmarkt are two remarkable apartment buildings. Designed by Otto Wagner in 1899, they represent the apex of Jugendstil style *(see pp56–9)*. No. 38 has sparkling gilt ornament, mostly by Kolo Moser. The façade of No. 40 has subtle flower patterns in pink, blue and green. Even the sills are moulded and decorated. No. 40, which is called the Majolikahaus after the glazed pottery used for the weather-resistant surface decoration, is the more striking. No. 42 next door, in historicist style *(see pp34–5)*, shows what Secession architects were reacting against.

❽ Mariahilfer Strasse

Map 3 A3 & 5 A5. Ⓤ Zieglergasse, Neubaugasse. Stiftkirche: **Open** 7:30am–6pm Mon–Fri, 7am–11pm Sat, 8:30am–9:30pm Sun. Mariahilfer Kirche: **Open** 8am–7pm Mon–Sat, 8:30am–7pm Sun.

This is one of Vienna's busiest shopping streets. On the corner of Stiftgasse is the Stiftkirche. The architect is unknown, but

the church dates from 1739. The façade is an austere pyramidal structure, rising to a bulbous steeple. Of particular interest, there are some lively Rococo reliefs set into the walls.

Across the street at No. 45 is the house where the playwright Ferdinand Raimund was born in 1790. Its cobbled courtyard is lined with shops.

Mariahilfer Kirche is named after a 16th-century cult of the Virgin Mary which was founded at the pilgrimage of Mariahilfer Kirche at Passau. The Viennese church is in the Baroque style and is dominated by two towers with bulbous steeples.

❾ Kaiserliches Hofmobiliendepot

Andreasgasse 7. **Map** 3 A2.
Tel 5243357. Ⓤ Zieglergasse.
Open 10am–6pm Tue–Sun. 🅿
Ⓦ hofmobiliendepot.at

The Imperial furniture collection, founded by Maria Theresa in 1747, gives an intimate portrait of the Habsburg way of life, as well as a detailed historical record of Viennese interior decoration and cabinet-making in the 18th and 19th centuries. Also included in the collection are pieces created by

artists and designers of the early 20th century. Room after room is filled with outstanding furnishings and royal domestic objects, ranging from a faithful recreation of Empress Elisabeth's Schönbrunn Palace apartments to a simple folding throne that was used while travelling. The exhibits, which range from the mundane to the priceless and often eccentric, provide a fascinating and evocative insight into the everyday lives of the imperial family.

❿ Haydn Museum

Haydngasse 19. **Map** 3 A3.
Tel 5961307. Ⓤ Zieglergasse.
Open 10am–1pm & 2–6pm Tue–Sun.
Closed Mon, public hols. 🅿
Ⓦ **wienmuseum.at**

As with many of the museums dedicated to composers, the Haydn Museum does not have a very comprehensive collection of exhibits: only a few copies of documents and scores, a piano and clavichord.

Haydn built this house in what was then a new suburb of Vienna with money he had earned from his successful visits to London between 1791 and 1795. He lived here from 1797 until his death in 1809 and it was here that he composed many of his major works, including *The Creation* and *The Seasons*. There is also a room that contains some furniture and mementoes belonging to Johannes Brahms.

Antique wheelchair in the Kaiserliches Hofmobiliendepot

BELVEDERE QUARTER

The Belvedere Quarter is a grandiose and extravagant district. From the Karlsplatz, with its gardens and statues, there is a lovely view of Johann Bernhard Fischer von Erlach's Baroque Karlskirche. East of this great church, visitors can see more delights, including the two palaces of the Belvedere, now public galleries, and the Schwarzenberg Palace. These huge palaces and beautiful gardens were designed by Johann Lukas von Hildebrandt, following the crucial defeat of the Turks in 1683. Only after the Turkish threat had been removed was it possible for Vienna to expand. The turbulent history of the city is excellently documented in the Wien Museum Karlsplatz. Just a few paces away is the Musikverein, home to the Vienna Philharmonic. There is also the Arnold Schönberg Center, containing a wealth of material relating to the great innovator's compositions, and also some of his paintings.

Sights at a Glance

Streets and Squares
7 Schwarzenbergplatz
10 Rennweg

Historic Buildings
3 Musikverein
4 Karlsplatz Pavilions
6 Imperial Hotel
9 Schwarzenberg Palace
13 Theresianum

Museums and Galleries
2 Wien Museum Karlsplatz
5 Künstlerhaus
8 Arnold Schönberg Center
11 *Palaces and Gardens of the Belvedere pp154–9*

Parks and Gardens
12 Botanical Gardens

Churches
1 *Karlskirche pp148–49*

See also Street Finder
maps 3, 4 and 6

| 0 metres | 250 |
| 0 yards | 250 |

Street-by-Street: Karlsplatz

This part of the city became ripe for development once the threat of Turkish invasion had receded for good in 1683 *(see pp28–9)*. The Ressel Park, at the front of the Karlskirche, gives an unobstructed view of this grandiose church, built on the orders of Karl VI. The park itself is lined with a variety of cultural institutions, notably the Wien Museum Karlsplatz and, across the road, the Musikverein.

❹ ★ **Karlsplatz Pavilions**
These pavilions were built as part of the underground system of 1899.

Underpass

To Karlsplatz U-Bahn

Ressel Park café

KARLSPL

The Technical University with its Neo-Classical façade (1816) fronts on to Ressel Park, which contains busts and statues of famous 19th-century Austrian scientists and engineers.

Ressel Statue

Key

— Suggested route

Henry Moore's Hill Arches were presented to the City of Vienna by the artist himself in 1978.

③ Musikverein
This Ringstrasse-style *(see p150)* concert hall, home of the Vienna Philharmonic Orchestra, is renowned for its superb acoustics.

Locator Map
See Street Finder, map 4

② ★ Wien Museum Karlsplatz
This museum houses relics of Roman Vienna, stained glass from the Stephansdom and the reconstructed rooms of celebrated Viennese such as Adolf Loos *(see p94)*.

KARLSPLATZ

DUMBASTRASSE

STRASSE

LOTHRINGER

MADERSTRASSE

MATTIELLISTRASSE

TECHNIKERSTR

USSHAUSSTRASSE

① ★ Karlskirche
Promised to the people during the 1713 plague, this is Vienna's finest Baroque church.

French Embassy

The Art Nouveau French Embassy

Built in 1904–12 by the French architect Georges Chédanne, the Embassy is typical of French Art Nouveau, resembling houses along Rue Victor Hugo in Paris. Unaccustomed to this foreign style, some thought the building was oriental, giving rise to a rumour that its plans had been mixed up with those of the French Embassy in Istanbul.

Art Nouveau façade of the French Embassy

| 0 metres | | 50 |
| 0 yards | | 50 |

❶ Karlskirche

During Vienna's plague epidemic in 1713, Emperor Karl VI vowed that as soon as the city was delivered from its plight he would build a church dedicated to St Charles Borromeo (1538–84), a former Archbishop of Milan and a patron saint of the plague. The following year he announced a competition to design the church, which was won by the architect Johann Bernhard Fischer von Erlach. The result was a richly eclectic Baroque masterpiece: the gigantic dome and portico are borrowed from the architecture of ancient Greece and Rome, while there are Oriental echoes in the gatehouses and minaret-like columns. Building took almost 25 years, and the interior was richly embellished with carvings and altarpieces by the foremost artists of the day, including Daniel Gran and Martino Altomonte.

The Pulpit
Two putti surmount the canopy of the richly gilded pulpit, decorated with rocailles and flower garlands.

★ High Altar
The high altar features a stucco relief by Albert Camesina showing St Charles Borromeo being assumed into heaven on a cloud laden with angels and *putti.*

KEY

① **Angel representing the Old Testament**

② **Pediment** reliefs by Giovanni Stanetti show the suffering of the Viennese during the 1713 plague.

③ **The two gatehouses** leading into the side entrances of the church are reminiscent of Chinese pavilions.

④ **Stairway (closed to public)**

⑤ **Cupola Cross**

⑥ **Angel representing the New Testament**

Main entrance

VISITORS' CHECKLIST

Karlsplatz, A-1040. **Map** 4 E2.
Tel 5056294. 🚌 4A.
Open 7:30am–7pm & 1–6pm
Mon–Fri, 8:30am–7pm Sat,
9am–7pm Sun. ✝ 6pm Mon–
Sat, 11am & 6pm Sun & hols.
🚫 ♿ 📷 to cupola.
🌐 **karlskirche.at**

Transport
Ⓤ Karlsplatz.

★ Frescoes in the Cupola
Johann Michael Rottmayr's fresco,
painted between 1725 and
1730, depicts the Apotheosis of
St Charles Borromeo. It was the
painter's last commission.

Johann Bernhard Fischer von Erlach

Many of Vienna's finest buildings, including the Trautson and
Schönbrunn Palaces, were
designed by Fischer von Erlach
(1656–1723). He died before he
finished the Karlskirche and his
son completed it in 1737.

★ The Two Columns
Inspired by Trajan's Column in
Rome, they are decorated with
spiralling scenes of St Charles
Borromeo's life. Qualities of
Steadfastness are illustrated on
the left, and Courage on the right.

Visitor entrance
and tickets

St Charles Borromeo
Lorenzo Mattielli's
statue of the patron
saint crowns the
pediment.

❷ Wien Museum Karlsplatz

Karlsplatz. **Map** 4 E2. **Tel** 50587470.
Ⓤ Karlsplatz. **Open** 10am–6pm Tue–
Sun & hols. **Closed** 1 Jan, 1 May,
25 Dec. ♿ 📷 Ⓦ **wienmuseum.at**

The Wien Museum Karlsplatz
moved to its current location
in 1959. The ground floor
usually has Roman and pre-
Roman items, as well as exhibits
from the Gothic period.
These include 14th- and
15th-century gargoyles and
figures, and stained glass from
the Stephansdom, and carved
portraits of early rulers of
Vienna. These displays are
sometimes moved to make
space for visiting exhibitions.

The first-floor 16th- and
17th-century exhibits include
prints depicting Turkish
sieges from 1529 onwards, as
well as a portrait of the Turkish
commander Kara Mustafa,
captured banners and weapons,
and prints of the celebrations
after Austria's victory. Here
too are Johann Bernhard
Fischer von Erlach's original
plans for the Schönbrunn
Palace *(see pp174–7)*, and the
original lantern from No. 6
Schönlaterngasse *(see p80)*.
On the second floor are a
reconstructed 1798 room from

The monumental, historicist-style façade of the Musikverein

the Caprara-Geymüller Palace in
Wallnerstrasse, panelled with
painted silks, and the apartment
of Austria's most famous poet,
Franz Grillparzer. There are
displays chronicling the
popularity of ballet, theatre
and operetta.

Exhibits from the 20th
century include Richard Gerstl's
portrait of Arnold Schönberg
(see p41) and portraits by Egon
Schiele and Gustav Klimt. There
is a room (1903) from Adolf
Loos's house *(see p94)* in
Bösendorferstrasse, silver- and
glassware by Josef Hoffmann,
designs from the Wiener
Werkstätte *(see p58)* and
pictures of Vienna over the
past hundred years.

❸ Musikverein

Bösendorferstrasse 12. **Map** 4 E2.
Tel 5058190. Ⓤ Karlsplatz.
Open for concerts only. 📷 ♿
Ⓦ **musikverein.at**

The Musikverein building – the
headquarters of the Society of
the Friends of Music – was
designed from 1867 to 1869 by
Theophil Hansen, in a mixture of
styles employing terracotta
statues, capitals and balustrades.
It is the home of the great
Vienna Philharmonic Orchestra
(see p229), which gives regular
performances here, and forms
the orchestra of the Opera
House. The concert hall seats
almost 2,000. Tickets are sold on
a subscription basis to Viennese
music lovers, but some are also
available on the day of the
performance. The most famous
annual event here is the New
Year's Day concert *(see p67)*.

❹ Karlsplatz Pavilions

Karlsplatz. **Map** 4 D2. **Tel** 5058747-
85177. Ⓤ Karlsplatz. **Open** Apr–Oct:
10am–6pm Tue–Sun & hols.
Closed Mon, 1 May.

Otto Wagner *(see pp56–9)* was
responsible for designing and
engineering many aspects of
the early underground system
in the late 19th century. Some
of these bridges and tunnels are
remarkable, but cannot match
his stylish pair of underground
railway exit pavilions (1898–9)
alongside the Karlsplatz, which
are among his best-known

Sunflower motifs on the façade of the Karlsplatz Pavilions

The enormous Hochstrahlbrunnen in Schwarzenbergplatz

❻ Imperial Hotel

Kärntner Ring 16. **Map** 4 E2 & 6 D5.
Tel 501100. Ⓤ Karlsplatz. ♿
Ⓦ **imperialvienna.com**

Along with the Hotel Sacher *(see p142)*, this is the best known of Vienna's sumptuous 19th-century hotels. You can sip tea to the sound of a pianist playing in the background or stay in the same room Richard Wagner occupied. Adolf Hitler made the Imperial Hotel his headquarters after the Anschluss *(see p38)*.

❼ Schwarzenberg-platz

Map 4 E2. Ⓤ Karlsplatz.

At the centre of this grand square is the equestrian statue (1867) of Prince Schwarzenberg, who led the Austrian and allied armies against Napoleon at the Battle of Leipzig (1813). The square combines huge office blocks, the Ringstrasse and the Baroque splendours of the Schwarzenberg and Belvedere palaces. Behind the fountain of Hochstrahlbrunnen (1873), at the intersection of Prinz-Eugen-Strasse and Gusshausstrasse, is the monument commemorating the Red Army's liberation of the city. It is none too popular with older Viennese, who still recall the brutalities endured in the Russian zone until 1955.

The Arnold Schönberg Center *(see p152)* lies at the eastern end of the square.

buildings. The green copper colour of the roofs and the ornamentation complement the Karlskirche beyond. Gilt patterns are stamped onto the white marble cladding and eaves, with repetitions of Wagner's beloved sunflower motif. But the greatest impact is made by the buildings' elegantly curving rooflines. The two pavilions face each other: one is now a café, the other is used for exhibitions.

❺ Künstlerhaus

Karlsplatz 5. **Map** 4 D2 & 6 D5.
Tel 5879663. Ⓤ Karlsplatz.
Open 10am–6pm Tue–Sun (to 9pm Thu). 📷 ♿ Ⓦ **k-haus.at**

Commissioned by the Vienna Artists' Society as an exhibition hall for its members, the Künstlerhaus was built in 1868. The society favoured grand, academic styles of painting in tune with the historicist Ringstrasse architecture. The Künstlerhaus itself is typical of this style, which is named after the Vienna boulevard where the look is most prevalent *(see pp34–5)*. Designed by August Weber (1836–1903) in a Renaissance palazzo style, the Künstlerhaus is now used for temporary art exhibitions.

Palazzo-style façade of the Künstlerhaus (1868)

Schwarzenberg Palace and Joseph Fischer von Ehrlach's fountain

❽ Arnold Schönberg Center

Schwarzenbergplatz 6 (entrance at Zaunergasse 1–3). **Map** 4 E2. **Tel** 712188. Ⓤ Karlsplatz . 🚌 4A. 🚃 71. **Open** 10am–5pm Mon–Fri. **Closed** public hols, 24 & 31 Dec. Ⓦ schoenberg.at

Vienna's Arnold Schönberg Center, established in 1998, is both a unique archive for music scholars and a cultural centre that is open to the general public. Schönberg – composer, painter, teacher, music theoretician and innovator – was born in Vienna in 1874 and died in Los Angeles in 1951. Something of a prodigy, he began composing at the age of 9. However, he later dismissed much of his early work as "imitative", gradually developing a more experimental and, for the times, daring approach to composition. This was to culminate in his highly influential twelve-tone composition technique.

Although Schönberg's work was much admired by fellow musicians, it baffled the general public. In 1913 he famously conducted what became known as the "Skandalkonzert" at Vienna's Musikverein *(see p150)*. This featured a programme of modern music so provocative that the audience rioted, bringing the concert to a halt.

The Center contains fascinating artifacts relating to Schönberg's life and work, a gallery of his paintings, a replica of his Los Angeles study and a

library on topics relating to the Viennese School. It also stages concerts, lectures, workshops and symposia. Visitors with an academic interest may be able to arrange access to Schönberg's music manuscripts, writings and correspondence.

Schönberg is buried in the Central Cemetery (see pp170–71). His grave has a striking Modernist monument by Fritz Wotruba.

❾ Schwarzenberg Palace

Schwarzenbergplatz 9. **Map** 4 E2.

The Palais Schwarzenberg was built by Johann Lukas von Hildebrandt *(see p154)* in 1697 and then altered by the Fischer

von Erlachs *(see p149)* in the 1720s. The main salon has a domed hall with a magnificent chandelier. Behind the palace are the lawns and shady paths of the park, focused around a pool and fountain designed by Joseph Emanuel Fischer von Erlach. In the past the main reception rooms were used as a venue for concerts and balls, and part of the building now houses a luxury hotel.

One wing is occupied by the Swiss embassy. The present head of the Schwarzenberg family served as an advisor to President Havel after the Velvet Revolution in Czechoslovakia in 1989 and was Czech foreign minister in 2007–2009 and 2010–2013.

❿ Rennweg

Map 4 E2. Ⓤ Karlsplatz. Gardekirche: **Open** 8am–8pm daily.

Rennweg runs from the Schwarzenbergplatz along the edges of the Belvedere palaces. At No. 3, a house built by Otto Wagner *(see p59)* in 1890 is now the (former) Yugoslav Embassy. Though the façade is in shabby condition, the house remains an interesting example of Wagner's work just as he was making the transition from Ringstrasse pomp to his later

Detail of the façade of the Salesianerinnenkirche in Rennweg

Jugendstil style of architecture. Next door at No. 5 is where Gustav Mahler *(see p41)* lived from 1898 to 1909. No. 5a is the Gardekirche (1755–63) by Nikolaus Pacassi (1716–99), Maria Theresa's court architect. It was originally built as the church of the Imperial Hospital and since 1897 has been Vienna's Polish church. A huge dome covers the entire interior, which adds to its spaciousness. One feature of interest is the gilt Rococo embellishment over the side chapels and between the ribs of the dome. Just beyond the Belvedere palace gates at No. 6a stands a Baroque mansion, while the forecourt at No. 8 has formed part of the Hochschule für Musik since 1988.

At No. 10, behind splendid wrought-iron gates, stands the Salesianerinnenkirche of 1717–30. The Baroque façade is flanked by monastic buildings in the same style. The upper storey has scrolled projections that serve as the base for statues. Like the Gardekirche, this church is domed, its design partly attributed to Joseph Emanuel Fischer von Erlach *(see p149)*. Apart from the pulpit, the interior is of little interest.

At No. 27, the present-day Italian Embassy is the palace where Prince Metternich *(see p32)* lived until he was forced to flee the city in 1848.

⓫ Palaces and Gardens of the Belvedere

See pp154–9.

⓬ Botanical Gardens

Rennweg 14. **Map** 4 F3. **Tel** 4277 54190. 🚋 71. **Open** 10am to 3:30–6pm, depending on season. May close in bad weather. ♿

The main entrance to the Botanical Gardens is on the corner of Prätoriusgasse and Mechelgasse. Other entrances are on Jacquingasse, and via a

The Botanical Gardens created by Maria Theresa in 1754

small gate at the rear of the Upper Belvedere which leads to the Alpine Garden and the Botanical Gardens. The latter contains more than 9,000 plant species. The Botanical Gardens were created in 1754 by Maria Theresa and her physician van Swieten for cultivating medicinal herbs. Expanded to their present shape in the 19th century, they remain a centre for the study of plant sciences as part of the University of Vienna's Institute of Botany. Of equal interest to amateurs, the gardens offer a quiet spot to sit and relax after sightseeing.

⓭ Theresianum

Favoritenstrasse 15. **Map** 4 E3. Ⓤ Taubstummengasse. **Closed** to public.

The original buildings of this former imperial summer palace date from the early 17th century, but were essentially rebuilt after the Turkish siege of 1683 in a Baroque style by the architect and theatre designer Lodovico Burnacini (1636–1707) and others. Known at that time as the Favorita, it became a favourite residence of emperors Leopold I, Joseph I and Karl VI. In 1746 Maria Theresa, who had moved into Schönbrunn *(see pp174–9)*, her summer palace, handed it over to the Jesuits. They established a college here for the education of children from less well-off aristocratic families – the sons of these families were trained to be officials.

Today, the Theresianum is still a school and, since 1964, has also been a college for diplomats and civil servants. In the Theresianum park on Argentinierstrasse stands Radio House. It has a beautiful entrance hall, which was designed by Clemens Holzmeister in 1935.

Theresianum, housing a school and a college for diplomats

⑩ Palaces and Gardens of the Belvedere

The Belvedere was built by Johann Lukas von Hildebrandt as the summer residence of Prince Eugene of Savoy, the brilliant military commander whose strategies helped vanquish the Turks in 1683. Situated on a gently sloping hill, the Belvedere consists of two palaces linked by a formal garden laid out in the French style by Dominique Girard. The garden is sited on three levels, each conveying a complicated programme of Classical allusions: the lower part of the garden represents the domain of the Four Elements, the centre is Parnassus and the upper section is Olympus.

★ **Upper Cascade**
Water flows from the upper basin over five shallow steps into the pool below.

Putti on the Steps (1852)
Children and cherubs representing the 12 months adorn the steps to the left and right in the middle area of the gardens.

Johann Lukas Von Hildebrandt

Hildebrandt became the court architect in Vienna in 1700 and was one of J B Fischer von Erlach's greatest rivals. In addition to the Belvedere, he designed the Schönborn Palace *(see p112)*, the Kinsky Palace *(see p112)* and the Maria-Treu-Kirche *(see p118)*.

Coloured etching of the Upper Belvedere and Gardens by Karl Schütz (1784)

Entrance to Lower Belvedere from Rennweg

1717–19 Dominique Girard landscapes the gardens

1720 Orangery built

1721–3 Upper Belvedere built

1714–16 Lower Belvedere built

1752 Habsburgs acquire the Belvedere

1779 Belvedere gardens open to the public

1765 Lower Belvedere becomes the barracks for the military guard

1781–1891 Belvedere houses the Imperial Picture Gallery, which opens to the public

1897 Archduke Franz Ferdinand, heir to the throne, moves to the Upper Belvedere

1923–9 The Baroque Museum, the 19th-century Gallery and the 20th-century Gallery open to the public

1953 Museum of Medieval Austrian Art opens to the public

1955 The Austrian State Treaty signed in the Marble Hall

Detail on Upper Cascade

1750 | 1800 | 1850 | 1900 | 1950

★ **Main Gate of the Upper Belvedere**
The Baroque iron gate (1728) by Arnold and Konrad
Küffner, with an "S" for Savoy and the cross of Savoy,
leads to the south façade of the Upper Belvedere.

VISITORS' CHECKLIST

Practical Information
Map 4 F3. Upper Belvedere:
see pp156–7. Lower Belvedere
and Orangery: *see pp158–9.*
Gardens: **Open** 6:30am–dusk
all year round.

**Entrance to Upper
Belvedere *(see
pp156–7)* and
gardens from
Prinz-Eugen-
Strasse**

★ **Upper Belvedere Façade**
The lively façade dominates the
sweeping entrance to the palace
(see pp156–7). The domed copper
roofs of the end pavilions
resemble the shape of Turkish
tents – an allusion to Prince
Eugene's victories over the Turks.

Statues of Sphinxes
With their lion bodies
and human heads, the
imposing sphinx
statues represent
strength and
intelligence.

Entrance to
Orangery

KEY

① Triumphal gate to Lower
Belvedere

② **Lower Belvedere** *(see pp158–9)*

③ **Statues of the Eight Muses**

④ *Bosquet* or hedge garden

⑤ **Lower cascade**

⑥ **Orangery** *(see p158)*

⑦ **Palace Stables**

Upper Belvedere

Standing at the highest point of the garden, the Upper Belvedere has a more elaborate façade than the Lower Belvedere: it was intended to be a symbolic reflection of Prince Eugene's glory. In addition to the impressive interiors of the Sala Terrena with its sweeping staircase, the chapel and the Marble Hall, the building now houses an Austrian art collection with works ranging from the Middle Ages to the present day.

★ Chapel
The centrepiece of this brown, white and gold interior is an altarpiece, *The Resurrection*, by Francesco Solimena (1723), set among statues of angels. Prince Eugene could enter the chapel from his apartments.

Viewing balcony for chapel

Laughing Self-Portrait
(1908)
This picture is by Richard Gerstl, the Viennese artist who was developing his own Expressionist style when he killed himself in his twenties.

Gallery Guide

The ground floor houses masterpieces of medieval and modern art. Baroque art and art from the fin-de-siècle to World War I is on the first floor. Nineteenth-century and Biedermeier art is on the second floor.

Key

- Neo-Classicism-Romanticism and Biedermeier
- Realism and Impressionism
- Baroque and early 19th-century art
- Vienna 1880–1914
- Medieval art
- Modern art: interwar period
- Non-exhibition space

Main entrance from gardens

★ Sala Terrena
Four Herculean figures by Lorenzo Mattielli support the ceiling vault of the Sala Terrena, while white stuccowork by Santino Bussi covers the walls and ceiling.

★ **Gustav Klimt Collection**
This marvellous Jugendstil collection by Gustav Klimt is considered by some to be the Belvedere's highlight. In the work here, *Judith I* (1901), Klimt depicts the Old Testament heroine as a Viennese *femme fatale*.

VISITORS' CHECKLIST

Practical Information
Prinz-Eugen-Strasse 27, A-1030.
Map 4 F4. **Tel** 79557134.
Open 10am–6pm daily. 🅿️ 📨
🚻 📷 🖥️ 🏛️ 🌐 **belvedere.at**

Transport
Ⓤ Südtirolerplatz. 🚌 69A. Ⓢ
Quartier Belvedere. 🚊 D, O, 18.

The Tiger Lion (1926)
This savage beast from the Modern art: interwar period section was painted by Oskar Kokoschka, a leading figure in Austrian Expressionism.

Second floor

Marble Hall

First floor

Stairs to 🚻

Ground floor

The Plain of Auvers (1890)
Van Gogh's airy landscape is part of a series inspired by the wheat fields around Auvers-sur-Oise, where the artist spent the last few months of his life.

Corpus Christi Morning (1857)
This bright genre scene is typical of the Austrian Biedermeier painter Ferdinand Georg Waldmüller.

Lower Belvedere and Orangery

The architect Johann Lucas von Hildebrandt (1668–1745) was commissioned by Prince Eugene of Savoy to build the Lower Belvedere in 1714, and it was completed in 1716. It previously housed the Museum of Austrian Baroque Art but now displays temporary exhibitions only. Attractions include the Marble Hall, the state bedroom of Prince Eugene of Savoy, the Hall of Grotesques and the Marble Gallery. The Lower Belvedere also incorporates the Orangery and the palace stables.

Exit to Orangery and stables

Prince Eugene's former bedroom

★ **Golden Cabinet**
A statue of Prince Eugene (1721) by Balthasar Permoser stands in this room, whose walls are covered with huge gilt-framed mirrors.

Hall of Grotesques
The hall is decorated with paintings of grotesques inspired by ancient Roman frescoes of fantastical creatures. They were created by the German painter Jonas Drentwett.

The Orangery

Next door to the Lower Belvedere is the handsome Orangery building, originally used to shelter tender garden plants in winter and now transformed into an exhibition hall retaining its original character. It previously housed the Museum of Austrian Medieval Art but now has regularly changing temporary exhibitions. Neighbouring the "White Cube", a unique exhibition space, the southern side gallery corridor offers a spectacular view of the Privy Garden and the Upper Belvedere.

The Palace Stables
Collected here are some 150 items of medieval art, including masterpieces of panel painting and sculpture.

The Orangery and gardens in winter

Lower Belvedere Palace
This impressive Baroque palace is set in beautiful landscaped gardens. The façade is adorned with Ionic columns and statues.

Gallery Guide

All works on display in the Lower Belvedere and Orangery are temporary. Exhibitions include traditional and contemporary painting and sculpture. Pieces are often loaned from galleries and museums worldwide, supplemented by the Belvedere's own collection.

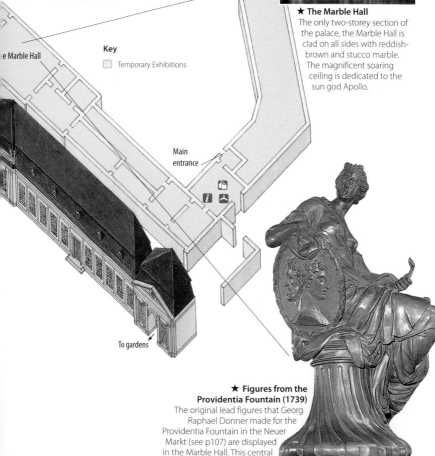

Key

▢ Temporary Exhibitions

e Marble Hall

Main entrance

To gardens

★ **The Marble Hall**
The only two-storey section of the palace, the Marble Hall is clad on all sides with reddish-brown and stucco marble. The magnificent soaring ceiling is dedicated to the sun god Apollo.

★ **Figures from the Providentia Fountain (1739)**
The original lead figures that Georg Raphael Donner made for the Providentia Fountain in the Neuer Markt (see p107) are displayed in the Marble Hall. This central statue represents Providence.

FURTHER AFIELD

For a city of over two million inhabitants, Vienna is suprisingly compact. Nonetheless, some of the most interesting sights are a fair distance from the city centre. At Schönbrunn sprawls the immense palace and gardens so loved by Maria Theresa, and the monastery at Klosterneuburg houses some of Austria's great ecclesiastical art treasures. Many parks and gardens, including the Prater, the Augarten and the Lainzer Tiergarten, all former private Habsburg domaines, are now open to the public.

Sights at a Glance

Churches and Monasteries
- **1** Wagner Villas
- **7** Karl-Marx-Hof
- **9** Augarten Palace and Park
- **11** Hundertwasserhaus
- **15** Favoriten Water Tower
- **16** Amalienbad
- **19** *Schönbrunn Palace and Gardens pp174–7*
- **20** Otto-Wagner-Hofpavillon Hietzing
- **21** Werkbundsiedlung

Churches and Monasteries
- **2** Kirche am Steinhof
- **6** Klosterneuburg
- **23** Wotruba-Kirche

Museums and Galleries
- **3** Geymüllerschlössel
- **10** Kriminalmuseum
- **13** *Heeresgeschichtliches Museum pp168–9*
- **18** Technical Museum

Parks and Gardens
- **8** Donaupark
- **12** *Prater pp164–5*
- **22** Lainzer Tiergarten

Historic Districts
- **4** Grinzing
- **5** Kahlenberg

Monuments
- **17** Spinnerin am Kreuz

Cemeteries
- **14** *Central Cemetery pp170–71*

Key
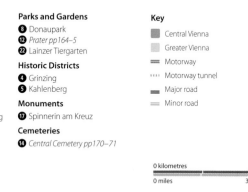
- Central Vienna
- Greater Vienna
- Motorway
- Motorway tunnel
- Major road
- Minor road

```
0 kilometres            5
0 miles                 3
```

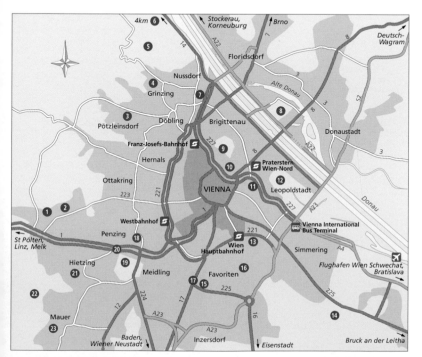

Detail of Ernst Fuchs' Brunnenhaus, next to Wagner Villas

① Wagner Villas

Hüttelbergstrasse 26, Penzing. **Tel**
9148575. **U** Hütteldorf. 43B, 52A,
52B. **Open** 10am–4pm Tue–Sat.
W ernstfuchsmuseum.at

The Villa Otto Wagner, designed
by Wagner from 1886 to 1888 as
his own residence, is stylistically
midway between his earlier
Ringstrasse architecture and
the decorative elements of
Jugendstil *(see pp56–9)*. The
house is built on a grand scale
and incorporates classical
elements such as Ionic columns,
and seems more suited to a
north Italian hillside than to
Austria. The present owner, the
painter Ernst Fuchs *(see p38)*, has
imposed his own personality on
the villa, adding a fertility statue
and garish colours.

The simpler villa next door
was built more than 20 years
later. Completed in 1913, the
house is of steel and concrete
rather than brick. It is very
lightly decorated in a severe
geometrical style with deep
blue panels and nailhead
ornament. The glass ornament
is by Kolo Moser *(see p59)*.

② Kirche am Steinhof

Baumgartner Höhe 1, Penzing.
Tel 9106011007. 48A.
Open 3–5pm Sat, noon–4pm Sun.
by appointment.

Completed in 1907,
this astonishing
church was Otto
Wagner's *(see
pp56–9)* last
commission. It is
set within the
grounds of the
Psychiatrisches
Krankenhaus, a
large mental
hospital. The
exterior is
marble-clad
with nailhead ornament and
has spindly screw-shaped pillars,
topped by wreaths, supporting
the porch. Four stone columns
on the façade are adorned with
angels by Othmar Schimkowitz
(1864–1947). The statues at
each corner of the façade are of
St Leopold and St Severin to the
left and right respectively. They
were designed by Richard
Luksch and are seated in chairs
by Josef Hoffmann *(see pp58–9)*.

The interior is a single space
with shallow side chapels. The
main decoration consists of gold
and white friezes and square roof
panels ornamented with gilt
nailhead. Illumination is provided
by daylight shining through
lovely blue glass windows by
Kolo Moser *(see p59)*.

③ Geymüller-schlössel

Khevenhüllerstrasse 2, Währing.
Tel 71136231. 41A. 41. **Open**
May–Nov: 11am–6pm Sat & Sun.

The Geymüllerschlössel in
Pötzleinsdorf, northwest of the
city, is a temple to Biedermeier
style *(see pp32–3)*. Dating from
1808, the house was built for
Johann Heinrich von Geymüller,
a rich banker. Now a branch
of the Austrian Museum of
Applied Arts *(see pp84–5)*, it
has a collection of intricate
Biedermeier and Empire
furniture, such as an apparently
simple desk that combines a
writing desk with a water-
colour cabinet. Gadgets
abound: spittoons, still-lifes
painted on porcelain, bowls, as
well as 200 clocks dating from
1780 to about 1850, the heyday
of Viennese clock manufacture.

Jugendstil angels by Othmar Schimkowitz adorning the façade of the
Kirche am Steinhof

➍ Grinzing

🆄 Heiligenstadt. 🚌 38A. 🚋 38.

Grinzing is the most famous *Heuriger* village *(see pp188–9)*, but it is also the most touristy, as many of the inns here cater to very large groups of visitors. It is nonetheless very pretty.

It is divided into the Oberer Ort and Unterer Ort (upper and lower towns), the lower town being where you will find more authentic *Heurige* along such lanes as Sandgasse.

Grinzing was repeatedly destroyed by Turkish troops during the many sieges of Vienna *(see p28–9)*, and was again damaged by Napoleon's forces in 1809 *(see p32)*.

➎ Kahlenberg

🚌 38A.

Kahlenberg, at 484 m (1,585 ft), is the highest point of the Vienna Woods *(see pp178–9)*. It has a television mast at the top, as well as a church, an observation terrace and a restaurant. The views over the vineyards below and the city beyond are fabulous, with the Danube bridges to the left and the Vienna Woods to the right. The Kahlenberg played a crucial part in the city's history, in 1683 when the Polish king, Jan Sobieski, led his troops down from this spot to the rescue of Viennese forces who were fighting for the city.

➏ Klosterneuburg

Stift Klosterneuburg. **Tel** 22434110.
🆄 Heiligenstadt. 🅂 Franz-Josefs-Bahnhof to Klosterneuburg-Kierling.
🚌 238, 239. **Open** 9am–5pm daily. 📷 Daily tours include the Monastery Museum and Imperial Apartments. 📷 🆆 **stift-klosterneuburg.at**

Above the Danube, 13 km (8 miles) north of Vienna, stands the vast monastery and fortress of Klosterneuburg. Dating originally from the 12th century, it houses the

The peach- and salmon-coloured façade of the Karl-Marx-Hof

astonishing Verduner Altar, whose 51 panels were completed in 1181 *(see p25)*. In the 18th century it was expanded by Karl VI, who intended to build a complex on the same grand scale as the Escorial palace near Madrid. The work was halted after his death in 1740.

Statue in Grinzing

➐ Karl-Marx-Hof

Heiligenstädterstrasse 82–92, Döbling.
🆄 Heiligenstadt. 🚋 D. **Closed** to the public.

The Kar-Marx-Hof, dating from 1927 to 1930, is an immense council block, which contains 1,382 flats. It is the most celebrated of the municipal housing developments built during the period of Red Vienna

(see p38), when 63,000 new dwellings went up across the city between 1919 and 1934. The architect of the Karl-Marx-Hof was Karl Ehn, a pupil of Otto Wagner *(see p56–9)*.

➑ Donaupark

🆄 Kaisermühlen. 🚌 20B. **Open** 24 hrs daily. Donauturm: **Tel** 2633572. **Open** 10am–11:30pm daily. ♿

Adjoining UNO-City *(see p39)*, the complex of United Nations agencies, is the Donaupark. Laid out in 1964, the park has cycle paths, cafés and other amenities. Rising 252 m (827 ft) above the park is the Donauturm, with two revolving restaurants and an observation platform. The park and the surrounding area have been redeveloped as the Donau City housing project, encompassing the Millennium Tower.

View of the Klosterneuburg monastery with its Baroque dome

⑫ Prater

Originally an Imperial hunting ground, these woods and meadows between the Danube and its canal were opened to the public by Joseph II in 1766. The central avenue, or Hauptallee, was for a long time the preserve of the nobility and their footmen. During the 19th century the western end of the Prater became a massive funfair with booths, sideshows, beer gardens and *Wurst* stands catering for the Viennese workers.

The Miniature Railway
The Liliputbahn travels a 4-km (2.5-mile) circuit.

To Praterstern station

★ **Ferris Wheel**
The huge wheel circulates very slowly at a speed of about 75 cm (2.5 ft) per second, allowing riders spectacular views over the park and funfair.

★ **Volksprater Funfair**
An amusement park has existed here since the last century. Today the enormous funfair is full of high-tech rides ranging from dodgem cars to ghost trains.

KEY

① *Tennisplätze* (tennis courts)
② Planetarium
③ *Messegelände* exhibition centre
④ *Stadion* (stadium)
⑤ *Stadionbad* (swimming pool),
⑥ Cycle paths
⑦ Maria Grun Kirche
⑧ *Golfplatz* (golf course)

The Trotting Stadium
Built in 1913, the Krieau Stadium is the scene of exciting regional and international trotting races from September to June *(see p231).*

The History of the Ferris Wheel

One of Vienna's most famous landmarks, the giant Ferris Wheel was immortalized in the film of Graham Greene's *The Third Man*. It was built in 1896 by the English engineer Walter Basset, but it now has only half the original number of cabins, as a fire destroyed many of them in 1945.

0 metres   800
0 yards   800

VISITORS' CHECKLIST

Practical Information
Funfair: **Open** 15 Mar–end Oct: 10am–11pm daily. Ferris Wheel: **Tel** 7295430. **Open** daily (times vary). Planetarium: **Open** 8:30am–noon, 1–2:30pm Tue, Thu; 8:30am–noon, 6–8pm Wed; 1:45–8pm Fri; 2:15–7pm Sat, Sun & hols. Miniature railway: **Open** end Mar–end Oct: 10am–11pm daily. Golf course: **Open** 8am–4pm Mon–Thu. Stadionbad: **Open** May–Sep: 9am–7pm Mon–Fri (to 8pm Jul & Aug), 8am–7pm Sat, Sun & hols (to 8pm Jul & Aug). Maria Grun Kirche: **Open** 10am–3pm Sun. Lusthaus: **Open** Jan–Mar: noon–5pm Sat–Tue; Apr–Sep: noon–10pm Mon, Tue, Thur & Fri (to 6pm Sat, Sun & hols); Oct–Dec: noon–5pm Thu–Tue. **Tel** 7289565.
W **praterservice.at/en**

Transport
U S Praterstern. 77A, 80A. 0, 1 (park), 5 (funfair).

★ Hauptallee
The avenue lined with chestnut trees stretches for 5 km (3 miles) through the centre of the Prater.

Lusthaus
The 18th-century octagonal pavilion is a former hunting lodge which now houses a restaurant.

Baroque façade of the Augarten Palace set amid 18th-century parkland

❾ Augarten Palace and Park

Obere Augartenstrasse 1. **Map** 2 E2.
Tel 21124201. Ⓤ Taborstrasse. 🚌 5A,
5B. 🚋 5, 31. Park: **Open** 6am–9pm
daily. Porcelain Museum: **Open** 10am–
6pm Mon–Sat. Augarten Contemporary:
Open 11am–7pm Thu–Sun. ♿

There has been a palace on this
site since the days of Leopold I,
when it was known as the Alte
Favorita, but it was destroyed by
the Turks in 1683 and then
rebuilt around 1700 to a design
attributed to Johann Bernhard
Fischer von Erlach *(see p149)*.
Since 1948 it has been the
home of the Vienna Boys' Choir
(see p41) and consequently it is
inaccessible to the public.

The park was planted in the
second half of the 17th century,
renewed in 1712, and opened
to the public in 1775 by Joseph
II. The handsome gates by
which the public now enters

the gardens were designed by
Isidor Canevale in 1775. Mozart,
Beethoven, and Johann Strauss I
all gave concerts in the park
pavilion. The Augarten was also
used for royal receptions and
gatherings while the Congress
of Vienna *(see p32)* was taking
place in 1815. The pavilion used
to be the imperial porcelain
factory, founded in the 18th
century, but has been run since
the 1920s by the municipal
authorities. Its showroom has
displays showing the history of
Augarten porcelain. Behind the
pavilion is the studio of the early
20th-century sculptor Gustinus
Ambrosi, open to the public as
the Augarten Contemporary.

The Augarten has the oldest
Baroque garden in Vienna, with
topiary lining long paths shaded
by walls of foliage. In the
distance, you can see two of the
huge and terrifying flakturms
that the Viennese are unable to

rid themselves of. Built by
German forces in 1942 as
defense towers and anti-aircraft
batteries, these enormous
concrete monoliths could
house thousands of troops.
So thick are their walls that
any explosives powerful
enough to destroy them would
have a similar effect on the
surrounding residential areas.
There are four other such
flakturms still standing in other
parts of the city.

❿ Kriminalmuseum

Grosse Sperlgasse 24. **Map** 6 E1.
Tel 6643005677. Ⓤ Taborstrasse. 🚌
5A. 🚋 1. **Open** 10am–5pm Thu–Sun.

Since 1991, this house of
medieval origin has been the
home of Vienna's museum of
crime. Once known as the
Seifensiederhaus (the soap
boiler's house), this museum's

⓫ Hundert-wasserhaus

Löwengasse/ Kegelgasse. Ⓤ
Landstrasse. 🚌 4A Löwengasse.
🚋 1 Hetzgasse. **Closed** to the public.

The Hundertwasserhaus is a
municipal apartment block
created in 1985 by the artist
Friedensreich Hundertwasser
(see p39), who wished to strike
a blow against what he saw as
soulless modern architecture.
The resulting building, with its
irregular bands of colour and
onion dome cupolas, has
been controversial since its
construction. While it is loved by
some, others think it is more like
a stage set than a block of flats.

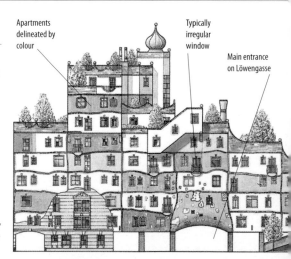

Apartments
delineated by
colour

Typically
irregular
window

Main entrance
on Löwengasse

20 rooms mostly chronicle violent crime, charting the murderous impulses of Vienna's citizens from the Middle Ages to the 20th century, and the history of the judicial system.

Many of the exhibits come from the archives of the Viennese police force and are distinctly gruesome; there is a wide selection of murder weapons, mummified heads of executed criminals, death masks and case histories illustrated with photographs and prints. Many of the more unsettling exhibits give a notion of how the Viennese poor of earlier centuries were involved in crime. Political crimes, such as the lynching of a government minister during the revolution of 1848 *(see p32)*, are also covered.

This interesting museum provides visitors with a blend of documentary social history and a chamber of horrors which portrays the darker side of Viennese life with gusto.

Painting depicting a 1782 robbery

⓬ Prater

See pp164–5.

⓭ Heeresgeschicht- liches Museum

See pp168–9.

⓮ Central Cemetery

See pp170–71.

⓯ Favoriten Water Tower

Windtenstrasse 3, Favoriten. **Tel** 5995931070. Ⓤ Reumannplatz. 🚌 15A, 65A. 🚊 1. **Open** for guided tours (phone to arrange).

A complex known the Favoriten pumping station was constructed in 1889 by Franz Borkowitz as part of a municipal scheme for the transportation of drinking water from the Alpine foothills to the rapidly growing city. By 1910 the construction of other installations around Vienna meant that the operations of the complex had to be scaled down, and of the seven original buildings only the highly decorative yellow-and-red-brick water tower remains. The fascinating feature

of this incongruous-looking tower that soars 67 m (220 ft) into the sky is the original pumping equipment which is still in place. Its utilitarian appearance provides a stark contrast to the ornate turrets, pinnacles and tiles of the building's superstructure. The interior has been restored and guided tours are available to the public. Nearby is the small children's funfair, the Böhmische Prater *(see p234)*.

Favoriten Water Tower

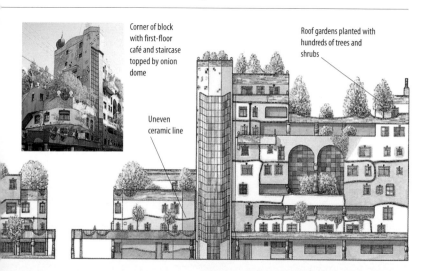
Corner of block with first-floor café and staircase topped by onion dome

Uneven ceramic line

Roof gardens planted with hundreds of trees and shrubs

⓭ Heeresgeschichtliches Museum

This impressive museum of army history is housed in a single block of the military complex known as the Arsenal. It was completed in fortress style in 1856. Theophil Hansen designed the museum itself *(see façade, below)*, which chronicles Austria's military prowess from the 16th century onwards. Exhibits relate to the Turkish siege of 1683, the French Revolution and the Napoleonic wars. Visitors should not miss seeing the car in which Archduke Franz Ferdinand was assassinated, or the modern armaments used in the war that the murder precipitated.

Radetzky
1848–1866

Façade of Heeresgeschichtliches Museum

Ground floor

Sea Power Austria

Republic and Dictatorship 1918–1945

Tank Park
Situated behind the museum are the armoured vehicles used in the Austrian army from 1955 as well as those that belonged to the German army that occupied Austria.

Main entrance from Ghegastrasse

The Assassination of Franz Ferdinand

On 28 June 1914 the heir to the throne, Archduke Franz Ferdinand, and his wife Sophie von Hohenberg paid a visit to Sarajevo. Gavrilo Princip, a Serbian nationalist, assassinated the couple, provoking an international crisis that later resulted in World War I. The museum houses the car in which the couple were killed.

Museum Guide

The museum is housed on two floors. To view it in chronological order, begin on the first floor on the left, where exhibits relating to the Turkish siege are displayed. Other rooms chronicle the various 18th-century wars and Napoleon's victory over Austria. The 19th and 20th centuries, including heavy artillery used in World War I, are covered on the ground floor. There is also a tank park.

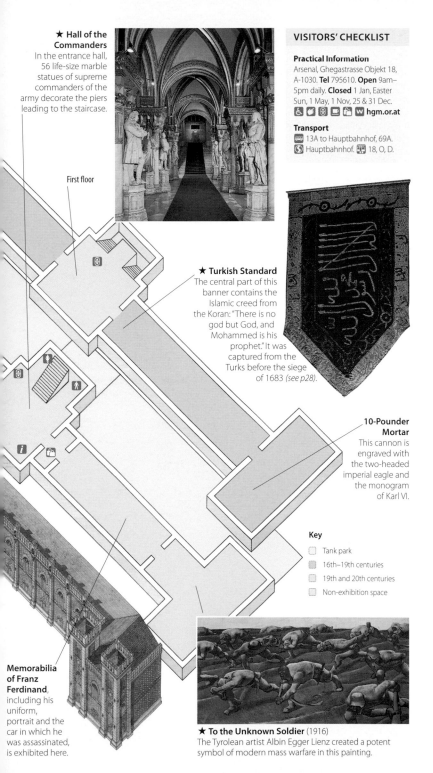

★ Hall of the Commanders
In the entrance hall, 56 life-size marble statues of supreme commanders of the army decorate the piers leading to the staircase.

First floor

VISITORS' CHECKLIST

Practical Information
Arsenal, Ghegastrasse Objekt 18, A-1030. **Tel** 795610. **Open** 9am–5pm daily. **Closed** 1 Jan, Easter Sun, 1 May, 1 Nov, 25 & 31 Dec.
♿ 🅿 🕒 🛗 📷 👜 🌐 hgm.or.at

Transport
🚌 13A to Hauptbahnhof, 69A.
🚆 Hauptbahnhof. 🚊 18, O, D.

★ Turkish Standard
The central part of this banner contains the Islamic creed from the Koran: "There is no god but God, and Mohammed is his prophet." It was captured from the Turks before the siege of 1683 *(see p28)*.

10-Pounder Mortar
This cannon is engraved with the two-headed imperial eagle and the monogram of Karl VI.

Key
- ☐ Tank park
- ▨ 16th–19th centuries
- ☐ 19th and 20th centuries
- ☐ Non-exhibition space

Memorabilia of Franz Ferdinand, including his uniform, portrait and the car in which he was assassinated, is exhibited here.

★ To the Unknown Soldier (1916)
The Tyrolean artist Albin Egger Lienz created a potent symbol of modern mass warfare in this painting.

⑭ Central Cemetery

Austria's largest burial ground, containing two and a half million graves, was opened in 1874 on the city's southern outskirts. The central section includes graves of artists, composers, architects, writers and local politicians. Funerals are usually quite lavish affairs, as the Viennese like to be buried in style, with the pomp appropriate to their station in life. The cemetery contains a vast array of funerary monuments varying from the humble to the bombastic; a museum on site also pays tribute to the city's enduring obsession with death.

★ Luegerkirche
Max Hegele, a pupil of Otto Wagner, designed this church dedicated to Vienna's mayor in 1907–10.

Presidential Vault
This contains the remains of Dr Karl Renner, the first President of the Austrian Republic after World War II.

Cemetery Layout

The cemetery is divided into specific numbered sections: apart from the central garden of honour where VIPs are buried, there are old and new Jewish cemeteries; a Protestant cemetery; a Russian Orthodox section and various war graves and memorials. It is easier to take the circulating bus that covers the whole area than to walk.

The Monument to the Dead of World War I is a powerful depiction of a mother lamenting by Anton Hanak.

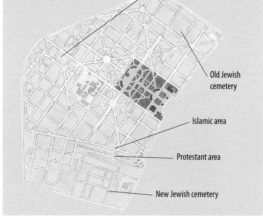

Old Jewish cemetery

Islamic area

Protestant area

New Jewish cemetery

Arnold Schönberg's Cube
The grave of the modernist Viennese composer Arnold Schönberg is marked with this bold cube by Fritz Wotruba.

Key

① Arcades around the Luegerkirche

② **Fritz Wotruba's grave** (see p173)

③ **Monument to Dr Johann Nepomuk Prix** by Viktor Tilgner (1894)

④ **Bestattungsmuseum**, the Undertakers' Museum, gives a fascinating insight into the history of Vienna's love affair with stylish burials.

Theophil Hansen's Grave
The architect of Vienna's Parliament building *(see p123)* lies near other artists and architects. Hansen died in 1891.

VISITORS' CHECKLIST

Practical Information
Simmeringer Hauptstrasse 234, Tor 2, A-1110. **Tel** 760410. **Open** daily; Nov–Feb: 8am– 5pm; Mar, Oct: 7am–6pm; Apr, Sep: 7am–7pm; May–Aug: 7am–8pm.

Transport
Ⓢ Zentralfriedhof, Kledering.
6, 71.

The Arcades
Some spectacular monuments are to be found carved in the semi-circular arcades that face the main entrance, including this memorial to the miner August Zang. It shows the entrance to a mine and is dated 1848.

Main Entrance from Simmeringer Hauptstrasse

★ Musicians' Graves
Among the city's musicians buried in this area are Johann Strauss I and II (grave pictured left), Beethoven, Brahms and Schubert. There is a monument to Mozart, who was buried in St Marx cemetery.

Russian Orthodox Chapel
Built in traditional Russian Orthodox style and completed in 1894, this chapel is used by Vienna's Russian community.

⓰ Amalienbad

Reumannplatz 23, Favoriten. **Tel** 6074747. Ⓤ Reumannplatz. 🚌 7A, 14A, 66A, 67A, 68A. 🚊 6, 67. Swimming pool: **Open** 9am–6pm Tue, 9am–9:30pm Wed & Fri, 7am–9:30pm Thu, 7am–8pm Sat, 7am–6pm Sun. Sauna: **Open** 1–9:30pm Tue, 9am–9.30pm Wed–Fri, 7am–8pm Sat, 7am–6pm Sun. ♿

Public baths may not seem like an obvious tourist destination, but the Jugendstil Amalienbad (1923–6) shows how the municipal administration in the 1920s not only provided essential public facilities, but did so with stylistic vigour and conviction. The two designers, Otto Nadel and Karl Schmalhofer, were employees of the city's architectural department.

The magnificent main pool is covered by a glass roof that can be opened in minutes and is surrounded by galleries overlooking the pool. Elsewhere in the building are saunas and smaller baths and pools used for therapeutic purposes.

When first opened, the baths were one of the largest of their kind in Europe, designed to accommodate 1,300 people. The interior is enlivened by imaginative mosaic and tile decoration, which is practical as well as colourful.

The baths were damaged in World War II but were impeccably restored in 1986.

Spinnerin am Kreuz

⓱ Spinnerin am Kreuz

Triesterstrasse 10, Meidling. Ⓤ Meidling. 🚌 15A, 65A. 🚊 1.

A medieval column marks the southernmost boundary of Vienna's inner suburbs. Built in 1452 and carved on all sides, it stands on the spot where, according to legend, a woman sat spinning for years awaiting her husband's return from the Crusades. Known as the Spinner at the Cross, it was designed by Hans Puchsbaum. Pinnacled canopies shelter groups of statuary, including a crucifixion and a grotesque figure placing the crown of thorns on the head of Christ.

⓲ Technical Museum

Mariahilfer Strasse 212, Penzing. **Tel** 899980. 🚌 10A 🚊 10, 52, 58. **Open** 9am–6pm Mon–Fri, 10am–6pm Sat, Sun & public hols. 🅿 ♿ Ⓦ tmw.ac.at

Franz Joseph founded the Technisches Museum Wien in 1908, using the Habsburgs' personal collections as core material; it opened its doors 10 years later. It documents all aspects of technical progress, from domestic appliances to large turbines, and includes exhibitions on heavy industry, energy, physics and musical instruments.

A major section of the museum features interactive displays on computer technology and oil and gas drilling and refining, as well as a reconstruction of a coal mine.

The Railway Museum forms an integral part of the Technical Museum. It houses an extensive collection of imperial railway carriages and engines. One of the prize exhibits is the imperial carriage that was used by Franz Joseph's wife, the Empress Elisabeth.

⓳ Schönbrunn Palace and Gardens

See pp174–7.

Decorative, geometrically-patterned tiling from the 1920s in the Amalienbad

⓴ Otto-Wagner-Hofpavillon Hietzing

Schönbrunner Schlossstrasse 13, Hietzing. **Tel** 8771571. Ⓤ Hietzing. 🚌 10A, 51A, 56B. 🚋 10, 58, 60. **Open** by appointment only.

Otto Wagner *(see p59)* designed and built this railway station for the imperial family and royal guests in 1899. This lovely building is in the shape of a white cube with green iron-work and a copper dome. Its waiting room is panelled with wood and glass, and adorned with a peach and russet asymmetrical carpet and a marble and brass fireplace. The cupola is decorated with glass and gilt flower and leaf motifs.

Wagner built the pavilion without a commission from the emperor in an attempt to showcase his work. Unfortunately, Franz Joseph used the station only twice.

The Hofpavillon Hietzing

㉑ Werkbund-siedlung

Jagdschlossgasse, Veitingergasse and Woinovichgasse, Hietzing. 🚌 54B, 55B. 🚋 62.

In the 13th district you can find the 30 or so fascinating "model" houses of the *Werkbundsiedlung* (housing estate) built in the early 1930s for the municipality by some of Europe's leading architects. They are neither beautiful nor lavish, since the idea was to produce a formula for cheap housing, with

Hermesvilla in the grounds of the Lainzer Tiergarten

two bedrooms, that was plain and functional. No. 19 Woinovichgasse is by Adolf Loos *(see p94)*, and Nos. 83–5 Veitingergasse are by Josef Hoffmann *(see p58)*. Each architect had to design a single building, placed side by side with the rest in order to evaluate the different qualities of each. Although intended to be temporary, they have luckily survived.

㉒ Lainzer Tiergarten

Lainzer Tiergarten, Hietzing. Tiergarten: **Tel** 400049200. 🚌 60B. 🚋 60. **Open** mid-Feb–mid-Nov: 8am–dusk daily. Hermesvilla and Garden: **Tel** 8041324. **Open** for exhibitions 10am–6pm Tue–Sun & public hols. **Closed** 27 Oct–24 Mar. 🅿

The Lainzer Tiergarten is a former Habsburg hunting ground which has been converted into an immense nature reserve in the Vienna Woods *(see p178)*. The Tiergarten was opened to the public in 1923 and is still encircled by its 24-km (15-mile) stone wall, protecting its herds of deer and wild boar. From the entrance, a 15-minute walk along paths through woods and meadows brings you to the Hermesvilla, built by Karl von Hasenauer in 1884. It became a retreat for the imperial family, notably the Empress Elisabeth and her husband Franz Joseph, who had a suite of rooms on the first floor. Inside are murals of scenes from *A Midsummer Night's Dream*, as well as art and historical exhibitions.

㉓ Wotruba-Kirche

Georgsgasse/Rysergasse, Mauer. **Tel** 8885003. 🚌 60A. **Open** 2–8pm Sat, 9am–4:30pm Sun & hols or **Tel** 0650 3324833 to make an appointment to see the church.

Built between 1965 and 1976 in uncompromisingly modern style, this church stands on a hillside very close to the Vienna Woods. It forms a pile of uneven rectangular concrete slabs and glass panels, some of the latter rising to the height of the church. They provide its principal lighting and views for the congregation out on to the woods and hills. The building is raw in style, but powerful and compact. Designed by the sculptor Fritz Wotruba (1907–75), the church looks different from every angle and has a strong sculptural quality. It accommodates a congregation of up to 250.

The exterior of the Wotruba-Kirche by Fritz Wotruba, not unlike a modern sculpture

⑲ Schönbrunn Palace and Gardens

The former summer residence of the imperial family takes its name from a beautiful spring that was found on this site. An earlier hunting lodge was destroyed by the Turks, so Leopold I asked Johann Bernhard Fischer von Erlach to design a grand Baroque residence here in 1695. However, it was not until Maria Theresa employed Nikolaus Pacassi that the project was completed in the mid-18th century. The strict symmetry of the architecture is complemented by the gardens with fountains and statues framed by trees and alleyways.

KEY

① Theatre
② Orangery
③ Obelisk Cascade
④ Public swimming pool
⑤ Japanese Gardens
⑥ Hietzing Gate

Maze
The maze was a favourite element of many European stately gardens. This one at Schönbrunn provides a puzzling detour for visitors.

Main entrance

★ Coach Museum
The former Winter Riding School houses the coaches, sleighs and sedan chairs that were used to transport the imperial family.

1683 First hunting lodge on site destroyed during the Turkish siege

1705 Jean Trehet lays out the gardens

1730 Palace is completed

1744–9 Nikolaus Pacassi adapts the building for Maria Theresa

1916 Emperor Franz Joseph dies here, aged 86

1918 Emperor Karl I abdicates Austrian throne in the Blue Chinese Salon (p176)

| 1650 | 1700 | 1750 | 1800 | 1850 | 1900 | 1950 |

1696 Leopold I commissions J B Fischer von Erlach to design a new palace

Emperor Leopold I

1775 Gloriette is built

1805 and 1809 Napoleon uses palace as headquarters

1752 Maria Theresa's husband, Franz Stephan, founds a menagerie, now the zoo

1952 Reconstruction is completed after war damage

1882 Palm House is built

★ Gloriette
This Neo-Classical arcade, designed by Ferdinand von Hohenberg and built in 1775, is the crowning glory of the hill behind the palace.

Neptune Fountain
This exuberant fountain and basin, at the foot of the hill, was sculpted in 1780 by Franz Anton Zauner.

Schönbrunn Zoo
Founded in 1752 at the order of Franz Stephan, the historic zoo has an octagonal pavilion.

★ Palm House
A vast collection of exotic plants flourishes in the magnificent tropical greenhouse that was erected in 1882.

Façade of Schönbrunn Palace seen from the gardens

Inside Schönbrunn Palace

The Rococo decorative schemes devised by Nikolaus Pacassi dominate the Schönbrunn state rooms, where white panelling, often adorned with gilded ornamental framework, tends to prevail. The rooms vary from extremely sumptuous – such as the Millionenzimmer, panelled with fig wood inlaid with Persian miniatures – to the quite plain apartments occupied by Franz Joseph and Empress Elisabeth.

★ Round Chinese Cabinet
Maria Theresa used this room for private discussions with her State Chancellor. The walls are adorned with lacquered panels and vases.

★ Great Gallery
Once the venue for imperial banquets, the gallery was used for state receptions until 1994.

Hidden staircase which leads to the apartment of the State Chancellor on the floor above and was used for access to secret conferences.

Blue Chinese Salon
The room where Karl I abdicated in 1918 has hand-painted wallpaper with blue insets showing Chinese scenes.

Napoleon Room

Millionenzimmer

Memorial Room

First Floor

★ Vieux-Lacque Room
During her widowhood, Maria Theresa lived in this room, which is decorated with exquisite oriental lacquered panels.

Main entrance

Large Rosa Room
Landscape scenes of Switzerland and northern Italy by Joseph Rosa give this room its name. The paintings are surrounded by Rococo gilded panels.

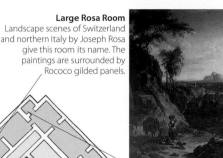

Breakfast Room
The imperial family's breakfast room has white wood panelling inlaid with appliqué floral designs worked by Maria Theresa and her daughters.

The Blue Staircase (so-called due to its original decorative scheme) leads to the entrance for guided tours of state rooms.

Room Guide

The state rooms open to the public are on the first floor. The suite of rooms to the right of the Blue Staircase were occupied by Franz Joseph and Elisabeth. Two galleries divide these from rooms in the east wing, which include Maria Theresa's bedroom and rooms used by Grand Duke Karl. Two guided tours, the Imperial and the Grand Tour, cover several rooms.

Key

☐ Franz Joseph's apartments

▨ Empress Elisabeth's apartments

☐ Ceremonial and reception rooms

▨ Maria Theresa's rooms

☐ Grand Duke Karl's rooms

☐ Non-exhibition space

Portrait of Napoleon

Portrait of Maria Louisa

Maria Louisa and the King of Rome

After Napoleon's fall from power, his young son by his Austrian wife Maria Louisa was kept a virtual prisoner in Schönbrunn Palace. In 1832 at the age of 21, after a lonely childhood, he died of consumption in what is known as the Napoleon Room. He was called the Duke of Reichstadt, or the King of Rome, and the Memorial Room contains his portrait as a five-year-old and his effigy. There is also a crested larch under a glass dome; the unhappy boy claimed that he never had a single friend in the palace apart from this bird.

Day Trips from Vienna

Within an hour or two's journey from Vienna there is an astonishing range of countryside from Hungarian-style plains to alpine mountains, majestic rivers and idyllic lakes. Vienna is at the centre of Austria's wine-growing country and is surrounded by historic castles and churches, among which nestle picturesque wine-producing towns and villages. All the sights are accessible by bus or train and trips such as Baden and Mayerling can easily be combined.

Among the trees of Vienna Woods, a popular recreation area

❶ Mayerling and the Vienna Woods

Vienna Sightseeing organizes trips *(see p251).* 🚌 552 or 1130 from Südtiroler Platz to Alland Hauptplatz, then 365 to Mayerling Altes Jagdschloss and Heiligenkreuz. Mayerling Chapel: **Tel** 02258 2275. **Open** Open 9am–1pm & 1:30–6pm daily (to 5pm Nov–Mar); 9am–12:30pm 24 Dec, Maundy Thu. **Closed** Good Fri, Holy Sat. Heiligenkreuz Abbey: **Tel** 225 887030. **Open** daily for tours. 📷 10am, 11am, 2pm, 3pm & 4pm Mon–Sat, 11am, 2pm, 3pm & 4pm Sun & hols.

The Vienna Woods extend from within the western bounds of the city and make excellent walking country. A turn around the Lainzer Tiergarten *(see p173)* makes a convenient half- or full-day outing from Vienna. Further on, where the Vienna Woods stretch out towards the lower slopes of the Alps, there are several interesting sights.
    The Mayerling hunting lodge, now the chapel, was the scene in 1889 of the double suicide of Crown Prince Rudolf *(see p34)* and his 17-year-old lover Mary Vetsera, daughter of the diplomat Baron Albin Vetsera.

Their tragic deaths shook the Austro-Hungarian empire. After his son's death, the Emperor Franz Joseph gave the hunting lodge to a Carmelite convent and it was completely rebuilt.
    A few miles north of Mayerling is the medieval Cistercian abbey of Heiligenkreuz. Much of the abbey was rebuilt in the Baroque period, having been destroyed by the Turks in 1529 and 1683. Inside is a 12th-century nave and a 13th-century chapter house. Fine Baroque features include the bell tower and Trinity Column. The abbey houses the tombs of 13 of the Babenbergs who ruled in Austria during the medieval period *(see pp24–5).*

❷ Baden

🚌 360 from Karlsplatz/Oper. 🚇 S2 or 🚆 R2335 or 2337 from Hauptbahnhof. 🚋 Badner Bahn (WLB) from Karlsplatz/Oper. **Tel** 02252 22600600.

To the south of Vienna are several spas and wine-growing towns in the hills of the southern Vienna Woods. The most famous is Baden, a spa with curative hot springs dating back to Roman times. As well as bathing in sulphurous water and mud to treat rheumatism, you can enjoy hot pools of 36°C (97°F).
    In the early 19th century Baden was popular with the Imperial Court of Vienna. Then many elegant Biedermeier villas, baths, town houses and a square were built, and the gardens of the Kurpark laid out. The park extends from the town centre to the Vienna Woods and has a rose garden and a memorial museum to Beethoven and Mozart. Today you can sample local wines in Baden's restaurants.

❸ Schloss Hof

🚌 Shuttle bus operated by Blaguss-Reisen Apr–Oct: Sat, Sun & hols from Marchegg station. Book by phone or online. **Tel** 61090200. 🅦 **blaguss.at Open** Apr–Oct: 10am–6pm daily. **Tel** 02285 200000. 🅦 **schlosshof.at**

After extensive restoration, Schloss Hof is an appealing destination. In 1725 Prince Eugene made it his principal country seat and laid out the present formal garden. Extended a generation later under Empress Maria Theresa, the palace contains private and state rooms from both periods.

Schloss Esterházy, the 17th-century residence of the Esterházy princes

Sights at a Glance

Day Trips

Key

◾ City centre
☐ Greater Vienna
═══ Motorway
▬▬▬ Major road
═══ Minor road
──── Railway
▬ ▪ International border

0 kilometres   25
0 miles   25

❹ Eisenstadt

🚌 566 from Hauptbahnhof. 🚆 REX 7618 from Hauptbahnhof to Müllendorf Bahnhof, then Bus 563. 🛈 02682 67390. Schloss Esterházy: **Tel** 02682 63004401. **Open** 15 Mar–11 Nov: 9am–6pm daily; 15 Nov–30 Dec: 9am–5pm Fri–Sun & hols. 📷 only. Haydn Museum: **Tel** 02682 7193011. **Open** Mar–May & Oct–mid-Nov: 9am–5pm Tue–Sat, 10am–5pm Sun & hols; Jun–Sep: 9am–5pm Mon–Sat, 10am–5pm Sun & hols. Jewish Museum: **Tel** 02682 65145. **Open** May–Oct: 10am–5pm Tue–Sun; Nov–Apr: by appt only (groups only).

Schloss Esterházy, built for Prince Paul Esterházy in 1663–73, lies southeast of Vienna in Eisenstadt. It contains the Haydnsaal, a great hall of state in which Joseph Haydn *(see pp40–41)* conducted the prince's orchestra. He lived nearby on Haydngasse and his house is now a museum. Also nearby is a Jewish Museum.

❺ Rust and Lake Neusiedl

🚌 566 or 765 from Hauptbahnhof; 566 from Eisenstadt. 🛈 7909100.

Lake Neusiedl, part of which is in Hungary, is surrounded by reeds, the home of dozens of species of wild birds. The reeds are used locally for crafts from thatching to basketwork. Around the lake are several wine villages and resorts; the prettiest is Rust, known for the storks which nest on its roofs and towers.

❻ Mariazell

🚌 552 or 1130 from Wien Hauptbahnhof. 🚆 from Westbahnhof, change at St Pölten to Mariazell alpine railway. 🛈 03882 2366. Basilica: **Open** Nov–Apr: 7:30am–7:15pm daily; May–Oct: 7am–8pm Sun–Fri, 7am–9:30pm Sat. 📷 **Tel** 03882 25950 for tours. Steam tram: **Tel** 0388 23014. **Open** Jul–Sep: 9:30am–4:30pm hourly Sat, Sun & hols.

The journey to Mariazell from St Pölten is by the Mariazell alpine railway. The town has long been the main Catholic pilgrim site of Central Europe, to which a Gothic and Baroque basilica bear witness. Inside the basilica, which was enlarged in the 17th century, is a wealth of Baroque stucco, painting and decoration. The treasury also forms part of the church.

A cable car up the mountain leaves every 20 minutes from the town centre. An additional attraction in summer is to ride the world's oldest steam tram, built in 1884, and running between Mariazell railway station and a nearby lake.

❼ River Trip from Krems to Melk

See pp180–81.

View of Mariazell, an important Marian shrine since 1377

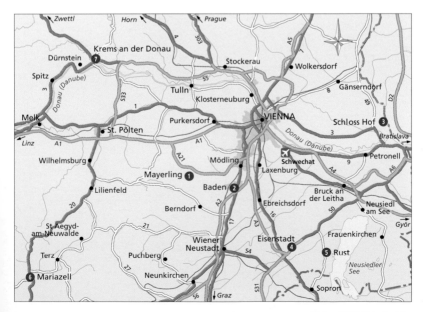

❼ River Trip from Krems to Melk

Some 80 km (50 miles) west of Vienna is one of the most magnificent stretches of river scenery in Europe. Castles, churches and wine-producing villages rise up on either side of the Danube valley and breathtaking views unfold. Redolent with history (it has been settled for over 30,000 years), this stretch from Krems to Melk is called the Wachau. A river trip is the best way to take in the landmarks, either with one of the tours organized by Cityrama, Vienna Line, Vienna Sightseeing or DDSG–Blue Danube *(see p251)*, or independently *(see box)*.

Wine-producing towns from Rossatz to Wösendorf

On the opposite bank to Dürnstein lies Rossatz ⑤, which has been making wine for centuries and was once a busy port. Findings of Neolithic and Roman remains testify to early settlement. In the 10th century it belonged to a Bavarian convent, but passed to the Babenbergs and

④ The perfectly-preserved medieval town of Dürnstein

Krems to Dürnstein

The beautiful Renaissance town of Stein has in modern times merged into one with Krems, which has a medieval centre ①. At the end of Steinerstrasse is the house of the Baroque artist Kremser Schmidt. Climb one of the narrow hillside streets and look across the Danube for a fine view of Göttweig Abbey ②, an excellent example of Austrian Baroque, and in the 17th century a centre of the Counter-Reformation. You can also see the small town of Mautern ③, which

developed from a 1st-century Roman fortification, and now boasts the gourmet restaurant Bacher in Südtirolerplatz.

Once on board, after about 8 km (5 miles) you will pass the perfectly-preserved medieval town of Dürnstein ④, with a Baroque church overlooked by the ruins of a castle. From 1192 to 1193, after his return from the Third Crusade, England's King Richard the Lionheart was held prisoner in the castle by Duke Leopold V of Babenberg *(see p25)*. He was released only on payment of a huge ransom. Dürnstein has conserved much of its medieval and Baroque character and has splendid river views and side streets leading to charming river walks. A separate visit is advisable if you want to see the town at leisure.

0 km   5

0 miles   3

Key

— Railway line

〜 River

▬ Major road

▭ Minor road

⑦ The church at Weissenkirchen which was fortified to hold off the Turks

became part of their Austrian domain. The Renaissance castle and Gothic church were transformed to Baroque around 1700.

At Weissenkirchen ⑥ the church dates mainly from the 15th and 16th centuries. The town is also renowned for its wine, as are Joching ⑦ and Wösendorf ⑧.

Churches and ruins

Clearly visible on top of a hill, the fortified Church of St Michael ⑨ was built between 1500 and 1523. An unusual architectural detail is the stone hares on its tower. Local folklore tells how, once, so much snow fell here that hares were able to leap onto the roof.

On the same side of the river is a ruined arch on a hill, Das Rote Tor ⑩, a fragment of a 14th-century gate through which the Swedes walked on their way to Spitz in 1645 during the 30 Years War (see p25). The town of Mitterarnsdorf ⑪ has Roman remains.

⑯ The ruined castle above the river at Aggstein

Spitz to Aggsbachdorf

Spitz ⑫ is another pretty wine town and was also a Protestant stronghold during the Reformation. It lies at the foot of the 1,000-Eimer Berg (1,000-Bucket Mountain), so called because it is claimed that in a good year the vine-clad hills can produce enough wine to fill 1,000 buckets.

Further on is a wall-like rocky precipice jutting out from the bank, the Teufelsmauer or Devil's Wall ⑬. It has given rise to a number of legends. One tells how the devil's grandmother wanted to stop pilgrims and crusaders by creating a dam. At Schwallenbach ⑭ the church was rebuilt after the Bohemians devastated the village in 1463. Although you cannot see it from the boat, you will pass very close to the village of Willendorf ⑮, famous for the prehistoric findings made nearby, including the statue and fertility symbol Venus of Willendorf (see pp22 and 130).

Aggstein ⑯ has a ruined castle high above the river. Jörg Scheck von Wald, follower of Duke Albrecht I, rebuilt and enlarged the original castle in 1429. Legend has it that he called a rock, placed at the highest point of the castle, his rose garden. He would force his imprisoned enemies to leap to their deaths if the ransom he demanded failed to arrive. Aggsbachdorf ⑰ was settled by the Romans in the 2nd century and owned by the Kuenringer robber-barons during the Middle Ages.

Schönbühel Castle to Melk

The picturesque castle of Schönbühel ⑱ stands on a rocky outcrop overlooking the Danube. Although it has been on record since the 9th century, its present form dates from the early 19th century. Further on,

⑳ The Benedictine abbey of Melk dominates the river and town

at the mouth of the 70-km long (43-mile) River Pielach ⑲, 30 Bronze Age tombs and the foundations of a Roman tower have been excavated.

The high point of the trip is the Benedictine abbey of Melk ⑳. The pretty town has Renaissance houses, romantic little streets, old towers and remnants of a city wall built in the Middle Ages. The Baroque abbey, where Umberto Eco's novel *The Name of the Rose* begins and ends, is a treasure trove of paintings, sculptures and decorative art. The great library contains 2,000 volumes from the 9th to the 15th centuries alone. The church has a magnificent organ, and skeletons dressed in luxurious materials inside glass coffins. Some of the Abbey's treasures are not on permanent view.

Tips for Independent Travellers

Starting points: Krems, Dürnstein, Melk or any river trip boarding point. River trip tickets are on sale at these points.
Getting there: Take the national network train from Franz-Josefs-Bahnhof to Krems or Dürnstein. For Melk, depart from Westbahnhof.
Stopping-off points: Dürnstein has restaurants and shops.
Melk Abbey Tel 02752 555232.
Open Palm Sunday–1st Sun after All Souls: 9am–4:30pm (May–Sep: 9am–5:30pm). 🎧 in English: 10:55am & 2:55pm May–Oct.
Cycling: A cycle path runs along the Danube. Hire bikes at Krems, Melk, Spitz and Dürnstein train stations (reduction with train ticket), or from river trip boarding points. Take your passport for identification. **W** stiftmelk.at

THREE GUIDED WALKS

Vienna is a comparatively small city, with several main attractions within easy walking distance of each other. All six sightseeing areas in this guide have a suggested short walk marked on a Street-by-Street map. Yet the city's suburbs are also worth exploring on foot. The following guided walks take you through some of the best walking areas in and around the city, all easily accessible by public transport. The first walk takes you through the town itself. Starting in the Stadtpark, it continues past the Karlskirche to the elegant Wagner Apartments and the colourful Naschmarkt on the Linke Wienzeile. Hietzing, on the western edge of the grounds of Schönbrunn Palace, is our second walk.

The former village's quiet streets are lined with an interesting mix of Biedermeier and Jugendstil villas. Towards the end of the walk is Schönbrunn Palace Park, with an area of woodland and the more formally planted Botanical Garden. The third walk takes you to the old wine village of Grinzing, with its many *Heurige*. The route goes through Heiligenstadt, where there are a number of buildings by well-known 20th-century architects. In addition to the walks that are suggested on these pages, there are signposted routes through the Vienna Woods and the Prater, marked *Stadtwanderwege*. For details of these, visit or contact the Vienna Tourist Board offices *(see p238)*.

A Two-Hour Walk to Grinzing *(see pp188–9)*

The Fillgrader Steps on the City Walk

Heiligenstädter Park, on the way to Grinzing

A 90-Minute Walk Around Hietzing *(see pp186–7)*

A Two-Hour City Walk *(see pp184–5)*

Key

••• Walk route

0 kilometres 2
0 miles 1

◄ Detail of the Art Nouveau façade of the Kirche am Steinhof, designed by Otto Wagner

A Two-Hour City Walk

This walk skirts the southwestern perimeter of the inner city, following part of the course of the River Wien. It begins with a leisurely stroll through the Stadtpark, which was laid out in English landscape style when the Ringstrasse was built (*see p34*). Continuing past Schwarzenbergplatz and Karlsplatz through the lively Naschmarkt, it ends with a glance at some masterpieces of Jugendstil architecture on the Linke Wienzeile.

⑪ Jugendstil portal in the Stadtpark, built in 1903–4 as part of the flood defences along the river

The Stadtpark

Begin the walk at the entrance to the Stadtpark opposite Weihburggasse. Almost facing you is an impressive side entrance ① with sculpted portals, which was designed between 1857 and 1862.

On the city side, the park contains many monuments to musicians and artists. The first is the gilded statue of Johann Strauss II (*see p41*) playing his violin (1921) ②. Go left past this monument, and left again, into a paved circular seating area with a fountain dedicated to the Sprite of the Danube ③. Turn right out of this area and you come to an iron bridge across the River Wien, from the middle of which you get a view of the embankments ④.

Walk back to the nearby lake ⑤. On its southern side a statue of the Viennese landscape painter Emil Jakob Schindler (1895) ⑥ sits in the bushes. Follow the path

㉑ No. 38 Linke Wienzeile

until it peters out into a culvert then go left across the bridge. Turn left again until you come to a monument to Franz Schubert (1872) by Carl Kundmann ⑦. Take the path past the lake and turn right at the clocktower. The painter Hans Makart, who dominated the visual arts in Vienna in the 1870s and 1880s, strikes a rhetorical pose in Viktor Tilgner's 1898 statue ⑧. Walk on past the entrance to the park. On the

right is the bust of Franz Lehár, composer of *The Merry Widow* ⑨. Walk towards the Kursalon ⑩, which opened for concerts, balls and waltzes in the 1860s. Continue past the Kursalon, leaving the park through one of the Jugendstil portals (*see p59*) ⑪.

⑯ Statue of Johannes Brahms (1908) by Rudolf Weyr, in the Ressel Park

Tips for Walkers

Starting point: Weihburggasse Tram 2 (on Parkring).
Length: 3 km (1½ miles).
Getting there: Tram 2, which circulates around the Ringstrasse and Franz-Josefs-Kai; or Stubentor U-Bahn, then walk.
Stopping-off points: The Kursalon in the Stadtpark serves tea, coffee and cakes on the terrace and has a beer garden to one side. There are also many benches where you can rest. There are cafés in Ressel Park and the Naschmarkt; towards the end of the walk you will find Café Sperl on Gumpendorfer Strasse.

Schwarzenbergplatz

Walk straight ahead, crossing the road into Lothringerstrasse. A monument to Beethoven (1880), showing the composer surrounded by figures alluding to the Ninth Symphony, stands on the right ⑫. Cross the road to the Konzerthaus (1912–13), home to the Vienna Symphony Orchestra (see p228) ⑬.

Cross the busy intersection to get a striking vista of Schwarzenbergplatz to your left, at the end of which is a fountain. It was erected in 1873 to celebrate the city's supply of pure drinking water, which comes from the mountains. Behind it is the Memorial to the Red Army which liberated Austria in 1945 ⑭.

⑩ The Neo-Renaissance Kursalon

Apartments (see p143) with golden medallions by Kolo Moser at No. 38 ㉑, and the Majolikahaus at No. 40, so called because of its floral tiles ㉒. As you turn into Köstlergasse alongside No. 38 it is worth pausing to admire the entrance.

⑰ Confession box, Karlskirche

Key

• • • Walk route

0 metres 250
0 yards 250

Ressel Park

Continue along Lothringerstrasse, past the Wien Museum Karlsplatz (see p150) ⑮, into Ressel Park. On the left is a statue of Brahms with his muse at his feet (1908) by Rudolf Weyr ⑯. Look left past Brahms to the Karlskirche (see pp148–9) ⑰. Go on, noting Otto Wagner's pavilions (see p150) at road level ⑱. Pass the Neo-Classical Technical High School ⑲ to leave the park. Cross Wiedner Hauptstrasse, go straight ahead then left into Operngasse, crossing the road. Walk through Bärenmühlendurchgang passage in the building facing you and cross the road into the Naschmarkt ⑳.

Naschmarkt

A lively food market (see p142), originally held in the Karlsplatz, moved here after this part of the river was paved over in the late 19th century. It is a good vantage point from which to admire the elegant 19th-century buildings along the left bank, or Linke Wienzeile. Leave the market and cross the road to look at Otto Wagner's

㉕ Papageno Gate of the Theater an der Wien

Gumpendorfer Strasse

Turn right at the end of Köstlergasse and walk up Gumpendorfer Strasse. Look left up Fillgradergasse for a glimpse of the Fillgrader Steps ㉓. Continue on to the historic Café Sperl (see p60), once the haunt of the composer Lehár ㉔. Go on and turn right into Millöckergasse to see the famous Papageno Gate of the Theater an der Wien (see p142) ㉕. The sculpture above the entrance shows the theatre's first owner, Emanuel Schikaneder, in the character of Papageno from Mozart's The Magic Flute. Continue down Millöckergasse to the Linke Wienzeile. Bear left, passing the Secession Building (see p142) ㉖, and go on to Karlsplatz U-Bahn.

For map symbols see back flap

A 90-Minute Walk Around Hietzing

The former village of Hietzing runs along the western edge of the extensive grounds of Schönbrunn Palace *(see p174–7)*. In Maria Theresa's time it was a fashionable area where the nobility went to spend their summers; later it became a suburb for the wealthy middle classes. The quiet streets contain a marvellous mix of Biedermeier and Jugendstil villas, while the square around the parish church retains an intimate small-town atmosphere.

⑥ The Kaiserstöckl opposite the Park Hotel, now a post office

From the station to Am Platz

Take the Hadikgasse exit from Hietzing U-Bahn ① and cross the tram tracks and road to Kennedybrücke. Turn right down Hadikgasse and after a minute you arrive at Otto-Wagner-Hofpavillon Hietzing *(see p173)* ②, a former station designed for the use of the imperial family when they were at Schönbrunn. Retrace your steps to the U-Bahn and cross the road into Hietzinger Hauptstrasse. Notice the attic of No. 6 with cherubs hugging the columns. The building dates from 1901–2, but the lower storey has been altered to accommodate shops ③. On your left through the railings are long avenues of trees at the side of Schönbrunn ④. Just across the road is the Park Hotel, its ochre façade echoing that of the palace buildings ⑤. Facing it is the Kaiserstöckl (1770) or Emperor's Pavilion ⑥. Today it is a post office, but it used to be the holiday venue of Maria Theresa's foreign ministers. Continue to Am Platz with its plague column dating from 1730 ⑦. Next door to this is the parish church of Maria Geburt ⑧, originally built in the 13th century, and remodelled in the 17th century. The Baroque interior contains altars by the sculptor Matthias Steindl and ceiling frescoes by Georg Greiner. The church was used by Maria Theresa when she was in residence at Schönbrunn, and her box can be seen in the right-hand wall of the choir. In front of the church stands a statue of Franz Joseph's brother Maximilian, the Emperor of Mexico who

Key

• • • Walk route

⑤ Façade of the Park Hotel

⑧ Elaborate altar by Matthias Steindl in the Maria-Geburt-Kirche

Tips for Walkers

Starting point: Hietzing U-Bahn.
Length: 5 km (3 miles).
Getting there: U-Bahn U4; tram 10, 58, 60; bus 51A, 56B, 58B, 156B. **Note:** On Sundays you may need to retrace your steps a short distance if the Maxing Gate is locked. **Stopping-off points:** the BAWAG café in Hietzing's Am Platz is a pleasant place for a coffee. Bezirksmuseum Hietzing: **Open** 2–6pm Wed, 2–5pm Sat. **Closed** Jul–Aug. Schönbrunn Palace and Park: *see pp174–7.* Villa Primavesi: **Closed** to public.

was executed in 1867 ⑨. Nearby is a Neo-Classical building housing the Bezirksmuseum Hietzing ⑩, and outside the museum is Vienna's last gas lamp.

Trauttmansdorffgasse and Gloriettegasse

Turn left into Maxingstrasse, named after Maximilian, then right into Altgasse. Almost facing Fasholdgasse is an old *Heuriger*, a Biedermeier building with ochre walls ⑪.

⑲ Detail from the majolica façade of the Lebkuchenhaus

road, at No. 27, is the house where the composer Alban Berg *(see p41)* once lived ⑬. Nos. 48 and 50 are contrasting examples of Viennese turn-of-the-century architecture ⑭. More examples of Biedermeier style can be seen at Nos. 54 and 56 ⑮. At the end of the road, turn right into Gloriettegasse. On the right at Nos. 14 and 16 is a villa with monumental sculpted figures resting in the pediments, built in 1913–15 by Josef Hoffmann for the financier Robert Primavesi ⑯. Cross the road to pass a terrace of Biedermeier houses – Nos. 38 and 40 have lunettes above the windows ⑰. No. 21 is the Villa Schopp, designed by Friedrich Ohmann in 1901–2 ⑱. Turn left down Wattmanngasse to see No. 29, the extraordinary Lebkuchenhaus (Gingerbread House) ⑲, so-called because of its dark brown decoration in majolica. It was built in 1914 to designs by a pupil of Otto Wagner *(see pp56–9)*. Turn back into Gloriettegasse. At its southern junction with Wattmanngasse, at No. 9, is the house that

belonged to Katharina Schratt, the actress and confidante of Emperor Franz Joseph during his later years. It is said that the Emperor was in the habit of arriving here for breakfast ⑳.

Maxing Park and Schönbrunn Park

Walk to the end of Gloriettegasse, then turn right up Maxingstrasse and cross the road at Maxing Park. If you would like to add another half hour to the walk, Hietzing cemetery, a little further up the hill, contains the graves of Otto Wagner, Gustav Klimt, Kolo Moser and Franz Grillparzer, among others. Alternatively, enter Maxing Park ㉑ and follow the main path upwards towards the right. At the top, go through the gates marked *Zum Tiergarten Schönbrunn*, passing the forestry research institute on your left. Although you are actually in the grounds of Schönbrunn, this heavily wooded area feels very remote from the formal gardens and you may catch a glimpse of deer. At the crossroads in the path turn left, signposted to the Botanical Garden. You soon arrive at a little wooden hut, which was Crown Prince Rudolf's playhouse ㉒.

The path eventually leads to the formally planted Botanical Garden ㉓, which was laid out in 1848 under Emperor Franz I. Take the path through the garden, keeping to the boundary wall with Hietzing. Exit into Maxingstrasse (this gate may be locked on Sundays) and continue north. At No. 18 is the house where Johann Strauss II wrote *Die Fledermaus* in 1874 ㉔. Carry on north along Maxingstrasse and retrace your steps to Hietzing U-Bahn.

HADIKGASSE

NISSELG

GYROWETZG

Hietzing U ①
②
③
⑤ ④
⑥
⑧

SCHÖNBRUNNER SCHLOSSSTR.

SCHÖNBRUNN PARK

㉒

Turn down Fasholdgasse into Trautt-mansdorffgasse, a street full of interesting houses. No. 40 is a beautifully-restored, long and low Biedermeier villa ⑫, while across the

SECCENDORFF-GUDENT-WEG

⑯ Sculpted figure in a pediment of the Villa Primavesi

For map symbols *see back flap*

A Two-Hour Walk to Grinzing

This walk through part of Vienna's 19th district begins at the site of one of the most important monuments of 20th-century Vienna, the public housing development of the Karl-Marx-Hof. It then takes you through a pretty 19th-century park to the old wine village of Grinzing. Although the village suffered destruction at the hands of the Turks in 1529 and 1683 and from Napoleon's army in 1809, and is now feeling the effects of modern tourism, its pretty main street preserves its charm.

⑮ Façade of the 16th-century Reinprecht *Heuriger*

Karl-Marx-Hof to Heiligenstädter Park

Facing you as you step out of Heiligenstadt station is the long ochre, terracotta and mauve façade of the Karl-Marx-Hof *(see p163)*, a huge housing project designed by the city architect Karl Ehn and built from 1927 to 1930 during the Red Vienna period ①. It sprawls for 1.2 km (3/4 mile) and has 1,272 flats.

Cross the road and pass through one of the four arches facing you into 12 Februar Platz to see the main façade from the other side. On the keystone of each arch stands a large figure sculpture by Joseph Riedl (1928) ②. Continue through the square, past a statue (1928) by Otto Hofner of a man sowing seeds ③, and you come to Heiligenstädter Strasse. Turn right, cross the road at the second pedestrian crossing and walk through the square opening in the building facing you. Go up the steps and take the path on the left into Heiligenstädter Park. When you come to a fork, take the left path that winds up a hill, going through woods. Turn right at the top into the formal part of the park ④. From here, you get a good view of the vine-clad slopes of the Kahlenberg ⑤.

① Figure on the Karl-Marx-Hof

Steinfeldgasse

Take the second small path on the right, which descends gradually into Steinfeldgasse, where there is a cluster of

houses built by the Secessionist designer Josef Hoffmann. The first one you come to is the Villa Moser-Moll at Nos. 6–8, designed for Carl Moll and Kolo Moser ⑥. Next to it is the Villa Spitzer ⑦, then the more classical Villa Ast, built in 1909–11 ⑧. Where Steinfeldgasse meets Wollergasse is the Villa Henneberg of 1901 ⑨, and at No. 10 Wollergasse ⑩ is the

Moll House II of 1906–7. Its black and white details are charming.

Steinfeldgasse to Grinzinger Strasse

At the point where Steinfeldgasse and Wollergasse meet, there is a path leading down through some woods. Follow this and descend the steps to the Church of St Michael, Heiligenstadt ⑪, which has striking modern stained-glass windows. Walk past the church, cross Hohe Warte and go up Grinzinger Strasse. You quickly arrive at No. 70, the house where Albert Einstein was a guest several times ⑫. On the same side of the road is No. 64, the late 18th-century house where Beethoven and the Viennese playwright Franz Grillparzer lodged during the summer of 1808 while Beethoven was composing

④ Lawns and trees in the Heiligenstädter Park

the Pastoral Symphony ⑬. Continue up Grinzinger Strasse, passing a number of attractive Biedermeier houses, until you arrive at Grinzinger Allee. Turn right past a series of wine gardens and immediately right again to get a quick glimpse of the upper part of Sandgasse, where there are a number of less touristy *Heurige* ⑭.

Grinzing

Turning back on yourself and towards the centre of Grinzing, ascend

Cobenzlgasse, Grinzing's main street

⑰ Courtyard at the Passauer Hof, an old wine press house

Tips for Walkers

Starting point: Heiligenstadt station. **Length:** 3.5 km (2 miles). **Getting there:** Heiligenstadt station is served by U-Bahn line U4, trains S40 and S45 and buses 10A, 11A, 38A and 39A. Tram D stops on Heiligenstädter Strasse. **Stopping-off points:** There are numerous *Heurige* (usually open from 4pm), coffee shops and restaurants in Grinzing. Avoid the larger *Heurige* – the smaller ones sell their own wine. Those at the top of Sandgasse are good.

Key

• • • Walk route
═══ Railway line

Cobenzlgasse, the upper fork of Grinzing's main street. The Reinprecht *Heuriger* at No. 22 Cobenzlgasse is a 16th-century house, the façade of which has a tablet commemorating the composer Robert Stolz ⑮. No. 30 Cobenzlgasse is the Baroque Trummelhof, standing on the site of an 1835 brewery ⑯. Further up on the left, at No. 9, is the Passauer Hof, an old wine press house that contains fragments of a far older, Romanesque building ⑰. On the corner of Cobenzlgasse and Feilergasse is the Altes Presshaus, whose cellar contains an old wine press ⑱.

Turn left into Feilergasse, and you soon come face to face with the impressive white Jugendstil façade of Nos. 41–3

Himmelstrasse ⑲. Continue down Himmelstrasse to No. 35, another *Heuriger*, Das Alte Haus, which has a charming plaque of the Virgin Mary above its door ⑳. There is a another such painting at No. 31, which shows a holy man carrying various items ㉑. No. 29 ㉒ is another *Heuriger* with a tablet to Sepp Fellner, a *Schrammel* musician *(see p41)* described as "The Schubert of Grinzing". Ironically, at No. 25, a grand building with shields above the doorway, there is a memorial to the real Schubert, described as "The Prince of Song, who loved to tarry in Grinzing" ㉓. Grinzing also has an attractive late Gothic church with a copper cupola and much-restored interior ㉔. Continue down the road to the tram terminus, where the No. 38 tram goes back to town.

㉑ Plaque of a holy man on the façade of No. 31 Himmelstrasse

A typical old street in central Vienna ▶

TRAVELLERS' NEEDS

WHERE TO STAY

With more than 500 hotels and pensions, Vienna offers accommodation to suit travellers on every budget. From palaces to simple lodgings, it has some of the grandest European city hotels as well as numerous small boarding-houses and self-catering establishments. Hotels are generally larger and better equipped to cater to a mix of business and leisure clientele while Vienna's numerous pensions offer simple bed-and-breakfast accommodation. The hotels on pages 196–9 include a selection of the best boutique, contemporary, family-friendly, luxury and pension accommodation, listed by area and in order of price category.

Baroque façade of the Mailberger Hof in Stephansdom Quarter *(see p197)*

Where to Look

One of the thrills of visiting Vienna is that guests can stay in either grand or modest accommodation right in the city centre. Many of the most famous historic hotels, such as the **Sacher**, **Bristol** and **Imperial** *(see p199)* are on or just off the Ringstrasse, as are many of the large chain hotels.

There are also a number of less expensive, comfortable hotels and pensions in the city centre, most on fairly quiet side streets. The Museum and Townhall Quarter has some good small hotels and offers affordable lodgings for budget travellers. A few hotels on Vienna's outskirts are also included in the listings.

The **Österreich Werbung** (Austrian Tourist Board) publishes information on over 500 hotels and pensions.

Hotel Prices

Accommodation can be expensive with prime locations highly priced year-round. However, guests can expect to pay approximately a fifth to a quarter less for a room in an establishment just outside the Ringstrasse, and less still if they are prepared to stay further afield.

Many traditional hotels offer a range of rooms at a variety of prices depending on their size, aspect and, in pensions, whether they have en suite bathrooms. Single rooms are about three-quarters the cost of double rooms. Some places will put an extra bed in the room on request, which can cost less than the price of a single room. Other hotels offer family or triple-bed rooms.

Vienna's low season is November–March (excluding Christmas and New Year) and July–August. Few hotels drop prices in summer, although some lower their winter rates by 25 per cent. Most of the large chain hotels reduce the room tariff during quiet periods and offer weekend specials. During off-season, it is worth asking for

Penthouse suite No. 663 in the Hotel Bristol in Belvedere Quarter *(see p199)*

a discount for payment in cash. Many places also offer discounts for longer stays, and it is possible to find packages such as three nights for the price of two. Ask for a rate reduction if your room does not have air conditioning.

Hidden Extras

Apart from some five-star hotels, breakfast is included in the tariff for most establishments. Rates will always include taxes such as VAT (or MWSt).

Some hotels have private garages and most will suggest a nearby underground car park.

Opulent lobby of the Imperial Hotel in Belvedere Quarter *(see p199)*

Room with contemporary design at Hollmann Beletage, a boutique hotel in Stephansdom Quarter *(see p196)*

Be warned – designated spaces for hotel guests are generally offered at sky-high prices. Parking fees are expensive with street parking within the Ringstrasse restricted to 90 minutes. Outlying districts do not have such stringent street parking restrictions, and garage parking is cheaper.

Making phone calls from the hotel room is extremely costly. Most hotels charge a flat rate plus a surcharge that can amount to three and a half times the standard rate. If you make a lot of calls, consider buying a pay-as-you-go mobile phone or a SIM card from a local provider.

Many hotels allow pet dogs to stay in the rooms – for a charge.

Facilities

Sign of a the famous Hotel Bristol

Hotels are rated one to five stars and pensions have a four-star system; a three-star hotel corresponds to a four-star pension. The rating also attempts to cover the quality and ambience of the hotel or pension. Five-star hotels are upmarket and well-run. Many three- and four-star hotels refer to themselves as *Palais*, which equates to a fine town house. At the cheaper end of the scale, small pensions above two stars are often more salubrious than cheap hotels. One- or two-star hotels and pensions are generally very basic and tend to cater for travellers on a budget.

Large hotels have a full range of public rooms – restaurant, bar, coffee shop and sitting room. Smaller establishments usually have lounge seating in the foyer. Even if there is no bar, drinks are often served. Almost all hotels and pensions have a breakfast room, with lower-priced establishments serving a continental breakfast and pricier hotels offering hot and cold breakfast buffets.

Hotels set in old buildings have character and no two bedrooms are the same. Rooms almost always have a phone, and usually have a TV. Mid-range hotel rooms often have cable TV, mini-bar and a bathroom with either a shower or bathtub. Many Viennese buildings look on to quiet courtyards so you can select a peaceful room, or one with a view.

In the 19th-century there was a restriction on building heights. To circumvent the regulation, lower floors were (and still are) called *Hochparterre* and *Mezzanin*. Consequently, guests may find that the "first floor" is up three flights of stairs. Additionally, in pensions a communal lift serves the whole building.

The quality of service in the best luxury hotels is as good as anywhere in the world. Wherever you stay, it could be well worth befriending the concierge (an early tip may help) as their local knowledge and contacts are invaluable – from helping guests find interesting restaurants and bars or conjuring tickets for the opera. Most hotel staff speak good English.

How to Book

Easter, May, June, September, October, Christmas and New Year are considered peak season during which accommodation may be fully booked as early as three months in advance – especially if an opera, ballet or conference draws foreign visitors.

Making direct hotel reservations is easy, since many hotel personnel speak English. A phone call to book will suffice; written confirmation by email and a credit card number may be requested. If you cancel once the booking is made, you may be charged for the room. Check in advance. If arriving after 6pm, let the hotel know or they may give the room to someone else. **Wiener Tourismusverband** (Vienna Tourist Board), which is located on the corner of Albertinaplatz, Tegethoffstrasse and Meysedergasse, can reserve hotel rooms in advance on your behalf.

Imposing lobby at Sans Souci in Museum and Townhall Quarter *(see p198)*

city centre. Most campsites have kitchen facilities; some have a supermarket. For additional camping information, contact **Wiener Tourismusverband**, **Camping und Caravaning Club Austria**, and **Österreichischer Camping Club**. Wiener Tourismusverband also produces a camping and youth hostel brochure that provides more details on these sites.

Self-Catering

For those who are keen to "go it alone" there are opportunities for self-catering in the city. **Ferienwohnungen Wien** has a range of large and small apartments for rent in and around Vienna. Its website has all the details. It puts clients directly in touch with the landlord of the property and does not charge commission fees. Some apartments have a combined living and sleeping space. Expect to pay less than the price of a pension.

Private Homes

It is possible for travellers to book a stay in a private home through **Wiener Tourismusverband**, but the booking has to be made in person. **Odyssee Reisen/ Mitwohnzentrale**, a private company, offers the same service. Normally it is necessary to stay a few nights and you should expect to pay around €36 per person per night.

Travelling with Children

An increasing number of hotels in Vienna are family friendly and offer child facilities such as bottle sterilizers, cots (some hotels charge extra for these) and baby-sitting services, as well as family-sized rooms.

Travellers with Disabilities

Information concerning wheelchair access to hotels relies on the individual hotel's assessment of their suitability and it is advisable to check before travelling. **Wiener Tourismusverband** publishes a detailed leaflet.

Youth Hostels

Youth hostel organisations such as **Österreichischer Jugendherbergsverband** have accommodation in Vienna. The Wiener Tourismusverband's youth hostel and camping brochure lists their facilities. Those with a better amenities cost around €10–€15 per night including breakfast. Most expect residents to be in by midnight. An International Youth Hostel Federation membership card is required, which can be obtained in advance or at the hostel.

Saisonhotels

From 1 July to 30 September, two dozen student hostels become Saisonhotels, or seasonal hotels, rated on a scale of one to three stars. At the three-star level expect fairly decent rooms. You may make enquiries at any time of the year at two of the main chains, **Academia Hotels** and **Sommerhotel Wieden**. Reserve well in advance and expect to pay up to €75 for a double room in one of the better venues.

Camping

Five well-equipped campsites can be found within a radius of 8–15 km (5–9 miles) from the

View of a campsite at No. 40 Hüttelbergstrasse

Chain Hotels

Almost all of the famous large hotel chains are well represented in Vienna. Marriott hotels include the **Vienna Marriott** *(see p197),* **Imperial Riding School Renaissance Vienna** *(see p199)* and **Renaissance Hotel Wien**. Other familiar names are **InterContinental** *(see p198),* **Hilton** and **Hotel Novotel City**, all of which are centrally located.

Chain hotels are often geared up for executive travellers and offer the best range of business services. Room rates usually vary according to their level of occupancy, rather than the season. Examples of these are **Lindner Hotel Am Belvedere** *(see p197)* and **Radisson Blu Palais Hotel** *(see p198).*

Recommended Hotels

The hotels listed on pages 196–9 are among the best in the historic centre of Vienna

Elegantly furnished room at the luxurious Hotel Sacher in Opera and Naschmarkt *(see p199)*

and its more bohemian outlying districts. The listings cover a variety of accommodation types in several price categories, ranging from simple pensions and family-friendly hotels to classy five-star chains, luxury palaces, characterful boutique hotels and contemporary options with minimalist decor and the latest high-tech gadgets.

Throughout the listings some establishments have been highlighted as DK Choice. These offer something particularly special for a memorable stay, such as a historic landmark building, exceptional art or design features, superlative service and amenities, a fantastic spa, outstanding city views, eco-friendly credentials or any combination of these qualities.

DIRECTORY

Where to Look

Österreich Werbung
Zollamtsstrasse 13, 1030.
Tel 588 66 0.
W austriatourism.com

How to Book

Wiener Tourismusverband
1, Albertinaplatz/
Meysedergasse, 1010.
Map 5 C4. **Tel** 245 55.
W wien.info

Youth Hostels

Österreichischer Jugendherbergs-verband
Zelinkagasse 12, 1010.
Map 2 D4.
Tel 533 53 53.
W oejhv.at

Saisonhotels

Academia Hotels
Pfeilgasse 3A, 1080.
Map 1 A5.
Tel 401 76 55.
W academiahotels.at

Sommerhotel Wieden
Schelleingasse 36, 1040.
Map 4 E1.
Tel 576 66 76.
W sommerhotel wieden.at

Camping

Camping und Caravaning Club Austria
Donaustadtstrasse 34, 1220.
Tel 123 22 22.
W cca-camping.at

Österreichischer Camping Club
Schubertring 1–3, 1010. **Map** 6 D5.
Tel 713 61 51.
W campingclub.at

Self-Catering

Ferienwohnungen Wien
Schubertgasse 11, 1090.
Map 1 B2.
Tel 699 122 65 721
W ferienwohnungen wien.com

Private Homes

Odyssee Reisen/ Mitwohnzentrale
Westbahnstrasse 19, 1070.
Map 3 A2. **Tel** 402 60 61.
W odyssee-reisen.at

Chain Hotels

Hilton
Am Stadtpark, 1030.
Map 6 F4. **Tel** 717 00 0.
W hilton.com

Hotel Novotel City
Aspernbrückenstrasse 1, 1020. **Map** 1 B5.
Tel 903 03 0.
W accorhotels.com

Imperial Riding School Reinaissance Vienna
Ungargasse 60, 1030.
Map 4 F1. **Tel** 711 75 0.
W marriott.com

InterContinental
Johannesgasse 28, 1037.
Map 6 E5. **Tel** 711 22 0.
W vienna.international. com

Lindner Hotel Am Belvedere
Rennweg 12, 1030.
Map 4 E2.
Tel 794 77 0.
W lindner.de

Radisson Blu Palais Hotel
Parkring 16, 1010.
Map 6 E4.
Tel 515 17 0.
W radissonblu.com

Renaissance Hotel Wien
Ullmannstrasse 71, 1150.
Tel 891 02.
W marriott.com

Vienna Marriott
Parkring 12A, 1010.
Map 6 E4.
Tel 515 18 0.
W marriott.com

Where to Stay

Boutique

Stephansdom Quarter

Alma Boutique Hotel €
Hafnersteig 7, 1010
Tel *533 29 61*   **Map** 6 E2
ⓦ hotel-alma.com
This elegant Art Nouveau hotel
has beautifully furnished rooms
and a roof terrace with a sun deck.

Hotel Kärntnerhof €
Grashofgasse 4, 1010
Tel *512 19 23*   **Map** 6 E3
ⓦ karntnerhof.com
Built around 1900, this charming
hotel has spacious rooms and
suites, and a roof garden.

> ### DK Choice
>
> **Hollmann Beletage** €€
> *Köllnerhofgasse 6, 1010*
> **Tel** *961 19 60*   **Map** 6 E2
> ⓦ hollmann-beletage.at
> With its sleek tangerine and
> granite decor, and 25 spacious
> rooms boasting an array of
> gadgets, this family-run hotel in
> a renovated 19th-century
> building is an absolute gem.
> Mammoth breakfasts, friendly
> staff and a sauna are just a few
> of the many highlights.

Hotel Am Schubertring €€
Schubertring 11, 1010
Tel *717 02 0*   **Map** 6 D5
ⓦ schubertring.at
Enjoy old Vienna charm at this
four-star hotel with beautifully
furnished rooms and helpful staff.

> ### DK Choice
>
> **The Ring** €€€
> *Kärntner Ring 8, 1010*
> **Tel** *221 22*   **Map** 6 D5
> ⓦ theringhotel.com
> Behind this hotel's sober 19th-
> century façade lies a warm
> interior with sensual fabrics,
> bold designs and luxurious
> creative touches. Individually
> styled rooms blend historic
> details with contemporary
> design. The superb spa offers
> great city views. Excellent service.

Hofburg Quarter

Graben Hotel €
Dorotheergasse 3, 1010
Tel *512 15 31 0*   **Map** 5 C4
ⓦ kremslehnerhotels.at
Attentive service and huge
breakfasts are the highlights here.

Schottering and Alsergrund

> ### DK Choice
>
> **Hotel Boltzmann** €
> *Boltzmanngasse 8, 1090*
> **Tel** *354 50 0*   **Map** 1 C3
> ⓦ hotelboltzmann.at
> Named after the Viennese
> physicist Ludwig Boltzmann, this
> lovely good-value hotel boasts
> cosy rooms, some suitable for
> families. In summer, enjoy a
> hearty breakfast buffet in the
> quiet courtyard garden. Friendly
> staff. Book well in advance.

Museum and Townhall Quarter

Fleming's Deluxe Hotel €€
Josefstädter Strasse 10–12, 1080
Tel *205 99 0*   **Map** 1 B5
ⓦ flemings-hotels.com
State-of-the-art gadgets and
excellent service are to be found
at this luxurious hotel with sleek
and elegant decor.

Hotel Rathaus €€
Lange Gasse 13, 1080
Tel *400 11 22*   **Map** 1 B5
ⓦ hotel-rathaus-wien.at
This hotel is dedicated to wine
and wine culture – echoed in the
decor, bar menu and artworks.

Levant Parliament €€
Auerspergstrasse 9, 1080
Tel *228 28 0*   **Map** 1 B5
ⓦ thelevante.com
Super-stylish hotel, with a lovely
courtyard, an eye-catching glass
bar and a Finnish sauna.

Room with a view of the Stephansdom at
Hotel Am Parkring

> ### Price Guide
> Prices are for a standard double room
> per night in high season, inclusive of all
> taxes and service charges.
>
> | € | up to €150 |
> |---|---|
> | €€ | €150–€250 |
> | €€€ | over €250 |

Belvedere Quarter

Hotel Am Konzerthaus €
Am Heumarkt 35–37, 1030
Tel *716 16 0*   **Map** 4 F2
ⓦ mgallery.com
Located amongst Art Nouveau
landmarks, this arty hotel attracts
a sophisticated clientele.

Further Afield

Art Hotel Vienna €
Brandmayergasse 7–9, 1050
Tel *544 51 08*   **Map** 3 B5
ⓦ thearthotelvienna.at
Spacious, well-equipped rooms
and studios and a 24-hour bar
feature here.

> ### DK Choice
>
> **Boutique Hotel Stadthalle** €
> *Hackengasse 20, 1150*
> **Tel** *982 4272*
> ⓦ hotelstadthalle.at
> This family-run eco-hotel with a
> garden has homely touches
> such as DVD players, flowers and
> candles. Extras such as lotions,
> soaps and oils made with home-
> grown lavender from the pretty
> roof garden add to its charm.

Hein Boutique Hotel €
Mannswörther Strasse 94, 2320
Tel *707 19 50*
ⓦ heinhotel.at
Choose from individually styled
rooms, suites and apartments in
a tranquil setting.

Contemporary

Stephansdom Quarter

> ### DK Choice
>
> **Hotel Am Parkring** €€
> *Parkring 12, 1010*
> **Tel** *514 80 0*   **Map** 6 E4
> ⓦ schick-hotels.com
> Renowned for its high-quality
> Viennese restaurant and well-
> stocked wine cellars, this four-
> star hotel has comfortable rooms
> with balconies and terraces
> offering magnificent views of
> the city's major landmarks.

Room with integral bathroom at the modern DO & CO Hotel

Hotel Am Stephansplatz €€
Stephansplatz 9, 1010
Tel *534 05 0*   **Map** 6 D3
🅦 hotelamstephansplatz.at
This environmentally-friendly
establishment features works by
contemporary artists and warm
decor made of natural materials.

Hotel Wandl €€
Petersplatz 9, 1010
Tel *534 55 0*   **Map** 5 C3
🅦 hotel-wandl.com
Comfortable rooms and
commendable service can be
enjoyed at this family-run hotel.

DO & CO Hotel €€€
Stephansplatz 12, 1010
Tel *241 88*   **Map** 6 D3
🅦 doco.com
A luxury hotel for the discerning
traveller. High-tech rooms have
iPad docks. There is a wine bar
and 24-hour room service.

Hofburg Quarter

Best Western Plus Hotel
Das Tigra €€
Tiefer Graben 14–20, 1010
Tel *533 96 41 0*   **Map** 5 C2
🅦 hotel-tigra.at
The spacious rooms are well
equipped at this bright hotel.

Pension A und A €€
Habsburgergasse 3, 1010
Tel *890 51 28*   **Map** 5 C3
🅦 pensionaunda.at
A family-run guesthouse offering
eight rooms and a deluxe
apartment with minimalist decor.

Schottering and Alsergrund

Hotel Goldener Baer €
Türkenstrasse 27, 1090
Tel *317 51 11*   **Map** 1 C4
🅦 goldbearhotel.com
A good-value option with well-
equipped, sound-proof rooms
and generous breakfasts.

Museum and Townhall Quarter

Altstadt Vienna €
Kirchengasse 41, 1070
Tel *522 66 66*   **Map** 3 B1
🅦 altstadt.at
The stylish rooms and suites here
combine period character with
modern furnishings and artworks.

Cordial Theaterhotel €
Josefstädter Strasse 22, 1080
Tel *405 36 48*   **Map** 1 B5
🅦 cordial.at
The chic, comfortable rooms and
studios here are decorated in
understated elegance.

Hotel Korotan €
Albertgasse 48, 1080
Tel *403 41 93*   **Map** 1 A5
🅦 korotan.com
Bright artworks adorn the walls
here and a glass front provides a
"window" on the city. There are
baby-sitting services and a library.

Mercure Josefhof Wien €€
Josefsgasse 4–6, 1080
Tel *404 19*   **Map** 1 B5
🅦 josefshof.com
A large hotel with all the latest
facilities, a bar and terrace, and a
breakfast buffet until noon.

Opera and Naschmarkt

Le Meridien Vienna €€
Opernring 13, 1010
Tel *588 90 0*   **Map** 4 D1
🅦 lemeridienvienna.com
The elegant rooms at Le Meridien
have personalised touches such
as a choice of pillows. There is an
award-winning restaurant.

Belvedere Quarter

Clima Cityhotel €
Theresianumgasse 21A, 1040
Tel *505 16 96*   **Map** 4 E4
🅦 climacity-hotel.com
A stylish contemporary hotel with a gallery
displaying contemporary art.

Hotel Daniel Wein €
Landstrasser Gürtel 5, 1030
Tel *901 310*   **Map** 4 F4
🅦 hoteldaniel.com
This smart, minimalist hotel has a
bakery on site. Facilities include
iPad and Vespa hire.

Lindner Hotel Am Belvedere €€
Rennweg 12, 1030
Tel *794 77 0*   **Map** 4 E2
🅦 lindner.de
High-tech lounges and a stress-
busting wellness centre make this
popular with business travellers.

Further Afield

Gartenhotel Glanzing €
Glanzinggasse 23, 1190
Tel *470 42 72 0*
🅦 gartenhotel-glanzing.at
A hotel offering rooms and
apartments, some with balconies.
The sauna is open 24 hours.

Family-Friendly
Stephansdom Quarter

Hotel Post €
Fleischmarkt 24, 1010
Tel *515 83 0*   **Map** 2 E5
🅦 hotel-post-wien.at
The individually furnished rooms
have all mod cons.

Hotel Schweizerhof €
Bauernmarkt 22A, 1010
Tel *533 19 31*   **Map** 6 D2
🅦 schweizerhof.at
A family-run hotel, with three-
and four-bed rooms.

Marc Aurel €
Marc-Aurel Strasse 8, 1010
Tel *533 36 40 0*   **Map** 6 D2
🅦 hotel-marcaurel.com
This comfortable family-owned
hotel has a lovely pavement café.

Hotel Capricorno €€
Schwedenplatz 3–4, 1010
Tel *533 31 04 0*   **Map** 6 E2
🅦 schick-hotels.com
A hotel offering single and family
rooms. Helpful staff.

Mailberger Hof €€
Annagasse 7, 1010
Tel *512 06 41 0*   **Map** 4 E1
🅦 mailbergerhof.at
Choose from rooms and
apartments at this grand palace
with a Baroque façade.

Vienna Marriott €€
Parkring 12A, 1010
Tel *515 18 0*   **Map** 6 E4
🅦 marriott.com
A large hotel with rooms, suites, a
sauna, gym, bars and restaurants.

For more information on types of hotels *see pages 192–5*

Individually designed suite at the fashionable Sans Souci

Schottering and Alsergrund

Harmonie €
Harmoniegasse 5–7, 1090
Tel *317 66 04* **Map** 1 C3
Ⓦ bestwestern-ce.com
Famous for its huge breakfast buffet. Other highlights include a café, bar and concert ticket office.

Hotel Mozart €
Julius-Tandler-Platz 4, 1090
Tel *317 15 37* **Map** 1 C2
Ⓦ hotelmozart-vienna.at
Free bike storage, cycle maps and eco-friendly bathrooms are offered at this family-run hotel.

Opera and Naschmarkt

Hotel Beethoven €€
Papagenogasse 6, 1060
Tel *587 44 82 0* **Map** 3 C2
Ⓦ hotel-beethoven.at
Owned by a culturally committed family, Hotel Beethoven hosts year-round art and music events.

Belvedere Quarter

Hotel Erzherzog Rainer €€
Wiedner Hauptstrasse 27–29, 1040
Tel *221 11* **Map** 4 D3
Ⓦ schick-hotels.com
A range of rooms is offered here. Extra beds and cots are provided without fuss. Popular restaurant.

Further Afield

Hostel Ruthensteiner €
Robert Hamerlinggasse 24, 1150
Tel *893 42 02*
Ⓦ hostelruthensteiner.com
A budget option that is popular with families and backpackers for its friendly, laid-back charm.

Hotel Capri €
Praterstrasse 44–46, 1020
Tel *214 84 04* **Map** 2 F4
Ⓦ hotelcapri.at
Choose from well-appointed rooms, suites and apartments at this pet-friendly budget hotel.

Hotel Jäger €
Hernalser Hauptstrasse 187, 1170
Tel *486 66 20 0*
Ⓦ hoteljaeger.at
This hotel has comfortable rooms and apartments. A breakfast buffet is served on the terrace.

Luxury

Stephansdom Quarter

InterContinental €€
Johannesgasse 28, 1037
Tel *711 22 0* **Map** 6 E5
Ⓦ vienna.intercontinental.com
Breathtaking views across the city, a classic restaurant and a spa are some of the highlights here.

Kaiserin Elisabeth €€
Weihburggasse 3, 1010
Tel *515 26 0* **Map** 6 D4
Ⓦ kaiserinelisabeth.at
The well appointed rooms have elegant, traditional decor and a host of state-of-the-art amenities.

König von Ungarn €€
Schulerstrasse 10, 1010
Tel *515 84* **Map** 6 D3
Ⓦ kvu.at
This historic, comfortable hotel has hosted many public figures.

Grand, Neo-Renaissance façade of Hotel Beethoven

Radisson Blu Palais Hotel €€
Parkring 16, 1010
Tel *515 17 0* **Map** 6 E4
Ⓦ radissonblu.com/palaishotel-vienna
The elegant rooms are decorated in old-world splendour at this hotel set in two beautifully restored 19th-century palaces.

Schlosshotel Romischer Kaiser €€
Annagasse 16, 1010
Tel *512 77 51 0* **Map** 6 D4
Ⓦ bestwestern.at/roemischerkaiser
Family owned since 1904, this historic hotel housed in a baroque palace offers rooms with grand architectural features.

Palais Coburg €€€
Coburgbastei 4, 1010
Tel *518 18 0* **Map** 6 E4
Ⓦ coburg.at
Stay in opulence in this historic building with lavish rooms, a gourmet restaurant and a spa.

Ritz-Carlton Vienna €€€
Schubertring 5–7, 1010
Tel *311 88* **Map** 6 D5
Ⓦ ritzcarlton.com
Housed in four 19th-century palaces, this hotel offers lavishly appointed rooms and suites boasting spectacular views over the city, and an indoor pool.

Hofburg Quarter

Hotel Steigenberger Herrenhof €€
Herrengasse 10, 1010
Tel *534 04 0* **Map** 5 B3
Ⓦ steigenberger.com
Experience ultimate comfort at this excellent-value hotel with modern rooms and suites, a fitness centre and a spa.

Museum and Townhall Quarter

Palais Hansen Kempinski €€€
Schottenring 24, 1010
Tel *236 10 00* **Map** 2 D4
Ⓦ kempinski.com
One of the city's most prestigious hotels, the glamorous Palais Hansen Kempinski features opulent rooms, high-tech facilities and a ballroom.

Sans Souci €€€
Burggasse 2, 1070
Tel *522 25 20* **Map** 3 B1
Ⓦ sanssouci-wien.com
With Philippe Starck-inspired decor, this trendy hotel is packed with original works of art. As well as a restaurant, cocktail bar and lounge, it has a superb spa.

Opera and Naschmarkt

DK Choice

Hotel Sacher €€€
Philharmonikerstrasse 4, 1010
Tel *514 56 0* **Map** 4 D1
W sacher.com
Opened in 1876 by the son of the inventor of the original *Sachertorte (see p206)*, Vienna's iconic landmark hotel offers one of the city's most historic and sumptuous places to stay, with prices to match.

Belvedere Quarter

NH Belvedere €
Rennweg 12A, 1030
Tel *206 11* **Map** 4 F3
W nh-hotels.com
An Art Nouveau hotel with plush rooms and deluxe furnishings.

**Imperial Riding School
Renaissance Vienna** €€
Ungargasse 60, 1030
Tel *711 75 0* **Map** 4 F1
W marriott.com
A large historic hotel with several lounges, bars, gardens and an indoor pool. The opulent rooms have all modern conveniences.

Hotel Bristol €€€
Kärtner Ring 1, 1010
Tel *515 16 0* **Map** 4 D2
W bristolvienna.com
This grand five-star hotel steeped in history is filled with antique art.

Imperial €€€
Kärtner Ring 16, 1015
Tel *501 10 0* **Map** 4 D2
W imperialvienna.com
Sumptuous accommodation is offered in this palatial building, dating to1863. The suites have butler service.

Further Afield

Landhaus Fuhrgassl-Huber €
Neustift/Walde 68, 1190
Tel *440 14 05*
W fuhrgassl-huber.at
This splendid country house on Vienna's outskirts is a good base to explore the city and beyond.

Pension

Stephansdom Quarter

Domzil €
Schulerstrasse 14, 1010
Tel *513 31 99* **Map** 6 D3
W hoteldomizil.at
Enjoy high comfort at a low price here; rooms have homely touches.

Pension Aviano €€
Marco-d'Aviano-Gasse 1, 1010
Tel *512 83 30* **Map** 5 C4
W aviano-pension-vienna.h-rez.com
This good-value, family-run B&B in a smart building has traditional Viennese decor.

Hofburg Quarter

Pension Nossek €
Graben 17, 1010
Tel *533 70 41 0* **Map** 5 C3
W pension-nossek.at
A lovely, family-run guesthouse with cosy rooms in chintzy floral prints. Great service.

Pertschy Palais Hotel €€
Habsburgergasse 5, 1010
Tel *534 49 0* **Map** 5 C3
W pertschy.com
A Baroque palace with a variety of tastefully furnished rooms full of character.

Schottering and Alsergrund

Pension Liechtenstein €
Nickelgasse 1, 1020
Tel *216 84 99* **Map** 2 E3
W pension-liechtenstein.at
Family-run, with a range of well-equipped apartments and rooms, this B&B is ideal for longer stays.

Pension Schottentor €
Hörlgasse 4, 1090
Tel *319 11 76* **Map** 1 C4
W pensionschottentor.whizrooms.com
Family-run three-star B&B with neat rooms and all basic amenities.

Museum and Townhall Quarter

Academia €
Pfeilgasse 3A, 1080
Tel *401 76* **Map** 1 A5
W academiahotels.at
This pleasant B&B is staffed by students and recent graduates. There is a delightful roof terrace.

Arpi €
Kochgasse 15/9, 1080
Tel *405 00 33* **Map** 1 B4
W hotelarpi.com
The small but clean rooms at Arpi have Wi-Fi and TVs. A buffet breakfast is included in the price .

Hotel-Pension Museum €
Museumstrasse 3
Tel *523 44 26* **Map** 3 B1
W hotelmuseum.at
The communal areas boast period furniture at this popular B&B with spacious rooms.

Opera and Naschmarkt

Pension Mariahilf €
Mariahilfer Strasse 19, 1060
Tel *586 17 81* **Map** 3 B2
W mariahilf-hotel.at
Quiet rooms of various sizes with private bathrooms, as well as apartments, are offered at this popular guesthouse.

DK Choice

Pension Suzanne €
Walfischgasse 4, 1010
Tel *513 25 07* **Map** 4 D1
W pension-suzanne.at
This family-owned, upmarket guesthouse boasts an impressive collection of antiques and works of art, including Freud's couch, Klimt's bench and Mahler's chair. Rooms are lovely with some facing a quiet, open courtyard. Warm, friendly service.

Further Afield

A & O Hostel €
Lerchenfelder Gürtel 9–11, 1160
Tel *4930 480 3900*
W aohostels.com
Rooms are clean and comfortable at this hostel. There is a stylish bar, a library and a lovely beer garden.

Hotel-Pension Continental €
Kirchengasse 1, 1070
Tel *523 24 18* **Map** 3 B2
W hotel-continental.at
Great-value rooms here range from singles to big family spaces. Buffet breakfasts are served.

Pension Baronesse €
Lange Gasse 61, 1080
Tel *405 10 61* **Map** 1 B5
W hotel-baronesse.at
Choose from 40 spacious and cosy rooms, including single, double, triple and family-size.

Luxuriously furnished room at the historic Hotel Sacher

For more information on types of hotels *see pages 192–5*

WHERE TO EAT AND DRINK

The Viennese know how to eat well. The staples of Vienna's cuisine are assimilated from the cooking styles of the Habsburg Empire, and include *Schnitzels*, originating as North Italian escalopes; dumplings that are a speciality of Bohemia; Hungarian goulash; and even *cevapcici* – Balkan grills and sausages. Balkan cuisine arrived with the post-World War II immigration that has multiplied the ethnic cuisines now available in the city. The range of gastronomy is vast, from gourmet nouvelle cuisine down to the

Würstelstände (booths selling sausages and beer on street corners). Diners can take their pick of atmosphere from old-fashioned sumptuous splendour to tavern gardens or Baroque wine cellars. Mealtimes are also flexible and in the city centre visitors will always find places serving hot meals between 11:30am and midnight. The restaurants on pages 210–19 are listed by area and by price, with the emphasis being on local cuisine, but there is a generous range of alternatives to choose from as well.

Types of Eating Place

The humble *Würstelstände* sell hot dogs and *Leberkäse* – a type of meat loaf made from finely ground corned beef or pork and bacon and onions. On a slightly higher level gastronomically, are the numerous small eateries selling sandwiches, filled rolls, pastries and soft drinks. Mouth-watering open sandwiches are a speciality of the popular and celebrated Austrian bakery Trzesniewski *(see p213)*. Order these with a coffee or a miniature Pfiff (1/8 of a litre) of beer to accompany them.

If something a little more substantial is required then the numerous *Stehbeisln* (stand-up counters) at some butchers' and food stores offer fresh dishes and sometimes a welcome

Wine cellar sign

bowl of hot soup, perfect on a winter's day. Some upmarket restaurants advertise a *Gabelfrühstück* (fork breakfast), serving brunch-style hot delicacies mid-morning. Another snack enjoyed by the Viennese is the *Jause* (cold meats and cheese, typically eaten between regular mealtimes). All these options are useful alternatives for the budget-conscious traveller to the museum restaurants and cafés which, however good, tend to be on the expensive side.

Vienna's self-service restaurants offer a range of cold and hot dishes, including grills made to order as well as pastas and salads. Try the bustling coffee-houses and wine cellars, especially appealing in the evenings.

Café-Restaurant Dunkelbunt *(see p218)*

Wine Cellars and Heurigen

Wine cellars represent good value, with cold buffets and a limited range of hot dishes to accompany local wines from the barrel. The atmosphere is informal, and even more so in the gardens of the *Heurigen* (taverns) at the periphery of the city, at Neustift am Walde, Grinzing and elsewhere. In theory, *Heurigen* serve only the wine from their own vineyards and of the current vintage. *Heuriger* has two meanings: it refers to the youngest available vintage of the local wine and it also refers to the venues that sell such wines by the glass. According to regulations laid down by Emperor Joseph II, pine twigs placed over or by the door *(ausg'steckt)* remained as long as the vintage lasted, after

Open sandwiches at Zum Schwarzen Kameel *(see p212)*

An array of delicious pastries and cakes at Café Mozart *(see p213)*

which they were removed and the tavern closed for the year. Visitors will still see such taverns, but in practice the larger ones are open all year and serve an extensive buffet with hot and cold cuts of meat. The wine is mostly white, often a blend of the *gemischter Satz* or local grapes, and is a true *Heuriger* until 11th November of the year after harvest. To sample a genuine local product, look for *Eigenbau* (meaning that the grower serves their own wine) by the entrance.

The Viennese Beisl

What the *trattoria* is to Italy the *Beisl* is to Vienna – a simple restaurant that offers local specialities in an agreeably informal atmosphere. The name is thought to be of Jewish origin – in the 18th century,

Typical sausage stand *(Würstelstand)* in the city centre

many innkeepers were Jewish. Unfortunately Many *Beisln* have gone upmarket and their prices have risen accordingly. All serve typical Viennese specialities such as *Tafelspitz* (boiled beef), *Vanillirostbraten* (pot roast with garlic), *Kalbsbeuschel* (calf's lung and heart), and of course *Wiener Schnitzel*, often in dauntingly large portions.

To follow are some pretty sturdy, but enticingly named desserts: *Powidltascherln* (pasta envelopes with plum jam) or *Zwetschkenknödel* (plums in potato dumpling). Viennese cooking also features some delicious soups. A popular soup is *Eierschwammerlsuppe*, made with chanterelle mushrooms.

Mid-Priced and Ethnic Restaurants

The top end of the *Beisln* merge with what Austrians somewhat misleadingly call "*gutbürgerliche Küche*", "good plain cooking", where the food is not just good but rather sophisticated as well. Many of the ethnic restaurants in the city offer extremely good-value dishes. Authentic Greek restaurants, such as Kostas *(see p216)*, tend to be inexpensive and there are a number of Asian restaurants that are good value, such as

Sri Thai Imbiss *(see p218)*, as well as the more upmarket and pricier Asian and Japanese venues.

Italian food is easy to find in Vienna and ranges from pizza slices to authentic dishes from the Lombardy or Tuscany regions. Vegetarian restaurants are on the increase; one of the longest-established is Wrenkh *(see p211)*. Lebenbauer *(see p215)* offers a particularly interesting range of vegetarian healthy dishes made from organic produce.

Café Sacher, known for its exquisite coffee and the *Sachertorte (see p216)*

The 7th-floor DO & CO restaurant *(see p212)*, with a splendid view of the Stephansdom

Café & Restaurant Imperial *(see p217)* and the Restaurant Bristol *(see p217)*. Steirereck *(see p212)*, located in the leafy surroundings of the Stadtpark, is considered one of the best gourmet eateries for gastronomes. The restaurant's menu has a strong Austrian theme. Trattoria Martinelli *(see p214)* serves traditional Tuscan specialities, which can be enjoyed in the Baroque ambience of the Harrach Palace.

Coffee Houses and Konditoreien

Vienna's legendary coffee houses *(see pp60–63)* are culturally specific: politicians favour Landtmann Café *(see p215)*, while the literati swap ideas in Café Hawelka *(see p210)*. Coffee is served in different ways varying in strength and the addition of hot milk or cream.

Prices vary according to location and type: a Ringstrasse café is more expensive than a smoke-filled den with a billiard table at the rear, or somewhere like the Café-Restaurant Ministerium *(see p210)*, patronised by the bureaucrats from the nearby ministries. While coffee houses serve a small range of simple hot dishes, the *Konditoreien* (confectioners) concentrate on pastries and cakes, though a few also do a good light lunch.

Luxury Restaurants

Gourmet eating in Vienna generally retains a local flavour. Seriously good cuisine may be found at luxury hotels such as the Café Sacher *(see p216)*, the

Reading the Menu

Generally, there are three main divisions of the menus: *kalte* or *warme Vorspeisen* (cold or hot hors d'oeuvres), *Hauptspeisen* (main course) and *Mehlspeisen* (desserts). There may be separate entries for *Suppen* (soups), *Fisch* (fish), *Rindfleisch* (beef) and *Schweinefleisch* (pork). Some restaurants have a children's menu or simply offer smaller portions. Menus may change with the season to make full use of the freshest produce. Most restaurants offer *Tagesangebot* (good-value daily specials) in addition to a standard menu. These are often worth ordering and can be particularly good value for money. The phrase *Fertige Speisen* also refers to dishes not on the fixed-price menu. Another is *Schmankerln*, which implies regional delicacies. Portions tend to be on the

Tables settings at the acclaimed fine-dining Restaurant at Eight *(see p212)*

generous side, although there is a trend toward light eating in the more upmarket establishments offering nouvelle cuisine.

The house wines are usually served in glasses, which hold exactly a quarter of a litre, though smaller glasses may also be served, and half a litre may come in a carafe. Most restaurants, at least in the city centre, have menus in English but if this is not the case, there is usually a member of staff who can help.

How Much to Pay

Vienna's restaurants generally represent good value for money. However, over-indulgence in tempting little delicacies can make a big dent in the wallet. Small items such as coffee are relatively inexpensive and a cup in one of the congenial old coffee houses or *Konditoreien* costs around €2.50 to €3. However, add in an alcoholic drink, such as apricot schnapps, and the price tag could easily double. Expect snacks and fast-food to cost around €5, with a modest meal in a self-service restaurant or a less touristy wine cellar likely to set you back around €10–€20. A reasonably priced *Beisl* might cost €20 a head with a glass of wine, but sticking to the fixed-price menu will probably reduce that significantly. There is a large group of restaurants where guests might expect a bill of up

Outdoor terrace of Vestibül, in the Burgtheater *(see p215)*

to €40 per person, while luxury and gourmet establishments have prices that accelerate well beyond the €50 mark. Prices can be more expensive in the evening or during peak tourist seasons and holidays.

Credit cards are widely accepted in restaurants with a regular international clientele. Smaller, local eateries will expect cash – so it is always best to check the payment method accepted in advance.

Booking and Service

Always telephone and confirm any special requests, such as facilities for the disabled or a menu for children. Facilities may be limited and some of the older establishments may have narrow corridors or steps. Booking a day ahead or even on the day is usually sufficient. Even a simple *Beisl* can be busy mid-week due to its faithful local clientele. Assiduous service is the hallmark of many Viennese restaurants. Tips are traditionally 10 per cent and are mandatory everywhere except in the few places where service is included.

Recommended Restaurants

The restaurants on pages 210–19 are listed by area and by price and represent a wide choice of establishments. They range from *Beisln* and *Heurigen* serving traditional local cuisine,

coffee houses offering typical Viennese savoury delicacies *(see pp204–5)* and superb cakes *(see pp206–7)* and restaurants with regional Austrian dishes *(see p204–5)*, to modern Austrian fusion cooking and international gourmet nouvelle cuisine. Asian and Japanese restaurants are popular and a number of these are listed, as are some Italian and Mediterranean options.

The restaurants highlighted as DK Choice have been chosen for one or more exceptional quality. This could be the historical setting, outstanding food, impeccable service, unique atmosphere or celebrated chefs. These special places come highly recommended by local clients and are worth seeking out.

Cosy decor of Griechenbeisl, Vienna's oldest inn *(see p210)*

Colourful dining room at the trendy Motto *(see p219)*

The Flavours of Vienna: Savoury Dishes

Austrian cuisine is a direct legacy of the country's imperial past, when culinary traditions from many parts of Europe influenced Viennese cooks. As a result, it is far more varied and flavoursome than most people realize. There are Italian and Adriatic influences, Polish- and Hungarian- inspired dishes, and even a rich seam of Balkan flavours running through much of the Austrian kitchen repertoire. *Schnitzel*, for example, may have come to Austria via Milan, which was once under Austrian control, while *Gulasch* is the Austrian version of a Hungarian dish that became popular in Vienna in the 19th century.

Chanterelle mushrooms

Cheese stall at a local Austrian farmers' market

Meat, Poultry and Dairy

Beef is narrowly ahead of pork as the nation's favourite meat. Austrian cattle farmers have a long and proud heritage of producing fine beef, which is used in many dishes, such as paprika-rich *Gulasch*. That most famous of Austrian dishes, *Wiener Schnitzel*, is traditionally made with veal. Pork is used primarily to make hams and sausages. The classic Austrian way with pork is to cure it, smoke it and leave it to mature for months in the clean air of the high Alpine pastures. The result is called *Speck*. Lean *Speck* is similar to Italian *prosciutto*, though with a distinctive smoky tang, while fattier cuts are more like *pancetta* or streaky bacon.

Bratwurst, made with beef, pork and veal, are Austria's preferred sausages, but other types such as *Frankfurters* are also common. Chicken is almost always served breaded (*Backhendl*), but *Grillhendl* is a whole chicken roasted over an open fire, or on a spit. Duck (*Ente*) is often served with sweet sauces, but sometimes with

Beef frankfurters
Bierwurst
Bratwurst
Pork frankfurters
Lean Speck
Speck

Selection of typical Austrian cured pork, sausages and salami

Austrian Dishes and Specialities

While most classic Austrian dishes (especially those originating in Vienna) are found all over the country, there are some regional differences. *Knödel* are more popular in the east, as are carp, game and pork, while beef and lamb appear more often the further west (and higher up the mountains) you travel. Beef is essential for *Tafelspitz*, often called the national dish. *Speck* is used to make *Speck Knödel*, small, dense dumplings, but the one part of the pig that Austrians do love to eat uncured is the knuckle, called *Stelze*, roasted and served chopped with heaps of sauerkraut. *Fischgröstl* is a mix of fish and seafood, fried together with onion, potato and mince (usually leftovers). It is rarely found on menus, but you may be lucky enough to try it in an Austrian home.

Paprika

Tafelspitz is silverside of beef, boiled with root vegetables and served thickly sliced with gherkins and sauerkraut.

Spectacular array of vegetables on display in a Viennese market

important to Austrians. That is truest of all for the nation's favourite, asparagus *(Spargel)*. Only local produce is used, and so is found on menus only during the harvesting season, from the end of April to early July. Austrians use asparagus in every way imaginable at this time of year. Wild mushrooms are another seasonal prize, especially chanterelles *(Eierschwammerl)*. Potatoes *(Erdäpfel)* feature widely, often in the form of *Knödel*. These are dumplings made of potatoes or stale white bread and are served with venison or pork dishes. White cabbage is often pickled *(Sauerkraut)* and red cabbage is served with venison and most game dishes.

sour accompaniments such as pickled red cabbage. Roast goose *(Gänsebraten)* is also popular, as are goose livers. The milk of Austrian dairy cows, grazed on sweet Alpine pastures, gives some excellent artisan cheeses, such as fruity Wälder.

Fish

While not great seafood lovers, Austrians have developed a number of their own fish dishes. Trout *(Forelle)* is the most popular fish, usually served grilled with boiled potatoes. Herring *(Hering)* is pickled and eaten as an appetizer. *Heringsschmaus*, a smoked herring and apple salad, is hugely popular at Easter. Carp *(Karpfen)* is a favourite Christmas dish, but is eaten all year, as is plaice *(Scholle* or *Goldbutt)*, which is

often served with a rich vegetable-based sauce.

Vegetables

Vegetables in Austria are of the highest quality and so, while imported produce is available all year round, seasonality is still

Bunches of pale spears of Austrian *Spargel* (asparagus)

SAVOURY SNACKS

Liptauer: Goat's or sheep's milk cheese is mixed with paprika, caraway seeds, capers, mustard, chives and onions to create this paste, a staple of Austrian wine bars.

Maroni: Roast chestnuts are a winter treat; the aroma of them, toasting over a brazier on a snowy day, is somehow quintessentially Vienna.

Blunzen: Blood sausage is marinated in vinegar and thinly sliced and served with brown bread. A popular "beer snack".

Schmalzbrot: Brown bread spread thickly with beef or pork dripping, and eaten with onions and pickles.

Wiener Schnitzel should classically be veal, breaded and fried. In Austria is is never served with sauce.

Rindsgulasch is the beef version of Hungarian goulash, a rich stew flavoured with paprika and caraway.

Forelle Blau, literally "blue trout", is made by poaching an unscaled fish in stock, which gives it a blueish hue.

The Flavours of Vienna: Sweet Foods

Few cities in the world can rival Vienna's devotion to all things sweet. The Viennese enjoy cakes mid-morning or afternoon, and set aside time for between-meal snacks. The finest *torten* (gâteaux), pastries and cakes tend to be found in *Konditoreien (see p202)* and are usually consumed with a cup of coffee. Traditional Viennese desserts can be found in all good restaurants, and are typically rich. From the classic Viennese *Apfelstrudel* to *Gugelhupf* from the Tirol, Austrian desserts all carry a regional influence. In Vienna, pastries take pride of place while, to the west, the Italian influence is strong and cakes, ice creams and meringues are preferred.

Poppy seeds

Relaxing over coffee and cake in an elegant Viennese café

Cakes

The Austrian tradition of cake-baking goes back centuries, with competition fierce between towns and cities to produce the finest. Even in small villages, bakeries would try to outdo each other with their sweet creations. Almost every Austrian city now has its trademark cake, with its citizens quick to boast that theirs is the best. The most famous Austrian cake is a Viennese creation, the *Sachertorte*, a rich chocolate cake invented by chef Franz Sacher for Chancellor Metternich in 1832. The signature dish of many an Austrian chef, it should be the first cake the visitor tries – with so much choice on offer, it will be difficult to decide on the second. While the Viennese rave about *Sachertorte*, over in Linz the locals insist their own *Linzertorte* – an almond based cake usually topped with raspberries – is superior. The people of Linz also say that the *Linzertorte* is older, dating back – legend has it – to the 17th century. Around the Hungarian border, they are proud of their *Dobostorte*,

Stollen   Sachertorte   Dobostorte   Esterházytorte

Linzertorte

Some of the many mouthwatering Austrian cakes available

Viennese Desserts

From *Topfentascherl* (curd cheese envelopes) to *Kastaniereis* (chestnut purée), Vienna's dessert cuisine uses rich and varied ingredients. The term *Mehlspeisen* is used to cover a broad range of puddings and pastries, including some that use ground hazelnuts or almonds in place of flour. Fruits such as plums and apples fill featherlight dumplings, pancakes, fritters and strudels. Whole or chopped nuts play a key role, especially hazelnuts and pine nuts, the latter often featuring in *Apfelstrudel*. More unusual desserts include sweet "pasta" served with poppyseeds to create *Mohnnudeln*, and *Böhmische Palatschinken* (Bohemian crepes) served with whipped cream and prune sauce. *Palatschinken* may also be a savoury snack.

Hazelnuts

Mohr im Hemd, a hazelnut and chocolate pudding, is served with chocolate sauce and whipped cream.

Display of traditional pastries and cakes in a *Konditorei*

named for the Budapest chef who created it in the 19th century. Its layers of sponge and chocolate butter cream are topped with a caramel glaze. From Salzburg, the cake of choice is baked meringue, known as *Salzburger Nockerl*, or Salzburg Soufflé. *Esterházytorte* also features meringue, layered with a rich hazelnut cream. Stollen is a marzipan-filled fruit bread originally from Germany and now an integral part of an Austrian Christmas. Regional or not, you'll now find all these classic cakes in Vienna and across the country.

Pastries

In the perfect global village, a place on the main street would always be reserved for an Austrian pastry and coffee shop. That the French collective name for sweet pastry is *Viennoiserie*

underlines the noble Viennese tradition of sweet baking. Austrian legend has it that the nation's café habit began when the Turks left all their coffee behind as they abandoned Vienna after the failed siege of 1529. The *Kipfel*, a light, crescent-shaped pastry (which later became famous as the croissant) also dates from the time of the

Entrance to one of the world-famous Mozart chocolate shops

Turkish siege, its shape being based on the crescent moon in the Ottoman flag. While such symbolism is often lost today, the importance of the café in Austrian society is not. Modern-day Austrians view cafés as extensions of their home, and spend hours reading, chatting and even watching television in them. Treats on offer in cafés will generally include a classic *Apfelstrudel*, *Cremeschnitte* (slices of puff pastry filled with custard and glazed with strawberry fondant), and *Punschkrapferl*, a calorie-packed, pink-fondant-topped pastry laced with rum.

Mozartkugel

Fine chocolates, presented in colourfully decorated boxes carrying the portrait of Mozart, are probably the quintessential Austrian souvenir. Known in Austria as *Mozartkugel*, the chocolates originated in Salzburg, where Mozart lived while composing *Cosi fan Tutti*, the opera in which he worships chocolate. In 1890, master confectioner Paul Fürst made the first Mozart chocolates by forming small balls of marzipan which he coated in a praline cream and then dipped in warm chocolate. Viennese confectioners soon adopted the technique and even today producers vie with one another as to whose *Mozartkugel* are the best and most authentic.

Apfelstrudel rolls paper-thin pastry with apple, sultanas, cinnamon and sometimes pine nuts or poppyseeds.

Palatschinken are fat, fluffy crêpes that may be filled with fruit or jam, or served with vanilla or chocolate sauce.

Topfenknödel are light curd cheese dumplings rolled in breadcrumbs and served with fruit compôte.

What to Drink in Vienna

Austria is a source of excellent wine and good rich beers. Vienna itself is a wine-growing region. It is surrounded by vineyards which supply the *Heurige (see p200–1)* in villages on the edge of the city with young local wines. Fine Austrian wines are found in good restaurants. Home-produced wine is mainly white but there are some excellent local red wines, especially from the Burgenland and Carnuntum districts. Sweet *Eiswein* is made from grapes left on the vines until the first frosts arrive, concentrating their juices. Fruit brandies and schnapps, many of them first class, are also produced.

Beyond the villages north and west of Vienna lie vineyards producing *Heurige* wines

Austrian Wines

The most popular wine in Austria is Grüner Veltliner *(see below)*. Other wines include superb dry Rieslings, especially from the Wachau, and rich Weissburgunder (Pinot Blanc) from Burgenland. Red wines tend to be soft and lush – robust reds come from the Blaufränkisch grape *(see below)*. Recent good vintages were 2002, 2003, 2006, 2007, 2009, 2010 and 2012.

Chardonnay from Styria and sparkling wine from Lower Austria

Riesling from the Wachau can be light, or full bodied like the Smaragd style.

Producer's name — **WIENINGER**

Grape variety — *Grüner Veltliner*

Vintage — **1991**

Level of ripeness — **Kabinett** *Auckenthal*

Producer's address — Weingut Wieninger, 1210 Wien, Stammersdorfer Straße 78

Style (dry) — Qualitätswein mit staatlicher Prüf-Nr. K 0005392, 11,0 %vol

ÖSTERREICH trocken

Alcohol level

Quantity — e 0,75 l

Grüner Veltliner is a fresh, fruity white wine. It is widely grown in Austria and is usually made in a dry style. It also makes excellent *Eiswein*.

St Laurent is a soft red wine; at its best it is rich and stylish.

Blaufränkisch is a quality local red – the best comes from Burgenland.

Krügel or ½ litre tankard

Seidl or standard
⅓ litre measure

Krügel or ½ litre of
pale beer

Pfiff or ⅛ litre
beer glass

Kaiser beer, a
light beer

Weizengold
wheat beer

Gösser Spezial
is rich

Austrian Beers

Vienna has been producing good malty beers for more than 150 years. Viennese lagers are bronze in colour and sweet in flavour. They make an excellent accompaniment to the hearty soups and stews found in *Beisln (see p201)*. The local Ottakring brewery's *Gold Fassl* is typical of the style, although lighter Bavarian-type beers such as *Weizengold* are also commonly available. One of Austria's most popular beers is *Gösser*, produced in Styria and found in the pubs and restaurants of Vienna. Speciality beers include the Styrian *Eggenberger Urbock 23°*, one of the strongest beers in the world. It is made by the Schloss Eggenberg brewery founded in the 17th century.

Bierhof beer mat
advertising a pub in
the Haarhof.

Null Komma Josef
is a local alcohol-
free beer.

Other Austrian Drinks

Austria offers a good range of non-alcoholic fruit juices such as *Himbeersaft* (raspberry syrup) or *Johannisbeersaft* (blackcurrant juice). Fruit is also the basis of many types of schnapps (sometimes called *Brand*). This powerful eau de vie is distilled from berries such as juniper and rowan as well as apricots *(Marillen)* and quince *(Quitten)*. It's worth paying the extra to sample the exquisite fruit schnapps produced by the dedicated specialists. *Almdudler* (herbal lemonade) is also a speciality. For a few weeks in autumn, fermenting grape juice, *Sturm*, is available. Milky in colour and quite sweet, it is more alcoholic than its grape flavour suggests.

Apricot
schnaps

The Wiener Rathauskeller is a popular restaurant serving
a number of beers

Where to Eat and Drink

Stephansdom Quarter

Akakiko €
Japanese Map 6 D3
Rotenturmstrasse 6, 1010
Tel *057 33 31 97*
Austria's largest Japanese restaurant chain offers a regularly changing menu of miso soups, sushi, maki, sashimi and teriyaki dishes, as well as other specialities.

Boehle Feinkost & Bistro €
Traditional Austrian Map 6 E3
Wollzeile 30, 1010
Tel *512 31 55* **Closed** *Sun*
Crammed to the rafters with fine cheeses, olive oils, charcuterie and hand-made breads, this miniscule deli-bistro uses only high-quality, natural ingredients.

Café Diglas €
Traditional Viennese Map 6 E3
Wollzeile 10, 1010
Tel *512 57 65*
Regulars descend on this friendly café for the hearty goulash and warm bread pudding, as well as salads, *Schnitzel* and wine – all at a decent price.

Café Hawelka €
Traditional Viennese Map 5 C4
Dorotheergasse 6, 1010
Tel *512 82 30*
Opened by Leopold Hawelka in 1939, this family-run café was a meeting point for post-war writers and critics. It is popular for its desserts, especially *Buchteln* (Austrian sweet roll).

Café Korb €
Traditional Austrian Map 6 D3
Brandstätte 9, 1010
Tel *533 72 15*
This lovely café is a great pitstop for breakfasts, sausages, *Schnitzel* or a bowl of beetroot soup.

Café Neko €
Japanese Map 6 D4
Blumenstockgasse 5, 1010
Tel *512 14 66*
Cat lovers will enjoy this unusual small café. Tame, resident cats roam freely, sleeping on seats or purring under tables as guests sip tea and eat the "cake of the day".

Café Prueckel €
Traditional Viennese Map 6 F3
Stubenring 24, 1010
Tel *512 61 15*
Head to this much-loved café for excellent coffee, meals and fresh pastries served by waiters in bow-tie garb. With its 1950s-style decor of velvet banquettes, it attracts a cool and arty crowd.

Gasthaus Poschl €
Traditional Austrian Map 6 D4
Weihburggasse 17, 1010
Tel *513 52 88*
Tuck into a crisp chicken *Schnitzel* and parmesan potatoes, accompanied by a newspaper and a glass of beer or chilled wine in this laid-back restaurant, which is popular with locals.

Griechenbeisl €
Traditional Viennese Map 6 D2
Fleischmarkt 11, 1010
Tel *533 19 77*
Vienna's oldest inn (dating from 1447) has signed, framed photos of famous guests, including politicians, artists, writers and musicians, lining the walls. It serves tasty wholesome dishes.

Café Frauenhuber €
Traditional Viennese Map 6 D4
Himmelpfortgasse 6, 1010
Tel *512 53 53*
Come here for simple, old-fashioned local cooking in a venue that found fame as the setting of Mozart's last public performance, in 1791.

Café-Restaurant Ministerium €€
Traditional Austrian Map 6 F3
Georg Coch-Platz 4, 1010
Tel *512 92 25* **Closed** *Sun*
This former ministerial dining room offers a good-value *Tageskarte* (daily changing menu) featuring dishes such as pork with stuffed cabbage, plus teas, coffee and snacks.

Photographs and autographs of famous guests on the walls at Griechenbeisl

Cantinetta Antinori €€
Italian Map 6 D3
Jasomirgottstrasse 3–5, 1010
Tel *533 77 22*
Famous for its tasty northern Italian specialities, favourites on the menu here include succulent oven-roasted rack of Tuscan lamb and steak Florentine, beautifully paired with Antinori wines.

Enoteca Cinque Terre €€
International Map 6 D2
Marc-Aurel-Strasse 10, 1010
Tel *533 38 26 5* **Closed** *Sun*
Dine in this family-friendly eatery from a large menu featuring dishes from all over the world, including sirloin steaks, grilled seabass and an exotic option – llama meat.

Figlmüller €€
Traditional Viennese Map 2 E5
Wollzeile 5, 1010
Tel *512 61 77*
Open since 1905, this restaurant is popular with locals and visitors alike. Flavourful delicacies include *Schnitzel*, rabbit casseroles, veal goulash and roast boar dishes. The *Powidltascherl* (dumplings filled with plum jam) are delicious.

Haas & Haas €€
International Map 6 D3
Stephansplatz 4, 1010
Tel *512 26 66*
A Vienna institution, this friendly teahouse is renowned for its lovely courtyard. It expertly delivers a wide-ranging menu for brunch, lunch and afternoon tea.

Hansen €€
Austro-Mediterranean Map 5 C2
Wipplingerstrasse 34
Tel *532 05 42* **Closed** *Sun*
In the high halls of a historic covered market, chef Tom Frötsch and his team lighten traditional Viennese cuisine with Mediterranean touches. Try the formidable risotto.

Hollmann Salon €€
Traditional Austrian Map 6 E3
Grashofgasse 3, 1010
Tel *9611 960 40* **Closed** *Sun*
Reserve a table in the stunning Baroque courtyard with its medieval arched vaults, and

enjoy wonderful food and friendly service in one of the city's most beautiful settings.

König von Ungarn €€
Traditional Viennese **Map** 6 D3
Schulerstrasse 10, 1010
Tel *515 84*
The restaurant in Vienna's oldest hotel, founded in 1746, serves hearty cuisine and is popular with families. The highlight is the beef trolley.

Le Loft €€
French-Austrian **Map** 6 F2
Praterstrasse 1, 1020
Tel *906 16 0*
At the top of the Sofitel Hotel, sparkling decor plus dazzling city views create a wonderful atmosphere to go with Le Loft's excellent menu. A huge selection of wines adds to the experience.

Le Siècle €€
International **Map** 6 E4
Parkring 16, 1010
Tel *515 17 34 40*
This award-winning restaurant is renowned for decadent dining. A la carte dishes from the extensive menu include caviar, suckling pig, herb-rubbed roast lamb and Châteaubriand steak.

Meierei am Stadtpark €€
Traditional Viennese **Map** 6 F4
Am Heumarkt 2A, 1030
Tel *713 31 68*
The sister restaurant of the much-acclaimed Steirereck *(see p212)*, this eatery is equally good and offers the perfect setting for breakfast, lunch or dinner.

Ofenloch €€
Traditional Austrian **Map** 5 C2
Kurrentgasse 8,1010
Tel *533 88 44* **Closed** *Sun*
Do not dismiss this restaurant as yet another traditional Austrian food joint – the menu may

Tables on the terrace for alfesco dining at Ofenloch

comprise the usual soups, *Schnitzel* and potato dumplings, but the service is a cut above the rest.

Österreicher im MAK €€
Modern Austrian **Map** 6 F3
Stubenring 5, 1010
Tel *714 01 21*
Although it offers an excellent set lunch menu at a great price, it is the more expensive but elaborate Sunday brunch spread that really pulls the crowds here.

Parkring Restaurant €€
International **Map** 6 E4
Parkring 12A, 1010
Tel *515 18 68 00*
Choose from several set-price menus, mouthwatering à la carte options and a remarkable six-course gastronomic meal at the restaurant of the Vienna Marriott.

Restaurant das Schick €€
Austro-Spanish **Map** 6 E4
Parkring 12, 1010
Tel *514 80 41 7*
Chef Johannes Reiser creates a unique culinary mix combining Austrian tradition and Spanish flair. There is an amazing choice of rice, casserole and roast dishes made using Mediterranean produce, seafood and local meats.

Salut €€
French Fusion **Map** 6 D3
Wildpretmarkt 3, 1010
Tel *533 13 22* **Closed** *Sun & Mon*
The candlelit rooms create a warm, inviting atmosphere at Salut. Remarkable wines complement a menu that draws on French cuisine with Arabian and Asiatic influences.

Salzamt €€
Austrian/International **Map** 6 D2
Ruprechtsplatz 1,1010
Tel *533 53 32*
The menu at Salzamt offers a wide variety of dishes together with local and international

wines, beers and spirits. Sample the delicious tenderloin steak with pink pepper sauce.

Schönbichler €€
Teashop **Map** 6 D3
Wollzeile 4, 1010
Tel *512 18 16* **Closed** *Sun*
Enjoy an extensive selection of fine, aromatic teas from all over the world, as well as scones and sandwiches in the tea gallery inside this shop. Regulars rave about the care with which the tea is made and the great service.

Tian €€
Vegetarian **Map** 6 D4
Himmelpfortgasse 23, 1010
Tel *890 46 65* **Closed** *Sun*
This pretty diner is a meat-free gem in the city's carnivorous dining scene. All dishes make use of produce grown in the restaurant's own organic garden.

Toko-Ri €€
Japanese **Map** 6 D2
Salztorgasse 4, 1010
Tel *532 77 77* **Closed** *Sun*
Sizzling-hot plates of spicy noodles, tempura prawns and large trays of sushi to share are served at this restaurant with sleek minimalist decor.

Weibels Wirtshaus €€
Traditional Austrian **Map** 6 E3
Kumpfgasse 2, 1010
Tel *512 39 86*
Tucked away along a cobbled street, this quaint restaurant serves high-quality, wholesome sausage and *Schnitzel* dishes that never fall short on taste.

Wrenkh €€
Vegetarian **Map** 6 D3
Bauernmarkt 10, 1010
Tel *533 15 26* **Closed** *Sun*
The no-frills menu at Wrenkh puts an emphasis on using organic produce in their vegetarian dishes. Try the mango and quinoa salad.

Dining room and bar area of Wrenkh, which specialises in vegetarian dishes

For more information on types of restaurants *see pages 200–203*

Chic interior of the DO & CO restaurant, overlooking the Stephansdom

Zum Basilisken €€
Traditional Austrian   Map 6 E5
Schönlaterngasse 3
Tel *5133123*
This restaurant with low lighting is filled with oversized furniture from a bygone age. Savour the pork belly with red cabbage for old-style comfort food at its finest.

DO & CO €€€
International   Map 6 D3
Stephansplatz 12, 1010
Tel *535 39 69*
On the top floor of the upscale DO & CO hotel, this restaurant serves fine dishes prepared with care and creativity. Try the gourmet *Schnitzel*.

DSTRIKT €€€
Modern Austrian   Map 6 D5
Schubertring 5–7, 1010
Tel *311 88 15 0*
Award-winning culinary wizard Wini Brugger delivers the best in local cuisine mixed with international flair at this upmarket diner in the Ritz-Carlton Vienna. Reservations recommended.

Fabios €€€
Mediterranean   Map 5 C3
Tuchlauben 4–6, 1010
Tel *532 22 22*   **Closed** *Sun*
Stunning architecture and dramatic glass and orange-tinted lighting create the mood at Fabios. The food is outstanding – try the venison with sage gnocchi.

Kervansaray Hummerber €€€
Seafood   Map 4 E1
Mahlerstrasse 9, 1010
Tel *512 88 43 0*   **Closed** *Sun*
Revel in a seafood menu that ranks among Vienna's finest and features succulent Norwegian lobster, salmon caviar, crayfish and beautifully sweet sole fillet.

Oswald & Kalb €€€
Traditional Austrian   Map 6 D3
Backerstrasse 14, 1010
Tel *512 13 71*
This exciting eatery in a vaulted medieval house offers some unusual home-made breads and herb-infused oils. The changing menu boasts classic regional dishes with creative touches.

Plachutta €€€
Traditional Viennese   Map 6 E3
Wollzeile 38, 1010
Tel *512 15 77*
Numerous Austrian soap stars and other VIPs eat at Plachutta. Savour fantastic dishes such as their famous *Tafelspitz* (boiled beef).

DK Choice

Restaurant at Eight €€€
Modern Austrian   Map 6 D5
Kärntner Ring 8, 1010
Tel *221 22 38 30*
This slick restaurant has a dual personality – light, airy and bustling by day; sophisticated and intimate by night. Thanks to the magic performed by head chef Daniel Kraft, the restaurant has been deluged by accolades. Austrian classics are transformed into chic, exquisite morsels with a variety of flavours to create an "aroma cuisine". Impeccable service.

Steirereck €€€
Modern Austrian   Map 6 F5
Am Heumarkt 2A/ Stadtpark, 1030
Tel *713 31 68*   **Closed** *Sat & Sun*
Steirereck offers an incredible seven-course tasting menu – a luxurious feast of seafood, game and poultry accompanied by honey, rye and lavender bread.

Walter Bauer €€€
Modern Austrian   Map 6 E3
Sonnenfelsgasse 17, 1010
Tel *512 98 71*   **Closed** *Sat & Sun*
Exuding old Viennese charm, this first-class restaurant is famed for its modern interpretation of local culinary classics. The smoked eel and venison dishes are a must.

Zu Den 3 Hacken €€€
Traditional Austrian   Map 6 D4
Singerstrasse 28, 1010
Tel *512 58 95*   **Closed** *Sun*
Grab an aperitif in the bar at one of Vienna's oldest inns before heading to the wood-panelled restaurant for terrines of berry-topped game stew and platters of roast meats.

Zum Schwarzen Kameel €€€
Austrian/International   Map 5 C3
Bognergasse 5, 1010
Tel *533 81 25 11*   **Closed** *Sun*
Be wowed in this Jugendstil restaurant by an 800-strong wine list. Choose from dozens of sandwiches on a first-class menu. For a more substantial dish, the wild boar with red wine is superb.

Hofburg Quarter

Café Hofburg €
Traditional Austrian   Map 5 B4
Michaelerkuppel, Hofburg, 1010
Tel *24 100 400*
This charming grand café is a great stop-off point for coffee, snacks or lunch before or after a visit to the imperial palace. There is live classical piano music every afternoon.

Konditorei Gerstner €
Tradtional Austrian   Map 5 C5
Kärntner Strasse 13–15, 1010
Tel *512 49 63*
One of the city's greatest pastry makers and chocolatiers, Gerstner is a favourite with locals and

Tables on the terrace at the fine-dining Restaurant at Eight

visitors. Indulge your tastebuds with heavenly macaroons, cupcakes and poppy pie.

Reinthaler's Beisl €
Traditional Austrian   Map 2 D5
Dorotheergasse 2–4, 1010
Tel *5131249*
Expect a reliable menu of typical, hearty food in generous portions at this informal restaurant. The classic dishes such as *Wiener Schnitzel* and goulash are superb.

Trzesniewski €
Traditional Austrian   Map 5 C3
Dorotheergasse 1, 1010
Tel *512 32 91*   **Closed** *Sun*
Follow your nose to find this renowned, aromatic bakery, which offers a superb range of local breads and delicious pastries, muffins, bagels and cakes.

Beaulieu €€
Mediterranean   Map 5 B2
Herrengasse 14, 1010
Tel *532 11 03*
The *coq au vin* and seafood risotto with saffron are a popular draw at this bistro. Look out too for the "dish of the day" or the plate of delectable cheeses and breads, paired with local wines.

Café Bräunerhof €€
Traditional Viennese   Map 5 C4
Stallburggasse 2, 1010
Tel *512 38 93*
This coffee house offers all the typical local delicacies. The 1920s furnishings and a fascinating clientele of intellectuals and academics bolsters its appeal.

Café Central €€
Traditional Austrian   Map 5 B3
Herrengasse 14, 1010
Tel *533 37 63*
Once a gathering place for luminaries in art, literature, politics and science, this café boasts a rich history and serves an excellent two-course lunch.

Café Demmel €€
Traditional Viennese   Map 5 C3
Kohlmarkt 14, 1010
Tel *535 17 17 0*
Oozing with style, and blessed with finesse and grandeur, Café Demmel has been serving glorious cakes, scones, sweets and pastries since 1786.

Café Mozart €€
Traditional Austrian   Map 5 C4
Albertinaplatz 2, 1010
Tel *24 100 200*
An excellent €12 set lunch menu means that this lovely café can be packed out at times. Graham Greene worked on the

screenplay of Vienna's signature movie, Orson Welles's *The Third Man*, here.

Ephesus €€
Turkish   Map 5 C3
Bräunerstrasse 8, 1010
Tel *533 90 91*   **Closed** *Sun*
Order olives and a glass of *raki* while choosing from the menu of grilled meats, fish and chicken at Ephesus. Try the delicious *Iskender* (a dish of meat, tomatoes, herbs and yogurt cooked on a flatbread).

DK Choice

Ilona Stüberl €€
Austro-Hungarian   Map 5 C3
Bräunerstrasse 2
Tel *533 90 29*
Founded in 1957, this family-run restaurant is a highly regarded part of Vienna's culinary scene. A menu in eight languages comprises veal, pork, fish, beef and vegetarian dishes, as well as salads, pastas, soups and hearty desserts. Learn about the 1867 unification of Austria and Hungary under Emperor Franz Josef from the friendly waiters who are amateur historians.

Oberlaa €€
Bakery   Map 5 C4
Neur Markt 16, 1010
Tel *513 29 36 0*
A treasure trove for the sweet-toothed, this charming bakery dishes out gorgeous cakes and fruit-topped pastries. Do not miss delights such as *Dobostorte* and *Apfelstrudel (see pp206–7)*. It has a lovely outdoor terrace.

Restaurant Kanzleramt €€
Traditional Viennese   Map 5 B3
Schauflergasse 6, 1010
Tel *533 13 09*   **Closed** *Fri & Sun*
Sip a glass of Austrian wine or fresh local draft beer while choosing from a wide range of

specialities such as calves' liver with parsley potatoes and pork steak with cream sauce.

Yugetsu/Senkoma €€
Japanese   Map 5 C4
Kärntner Strasse 44
Tel *587 20 23*   **Closed** *Sun*
Enjoy sushi, teriyaki and tempura dishes before visiting the karaoke rooms, with Japanese, English, Korean and Chinese songs. Limited seating; arrive early.

Limes Restaurant €€€
Italian   Map 5 C3
Bräunerstrasse 11, 1010
Tel *905 80 0*   **Closed** *Sun*
This lovely restaurant offers set menus plus à la carte options, ranging from goat's cheese salad to monkfish fettucine with dill crostini, in a stylish setting.

Palmenhaus €€€
International   Map 5 B4
Burggarten 1, 1010
Tel *533 10 33*
In a Jugendstil greenhouse, this is one of Vienna's plushest venues and has a menu to match. Opt for the "Carpe Diem" breakfast consisting of fresh pineapple, rye breads, goat's cheese omelette and rolls with jam.

Regina Margherita €€€
Italian   Map 5 B3
Wallnerstrasse 4, 1010
Tel *533 08 12*
The hand-made pizzas at Regina Margherita are topped with the freshest produce and high-quality olive oil. The menu also includes pastas, grilled meats and fish as well as some Neapolitan dishes.

Restaurant im Ambassador €€€
International   Map 6 D4
Kärntner Strasse 22, 1010
Tel *961 610*
The Ambassador hotel's restaurant has established itself as a strong force in the city's culinary circles with its flavourful, wide-ranging dishes.

Dining on the outdoor terrace at Café Mozart

For more information on types of restaurants *see pages 200–203*

Sapori Restaurant €€€
Mediterranean Map 5 B2
Herrengasse 12, 1010
Tel *227 80 0* **Closed** *Sat & Sun*
The delicious modern take on
flavourful Mediterranean fare at
Sapori includes braised lemon
chicken with almond polenta,
and pumpkin and beetroot and
anchovy salad with Dijon mustard.

Sky Restaurant €€€
International Map 5 C5
Kärtnerstrasse 19, 1010
Tel *513 17 12*
Enjoy gourmet heaven on the
top floor of the Steffl department
store, with spectacular views
over the city. The menu offers
Mediterranean and Asian dishes
as well as Viennese classics.

Schottering and Alsergrund

Konzert-Café Weimar €
Traditional Viennese Map 1 B3
Währinger Strasse 68, 1090
Tel *317 12 06*
One of the last Viennese classic
coffee houses run in traditional
style serves coffee, pastries, cakes,
snacks and *Schnitzel* dishes.

CaffèCouture €€
International Map 1 B4
Garnisongasse 18, 1090
Tel *0676 33 22 076* **Closed** *Sat & Sun*
This hip café uses a state-of-the-
art coffee machine to serve
amazing coffees in a convivial
atmosphere. Guests share a large
communal table.

Café Schottenring €€
Traditional Austrian Map 5 B1
Schottenring 19, 1010
Tel *315 33 43*
Opened in 1879, this café serves
hearty breakfasts, sandwiches and
cakes, as well as great coffees.

Delicious cakes at the trendy
CaffèCouture

Cosy dining room of the historic
Café Schottenring

I Vecchi Amici €€
Italian Map 1 C3
Lichtensteinstrasse 24, 1090
Tel *319 12 86*
Experience the warmth of the
Mediterranean, both in the food
and the tangerine-coloured walls,
at I Vecchi Amici. The chalkboard
menu lists freshly cooked pizzas,
pastas and seasonal specials.

Orlando di Castello €€
International Map 5 B2
Freyung 1, 1010
Tel *533 76 29*
Enjoy a memorable dining
experience in this beautiful, chic
venue. Choose from a menu of
robust Spanish cheeses, steak
tartare, gourmet hand-made
burgers and Thai-style soups.

Rembetiko €€
Greek Map 1 C3
Porzellangasse 38, 1090
Tel *317 64 93*
This blue-and-white-tiled
taverna transports diners to the
cobbled backstreets of Athens.
Fresh pork kebabs, feta salads
and lamb chops are cooked to
order in a rustic kitchen.

Servitenwirt €€
Traditional Viennese Map 2 D3
Servitengasse 7, 1090
Tel *315 23 87*
The outdoor seating at
Servitenwirt's wooden benches
and tables is popular once spring
arrives – so arrive early for lunch
here. The menu changes daily.

Stomach €€
Modern Austrian Map 1 C3
Seegasse 26, 1090
Tel *310 20 99* **Closed** *Mon & Tue*
This intimate, hole-in-the-wall
diner with gorgeous bloom-filled
gardens is a well-hidden secret.

Choose from modern
interpretations of Austrian
classics in fresh, light
portions. Cash only.

Trattoria Martinelli €€
Italian Map 2 D5
Freyung 3, 1010
Tel *533 67 21*
For breakfast lunch and
dinner, this beautiful courtyard
restaurant offers a fantastic
menu, superlative service and
plenty of charm. There is
indoor seating too inside
the historic building. The
beefsteak is a highlight.

Kim Kocht €€€
Asian fusion Map 1 B2
Lustkandlgasse 4, 1090
Tel *319 0242* **Closed** *Sat–Mon*
Highly-acclaimed Asian chef
Kim Kocht creates exquisite
dishes fusing eastern and
western flavours at this sleek
modern restaurant. Tables are
booked up weeks in advance for
Kocht's signature €67 evening
"surprise dinner".

Livingstone €€€
Steakhouse Map 2 D4
Zelinkagasse 4, 1010
Tel *533 33 93 0*
Slow-moving ceiling fans, giant
potted palms and wooden floors
create distinctive plantation-style
interiors reminiscent of 19th-
century America. Livingstone
serves the best steaks in
Vienna and a selection of
over 500 different wines.

Museum and Townhall Quarter

Café Eiles €
Traditional Viennese Map 1 B5
Josefstädter Strasse 2, 1080
Tel *405 34 10*
This café remains a favourite
haunt of writers, actors, dancers
and theatre critics. Choose from
breakfasts, light meals, cakes
and coffees in an unassuming
setting. Faded black-and-white
photographs adorning the walls
chronicle a fascinating past.

Café Maria Haag €
Traditional Viennese Map 5 B2
Helferstorferstrasse 2
Tel *533 58 66* **Closed** *Sun*
Stop by at this warm little café
for coffees, teas and freshly
baked cakes and pastries. The
menu changes daily, depending
on seasonal fruits. The apricot
tarts and strudels are
particularly recommended.

For key to prices *see page 210*

Elegant dining room of Vestibül inside the Burgtheater

Amerlingbeisl
Traditional Viennese   €€   Map 3 B1
Stiftgasse 8, 1070
Tel *526 16 60*
The small seasonal menu at Amerlingbeisl includes cocktails and specials. The pasta with smoked salmon and white wine cream is particularly good.

Café Bellaria
Traditional Viennese   €€   Map 3 C1
Bellariastrasse 6, 1010
Tel *523 53 20*
For superb coffee and blissful piano music, visit this typical café where the owner hosts operetta and Lieder evenings. The traditional dishes are served by charming waiters.

Café Leopold
International   €€   Map 3 C1
Museumsplatz 1, 1070
Tel *523 67 32*
This café in the Leopold Museum has an inventive menu – try the tandoori chicken wrap or the falafel with hummus and olives. It has a club atmosphere on weekend nights, with live DJs and music.

Centimeter II am Spittelberg   €€
Traditional Austrian   Map 3 B1
Stiftgasse 4
Tel *470 0606*
Gorge on the delicious, monster-sized ribs served here, or take a pick from the numerous sausage varieties, giant burgers and succulent steaks.

Halle Café
International   €€   Map 3 C1
Museumsquartier 1, 1070
Tel *523 70 01*
A popular Museum quarter restaurant, Halle Café in the Kunsthalle Wien serves food from morning until late. On the menu are good-value daily specials such as pork with red cabbage and *Rösti*, along with salads, snacks and desserts.

Kunsthistorisches Museum Café & Restaurant
Traditional Austrian   €€   Map 3 C1
Burgring 5, 1010
Tel *649 66 45 46*   **Closed** *Mon*
The beautiful, opulent Cupola Hall of the Kunsthistoriches Museum provides an idyllic setting for the popular Sunday brunch or a romantic fine-dining supper.

Lebenbauer
Vegetarian   €€   Map 1 C5
Teinfaltstrasse 3, 1010
Tel *533 55 56*   **Closed** *Sat & Sun*
One of Vienna's most upmarket vegetarian restaurants, Lebenbauer boasts an especially creative meat-free menu. Its recipes use mainly organic produce and are cooked without fat, eggs or flour. The pumpkin risotto is a menu highlight.

Lux
Viennese   €€   Map 3 B1
Schrankgasse 4 / Spittelberggasse 3, 1070
Tel *526 94 91*
Come here for tasty, gourmet home-made sausages, mouth-watering sauces and freshly baked rolls. Soups, salads and an ever-changing specials board make this a great find.

Pizzeria-Osteria Da Giovanni   €€
Italian   Map 3 B1
Sigmundsgasse 14
Tel *523 77 78*
At this simple and welcoming restaurant guests can choose from bruschetta, soups, salads, pastas and pizzas, made from fresh ingredients. The home-made traditional desserts are delicious.

Spatzennest
Traditional Austrian   €€   Map 3 B1
Sankt-Ulrichs-Platz 1, 1070
Tel *526 16 59*   **Closed** *Fri & Sat*
Diners here rave about the mouth-watering potato dumpling dish with bacon, cheese and onions. Choose from a good stock of local beers. There are some outdoor tables.

Zu ebener Erde und erster Stock
Traditional Viennese   €€   Map 3 B1
Burggasse 13, 1070
Tel *523 62 54*   **Closed** *Sat & Sun*
This delightful café built in the Biedermeier style offers an authentic Viennese experience, from candlelight à la carte dinners to set-price meals of *Schnitzel* and potato dumplings.

Landtmann Café
Traditional Viennese   €€€   Map 1 C5
Universitätsring 4
Tel *241 00 10 0*
Sigmund Freud, Hillary Clinton, Sir Paul McCartney and other famous figures have graced this elegant café dating back to 1873. There is live piano music on Monday and Tuesday evenings.

Schnattl
International   €€€   Map 1 B5
Lange Gasse 40, 1080
Tel *405 34 00*   **Closed** *Sat & Sun*
Discerning gourmets visit Schnattl for its extensive three- or nine-course tasting menus. There is a lovely courtyard terrace.

DK Choice

Vestibül
Modern Austrian   €€€   Map 1 C5
Universitätsring 2, 1010
Tel *532 49 99*   **Closed** *Sun*
This accolade-winning restaurant in the Burgtheater specializes in wholesome dishes made with seasonal ingredients. Everything is home-made from scratch, from stock to elderberry juice. Buy a sauce from the kitchen to recreate favourite recipes at home.

Opera and Naschmarkt

Café Drechsler
Traditional Viennese   €   Map 3 C2
Link Wienzeile 22 / Giradigasse 1, 1060
Tel *581 20 44*
Despite a 21st-century style make-over, Drechsler retains its classic charm. It offers breakfasts, coffee and hot meals, and has Wi-Fi.

Café Ritter €
Traditional Viennese **Map** 3 B2
Mariahilfer Strasse 73, 1060
Tel *587 82 38* **Closed** *Sun*
Choose from a wide range
of breakfasts as well as snacks,
lunches, afternoon teas and
dinner. Special dishes include
superb grilled bream with
spinach. Excellent wine list.

Café Sperl €
Traditional Viennese **Map** 3 C2
Gumpendorferstrasse 11, 1060
Tel *586 41 58*
Come to Café Sperl for a simple
breakfast of ham, eggs and
freshly baked breads. It also
serves snacks, lunches and
dinners, from dumpling soups to
rabbit stews, and has a long
menu of cream-topped coffees.

Café Westend €
Traditional Viennese **Map** 3 A3
Mariahilfer Strasse 128, 1070
Tel *523 31 83*
This quirky café serves good
coffee, pastries and basic dishes,
It often has art displays.

Neni €
International **Map** 3 C2
510 Naschmarkt, 1060
Tel *585 20 20*
Open 24 hours a day, Neni is a
lively, simple restaurant, which
uses Middle-Eastern ingredients
in its Mediterranean and
European cooking. Try the
flatbreads with *hummus*, tahini
and olives, lamb *shish kebab*,
Israeli salad or lentil soup.

Tewa €
International **Map** 3 C2
672 Naschmarkt, 1040
Tel *676 84 77 41 211* **Closed** *Sun*
Enjoy fresh and exciting food at
this trendy restaurant. Try honey
toast or croissants for breakfast
and wash them down with
mango lassi. The lunchtime
wraps and soups are great.

DK Choice

Café Sacher €€
Traditional Viennese **Map** 4 D1
Philharmonikerstrasse 4, 1010
Tel *514 56 0*
One of Vienna's most stylish
venues, Café Sacher's speciality
is the original *Sachertorte*. This is
a popular meeting place for
exquisite coffees, classic cakes
(the *Apfelstrudel* is also highly
recommended) and dishes
such as *Wiener Schnitzel* in
an elegant historic setting.
There is a lovely open terrace
in summer.

Chandelier-lit dining room of the
traditional Café Sperl

Kostas €€
Greek **Map** 4 D2
Friedrichstrasse 6, 1010
Tel *5863729* **Closed** *Sun*
This friendly restaurant offers
diners a taste of authentic Greek
cuisine including delicious *gyros*
and crisp salads.

Restaurant Hofbräu €€
Traditional Austrian **Map** 3 B2
Mariahilfestrasse 47
Tel *941 2332* **Closed** *Sun*
Don't be fooled by the bright,
fun decor of this diner – it is very
serious about food. Try the
breaded cheese with plum
compote or venison ragout
with potato dumplings.

DK Choice

Saint Charles Alimentary €€
Vegetarian **Map** 3 C2
Gumpendorferstrasse 33, 1060
Tel *586 13 65* **Closed** *Sat & Sun*
Laid out like a dispensary with
medicine jars, pill bottles and
apothecary trappings, this
quirky restaurant focuses on
wellness cuisine. Dishes use
herbs, plants, nuts and seeds
with healing properties. Try the
aromatic wild root soup or spelt
with roast pumpkin and walnuts
for a meal that is truly healthy.

Anna Sacher €€€
Viennese **Map** 4 D1
Philharmonikerstrasse 4, 1010
Tel *514 56 0* **Closed** *Mon*
One of Vienna's best-loved
fine-dining venues, the
luxurious Anna Sacher has
exquisite four-, five- and six-
course menus, served with
complimentary wines.
Traditional dishes are given a
light contemporary touch.

Aux Gazelles €€€
French-Moroccan **Map** 3 C2
Rahlgasse 5, 1060
Tel *585 66 45* **Closed** *Sun*
This restaurant and well-being
centre is housed in a former brick
factory. Guests are invited to
smoke a hookah after dinner
before heading for the spa.

Shambala €€€
International **Map** 4 D1, 5 B5
Opernring 13, 1010
Tel *588 90 0*
An ideal venue for a lively Sunday
brunch, Shambala offers a
banquet of fruit, tea, coffee,
egg dishes, fish and meat
specialities, breads, pastries
and champagne – all at €38.

Belvedere Quarter

Café Dialog €
Traditional Viennese **Map** 5 E2
Renweg 43, 1030
Tel *712 62 08*
Eat and drink while reading the
newspapers at this authentic
café, popular with locals. Endless
coffee refills are offered in a cosy
atmosphere. Alcohol is served
20 hours a day.

Café Museum €
Traditional Viennese **Map** 4 D2
Operngasse 7, 1010
Tel *241 00 62 0*
Since 1899 this lovely café has
played host to numerous creative
talents, including artists Gustav
Klimt and Egon Schiele, composer
Oscar Straus and architects Otto
Wagner and Adolf Loos. Enjoy a
range of breakfasts and hearty
dishes, as well as live evening
piano music at weekends.

Tempting desserts on display at the
elegant Café Sacher

Café Schwarzenberg, a traditional Viennese coffee house

Kunsthalle Café €
Traditional Austrian   **Map** 4 D2
Treitlstrasse 2 / Karlsplatz, 1040
Tel *587 00 73*
Kunsthalle café is a great venue for enjoying hearty breakfasts and meals outside on the large patio. One of the trendy haunts of the city's hip nightlife scene, it hosts outdoor parties until dawn.

Bistro Menagerie €€
International   **Map** 4 F4
Prinz Eugen Strasse 27, 1030
Tel *172 04 46 5*
Indulge in creatively presented dishes here, including perfectly cooked pink seared tuna, juicy polenta-stuffed chicken and a mouthwatering array of exquisite Viennese desserts.

Café Schwarzenberg €€
Traditional Viennese   **Map** 4 E2
Kärntner Ring 17, 1010
Tel *512 89 98*
Choose from dozens of tea varieties as well as great coffees. The glass-fronted cabinet is full of tempting sugar-frosted buns, shiny tortes and yummy fruit pies. This is definite value for money.

Entler €€
Traditional Austrian   **Map** 4 D3
Schlüsselgasse 2, 1040
Tel *504 35 85*   **Closed** *Sun, Mon, hols*
After an appetizer of nutty rye bread and carrot dipped into a herby oil, savour main course highlights such as venison and duck at this informal diner with cheerful, warm decor.

Salm Bräu €€
Tradtional Austrian   **Map** 4 F3
Rennweg 8, 1030
Tel *799 59 92*
Try smoked venison and garlic bread or dumpling-topped brown beer soup at this popular

restaurant with a convivial atmosphere. The daily specials are good value.

Tenmaya €€
Japanese   **Map** 6 D5
Krugerstrasse 3, 1010
Tel *512 73 97*
This smart restaurant serves authentic dishes, including sushi, tempura and seafood. There are set meals as well as an à la carte menu and a long drinks list.

Wiener Wirtschaft €€
Traditional Viennese   **Map** 4 D3
Wiedner Hauptstrasse 27–29, 1040
Tel *221 11 36 4*
Popular with locals and visitors alike, this restaurant offers generous portions of well-prepared dishes, plus a variety of wines, draft beer and Austrian spirits including schnapps.

Café & Restaurant Imperial €€€
Traditional Viennese   **Map** 4 D2
Kärtner Ring 16, 1015
Tel *501 10 63 89*
Dine in a regal setting at tables laden with crystal under portraits of Austrian monarchs in this refined restaurant. The acclaimed Sunday champagne brunch is recommended.

DK Choice

Restaurant Bristol €€€
Modern Austrian   **Map** 4 D2
Kärntner Ring 1, 1010
Tel *515 16 54 6*
Enjoy some of the finest food in Vienna at this highly regarded restaurant where menu highlights run from pumpkin soup and venison goulash to delicately smoked fish. Revel in finely honed service born out of a lengthy gourmet tradition. The setting is grand, so dress up to the nines for a culinary treat.

Further Afield

Arjuna €
Indian
Payergasse 12, 1160
Tel *923 39 55*   **Closed** *Sun*
Choose from a tiny menu of freshly cooked Bengali dishes including soups, thalis (taster meals), breads, pakoras and samosas. Excellent value.

Café Aida €
Traditional Austrian
Schönthaler Gasse 1, 1210
Tel *262 58 11 0*
This confectioners boasts over 20 branches in the city. The theme is pink, from the cakes, cups, and sweets to the waitresses' outfits. Buy a box of chocolates to take home as a souvenir.

Café Cobenzl €
Traditional Austrian
Am Cobenzl 94, 1190
Tel *320 51 20*
A popular venue for cakes and excellent coffee, Café Cobenzl offers daily specials and serves its *Strudel* with a large dollop of whipped cream.

Café Cuadro €
International   **Map** 3 C4
Margaretenstrasse 77, 1050
Tel *544 75 50*
The chrome, beech and opaque glass decor lends this café a Scandinavian feel. It serves great-value breakfasts, burgers and cock-tails, and fills up quickly after dark.

Café San Marco €
Italian
Schwaigergasse 21, 1210
Tel *270 17 13*   **Closed** *Sun, hols*
This simply furnished restaurant offers generous plates of crisp wholesome salads, well-cooked pastas and delicious breads fragrant with garlic.

Restaurant Bristol, one of Vienna's most acclaimed eateries

For more information on types of restaurants *see pages 200–203*

Garden seating with mosaic-tiled tables at Café-Restaurant Dunkelbunt

Café Schmid Hansl €
Traditional Viennesei   **Map** 1 A2
Schulgasse 31, 1180
Tel *406 36 58*   **Closed** *Sat & Sun*
The menu at this restaurant away from the tourist hordes features standard dishes such as *Schnitzel*, and is popular with the locals. Check out the programmes of live music and recitals.

Café Schopenhauer €
Traditional Viennese   **Map** 1 A3
Staudgasse 1, 1189
Tel *406 32 88*
A huge variety of coffees along with teas, light bites and *Strudels* are served at charming pavement tables. For a big meal, order the ham and egg plate accompanied by chunks of warm bread.

Café-Restaurant Dunkelbunt €
Traditional Austrian
Weissgerberlände 14, 1030
Tel *715 26 89*   **Closed** *Sun*
In a tranquil oasis of raised gardens of plants and blooms, Dunkelbunt makes use of organic, fresh produce wherever possible, and is known for its great vegetarian dishes.

Café-Restaurant Residenz €
Traditional Austrian
Kavalierstrakt 52, 1130
Tel *241 00 30 0*
Grab a table on the terrace or sit in the relaxed dining area for hearty breakfasts, coffee, pastries or a hot meal of local delicacies. There is a fine range of game dishes on the menu.

Gasthaus Reinthaler €
Traditional Viennese
Stuwerstrasse 5
Tel *512 33 66*   **Closed** *Sat & Sun*
Locals flock to this friendly inn for tasty, home-cooked dishes such as juicy meat-filled cabbage rolls followed by

apricot dumplings served with vanilla ice cream. The daily specials are great value.

Rasouli €
International
Payergasse 12, 1160
Tel *403 13 47*   **Closed** *Mon*
Arrive early at Rasouli for a breakfast of feta cheese omelette or a pancake stack, or opt for a lunch of sausage with chickpeas. The chicken couscous is heavenly.

Restaurant Isola €
Traditional Austrian
Arena OG Top 925, Donauzentrum, 1220
Tel *203 47 19*   **Closed** *Sun*
A large open kitchen gives this restaurant a real energy, with plenty of amazing aromas. Specialities on the menu originating from all regions of Austria include couscous with lamb and Viennese sausages with fried potatoes.

Rote Rübe €
Vegetarian   **Map** 3 A1
Zieglergasse 37, 1070
Tel *791 38 60*   **Closed** *Sun, Mon, hols*
An arty café with a distinctive white-and-red decor, Rote Rübe boasts a completely meat-free menu. Crêpes and frittatas fuse Greek flavours with local produce for good-value delicious meals.

Sri Thai Imbiss €
Thai
Baumgasse 18, 1030
Tel *707 92 96*   **Closed** *Sun*
Diners can watch Mrs Sri herself cooking a range of authentic northern Thailand delicacies with fresh ingredients in the open kitchen. The menu features noodles, curries and rice dishes.

Vegetasia €
Vegetarian
Ungargasse 57, 1030
Tel *713 83 32*
A utopia for a hungry vegetarian in Vienna, this restaurant serves an amazing all-you-can-eat lunchtime buffet. Other meal options include lentil soups, olive breads, tofu stir-fry, aubergine stew and pesto pasta.

Wetter €
Italian
Payergasse 13, 1160
Tel *406 07 75*   **Closed** *Sun*
This former launderette has been transformed into a busy little eatery that is as distinctive in its industrial decor and rubber floor as its wholesome north-western Italian dishes and Ligurian wines.

Zum Schmankerlwirt €
Traditional Viennese
Salmgasse 23, 1030
Tel *961 94 64*   **Closed** *Sat & Sun*
The reliable menu here includes favourites such as *Schnitzel*, grilled pork and fried chicken served with potato salad. There is a superb selection of desserts – try the strawberries and vanilla ice cream with pumpkin-seed oil.

Café Dommayer €€
Traditional Viennese
Dommayergasse 1, 1130
Tel *877 54 65 0*
Revel in the classic decor of this stylish café and relax with a steaming cup of Melange in the shaded garden or on a comfortable red couch under crystal chandeliers.

Café Europa €€
Austrian   **Map** 3 B2
Zollergasse 8, 1070
Tel *526 33 83*
Excellent breakfasts are served 16 hours a day here. The *Schnitzel* is delicious. DJs spin club classics in the back room at weekends.

Café Goldegg €€
International   **Map** 4 E4
Argentinierstrasse 49, 1040
Tel *505 91 62*
This fine old café with leather chairs and a pool table serves full English breakfasts and club sandwiches as well as traditional local fare.

Café-Restaurant Ocktogon Am Himmel €€
Traditional Austrian
Himmelstrasse 125, 1190
Tel *328 89 36*   **Closed** *Mon & Tue*
Away from the bustle of the city, and nestled amid tumbling vines, rolling meadows and bird-filled

woods, this eatery is worth a visit for its picturesque setting. Expect staples such as *Schnitzel*, goulash and pork belly on the menu.

Dellago €€
Italian
Payergasse 10, 1160
Tel *957 47 95*
This lovely restaurant offers excellent breakfasts that draw crowds for the fresh fruit, big jugs of juice, coffee and freshly baked Viennese breads and pastries. The salmon fettuccine are superb too.

Kulinarium 7 €€
International   **Map** 3 B2
Sigmundsgasse 1, 1070
Tel *522 33 77*   **Closed** *Mon & Sun*
Choose from the à la carte or daily specials menu for beautifully presented dishes such as pork risotto, beef goulash or artichokes with parmesan. There is an extensive wine list.

Pan e Wien €€
Mediterranean   **Map** 4 F2
Salesianergasse 25, 1030
Tel *710 38 70*   **Closed** *Sat & Sun*
Dishes have a strong Italian accent at Pan e Wien, a pleasant restaurant with exposed brickwork, gilded mirrors and the hubbub of a busy kitchen.

Strandcafé €€
Traditional Austrian
Florian-Berndl Gasse 20, 1220
Tel 203 67 47
Big portions of hearty dishes are the trademark of this well-known waterfront restaurant. Choose a table out on the deck or in the pleasant interior for a menu of pork, steak, fish and pasta.

Taverna Lefteris €€
Greek
Hörnesgasse 17, 1030
Tel *713 74 51*   **Closed** *Fri & Sun*
Live music from popular local Greek musicians entertains diners at this vibrant side-street taverna. Select from hot and cold meze such as halloumi cheese, tzatziki, pork kebabs, hummus and well-seasoned lamb cutlets.

Xu's Cooking €€
Vegetarian
Kaiserstrasse 45, 1070
Tel *523 10 91*
Nutrition is taken very seriously at Xu's where the Chinese dishes are rich in proteins, vitamins and minerals and free from monosodium glutamate. Try the popular hot buffet, which is excellent value for money.

Dining Room €€€
Mediterranean
Maygasse 31, 1130
Tel *804 85 86*   **Closed** *Tue, Thu, Sat & Sun*
This elegant little restaurant in a handsome private home is one of the most inspired kitchens in Vienna. Ideal for guests who prefer intimate gastronomic experiences, the food is exquisite.

Flatschers Restaurant & Bar €€€
Steakhouse
Kaiserstrasse 113–115, 1070
Tel *523 42 68*
Dishes such as beef tartare, smoked meats, chilli steak wrap and burgers with a huge choice of toppings wow a loyal clientele at this popular venue. Try the superb signature dish of Argentine fillet steak.

Motto €€€
Asian fusion
Schonbrunerstrasse 30, 1050
Tel *587 06 72*
One of Austria's hippest restaurants, Motto is popular with the "in crowd" and is a renowed celebrity haunt. Its eclectic menu ranges from Viennese dishes to sushi, Thai curries and salads.

Mraz und Sohn €€€
International   **Map** 2 E1
Wallensteinstrasse 59, 1200
Tel *330 45 94*   **Closed** *Sat & Sun*
The creative cuisine here includes acclaimed saddle of lamb with barley, as well as a nine-course menu with wine pairings.

DK Choice

Noir €€€
International   **Map** 3 B2
Neubaugasse 8/II, 1070
Tel *800 10 19 99*   **Closed** *Sun & Mon*
A unique dining experience, Noir is a concept restaurant in which guests eat in complete darkness – the taste, texture and aromas of the food can be relished to achieve a heightened state of enjoyment. The gourmet menu includes meat, poultry, seafood and vegetarian options.

Restaurant Cobenzl €€€
Austrian
Am Cobenzl 94, 1190
Tel *320 51 20*
A menu highlight at this historic, romantic eatery with views over Vienna is a local delicacy – boiled beef fillet with mustard and herbs.

The bright, flashy decor of the fashionable Motto

For more information on types of restaurants *see pages 200–203*

SHOPS AND MARKETS

Since Vienna is a compact city, it is a pleasant place to shop. The main shopping area is pedestrianized and full of pretty cafés, and although it is not in the same league as London, Paris and New York when it comes to international stores, you can browse around at a more leisurely pace. Austrian-made glassware, food and traditional crafts all make for good buys. However, the shops tend to cater for comparatively conventional and mature tastes and purses. Vienna has a range of markets selling a variety of produce and wares from exotic fruit to old trinkets. The pedestrian shopping areas of Kärntner Strasse, the Graben and Kohlmarkt house the more expensive shops and are pleasant to wander around. For more details of shops and markets see the Directory on page 225.

Best Buys

Many of the best buys in Vienna are small and readily transportable: coffee addicts shouldn't forget to buy freshly ground coffee – the city imports some of the best.

If you have a sweet tooth, you couldn't be in a more appropriate city. It is justly famous for its cakes, pastries and *Torten (see p206–7)* and any good *Café-Konditorei* (cake shop and café) will post cakes back home for you. In November and December, try the buttery Advent *Stollen* available from **Julius Meinl am Graben** *(see p223)* or any good baker. Stuffed with fruit and nuts and dusted with icing sugar, it is a tasty Christmas loaf.

Alternatively, buy some prettily-packaged *Sachertorte (see p207)*, available year round. The specialist chocolate shops *(see p223)* are worth a visit, both for the unusual packaging and the chocolate itself.

Sweet *Eiswein* (so-called because the grapes are left on the vines until the first frosts) is an unusual and delicious dessert wine. **Zum Schwarzen Kameel** *(see p223)* sells the rarer red version as well.

Other Austrian-made goods include clothes manufactured in the felt-like woollen fabric known as *Loden (see p223)*. If you feel like treating yourself and have space in your car or suitcase, buy custom-made sheets or high-quality down pillows or duvets made in Austria *(see p222)*. Petit point embroidery, which adorns anything from powder compacts to handbags, is a Viennese speciality *(see p222)*.

Glassware – including superb chandeliers – and **Augarten** porcelain *(see p222)* tend to be highly original, although expensive. Many people collect crystal ornaments made by Swarovski. **Ostovics** *(see p222)* is a good cookery and glass shop for such items.

Trachten (Austrian costume) shops *(see p223)* are fun; they have a wide selection of hats, children's dresses, jackets and blouses. **INLIBRIS Gilhofer**

Chest of drawers chocolate box from Altmann & Kühne *(see p223)*

(see p223) stocks old prints and maps. Early editions of works by writers such as Freud, Kraus or Rilke can be found in Vienna's antique bookshops *(see p223)*.

Opening Hours

Shops usually open at 8:30 or 9 in the morning and close at 6 or 7 in the evening. Some of the smaller shops close for an hour at lunch time. Traditionally stores were required to close at noon on Saturday, though all now stay open until 5pm. Shops are still closed on Sundays and public holidays, although you can buy items such as groceries, flowers, camera film, books and newspapers at the major railway stations. The supermarkets at the airport and Wien Nord station are open seven days a week.

How to Pay

Vienna is now more credit (and debit) card-orientated, with many shops accepting the major cards. Some also take

J & L Lobmeyr's glass shop on Kärntner Strasse *(see p222)*

Eurocheques (with a card), but it is still wise to carry some cash as an alternative.

Where to Shop

The pedestrian shopping areas of Graben, Kohlmarkt and Kärntner Strasse have many of the most well-known and expensive shops in Vienna.

The more cheaply priced area is along Mariahilfer Strasse, with department stores selling household goods, and well-known chain stores such as H & M.

Rights and Services

If a purchase is defective you are usually entitled to a refund, provided you have proof of purchase. This is not always the case with goods bought in the sales – inspect them carefully before you buy. Many shops in Vienna will pack goods for you – and often gift-wrap them at no extra charge – and send them anywhere in the world.

VAT Exemption

VAT (value added tax) or MWSt (Mehrwertsteuer) is normally charged at 20 per cent. If you reside outside the European Union (EU), you are entitled to claim back the VAT on goods purchased in Austria. This is only the case, however, if the total purchase price (this can include the total cost of several items from one shop) exceeds €73. Take along your passport when shopping and ask the shopkeeper to complete Form U34 at the time of sale. This should also bear the shop's stamp and have the receipt attached. You may choose to have the refund credited to your credit card account, have it posted home, or pick it up at the airport.

Purchased goods must not be used prior to exportation. If you leave Vienna by air, present the form at Customs before checking in, and have it stamped as proof of export. You may also have to show your purchases at Customs, so pack

View down Kohlmarkt, one of Vienna's pedestrian shopping streets

them somewhere accessible. Then post the stamped form to the Austrian shopkeeper or collect the refund at the airport (there is a handling fee). If leaving by car or train, present the form to Customs at the border, where you can also claim a refund. If you are not disembarking the train at the border, there is sometimes a customs official on the train to stamp your form.

When you have goods sent directly to your home outside the EU, VAT is deducted at the time of purchase. However, since Austria is a member of the EU, EU citizens cannot claim back VAT.

One of the famous *Loden* coats from Loden-Plankl (*see p223*)

Sales

The bi-annual sales are held in January and July. The best bargains can usually be found in fashions. Electrical and household goods are also much reduced.

Shopping Centres

Shopping centres are a fairly recent innovation in Vienna. The most modern are the **Ringstrassen-Galerien**, the splendid **Haas-Haus** and the spruced-up **Generali-Center**. Built in the same style as the Café Central (*see pp60–3*), **Freyung Passage** is an arcade of elegant shops in the Palais Ferstel (*see pp110 and 112*).

Addresses

Generali-Center
Mariahilfer Strasse 77–79.
Map 3 A3.

Haas-Haus
Stock-im-Eisen-Platz 4.
Map 2 D5 & 5 C3.

Freyung Passage
Palais Ferstel 1, Freyung 2.
Map 2 D5 & 5 B2.

Ringstrassen-Galerien
Kärntner Ring 5–7.
Map 6 D5.

Shops and Boutiques

Even if Vienna does not boast the wide range of shops you find in many other European capitals, it does offer certain goods that are hard to beat elsewhere. Austrian glassware is justly famous and cut-glass gifts are of a high quality. A few shops, such as **Knize** (in the Graben), designed by Adolf Loos, are in themselves worth a visit simply to admire the Jugendstil architecture. It's best to speak English in shops unless you are fluent in German – you will probably receive quicker service!

Speciality Shops

Vienna still manufactures leather goods, although nowadays a lot are imported from Italy. **Robert Horn** designs and manufactures leather travel cases and accessories. He maintains that even he has been unable to improve on the design of a briefcase carried by Metternich at the Congress of Vienna, which he has only slightly modernized.

Petit point embroidery is another Viennese speciality. Some of the most attractive can be found at **Petit Point** (where even the shop's door handle is embroidered) and at **Maria Stransky**.

Kober *(see p232)* is a "serious" toy shop which sells well-made dolls and toys. Or combine a visit to the novelty and joke shop called **Witte Zauberklingl** with a trip to the Naschmarkt. It stocks masks, fancy dress outfits, and beautiful old-fashioned paper decorations that are ideal for festivals. **Metzger**, a shop specializing in beeswax, sells its own candles and candlesticks. It also stocks other gift items on the same theme, such as honey cakes and boxes of chocolates.

Music

As you would expect in "the City of Music", the range of recordings available is rich and varied. The shops with the widest range of classical CDs are **EMI** and **Gramola**. However, don't expect to find many bargains: CDs are more expensive in Austria than in other countries in Europe.

Arcadia specializes particularly in opera and operetta. The staff in all these shops are usually very knowledgeable. **Doblinger** focuses on contemporary Austrian music and is excellent for sheet music; it also has a second-hand CD department.

Jewellery

Viennese jewellers have long been famous for their fine workmanship. Fruit and flower brooches carved in semi-precious stones and sometimes studded with diamonds, are a more recent Austrian innovation. **Juwelier Wagner** always has a good selection. Both **Köchert** and **Heldwein** were jewellers to the Imperial Court and still produce beautiful jewellery in their own workshops today. Köchert also sells antique pieces and Heldwein are known for their multi-coloured chains of semi-precious stones. In 2010, one of the pieces designed by **Schullin** won the prestigious Diamonds International award organized by De Beers for innovative design. Their small window usually attracts a crowd of admirers to view their latest creations. Don't let that put you off – prices start at a reasonable level.

Glassware

The Chandeliers at Vienna's Opera House and the Metropolitan Opera in New York are by **J & L Lobmeyr**, as are the chandeliers in numerous palaces throughout the world – including the Kremlin. This company – now run by a fifth generation of the same family – has produced beautiful glasses and crystal chandeliers since the early 19th century, often commissioning famous artists. One range of glasses still in production today was designed by Josef Hoffmann *(see p56)* in Jugendstil style. Its famous *Musselinglas*, a type of glass so fine that it almost bends to the touch, is exquisite. There is a small but superb glass museum on the first floor and, apart from its own glassware, Lobmeyr also sells select items of Hungarian Herend porcelain.

Interiors

Albin Denk, founded in 1702, is the oldest porcelain shop in Vienna and was the official purveyor to the court. It has a vast range of beautiful objects. **Augarten**, the second oldest porcelain maker, was founded in 1718 and taken over by the House of Habsburg in 1744. Ever since, its products have been marked with their banded shield coat of arms. Each piece of porcelain at **Schloss Augarten** is still hand finished and painted: patterns and shapes are based on original models from the Baroque, Rococo, Biedermeier and Art Deco periods and on designs created by present-day artists. The Schloss Augarten factory is open to visitors. **Ostovics** stocks glass and porcelain as well as kitchenware, and is good for gifts.

Founded in 1849, **Backhausen** is known for its exclusive furnishing fabrics, woven in the original Jugendstil patterns, and for its silk scarves and matching velvet handbags. In addition it has a good selection of duvets and household linens. Quality bedding and linens are available at **Gans**, which conveniently has a shop at Vienna's Schwechat airport for last-minute purchases.

Gunkel stocks household linen and bath robes, and for generations the Viennese have patronized **Zur Schwäbischen**

Jungfrau, founded in 1720, where fine linens can be made to order as well as purchased ready-made.

Food and Wine

One of Vienna's most renowned and almost revered food and wine shops, Zum Schwarzen Kameel (see p212), sells mouthwatering produce. Julius Meinl am Graben food hall, on the pedestrianized Graben, also offers a wide selection of delicacies. Enter via its Lukullus Bar in Naglergasse if you decide you would like to stop for a snack and a drink. There is also a good chain of wine merchants called Wein & Co, one of which is situated on the Jasomirgottstrasse. Altmann & Kühne is famous for its tiny, handmade chocolates sold in beautiful boxes shaped like miniature chests of drawers, books, horses and angels.

Gifts

Successor of the famous Wiener Werkstätten, the outfit called Österreichische Werkstätten has a selection of almost exclusively Austrian goods. In stock are a range of enamelled jewellery designed by Michaela Frey, ceramics, mouth-blown glass, candles and, from late autumn onwards, Christmas tree decorations. The arts and crafts markets (see p224) are also good hunting-grounds for picking up knick-knacks. The Tirol-based firm of Swarovski produces high quality crystal. Their necklaces, pins and earrings are popular worldwide, as are their animal figurines and accessories.

Books

Located in the Jewish District is Shakespeare & Co, which stocks an extensive selection of books in English, as does Frick International. For music books in English, visit Doblinger (see p222). Rare old books – as well as new ones, including novels and autobiographies – can be

purchased at Heck. Old prints and maps are available at the specialist INLIBRIS Gilhofer.

Newspapers and Periodicals

Most newspaper kiosks located within the Ringstrasse stock foreign newspapers – and so do the best coffee houses, where they can be read free of charge. There is no English-language Viennese newspaper. Morawa sells a variety of newspapers and periodicals in practically any language.

Clothes and Accessories

Viennese clothes are well-made and tend to be quite formal. Loden-Plankl is famous for jackets, coats and capes made from Loden. This is a warm, feltlike fabric traditionally in dark green or grey, but now produced in a range of colours.

Tostmann is best known for traditional Austrian costumes or Trachten: its Dirndl (dresses) are made from a variety of fabrics including beautiful brocades. Its clothes for children are particularly delightful.

Fürnkranz has several branches throughout Vienna, but its main shop providing elegant day and evening wear is in Kärntner Strasse, with the shop at Neuer Markt stocking more sporty styles. Opened in 2011, the flagship store of Peek & Cloppenburg offers casual and sports wear as well as accessories. A trusted and old-established Viennese name is

Knize. In imperial times this was a famous tailoring establishment, but the shop now stocks ready-to-wear clothes for men and women. It also sells its own scent. Kettner – almost hidden down a nearby side street – stocks casual daywear for both men and women at all its branches.

Steffl department store offers fashion, toys and stationery over seven floors.

All the shoes at Bally are imported from Italy; the quality, as you would expect, is excellent. D'Ambrosio, which has several branches located in the first district, stocks trendy, up-market Italian-style shoes for both men and women at moderate prices. Kurt Denkstein is another shoe retailer with stock at reasonable prices.

Younger, trendier shoppers should head straight to Judengasse – this street has plenty of reasonably priced boutiques with styles to suit every taste. For menswear in particular, D G Linnerth stocks informal and sporty clothes designed for teenagers upwards. The branch of the trendy clothes chain H & M, on Graben, is worth a visit if only to view the gilded birdcage of a lift.

An optician called Erich Hartmann bought a shop with a large stock of horn and tortoiseshell back in 1980. Today he sells a range of handmade spectacles, combs and chains, all made from horn.

Size Chart

For Australian sizes follow British and American convention.

Women's clothes								
Austrian	36	38	40	42	44	46	48	50
British	10	12	14	16	18	20	22	24
American	8	10	12	14	16	18	20	22
Shoes								
Austrian	36	37	38	39	40	41	42	43
British	3½	4	5	5½	6½	7½	8	9
American	5	5½	6½	7	8	9	9½	10½
Men's shirts								
Austrian	44	46	48	50	52	54		
British	34	36	38	40	42	44		
American	S	M	M	L	XL	XL		

Antiques, Auctions and Markets

Many districts in Vienna have their own markets –and a few have several – where you can buy arts and crafts, food, flowers and imported and second-hand goods. The city is also known for its Christmas markets, popular with locals in the evenings. If you are interested in antiques and bric-a-brac, it is worth looking in both the specialist antique shops and the main auction house. Alternatively, enjoy browsing round the bustling ethnic stalls and mix of cultures in the Naschmarkt, Vienna's main food market.

Antiques

Vienna is justly famous for its antique shops. Most are located in the Stephansdom Quarter as well as along Schönbrunner Strasse, where stock ranges from valuable antiques to simply second-hand. The **Dorotheum** *(see Auctions)*, the **Kunst und Antikmarkt** and the Flohmarkt *(see Artisan Markets)* should not be missed. Jewellery and antique paintings can be particularly good finds. One of the best shops for antique jewellery is the **Galerie Rauhenstein**. It stocks rare and beautiful pieces up to and including the 1940s.

If you are interested in old jewellery and silver and other antiques, **Herbert Asenbaum** is worth a visit. For larger pieces and shops on a larger scale, try **Subal & Subal** on Spiegelgasse or **Reinhold Hofstätter** on Bräunerstrasse. They are both well established and have a good selection of fine antique furniture.

Auctions

Opened in 1707 as a pawn-brokers for the "new poor", and appropriately called the *Armen Haus* (poor house), Vienna's **Dorotheum** is now the city's most important auction house. In 1788 it moved to the site of a former convent called the Dorotheerkirche, which had an altar-piece of St Dorothea in it – hence the name. This is an interesting place to browse around, and since buying is not restricted to auction times, you can often purchase items over the counter. It has other branches dotted around the city.

Food Markets

Between the Linke and Rechte Wienzeile, the **Naschmarkt** *(see p142)* is worth visiting even if you don't buy anything. Exotic fruit and vegetables, notably Greek, Turkish and Asian specialities, crowd the stalls and are piled high in the shops. It is a fascinating place to wander around and observe life. Open all year round, it acts as a meeting point for people of different nationalities who come to buy and sell fruit and vegetables, tea, herbs and spices. The section near the Karlsplatz contains the more expensive Viennese-run stalls. These gradually give way to stands run by colourful Turkish stallholders as you move further towards the flea market.

In addition to the exotic food stalls, you will see Czechs selling hand puppets, Russians selling Babushka dolls and Turks with stalls piled high with eastern clothes. The market is also a good spot for late-night revellers to feast on highly spiced fish snacks in the early hours of the morning.

Food-lovers should not miss the farmers' market known as the **Bauernmarkt**. A whole range of organic and other country produce is on sale here on Saturday mornings.

Artisan Markets

Antique markets and arts and crafts markets are fairly new to Vienna, but the Flohmarkt (flea market) at the end of the **Naschmarkt** *(see p142)* and the **Kunst und Antikmarkt** are established hunting grounds for second-hand goods and antiques. The price quoted is probably not the price that you are expected to pay – it's usually assumed that you will bargain.

For the better quality hand-crafted goods, head to the Spittelberg market *(see p119)* near the Volkstheater. Here artists and craftspeople sell their own products rather than mass-produced factory goods. This is a fashionable and attractive part of Vienna and, although the market is small, you are likely to find gifts of good quality. There are also small galleries and cafés where artists exhibit their works.

The **Heiligenkreuzerhof** *(see p81)* art market is in a quiet, secluded courtyard where a small, select group of exhibitors is on hand should you wish to discuss the work. The stalls sell jewellery, ceramics and other handmade goods. Further entertainment and atmosphere is provided by an Austrian folk singer dressed in traditional clothes playing his accordion.

Festive Markets

Christmas markets in Vienna are very special, the most famous of all being the **Christkindlmarkt** *(see p66)* held in front of the Rathaus. Attractions vary from year to year, but there are always sideshows, decorated trees, per-formances on a temporary stage and lots of stalls, as well as a workshop for making Christmas presents and baking goodies. Items for sale include honey cakes, bees-wax candles, Christmas decorations and various crafts, although the main attraction is the joyous atmosphere. It is especially magical at night when everything is lit up.

The **Alt Wiener Christ-kindlmarkt** *(see p66)* at the Freyung is a smaller affair. Two weeks before Easter there is also an Easter market here with a large selection of blown and hand-painted eggs. Other Christmas markets take place in the Spittelberg area, Schloss Schönbrunn, Karlskirche, Heiligenkreuzerhof and on Maria-Theresien-Platz.

DIRECTORY

Speciality Shops

Kober
Wollzeile 16.
Map 6 E3.
Tel 5336018.

Maria Stransky
Hofburg Passage 2.
Map 5 C4.
Tel 5336098.

Metzger
Stephansplatz 7. Map 2
E5 & 6 D3. Tel 5123433.
One of two branches.

Petit Point
Kärntner Strasse 16. Map
4 D1 & 6 D4. Tel 5124886.

Robert Horn
Bräunerstrasse 7.
Map 5 C4. Tel 5138294.

Witte Zauberklingl
Linke Wienzeile 16.
Map 3 A4. Tel 5864305.

Music

Arcadia
Kärntner Strasse 40. Map
4 D2 & 5 C5. Tel 5139568.

Doblinger
Dorotheergasse 10.
Map 5 C3. Tel 515030.

EMI
Kärntner Str 30. Map 4 D1
& 6 D4. Tel 5137974.

Gramola
Graben 16. Map 2 D5 & 5
C3. Tel 5335034.

Jewellery

Heldwein
Graben 13. Map 5 C3.
Tel 5125781.

Juwelier Wagner
Kärntnerstrasse 32.
Map 4 D1. Tel 5120512.

Köchert
Neuer Markt 15. Map 5
C4. Tel 5125828.

Schullin
Kohlmarkt 7.
Map 2 D5 & 5 C3.
Tel 5339007.

Glassware

J & L Lobmeyr
Kärntner Str 26.
Map 2 D5 & 6 D4.
Tel 512050888.

Interiors

Albin Denk
Graben 13. Map 2 D5 & 5
C3. Tel 5124439.

Augarten
Stock-im-Eisen-Platz 3–4.
Map 2 D5 & 5 C3.
Tel 5121494.

Backhausen
Schwarzenbergstrasse 10.
Map 6 D5. Tel 514040.

Gans
Brandstätte 1–3. Map 4
D1 & 6 D3. Tel 5333560.
One of several branches.

Gunkel
Tuchlauben 11. Map 2 D5
& 5 C3. Tel 53363010.

Ostovics
Stephansplatz 9. Map 6
D3. Tel 5331411.

Schloss Augarten
Obere Augartenstrasse 1.
Map 2 E2. Tel 21124200.

Zur Schwäbischen Jungrau
Graben 26. Map 2 D5 & 5
C3. Tel 5355356.

Food and Wine

Altmann & Kühne
Graben 30. Map 2 D5 & 5
C3. Tel 5330927. One of
two branches.

Julius Meinl am Graben
Graben 19. Map 2 D5 & 5
C3. Tel 5323334.

Wein & Co
Jasomirgottstrasse 3–5.
Map 6 D3. Tel
0507063121.

Zum Schwarzen Kameel
Bognergasse 5.
Map 5 C3.
Tel 533812527.

Gifts

Österreichische Werkstätten
Kärntner Str 6. Map 4 D1
& 6 D4. Tel 5122418.

Swarovski
Kärntnerstrasse 24.
Map 6 D4. Tel 3240000.
One of several branches.

Books

Frick International
Schulerstrasse 1–3.
Map 6 D3.
Tel 5126905.

Heck
Kärntner Ring 14. Map 4
E2 & 6 D5.
Tel 5055152.

INLIBRIS Gilhofer
Rathausstrasse 19. Map 1
C5. Tel 40961900.

Shakespeare & Co
Sterngasse 2. Map 2 E5 &
6 D2. Tel 5355053.

Newspapers and Periodicals

Morawa
Wollzeile 11. Map 2 E5 &
6 D3. Tel 5137513450.

Clothes and Accessories

Bally
Graben 12. Map 5 C3. Tel
5130550.

D'Ambrosio
Jasomirgottstrasse 6.
Map 6 D3. Tel 532635225.
One of several branches.

D G Linnerth
Lugeck 1–2. Map 6 D3.
Tel 5138318.

Erich Hartmann
Singerstrasse 8, Corner of
Lilieng. Map 6 D3.
Tel 5121489.

Flamm
Neuer Markt 12. Map 5
C4. Tel 5122889.

Fürnkranz
Kärntner Str 39. Map 6 D4
& 5 C5. Tel 4884426. One
of several branches.

H & M
Graben 8. Map 2 D5 & 5
C3. Tel 0810909090. One
of several branches.

Kurt Denkstein
Stephansplatz 4. Map 6
D3. Tel 5127465.

Kettner
Plankengasse 7. Map 5
C4. Tel 5132239.

Knize
Graben 13. Map 2 D5 & 5
C3. Tel 5122119.

Loden-Plankl
Michaelerplatz 6.
wMap 5 C3. Tel 5338032.

Steffl
Kärntnerstrasse 19.
Map 6 D3. Tel 930560.

Tostmann
Schottengasse 3a. Map 5
B2. Tel 5335331.

Antiques

Galerie Rauhenstein
Rauhensteingasse 3. Map
6 D4. Tel 5133009.

Herbert Asenbaum
Kärntner Str 28. Map 4 D1
& 6 D4. Tel 522847.

Reinhold Hofstätter
Bräunerstrasse 12. Map 5
C4. Tel 5335069.

Subal & Subal
Spiegelgasse 8. Map 4 D1
& 5 C4. Tel 5131349.

Auctions

Dorotheum
Dorotheergasse 17. Map
4 D1 &5 C4. Tel 515600.

Markets

Alt Wiener Christkindlmarkt
Freyung. Map 2 D5 & 5
B2. Open 17 Nov–24 Dec:
9:30am–7:30pm daily.

Bauernmarkt
Freyung. Map 2 D5 & 5
B2. Open Mar–end Oct:
10am–6:30pm Tue & Thu.

Christkindlmarkt
At the Neues Rathaus.
Map 1 C5 & 5 A2. Open
Mid-Nov–24 Dec:
10am–7pm daily.

Heiligenkreuzerhof
Map 2 E5 & 6 E3. Open
Apr–Sep: first Sat & Sun of
each month; end Nov–
Mar: 10am–6pm Sat & Sun.

Kunst und Antikmarkt
Donaukanal-Promenade.
Map 6 F2. Open May–
end Sep: 2–8pm Sat,
10am–8pm Sun.

Naschmarkt
Map 3 C2. Open
6am–6:30pm Mon–Fri,
6am–6pm Sat.

ENTERTAINMENT IN VIENNA

Vienna offers a wide range of entertainment, particularly of the musical variety. There is grand opera at the Opera House – Staatsoper *(see pp140–41)* – or the latest musical at the Theater an der Wien *(see p142)*. Dignified orchestral concerts and elegant Viennese waltzes take place at the great balls during the Carnival season, and waltzes are played in the relaxed atmosphere of the Stadtpark. Even the famous Lipizzaner horses perform to Viennese music and no visit to the city is complete without a trip to the Spanish Riding School *(see pp100–101)*. Vienna also has excellent theatres, two of which perform in English, and several cinemas which specialize in classic films. Restaurants close early, but you can still be entertained around the clock at one of Vienna's many nightspots. Within the Ringstrasse, the city buzzes with late-night revellers enjoying jazz clubs, such as the Roter Engel, discos, casinos and bars with live music. Alternatively, you can end your day sipping coffee and nibbling pastries at a late-night café.

The stage of the Theater in der Josefstadt *(see p118)*

Practical Information

A monthly guide to Vienna is issued free by the Wiener Tourismusverband (main Vienna Tourist Office – *see p238*). Posters which list the weekly programmes for the opera houses and theatres are pasted on billboard columns and displayed in most hotel lobbies. They also list casts for all the performances. Each day the four main newspapers in the city, *Die Presse, Kronenzeitung, Standard* and *Kurier (see p245)* publish programme listings. All four also give details of daily cinema performances and concerts as well as the main sporting events.

Booking Tickets

You can buy tickets from online agencies such as culturall.com, viennaclassic.com, vienna concerts.com, viennaticket. com and wien-ticket.at, and also direct from the appropriate box office (check opening hours, since these vary),or reserve them on the telephone. The phone numbers and addresses for the booking offices are listed in the Music, Theatre and Cinema directories *(see pp229–30)*. The four state theatres, the Burgtheater *(see p134)*, the **Akademie-theater** *(see p230)*, the Opera House *(see pp140– 41)* and the **Wiener**

Volksoper *(see p229)*, all have one central booking office, the **Bundestheaterkassen** *(see p229)*. However, tickets for performances at any of these four theatres can also be purchased at the box office of the Wiener Volksoper and the Burgtheater.

Tickets usually go on sale two months before the performance. However, bear in mind that tickets for September performances of the Vienna State Opera are sold during the month of June.

Written applications for tickets for the state theatre must reach the Vienna State Opera ticket office (address as Bundestheaterkassen) no later than three weeks before the date of the performance. Standing-room tickets are sold at the evening box office one hour before the start of the performance.

Tickets for the state theatres, the Theater an der Wien *(see p142)*, the **Raimund Theater** *(see p229)* and **Konzerthaus** *(see p228)* can be used on public transport for two hours before, and six hours after, all performances. Agencies are reliable – try **Reisebüro Mondial** *(see p229)* – and hotel staff may be able to obtain tickets. Otherwise try the box office for returns.

At the Theatre

If you visit the theatre in person, you will be able to see the seating plan and

Billboard column

Busker beneath the Pestsäule

make your choice accordingly. The monthly programme for the state theatres also contains individual seating plans and it is a good idea to have them in front of you when booking your tickets by telephone. Most hotel porters will also have copies of seating plans for the principal venues.

If you book by telephone remember that *Parkett* (stalls) are in front and are usually the most expensive. In some theatres the front rows of the stalls are known as *Orchestersitze*. The *Parterre* (back stalls) are cheaper and the dress circle (the grand or royal circle) is called *Erster Rang*, followed by the *Zweiter Rang* (balcony). At the Burgtheater and Opera House, there are two extra levels called the *Balkon* and *Galerie*. The higher you go, the cheaper the seats are. Boxes are known as *Logen* and the back seats are always cheaper than the front seats.

At the **Wiener Volksoper** (see p229) they still have *Säulensitze*, seats where the view is partly obscured by a column. These cheap tickets are bought by music lovers who come to listen rather than to view. There are four tiers of boxes at the Volksoper, known in ascending order as *Parterre, Balkon, Erster Rang* and *Zweiter Rang*.

Buffets at Vienna's principal theatres provide alcoholic and non-alcoholic drinks, and tasty snacks which range from open sandwiches at the **Akademietheater** (see p230) and Volksoper to the more elaborate

concoctions at the Opera House and Burgtheater. Small open sandwiches with caviar, egg, smoked salmon, cheese and salami on Vienna roll-style bread are also common. Glasses of *Sekt*, a sparkling wine, are always available.

Buffets are usually open for up to one hour before the start of a performance and are often fairly empty. They are an ideal place for relaxing with a snack and a drink, and the coffee is extremely good.

It is not usual to tip ushers at theatres, unless you are being shown to a box, but you may round up the price of a theatre programme.

Coats and hats have to be left in the cloakroom before you go to your seat. There is usually no fixed charge, and tipping is at your discretion.

Facilities for the Disabled

A number of venues offer wheelchair access or help for those with hearing difficulties. Be sure to make your needs very clear when booking tickets.

A booklet, *Wien für Gäste mit Handicaps* (Vienna for handicapped guests), is published by the Wiener Tourismusverband (see p238) and provides information on facilities at entertainment venues, museums, hotels, restaurants, cafés, cinemas, post offices and so on.

Transport

Buses and trams run until around midnight, while the underground continues until about midnight (see *Getting Around Vienna, pp250–55*). Night buses are popular, with 20 routes operating around the city and into the suburbs. They start at 12:30am from Schwedenplatz, the Opera and Schottentor, and continue every half hour until 4am, 24hrs at weekends. Tickets

usually cost around €1 and are sold on the bus (see p254).

You can phone for a taxi from your venue, or take one from outside. Taxis usually line up outside theatres after a performance, otherwise you can go to one of the many taxi ranks which are found on most street corners. Taxis which do not stop when hailed are already booked.

Casino Wien in Esterházy Palace

Casinos

Casinos Austria has become the hallmark for superbly run casinos all over the world, but **Casino Wien** is a showcase. It is set in the Baroque Esterházy Palace (see p82) and you can play French or American roulette, baccarat and poker there. The complex includes a bar, a restaurant and the **Jackpot Casino**, which is a typically Viennese addition.

Casino Wien

Kärntner Strasse 41. Map 4 D1. Casino: **Open** 3pm–3am daily (to 4am Fri & Sat). Jackpot Casino: **Open** 11am–2:30am daily (to 3:30am Fri & Sat). **Tel** 5124836.

Dancing at the grand Opera Ball (see p141)

Music in Vienna

The Vienna Opera House (see pp140–41) is one of the greatest of its kind in the world and, like all four state theatres, is heavily subsidised. The acoustics are excellent – the world-famous conductor Arturo Toscanini advised on the rebuilding of the theatre after it was destroyed at the end of the last war. The house orchestra, the Wiener Philharmoniker, performs while the Opera House is open from September until June. Most operas are sung in the original language. The city supports two principal orchestras, the Wiener Philharmoniker and the Wiener Symphoniker. There are also a number of chamber music ensembles and visiting artists. Church music is often of concert quality. You can hear more informal music in the Stadtpark, where a small orchestra regularly plays waltzes in summer. Live rock music is popular in discos, and there is an annual jazz festival (see p65).

Opera and Operetta

Seat prices at the Vienna Opera House range from €12 to over €200. Tickets are sold one month in advance of a performance, except standing-room tickets, which are on sale one hour before the performance starts. These are good value, but because of this there is usually a long queue. After buying your ticket you can mark your space by tying a scarf around the rail, leaving you free to wander around. The New Year's Eve performance is always *Die Fledermaus* by Johann Strauss, and famous guests sometimes make surprise appearances during the second act.

The **Wiener Volksoper** is renowned for its superb operetta productions of works by composers ranging from Strauss, Millöcker and Ziehrer to Lehár and Kálmán. There are also performances of musicals and light opera by Mozart, Puccini and Bizet, sung in German. Prices can range from €3 to €86, and the season is exactly the same as the Opera House.

Concealed in a small side street in the Stephansdom Quarter is one of Vienna's great little opera houses the **Wiener Kammeroper**. Many international singers such as Waldemar Kmentt, Eberhard Waechter and Walter Berry started their careers here. You can expect anything to be performed here from the early

works of Rossini to classic operetta, as well as rock versions of familiar operas such as *Tales of Hoffmann* and *Carmen*, and opera parodies.

Another venue for opera is the **Theater an der Wien** (see p142). Musicals had previously been staged here. These are now put on at the historic **Ronacher**, once Vienna's most glamorous theatre, and the large **Raimund Theater**. In May and June, the Wiener Festwochen (see p64) presents theatre and music theatre productions in a variety of venues, most notably Halle G at the MuseumsQuartier.

July sees opera performances by **Oper Klosterneuburg** in the Kaiserhof courtyard of Klosterneuburg, the palatial religious foundation a short way north of Vienna. The festival **Seefestspiele Mörbisch** (see p65) takes place every weekend in July and August on a stage projecting on to Lake Neusiedl.

Classical Concerts

The principal venues for classical concerts are the **Musikverein** (including the Brahmssaal and the halls of Gläserner Saal and Steinerner Saal) and the concert halls of the **Konzerthaus**. Performances are also held in places such as Schubert's birthplace in Nussdorf (see p187) and in many historic palaces.

The New Year's Concert (see p67) is televised live from the Grosser Musikvereinsaal in the Musik-verein every year. You can apply for tickets by writing direct to the **Wiener Philharmoniker**. However, applications must be received on 2 January (not before, not after) for the next year's concert. You can order at www.wienerphilharmoniker.at.

Waltz concerts and operetta, which include stars from the Vienna Volksoper, can be heard at the Musikverein, the Neue Burg (see p97) and the Konzerthaus on Tuesdays, Thursdays and Saturdays from April until October. Mozart and Strauss concerts are performed on Wednesdays at the Neue Burg. All tickets are the same price, so the best thing to do is to get there early if you want to make sure of getting the best seat. The Konzerthaus and Musikverein concert seasons run from October to June (for events from July to September, see page 65).

Church Music

Details of the many church concerts performed in Vienna are published in all the daily newspapers. Look out particularly for details of Sunday mass at the following places: Augustinerkirche (see p104), Minoritenkirche (see p105), the Jesuitenkirche/Jesuit church (see pp72 and 79), Stephansdom (see p75) and Michaelerkirche (see p94). In July and August, many other churches hold organ recitals.

The Vienna Boys' Choir (see p41) can be heard during mass at the Burgkapelle (see p105) every Sunday and religious holiday at 9:15am except from July to mid-September. (Tickets are available from the Burgkapelle; the box office is open the Friday before). You can also hear them at the **Konzerthaus** every Friday at 5:30pm in May, June, September and October. Buy tickets from hotel porters and from **Reisebüro Mondial** or from the website of the Vienna Boys' Choir Concert Hall, www. muth.at. Book well in advance.

Informal Music

The description just outside **Konzertcafé Schmid Hansl** reads, "the home of Viennese song". The original owner of this small café, which serves hot food until it closes, was Hansl Schmid, a very fine singer and musician. Guests would often visit the café just to hear him sing, and sometimes a famous artist might join him in a duet or give a solo performance. The present owner, Hansl Schmid's son, once a member of the Vienna Boys' Choir, has kept up this tradition, and you may well encounter opera stars coming in to perform unexpectedly.

Another Viennese favourite is the **Wiener Kursalon**. Dinner and waltz evenings with the Johann Strauss Salonorchester are held daily throughout the year along with classical ballet performances. Concerts take place in the Stadtpark during the summer months.

Rock, Pop and Jazz

What is popular one week in Vienna's lively music scene may very well be out of fashion the next. Many discos have live music on certain nights or for a limited period.

U4 disco has a different style every night (from industrial to flower power); Monday is Open Stage night for upcoming acts. **Volksgarten Clubdiskothek** is the oldest disco in town, with music ranging from house to hip-hop and salsa. **Roter Engel** in the Bermuda Triangle has live music every night. The **Praterdome**, situated near the ferris wheel in Prater park, has popular theme nights.

Live concerts are held at **Chaya Fuera**, **Jazzland**, and on Sundays at **Chelsea**. The **Ost Klub** features live music from Eastern Europe, the Balkans and Russia.

A must for jazz fans is **Jazz & Music Club Porgy & Bess**, with live music and dancing, and the **Jazzfest** held in the first two weeks of July, with concerts in various venues such as the Opera House (see pp140–41), the Volkstheater (see p230) and the Neues Rathaus (see p132) as well as many open-air events.

All styles, electro and house as well as alternative music, can be found at **Café Leopold**, **Schikaneder Bar** and **Flex**.

DIRECTORY

Theatre and Cinema

Vienna has a good choice of theatres, with an eclectic mix of styles ranging from classical drama to the avant-garde. Some places, like the early 19th-century Theater in der Josefstadt *(see p118)*, are well worth visiting for their architecture alone. You can see productions in English at the English Theatre or, if you understand German, you can go and watch one of the many fringe performances. Some cinemas screen films in their original language. The classic film which is usually showing somewhere in the city is *The Third Man*, set in Vienna during the Allied occupation.

Theatres

Viennese theatre is some of the best in Europe and the **Burgtheater** *(see p134)*, one of the City's four state theatres, is the most important venue. Classic and modern plays are performed here and even if your understanding of German is limited, you will still enjoy a new production (which can often be avant-garde) of a Shakespeare play. For classic and modern plays go to the **Akademietheater**, part of the Burgtheater.

The **Theater in der Josefstadt** *(see p118)* is worth a visit for the interior alone. As the house lights slowly dim, the crystal chandeliers float gently to the ceiling. It offers excellent productions of

Austrian plays as well as classics from other countries, and the occasional musical. **Kammerspiele** is the Josefstadt's "little house". The old and well-established **Volkstheater** offers more modern plays as well as the occasional classic and some operetta performances.

Vienna has a wide range of fringe theatre from one-man shows to *Kabarett* – these are satirical shows, not cabarets – but reasonably fluent German is needed to appreciate them. German-speakers will also enjoy the highly recommended **Kabarett Simpl**, featuring top name cabaret acts.

Theatres that give performances in English

include **Vienna's English Theatre**. Plays staged here are cast and rehearsed in London or New York before opening in Vienna. Some run for a short period only, but they often feature famous international stars.

Cinemas

A cinema that screens the latest films in their original language is the **Burg Kino**, while the **Haydn Kino** and the **Artis International** show new releases in English only. Cinemas that specialize in showing old and new classics as well as more unusual films are the **Österreichisches Filmmuseum**, **Filmhaus Stöbergasse**, **Filmcasino**, and **Votiv-Kino** (which has a special cinema breakfast on Sundays). The Filmmuseum is a national cultural centre dedicated to the collection, preservation and restoration of films and film-related artifacts. It shows a programme of newly restored movie classics. The oldest film in its archive dates from 1883 and was produced by Thomas Edison. For new releases, the **Apollo Center** is a modern multiplex that boasts the largest cinema screen in Austria.

DIRECTORY

Theatres

Akademietheater
Lisztstrasse 1, A-1030.
Map 4 E2.
Tel 514444740.

Burgtheater
Dr Karl-Lueger-Ring, A-1014. **Map** 1 C5 & 5 A2.
Tel 514444145.
W burgtheater.at

Theater in der Josefstadt
Josefstädt Strasse 26, A-1080. **Map** 1 B5.
Tel 427000.
W josefstadt.org.at

Kabarett Simpl
Wollzeile 36, A-1010.
Map 2 E5 & 6 E3.
Tel 5124742.
W simpl.at

Kammerspiele
Rotenturmstrasse 20, A-1010.
Map 2 E5 & 6 E2
Tel 42700300.
W josefstadt.org.at

Vienna's English Theatre
Josefsgasse 12, A-1080.
Map 1 B5.
Tel 4021260.
W englishtheatre.at

Volkstheater
Neustiftgasse 1, A-1070.
Map 3 B1. **Tel** 52111400.
W volkstheater.at

Cinemas

Apollo Center
Gumpendorfer Strasse 63, A-1060. **Map** 3 A4 & 5 B5.
Tel 5879651.

Artis International
Schulgasse 5, A-1010.
Map 1 A2.
Tel 5356570.

Burg Kino
Opernring 19, A-1010.
Map 4 D1 & 5 B5.
Tel 5878406.
W burgkino.at

Filmcasino
Margaretenstrasse 78, A-1050.
Map 3 C3.
Tel 5879062.
W filmcasino.at

Filmhaus Stöbergasse
Stöbergasse 11–15, A-1070.
Map 3 B5.
Tel 5466630.

Haydn Kino
Mariahilfer Strasse 57, A-1060.
Map 3 B2.
Tel 5872262.
W haydnkino.at

Österreichisches Filmmuseum
Augustinerstrasse 1, A-1010.
Map 4 D1 & 5 C4.
Tel 5337054.
W filmmuseum.at

Votiv-Kino
Währinger Strasse 12, A-1090.
Map 1 C4.
Tel 3173571.
W votivkino.at

Sport and Dance

Outdoor activities are extremely popular. Football is followed by many locals – especially since the pre-war victories of the famous "Wonder Team". Visitors who enjoy swimming can take advantage of the pools the city has to offer. Horse racing and ice-skating also attract many locals. Flat racing takes place at the Freudenau in the Prater. The well-equipped **Stadthalle** is ideal for spectator sports like boxing and wrestling and houses its own pool, bowling alleys and ice rink. Many of Vienna's dance schools hold special waltz classes during the Carnival season *(see p67)*.

Ice-skating

Outdoor ice-skating is very popular in Vienna. Locals make good use of the open-air rinks at the Wiener Eislaufverein and Vienna Ice Dreams *(see p234)*.

Swimming

Vienna can be very warm in summer and has many outdoor pools, including the Schönbrunner Bad in the Schönbrunn Palace park *(see pp174–5)*. The **Krapfenwaldbad** has wonderful views over Vienna, and the **Schafbergbad** holds underwater gymnastics every Tuesday and Thursday. The **Thermalbad Oberlaa** has three open-air pools and an indoor pool. The Familienbad Augarten *(see p234)* is popular with children, and they can be left in the shallow pool to be watched by the attendants. Beach huts on the Alte Donau coast can be hired daily from **Strandbad Gänsehäufel** or **Strandbad Alte Donau**, where you can also hire boats. Strandbad Gänsehäufel has a beach, a heated pool, table tennis and Punch and Judy shows. For relaxing beaches, the world's longest water slide, barbecues and a night bus at weekends, visit **Donauinsel**.

Football

The Viennese are enthusiastic football fans, and there are two huge covered football stadiums in the city. The **Ernst Happel Stadion** (which seats 48,000) is in the Prater and the **Hanappi Stadion** (which seats 20,000) is at Hütteldorf.

Horse Racing

The Prater offers a wide range of activities *(see pp164–5)*, including trotting races at the **Krieau**.

Dancing and Dance Schools

During the Carnival season *(see p67)* many balls, and some fancy dress dances, are held in Vienna. Venues include the Hofburg, the Neues Rathaus *(see p132)* and the Musikverein *(see p229)*. The grandest event is the Opera Ball *(see p141)*, which takes place on the Thursday before Ash Wednesday. The opening ceremony includes a performance by the Opera House ballet. An invitation is not needed, you just buy a ticket. The Kaiserball is held at the Neue Burg on New Year's Eve *(see pp67 and 97)*. A special ball calendar is issued by the Wiener Tourismusverband – Vienna Tourist Office *(see p238)*.

The Summer Dance Festival *(see p65)* runs from July to August. You can learn a range of dances, including rock'n'roll, at some dance schools in the city. During the Carnival season, some schools hold Viennese waltz classes. The **Elmayer-Vestenbrugg** also teaches etiquette.

DIRECTORY

General

Stadthalle
Vogelweidplatz 15.
Swimming pool
Tel 98100433.
Open 8am–9:30pm Mon,
Wed, Fri, 6:30am–9:30pm
Tue & Thu, 7am–9:30pm
Sat, 7am–6pm Sun &
public hols.

Ice-skating

Wiener Eislaufverein
Lothringerstrasse 28.
Tel 7136353.
Open Nov–Feb: 9am–
9pm Tue–Fri, 9am–8pm
Sat–Mon & public hols.

Swimming

Donauinsel
U1 stop – Donauinsel.

Krapfenwaldbad
Krapfenwaldgasse 65–73.
Tel 32015010.
Open May–Sep:
9am–8pm Mon–Fri,
8am–8pm Sat & Sun.

Schafbergbad
Josef-Redl-Gasse 2.
Tel 4791593.
Open May–Sep:
9am–8pm Mon–Fri,
8am–8pm Sat & Sun.

Strandbad Alte Donau
Arbeiterstrandbad-
strasse 91.
Tel 2636538.

Open May–Sep:
9am–8pm Mon–Fri,
8am–8pm Sat & Sun.

Strandbad Gänsehäufel
Moissigasse 21.
Tel 2699016
Open May–Sep:
9am–8pm Mon–Fri,
8am–8pm Sat & Sun.

Thermalbad Oberlaa
Kurbadstrasse 14.
Tel 680099600.
Open 9am–10pm Mon–
Sat (8am–10pm Sun &
public hols).

Football

Ernst Happel Stadion
Meiereistrasse 7.
Tel 7280854.

Hanappi Stadion
Kaisslergasse 6.
Tel 9145519.

Horse Racing

**Krieau Prater:
trotting stadium**
Nordportalstrasse 247.
Tel 7280046 (enquiries).
(see pp66 & 164).

Dancing and Dance Schools

Elmayer-Vestenbrugg
Bräunerstrasse 13.
Map 5 C4.
Tel 06643535355
(3–8pm).
Open 3–8pm Mon–Sat,
5–10pm Sun.
Ⓦ elmayer.at

CHILDREN'S VIENNA

Traditionally, the people of Vienna have a reputation for preferring dogs to children. But negative attitudes towards children are gradually disappearing as the number of families has increased since the baby boom of the 1960s. Most restaurants serve children's portions, and in some of the more expensive places they can eat Sunday lunch at half price. Eating out at a *Heuriger* is less formal, and you can sit outside in summer. Vienna has many playgrounds and almost all museums offer tours that cater for children. Further out there are large parks, a zoo, swimming pools and ice rinks. Various children's activities are organized throughout the year.

Children pay half price on trams

Practical Advice

Traffic in Vienna can be fast and drivers are not automatically obliged to stop at pelican crossings. Always cross the road at traffic lights, and watch out for speeding cyclists in the bicycle lanes.

Children up to the age of six can travel for free on public transport. Those between the ages of six and 14 must buy a half-price ticket. During the summer holidays (the end of June to the end of August) children under 15 can travel free provided they can show some form of identification when buying a ticket.

It is a good idea to carry some small change, as you will need it to use public lavatories. These are usually clean.

In shops, the assistants may offer children boiled sweets, but do not feel obliged to accept these.

The concierges at many hotels, particularly the larger establishments, can arrange for a baby-sitter. If they cannot, they may be able to suggest a reliable local agency. If you get back from an evening out after about 10 or 11pm, you may have to pay for the baby-sitter's taxi home.

Children's Shops

Traditional Austrian clothing, which is still worn by some children in Vienna, can be purchased from **Lanz Trachtenmoden** on Kärntner Strasse. Traditional dress includes *Lederhosen*, leather shorts, for boys and the *Dirndl*, a traditional dress, for girls. The *Dirndl* is worn with a white lace blouse and an apron. A little bag is sometimes carried as well. Lanz Trachtenmoden also stocks a range of beautiful knitwear in a myriad of colours and designs. Children will particularly appreciate the fine embroidered woollen slippers made in the Tyrol.

Dohnal sells Austrian-made clothes for children up to the age of 16. In addition, the large international chains such as **012 Benetton**, **Jacadi** and **H & M** stock a wide selection of good-quality children's clothes.

Haas & Haas sells delightful craft-like presents, including wooden toys and puppets. They also have a conservatory-style tea house which is an ideal place to treat your children to lunch, or a delicious cake or *Palatschinken* (see pp206–7). A more

Children on a day out visiting Josefsplatz in the Hofburg

conventional toy shop is **Kober** on Wollzeile. Kober stocks a superb selection of toys and games, but at high prices.

Dressing up in traditional costume is popular during Fasching (see p67)

Eating Out

Generally speaking, the restaurants in Vienna are not as tolerant of noisy or boisterous children as establishments in many other cities, but there are still a large number of places where children are welcome. It is worth noting that some more expensive hotel restaurants offer special Sunday brunch buffets for families. The best is probably the **Vienna Marriott** (see p197), where children under 6 eat free and 6- to 11-year-olds eat half price. The hotel also provides a playroom with a child minder. The **Radisson Blu Palais Hotel** (see p198) offers a brunch deal, but does not have a playroom.

Heurige, where you can sit outside in summer, are usually less formal and therefore a better option for families with small children. The best time for families is from 4pm, when most of them open, as they are likely to get busier as the evening goes on. Heuriger

Visitors watching the penguins at Vienna's zoo

Zimmermann on Armbruster-
gasse in Grinzing (see pp188–9) has a small zoo where children
may stroke the animals.

There are also well-
known fast-food
restaurants, including
McDonald's and **Da
Bizi**, which are an
option you may decide
to go for if your children
are fussy about food. Most
of them have special
children's menus and some
offer free gifts for children,
especially on their birthdays.
The **Wienerwald** Viennese
chicken restaurants also
have a children's menu.
**Markt-Restaurant
Rosenberger** also caters
for children.

Delicious hot
chocolate

Sightseeing with Children

Vienna has an amazing variety
of attractions that will appeal to
children of all ages, including
theme parks, funfairs, museums,
sports and the zoo.

It usually costs around half the
adult entrance fee for children
to get into museums. However,
be warned that if children touch
or get too close to the exhibits,
the museum attendants are
likely to make a fuss.

Vienna has plenty of parks,
but some are designed more for
admiring from the pathways
than running around in. Watch
out for signs warning Bitte nicht
betreten, which means "Please

don't walk on the grass".
Details of some of the more
child-friendly parks and nature
reserves are given on page
234, and there are several
playgrounds along the first
stretch of the Prater
Hauptallee. A picnic in
one of these parks is an
ideal way to entertain
children. Picnic foods
and drinks can easily be
obtained from a super-
market, and the delicious
cakes and pastries that
Vienna is famous for can
be bought in a Konditorei
(café and cake shop), of
which there are many.
Children's play-
grounds in Vienna
are generally safe
and well equipped. However,
it is advisable to avoid the
Karlsplatz and Stadtpark play
areas because of drug dealing
in the vicinity.

see pp188–9

DIRECTORY

Children's Shops

012 Benetton
Kärntner Strasse 14. **Map** 5 C3.
Tel 5128773.

Dohnal
Kärntner Strasse 12. **Map** 4 D1 &
6 D4. **Tel** 5127311.

H & M
Kärntner Strasse 28.
Map 4 D1. **Tel** 810909090.

Haas & Haas
Teehandlung, Stephansplatz 4.
Map 2 E3 & 6 D3. **Tel** 5129770.

Jacadi
Trattnerhof 1. **Map** 5 C3.
Tel 5358866.

Kober
Wollzeile 16. **Map** 2 D5 & 5 C3.
Tel 5336018.

Lanz Trachtenmoden
Kärntner Strasse 10.
Map 4 D1 & 6 D4. **Tel** 5122456.

Eating Out

Da Bizi
Rotenturmstrasse 4. **Map** 6 D3.
Tel 5353457.

**Markt-Restaurant
Rosenberger**
Maysedergasse 2. **Map** 5 C4.
Tel 5123458.

McDonald's
Singerstrasse 4. **Map** 4 E1 &
6 D3. **Tel** 5139279.

Wienerwald
Annagasse 3. **Map** 4 D1 &
6 D4. **Tel** 5123766.
Goldschmiedgasse 6.
Map 6 D3. **Tel** 5354012.

Family out cycling, a familiar sight at the Prater

Elephants at Tiergarten Schönbrunn in the palace gardens *(see pp174–5)*

The Zoo, Parks and Nature Reserves

Situated in Schönbrunn Palace gardens *(see pp174–5)* is a fine zoo *(Tiergarten)* that combines historic features with a thoroughly up-to-date layout and the benefit of spacious reserves for the animals. The garden also has a superb maze, which was laid out between 1698 and 1740, and a labyrinth with various games and riddles. With its frescoed ceilings, the central pavilion serves as a charming café.

In the Vienna Woods, the Lainzer Tiergarten *(see p173)* is a nature reserve where children can see deer, wild boar and horses. There are playgrounds and a pond. An easy walk takes you to Hermesvilla hunting lodge, with its café and nature-based exhibitions.

Funfair and Children's City

An ideal venue for a family outing is the atmospheric **Prater** *(see pp164–5)*. Its big wheel is magical at night, and busier than by day. The Prater park also has sandpits, playgrounds, ponds and streams. **Minopolis** is a child-sized city, with a hospital, bank, supermarket, and fire and police stations where childen aged four to 12 can play at being adults.

Minopolis
Cineplexx Reichsbrücke, Wagramerstrasse 2. **Tel** 0810970270. **Open** Sep–Jun: 1–7pm Fri–Sun & hols except 1 Jan & 25 Dec; Jul & Aug: 1–7pm Wed–Sun & hols.

Children's Sports

Vienna has some excellent swimming baths, free for children under six, such as the Dianabad *(see p231)*. The **Familienbad Augarten** is a shallow pool and free for children between the ages of six and 15. However, it is not open to anyone else, except accompanying adults. The **Stadionbad** has three children's pools and a water slide and is generally free to children aged under 6.

In summer, you can swim in the Donauinsel coves *(see p231)*. During winter, you can bathe in the hot geysers at Thermalbad Oberlaa *(see p231)*.

In winter you can go ice-skating, at **Wiener Eislaufverein** or at **Vienna Ice Dreams** in front of the Rathaus. Then enjoy hot

chocolate in a Ringstrasse coffee house such as Café Prückel *(see pp60–63)* or Café Schwarzenberg *(see pp62–3)* on Kärntner Ring.

Vienna Ice Dreams
Rathausplatz. **Map** 5 A2. **Open** end of Jan–Mar: 9am–11pm daily.

Wiener Eislaufverein
Lothringerstrasse 28. **Map** 4 E2. **Tel** 71363530. **Open** mid-Oct–early Mar: 9am–9pm Tue, Thu, Fri, 9am–8pm Sat–Mon, 9am–10pm Wed.

Ice-skating at Wiener Eislaufverein

Entertainment

Although most theatre is performed in German, the **Märchenbühne der Apfelbaum** marionette theatre sometimes puts on shows in English of favourite fairy tales. Fairy stories with music and song can also be seen at the **Lilarum** puppet theatre. The **Wiener Konzerthaus** and Musikverein hold regular concerts for children six times a year on

The big wheel forms a familiar landmark in the Prater park *(see pp164–5)*

Saturday or Sunday afternoons. In November and December the Opera House *(see pp140–41)* and the Wiener Volksoper *(see p229)* have traditional children's programmes *(Kinderzyklus)*. Productions include Mozart's *The Magic Flute* and the most popular opera at the Volksoper, Engelbert Humperdink's *Hansel and Gretel*.

Several cinemas in Vienna show films in the original languages – look in the *Standard* newspaper's foreign films section. See also *Entertainment in Vienna* on pp226–31.

A Christmas market stall in front of the Rathaus *(see p132)*

Special Activities and Workshops

The Rathaus *(see p132)* has children's activities once a month (details from the town hall), and from mid-November there is a Christmas market *(see pp224–5)* which includes a children's train, pony rides and stalls selling toys, chestnuts and winter woollens. A Christmas workshop is held at the Volkshalle in the Rathaus from 9am to 7pm daily (to 4pm on 24 December). The activities include baking, silk painting and making decorations.

Attacus atlas at the Natural History Museum *(see pp130–31)*

Museums

Vienna has a range of museums that children will enjoy. The Natural History Museum *(see pp130–31)* boasts an impressive collection of fossils. The **Haus des Meeres** (Vienna Aquarium) contains over 3,000 sea creatures, including piranhas, crocodiles and sharks. Feeding time is 3pm.

Popular exhibits at the Völkerkundemuseum *(see p97)* include exotic musical instruments, African masks and figurines, and Montezuma's treasures. Children aged 10 and under are allowed to enter the **Kunst Haus Wien** free. Designed by Friedensreich Hundertwasser, this colourful private gallery has undulating

floors and bright paintings. The **Wiener Strassenbahnmuseum** (Vienna Tram Museum) houses the largest collection of vintage trams, light rail stock and buses in the world. The history of public transport in Vienna is shown through these vehicles, as well as through documents, a film and old photographs.

The Heeresgeschichtliches Museum *(see pp168–9)* contains a range of war memorabilia and the ZOOM Kindermuseum *(see p122)* offers interactive exhibits such as the Zoom Lab. Other options include the **Circus- und Clownmuseum**, just north of the Prater; dressing up events at the Sisi Museum in the Hofburg and at Schönbrunn Palace, experimenting with sight and sound at the Haus der Musik *(see p82)* and learning about the mechanics of theatre on a back stage tour at the Austrian Theatre Museum inLobkowitz Palace *(see p106)*.

Montezuma's headdress in the Völkerkundemuseum *(see p97)*

DIRECTORY

Swimming

Familienbad Augarten
Karl-Meissl-Gasse entrance, Augarten Park.
Map 2 E1.
Tel 3324258.
Open May–Sep: 10am–8pm daily.

Stadionbad
Prater, Krieau. **Tel** 7202102. **Open** May–Sep: 9am–7pm Mon–Fri (to 8pm Jul & Aug), 8am–7pm Sat, Sun & hols (to 8pm Jul & Aug) .

Entertainment

Lilarum
Göllnergasse 8. **Tel** 7102666.

Märchenbühne der Apfelbaum
Kirchengasse 41. **Map** 3 B1.
Tel 523172920.

Wiener Konzerthaus
Lothringerstrasse 20. **Map** 4 E2 & 6 E5. **Tel** 242002.

Museums

Haus des Meere
Esterházypark. **Map** 3 B2. **Tel** 5871417. **Open** 9am–6pm daily.

Kunst Haus Wien
Untere Weissgerberstrasse 13. **Tel** 7120491. **Open** 10am–7pm daily.

Wiener Strassenbahnmuseum
Ludwig-Kössler-Platz. **Tel** 790 946803. **Open** Year-round; see
W **wienerlinien.at for times.**

Circus- und Clownmuseum
Ilgplatz 7. **Tel** 6764068868.
Open, 10am–1pm Sun, 7–9pm every 1st or 3rd Thu of month.

Traditional horse-drawn open carriage, or Fiaker ▶

SURVIVAL
GUIDE

PRACTICAL INFORMATION

The best way to get around the centre of Vienna is on foot, because so many of the sights are in close proximity to each other. Museums and galleries are often crowded at weekends, so in order to avoid the tourist hordes, plan a visit during the week if possible. A useful map with up-to-date information on Vienna's museums and *Wien* *Programm*, a monthly listings guide, can be obtained free from tourist offices. Galleries and churches may be closed for refurbishment or special events, so it is wise to check opening hours in advance. Most shops in the city centre are open Monday to Friday from 8am to 6pm, and until 5pm on Saturdays. Embassy details are listed on page 239.

Visas and Passports

Austria is part of the Schengen common European border treaty, which means that travellers moving from one Schengen country to another are not subject to border controls. Schengen residents need only show an identity card when entering Austria. Visitors from the UK, Ireland, US, Canada, Australia or New Zealand will need to show a full passport. Travellers from these countries do not need visas for stays of up to three months. Non-EU citizens wishing to stay in the country longer than three months will need a visa, obtained from the Austrian embassy or consulate. These must be obtained in advance. All visitors should check requirements before travelling.

Customs Information

Nationals of EU countries, including Britain and Ireland, may take home unlimited quantities of duty-paid alcoholic drinks and tobacco goods as long as these are intended for their own consumption, and it can be proven that the goods are not intended for resale. Citizens of the US and Canada are limited to a duty-free

Tourist Information office in central Vienna

maximum of 200 cigarettes or 50 cigars. Americans may bring home 1 litre (33.8 fl oz) of wine or spirits, while Canadians are allowed 1.5 litres (50.7 fl oz) of wine, or a total of 1.14 litres (38.5 fl oz) of any alcoholic beverages, or 8.5 litres (287 fl oz) of beer or ale. Residents of other countries should ask their customs authority for more details. Information is included in the free *Zollinfo* brochure available at the Austrian border and allowances are listed on the Vienna Tourist Board website. The **Austrian Foreign Ministry** website also has information on tax-free goods.

Tourist Information

For help planning your visit you can contact the **Österreich Werbung** (Austrian National Tourist Office) and the **Wiener Tourismusverband** (Vienna Tourist Board). The main Tourist Board office is located on Albertinaplatz, just by the Hofburg palace complex. The information booth at Schwechat Airport *(see p246)* can provide maps, brochures, public transport schedules and assistance with hotel bookings. Tickets to musical and theatrical performances are sold at the Albertinaplatz office, including discounted rates for same-day events. The Austrian National Tourist Office can also assist with planning day trips from Vienna *(see pp178–81)*.

Wien Xtra-Youth Info offers plenty of multi-lingual information about cheap hostel accommodation, youth events, cinema, pop concert tickets and leisure activities.

Tourists walking near the Hofburg complex *(see pp98–103)*

Admission Fees and Opening Hours

Entrance prices vary considerably between museums. Any major temporary exhibition will involve an additional charge. Children pay roughly half price and there are also reductions for senior citizens and students with ID. Many sights are free for those under 19 years of age. Entrance fees are waived each year on 26 October – Austria's National Day. At the main entrance to the MuseumsQuartier *(see pp120–23)* you can buy combined tickets like the Duo (€17), which provides entry into the Leopold Museum and MUMOK, or the Kombi ticket (€25), which permits entry into these plus the Kunsthalle Wien and the Architekturzentrum Wien. Many museums close on Mondays or Tuesdays so check opening times in advance. For information on booking theatre and musical performances, see pages 226–9.

Accessibility to Public Conveniences

Viennese public toilets (signed as "WC") are clean, safe and well maintained. Most charge a nominal fee payable to an attendant or machine in small change. Many are open until late, especially those in underground stations. Vienna is famous for its "toilet art", and the beautiful Art Deco WC on the Graben, designed by Adolf Loos, is well worth a visit. Other lavatory highlights include the Opera Toilet at the Karlsplatz underground station and the Toilet of Modern Art in the Hundertwasserhaus housing estate.

Travellers with Special Needs

Vienna is relatively easy to navigate as a disabled traveller. Most of the major museums have special entrances and ramps for wheelchairs, and detailed information is available from the Vienna Tourist Office. Trams and buses are equipped with seats for disabled travellers *(see p254)*. Most major underground stations provide lifts unless otherwise indicated. Travellers who need assistance from airline staff should contact the airline at least 48 hours before they fly.

Senior Travellers

The Viennese are extremely respectful of older people. Senior travellers in Vienna are often given priority seating on public transport and many theatres, cinemas, attractions and museums offer generous discounts to travellers with senior ID. **Retired Backpackers** and **My Travel Companions**

serve independent world travellers over 50, including those headed for Austria.

Student Travellers

Vienna's main theatres offer cheap standing-room and unsold tickets at the box office before the performance. For popular shows, you may need to queue for several hours. A university identity card or international student card also entitles students to discounts on some museum admission fees and occasionally on rail tickets. Tourist offices provide a list of cheaper hotels as well as a list of Vienna's youth hostels *(see p195)*.

Electricity

Austria's voltage is 220V AC/50Hz and electrical sockets take European round 2-pin plugs.

Responsible Tourism

Austria is one of the world's leading destinations for sustainable tourism. About 70 per cent of energy is generated from renewable sources and about 60 per cent of all waste is recycled. In the capital itself, recycling bins are located throughout the city and there are numerous organic restaurants, food shops and even clothes stores that promote sustainable fashion.

The *Österreichisches Umweltzeichen* (Austrian Eco-Label) is a seal of approval awarded to hotels and restaurants that meet high environmental and waste-reduction standards. **Hotel Stadthalle**, near to Westbahnhof station, was the first hotel in Vienna to be awarded the *European Ecolabel* for its green credentials. This hotel uses solar panels to heat up water and collects rain water to flush its toilets.

For organic, locally grown produce, head to the market at Freyung in the 1st District open from 9am to 6pm every Friday and Saturday.

Market stall selling fruit and vegetables

DIRECTORY

Embassies and Consulates

Australia
Mattiellistrasse 2–4. **Map** 4 F2. **Tel** 506740.

Canada
Laurenzerberg 2. **Map** 6 E2. **Tel** 531383000.

Ireland
Rotenturmstrasse 16–18. **Map** 6 D3. **Tel** 7154246.

New Zealand
Mattiellistrasse 2–4/3. **Map** 4 F2. **Tel** 5053021.

United Kingdom
Jaurèsgasse 12. **Map** 4 F2. **Tel** 716130.

United States of America
Boltzmanngasse 16. **Map** 1 C3. **Tel** 313390.

Customs Information

Austrian Foreign Ministry
W bmeia.gv.at/en

Tourist Information

Austrian National Tourist Office London
9–11 Richmond Buildings, W1D 3HF. **Tel** 0845 101 1818.

Austrian National Tourist Office New York
120 West 45th Street, New York, NY 10036. **Tel** 212 575 7723.

Österreich Werbung
Margaretenstrasse 1. **Tel** 58866363.
W austriatourism.com

Wien Xtra-Youth Info
Babenbergerstrasse 1. **Map** 3 C1 & 5 B5. **Tel** 400084100.

Wiener Tourismusverband
Albertinaplatz. **Map** 4 D1 & 6 C4. **Tel** 24555 or 211140.

Senior Travellers

My Travel Companions
W mytravelcompanions.com

Retired Backpackers
W retiredbackpackers.com

Responsible Tourism

Hotel Stadthalle
Hackengasse 20, 1150. **Tel** 9824272.

Personal Security and Health

Vienna is one of Europe's safest capital cities and presents few risks to visitors who employ common sense. Crime rates are low and violence, delinquency and social disorder are rare. Austrian police are trusted and respected and are easy to contact for both minor incidents and in the case of an emergency. Most incidents involving visitors are crimes of opportunity, involving theft of personal belongings.

Police

Vienna's police are easily identifiable. They wear a blue uniform with a badge that reads Polizei (police) and an Austrian coat of arms and/or the Austrian flag, and will carry official ID. Most are helpful and many speak good English. Only surrender your passport and wallet, if needed, once at a police station. To report a crime, go in person to the nearest police station or call the emergency number, "133". You will need to give a detailed account of the incident and any items stolen. The police will prepare a statement, which you will need to sign. You can ask for an interpreter to translate any German language documents or terms you don't understand. Should the police need to detain you for questioning, be sure to request the services of a solicitor. You are also entitled to contact the local branch of your country's embassy or consulate for assistance (see p239).

Viennese police officers
in uniform

What to Be Aware Of

When looking after your personal safety use common sense. Be alert for pickpockets, particularly in the Prater at night, as well as at crowded markets, on public transport and at stations. Keep your cash in a discreet money belt and other valuables, such as cameras and mobile phones, well out of sight. Carry bags on your front with the strap worn across your shoulder.

There are a few places to steer clear of in Vienna. Unlit parks should be avoided at night. Illegal drug users often gather at Karlsplatz (underneath the Opera), but they generally present few problems for tourists. Prostitution is legal and is centred on the Gürtel ring-road near the Westbahnhof. Schwedenplatz can also be unsavoury after dark. Always avoid street gambling and illegal money changers, as they are likely to be using counterfeit notes. Street cons and late-night petty theft are common in the "Bermuda Triangle" area (see p86). Walking on Vienna's cycle lanes is forbidden and dangerous at any time of day or night.

Austria has experienced an increase in drug trafficking operations due to its strategic location in Europe. However, unlike some other European capitals, Vienna employs a zero-tolerance approach to drug misdemeanours. Anyone found in possession of drugs faces arrest and a court appearance followed by a heavy fine and/or a period of imprisonment.

English-speaking services and helplines available to visitors in Vienna include **Alcoholics Anonymous** and **Befrienders**, a helpline for anyone feeling lonely.

In an Emergency

Austrians are approachable, community-minded and often more than willing to help a person in need. Before you arrive in Austria, make a list of the emergency numbers you may require for events such as credit card theft, emergency repatriation or any specialized critical medical care you may need. Also take a photocopy of your passport, medical insurance and ID cards. Your country's consulate in Austria will be able to help in the first instance with most emergency situations. All underground stations have SOS points for emergencies from

Red Cross sign

which you can call the station supervisor or halt trains. Experienced and well-trained Red Cross (Rotes Kreuz) workers are also at hand to provide aid in the event of a natural disaster or emergency situation. For ambulance, fire and police emergency numbers, see the directory opposite.

Lost and Stolen Property

Victims of theft should visit the police station in **Stephansplatz** as soon as possile to file a crime report. The report will take some time to complete, but you will need a copy to claim against an insurance policy for stolen property. For items misplaced on the railways or the Schnellbahn, go to the lost-and-found office in person at the **Westbahnhof**. For lost or stolen credit cards, contact the issuing company's office (see p242). For items lost elsewhere, call the **Lost Property Bureau** (Fündburo) and consult your embassy for help (see p239).

Police car

Ambulance

Fire engine

Hospitals and Pharmacies

Vienna's many pharmacies are a good source of information on medicines and the treatment of minor ailments. To locate an *Apotheke* (pharmacy), look out for a bright red "A" sign; there is generally one on every major street. Pharmacies operate a night and Sunday rota system. Closed pharmacies will display the address of the nearest one open, and the number of the **Pharmacy Information Line**.

For more serious illnesses and injuries, call the **ViennaMed** doctors' hotline for visitors. Vienna has several private hospitals, clinics and medical centres, but the main facility is **Vienna General**, the largest hospital in Europe. Most doctors, paramedics, and clinic staff in Vienna speak English. An ambulance *(Rettungsdienst)* should be called in all medical emergencies by dialling "144" *(see Directory)*.

Minor Hazards

Most visitors to Vienna will only ever need medical advice for minor ailments. Commonly, these are sun-stroke during the city's hottest months, blisters from the excessive pavement-pounding and upset stomachs and headaches from too much rich food, wine and beer. Other annoyances over the summer include mosquitoes, noise from outdoor bars and clubs in the "Bermuda Triangle" and the pungent smells that bubble up from parts of the Danube Canal. Unlike some European cities, Vienna's water quality is excellent: freshly supplied from outlying mountains with purity assured.

Your hotel can recommend a walk-in clinic or doctor for minor medical issues.

Travel and Health Insurance

Medical care is expensive in Vienna, so it pays to be fully insured for health purposes, however short your visit. Britain, like many other European countries, has a reciprocal arrangement with Austria whereby emergency hospital treatment is free upon presentation of a British passport. Keep all receipts for medical services, as you may need to claim costs back after you return home. EU citizens must carry a European Health Insurance Card (EHIC) to make use of medical services. The card comes with a booklet of advice and information on the procedure for claiming free medical treatment.

A travel insurance policy will also provide cover for other expenses and losses. Health and travel policies vary dramatically, so be sure to shop around for a policy that suits your particular needs, especially if you are planning on participating in adventure sports, or if you have an existing medical condition.

Banking and Local Currency

As you'd expect from a thriving European capital city, the financial services available in Vienna are excellent and funds are easily accessible. Credit and debit cards are widely accepted in major establishments, including restaurants, theatres and hotels. However, it is not unusual for smaller stores and cafés to insist on cash. ATMs are easily found in the city centre around the main tourist and shopping areas, together with money-changing machines and a number of bureaux de change.

Banking and Bureaux de Change

The best place to change money is at a bank. Although you can use travel agents, hotels and bureaux de change (Wechselstuben), banks offer a better rate. Commission applies on all currency changed. The two banks that have the most branches – Bank Austria and Erste Bank – charge either 3% commission or a minimum handling fee of €5.50.

Exchanging a larger amount of money at one time can save on commission. You can also exchange foreign bank notes for euros at the automatic money-changing machines (Change-o-mats) found in the city centre and at main railway stations.

Most banks are open from 8am to 3pm Monday to Friday (to 5:30pm on Thursdays). Some banks, generally those located at the main railway stations and at airports (see Directory), stay open for longer.

The façade of Bank Austria in central Vienna

ATMs

ATMs are easy to find in Vienna's central shopping and main tourist areas. They accept a wide range of debit and credit cards; to find a cash point that accepts your card, check the logos on the machine. ATMs give instructions in German, English and French and increasingly also in Italian, Swedish and Spanish. The daily limit for withdrawals is usually £250. A fee is charged for each withdrawal. Charges for overseas usage vary, so check with your bank before you travel.

To use an ATM safely, only withdraw cash in daylight at a centrally located machine and never carry your PIN with your card. Use your body to shield the transaction from the queue behind. Don't count your money at the ATM or walk away with cash clearly exposed.

Credit Cards, Debit Cards & Traveller's Cheques

Credit cards, including **VISA, MasterCard, American Express** and **Diners Club**, are accepted in most hotels, shops and major restaurants. Many shops also accept debit cards. However, it is advisable to carry some cash, which is often preferred by smaller establishments such as side-street boutiques and cafés. Travellers planning to use a credit card should always check first to make sure it is accepted. Often a minimum expenditure applies (such as €10) when making a payment in this way. Credit card companies may also charge a fee for using the card overseas. These

charges can vary dramatically, so ask your credit card company about transaction costs before using your card abroad. Be sure to report lost or stolen cards to your own or nearest Austrian bank.

Although the popularity of traveller's cheques has declined, these fixed-amount cheques remain a safe way to carry large sums of money. A minimum commission applies, so it is uneconomical to change small sums. Cheques can be cashed at any bank or bureau de change. Choose a well-known name such as American Express. Traveller's cheques can usually be replaced if they are lost or stolen, as long as the issuing receipt showing the serial number of the cheque is retained.

Currency

The euro (€) is the common currency of the European Union. It went into general circulation on 1 January 2002, initially for 12 participating countries. Austria was one of those 12 countries taking the euro in 2002, with the Austrian schilling phased out in the same year.

EU members using the euro as sole official currency are known as the Eurozone. Several EU members have opted out of joining this common currency.

Euro notes are identical throughout the Eurozone, each denomination portraying designs of fictional architectural structures. The coins, however, have one side identical (the value side), and one side with an image unique to each country.

Bank Notes

Euro bank notes have seven denominations. The €5 note (grey in colour) is the smallest, followed by the €10 note (pink), €20 note (blue), €50 note (orange), €100 note (green), €200 note (yellow) and €500 note (purple). All notes show the stars of the European Union.

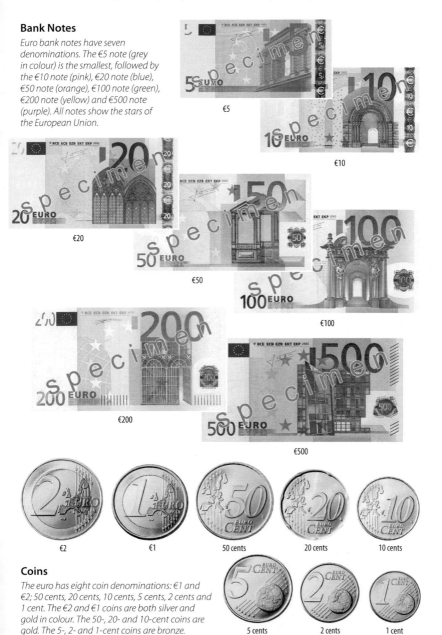

€5

€10

€20

€50

€100

€200

€500

€2

€1

50 cents

20 cents

10 cents

Coins

The euro has eight coin denominations: €1 and €2; 50 cents, 20 cents, 10 cents, 5 cents, 2 cents and 1 cent. The €2 and €1 coins are both silver and gold in colour. The 50-, 20- and 10-cent coins are gold. The 5-, 2- and 1-cent coins are bronze.

5 cents

2 cents

1 cent

Communications and Media

Staying in touch in Vienna is easy. Making national and international telephone calls is uncomplicated, thanks to well-organized networks of mobile and landline services. Post offices across the city offer a range of mailing options. Vienna is also saturated with high-speed Internet and Wi-Fi networks and well served by TV (terrestrial and satellite) and radio channels, plus a range of domestic and foreign-run newspapers and magazines.

Touch-screen public telephone

International and Local Telephone Calls

Making calls within Austria and to overseas numbers is straightforward but can be pricey. For international calls it is best to avoid phoning from hotels as they tend to add a hefty surcharge. Cheap-rate calling times for international calls from Austria is between 6pm and 8am and at weekends; for domestic calls it is between 8pm and 6am, and weekends. A cheap way to make calls to international numbers from a regular phone is with a phonecard, which can be purchased from any post office or from newsagents. Travellers are also increasingly using VoIP

(Voice over Internet protocol) services such as Skype. This system permits you to make phone calls anywhere in the world from a computer providing you have the right software installed and all the necessary adaptors and hardware.

Mobile Phones

To guarantee that your mobile phone will work in Austria, make sure you have a quad-band phone. Tri-band phones from outside the US are also usually compatible, but a US tri-band phone may have limited global coverage. Contact your service provider for clarification.

To use your mobile phone abroad, you may need to ask your provider to enable roaming on your phone. Bear in mind that you will be charged for both incoming and outgoing calls, and you pay a substantial premium for the international leg of the call. Remember, also, that Austrian electrical sockets take a European round 2-pin plug, and you may need an adaptor in order to charge your phone.

If your handset is unlocked, you may be able to purchase a SIM card from one of the local mobile

phone providers, such as **A1 Telekom, tele.ring** or **Yesss**. Pay-as-you-go handsets can be bought from supermarkets such as Merkur or Hofer for around €15–20.

Public Telephones

As in other parts of the world, public payphones are now not easily found in Vienna, but transport hubs such as main railway stations still have them. They usually take debit or credit cards, as well as 10-, 20- and 50-cent, and €1- and €2- coins.

Most public phones have instructions in English and other languages. Directories are usually missing or too tatty to use. Post offices have directories in good condition; your hotel may help you find a number, or contact directory enquiries *(see Reaching the Right Number, below)*.

Internet Access

Almost every major hotel, restaurant and public space in Vienna is a Wi-Fi hotspot. For an up-to-date list of locations, visit the **Freewave** website. A number of hotels charge a daily fee for Wi-Fi access but many provide it free for guests. Some

Tourists using Internet café in central Vienna

Reaching the Right Number

- For directory enquiries (including EU numbers), dial 118877.
- For international directory enquiries (excluding EU numbers), dial 0900 118877.
- All directory enquiries cost €2.17 per minute.
- For wake-up service, dial 0900 979720.
- To phone the **USA**, dial 001 followed by the number.
- To ring the **UK**, dial 0044 followed by the number (omit the 0 from the area code).

- To ring **Australia**, dial 0061 followed by the number.
- To ring **New Zealand**, dial 0064 followed by the number.
- To ring the **Irish Republic**, dial 00353 followed by the number.
- The front pages of the A–Z telephone directory list codes for each country.

of the best spots in which to log on for free are the many bars, restaurants and coffee shops around the MuseumsQuartier. Vienna also boasts a rich supply of Internet cafés. Some popular options in or near Innere Stadt include **BIGnet Internet**, **Café Einstein**, **Café Stein**, **Café-Bar Blue Box** and **Surfland Internet Café**. Tourists may also use computers in public facilities such as libraries and business centres, where access is usually charged at an hourly rate.

Postal Services

Austrian post offices are clearly identifiable by their bold yellow signs. They provide postage stamps *(Briefmarken)* and registered letters, and arrange the delivery of packages. Phonecards and collectors' stamps are also sold. Other services include *Post Restante* or *Postlagernd* (to be called for) and the cashing of travellers' cheques and giro cheques up to a maximum of €180 per cheque. Foreign currency is handled by the larger post offices.

The Austrian postal system is reliable and efficient. Postage is charged by weight. Customers can choose between two postal tariffs: priority and economy. For quick delivery of a package, international couriers such as **DHL** and **FedEx** offer a reliable service.

Post office opening hours are generally between 7am and 7pm Monday to Friday. Larger post offices are also open on Saturday mornings (not for financial dealings). The Innere Stadt's **Central Post Office** is open 7am–10pm Monday–Friday and 9am–10pm Saturday and Sunday. The post office at Westbahnhof is open 7am–9pm Mon–Fri, 9am–6pm Saturday and 9am–2pm Sunday. The post office at Schwechat Airport is open 8am–8pm daily.

Postage stamps are also sold at newsagents. Letters for Europe weighing up to 20g cost 70 cents, as do postcards. You'll need a €1.40 stamp for the rest of the world. Registered letters cost €2.85.

Newspapers and Magazines

Tabloid *Kronen Zeitung* is, by far, Austria's most widely read newspaper. The second-largest, *Der Kurier*, is less sensationalist and focuses on national and international news, politics and current affairs. *Die Presse* is the oldest of Austria's national dailies, as well as the best-selling quality paper, while independent broadsheet *Der Standard* is popular with university students. *Falter* is Vienna's main listings magazine. Papers, including foreign language magazines and periodicals, can be bought from a *Tabak Trafik* (newsagent), kiosks or, on Sundays, street vendors. Online news magazines, such as the monthly English-language *viennareview.net*, are increasingly popular.

TV and Radio

Austria has two main radio stations. Ö1 specializes in classical music and Ö3 plays popular tunes. Radio FM4 broadcasts in English from 1am to 2pm daily on 103.8 MHz. Vienna Cable Radio transmits on FM100.8. Although terrestrial broadcast TV is German-language, many international films are shown with subtitles. Almost every hotel and sports bar has satellite television, on which large numbers of international programmes and English-language channels are broadcast.

Distinctive yellow sign outside one of Vienna's post offices

National and foreign newspapers on sale at a street kiosk

DIRECTORY

Mobile Phones

A1 Telekom
W a1.net

tele.ring
W telering.at

Yesss
W yesss.at

Internet Access

BIGnet Internet
Hoher Markt 8. **Map** 2 E5 & 6 D2.
Tel 5332939.
W bignet.at

Café Einstein
Rathausplatz 4. **Map** 1 C5 & 5 A2.
Tel 4052626.
W einstein.at

Café Stein
Währingerstrasse 6-8. **Map** 1 A2 &
5 A1.Tel 3197241.
W cafe-stein.com

Café-Bar Blue Box
Richtergasse 8. **Map** 3 A2.
Tel 5227048.
W bluebox.at

Freewave
Tel 8040134. W freewave.at

Surfland Internet Café
Krugerstrasse 10. **Map** 6 D5.
Tel 5127701.
W surfland.at

Postal Services

Central Post Office
Fleischmarkt 19. **Map** 2 E5 & 6 D2.
Tel 05776771010 or 0810010100
(for general information).
W post.at

DHL
Tel 0820550505. W dhl.at

FedEx
Tel 0800123800.
W fedex.com/at

GETTING TO VIENNA

Forming a strategic commercial and transit hub between Eastern and Western Europe, Vienna is well served by air, water and rail. Direct flights link to every major European city as well as to North America, Canada, Japan and Australia. An efficient hydrofoil runs between Vienna and Bratislava and river cruises arrive from Romania, Bulgaria, Germany, Budapest, Slovakia and Prague. Vienna has good motorway routes to the rest of Europe, but if you are arriving from neighbouring Germany, note that the Austrian motorway speed limit is only 130 km (80 miles) per hour. Flights into Bratislava, just 65 km (40 miles) from the centre of Vienna, arrive frequently and are often competitively priced. Taxis, trains and airport shuttle buses transfer arriving air travellers from Bratislava Central Station to Vienna.

The modern exterior of Schwechat International Airport

Arriving by Air

Vienna's main airport is well served by most international airlines. Several flights per day link London Heathrow with Vienna's airport at Schwechat. The main airlines with regular direct flights between the UK and Vienna are **British Airways** and **Lufthansa**, along with several low-cost carriers such as **easyJet** and **airberlin**. The main Austrian carrier is **Austrian Airlines**.

   Travellers from the United States can choose direct flights with **United** from New York, Orlando and Atlanta. Austrian Airlines flies direct to New York and Chicago. There are also direct flights from Toronto.

   As an alternative to arriving at Schwechat, and often with cheaper airfares, Bratislava's Milan Rastislav Štefánik Airport is less than 2 hours' drive from central Vienna with regular domestic and international flights from Europe, the Middle East and North Africa.

Schwechat Airport

Schwechat International, Vienna's only airport, is located 19 km (12 miles) southeast of the city centre. With two terminals, the airport is used by over 100 airlines. As one of Europe's most modern airport facilities, Schwechat International is served by the super-efficient CAT (City Airport Train), which runs to and from Wien Mitte station.

   A well-maintained road also connects with central Vienna, and drivers will find a fuel station, auto repair shop, parking and several car rental outlets onsite. The airport itself is clearly signed and easy to navigate, with all the facilities that you would expect, including restaurants, duty free shops, a supermarket, banks and tourist information offices. The well-stocked supermarket is open 7 days a week from 6:30am until 10pm, including holidays. The airport is fully equipped for disabled travellers.

Bratislava Airport

With its close proximity to Vienna, Bratislava's upgraded Milan Rastislav Štefánik Airport has become a popular transit point for visitors to the Austrian capital. Located 9 km (5.6 miles) northeast of Bratislava, Milan R Š is Slovakia's main international airport.

   Scheduled flights, operated by **Travel Service Airlines Slovakia** (as Smart Wings)**, Air Onix, Danube Wings, Norwegian Air Shuttle** and **Ryanair**, connect to Europe and the Middle East.

   Most nationalities do not need a visa to enter Slovakia. You will, however, need a valid passport or identity card. For detailed information, check with your consulate before travelling.

Tickets and Fares

To get the best deal on air fares, shop around and book well in advance. Cheaper tickets on scheduled flights can often be booked up to six months before the date of travel. Discount agencies also sell cut-price APEX tickets at less than the normal full fare. Charter flights are often available at very competitive prices. No-frills budget airlines represent excellent value for money, although many charge extra for checked luggage, stowed sporting equipment, priority boarding and other services. Meals are also an additional charge. Being flexible on the date and time of travel allows passengers to get the best from low-cost airlines. Another

Shopping mall at Schwechat International Airport

option is a weekend package, which will often include a two-night stay at a good Viennese hotel for less than the price of an economy-class airline ticket.

Transport from Airport into Town

From Schwechat International, you can get to Vienna city centre either by taxi or **CAT (City Airport Train)**. Taxis take about 20 minutes to reach central Vienna and cost around €32. The CAT train departs every 30 minutes from the basement level of the airport to Wien Mitte. It costs €14 each way if you pay on the train, or €11 if booked in advance online.

The cheapest means of transport into the city is the Schnellbahn train, which also departs from the basement level of the airport. Running every half hour, the train takes roughly 30 minutes to connect with Wien Mitte and stops at Praterstern-Wien Nord. Tickets cost €4.20. Buses run from about

6am–midnight every 30 minutes to Schwedenplatz, Meidling and Westbahnhof stations. A one-way ticket costs around €8; pay the driver on board.

From Milan Rastislav Štefánik Airport, bus shuttle transfers take 75 minutes and cost €7.70 each way. Shuttle buses depart from the terminal building at about 30-minute intervals from 6am to 11pm. Seasonal services offer the option of the **Twin City Liner** catamaran, which takes 75 minutes and costs €20–€35 one way. However, a year-round train service remains the fastest option at around 1 hour. Trains run from 4.24am to 11.20pm nearly every hour. A single journey costs €21.20. Taxis from the airport cost around €90 per person.

Slovakia is part of the Schengen agreement, which means residents from other Schengen countries are not subject to border controls. Other nationalities will need to show their passport when crossing the border.

CAT (City Airport Train) linking Schwechat to the centre of Vienna

Arriving by Rail

Vienna's rail network is in the process of being restructured and construction is under way for a main railway station to replace the former Südbahnhof. The new station, called the Wien Hauptbahnhof, will serve all international routes into Vienna and is located at Südtirolerplatz, south of the city centre. It is already partly operational and is due to be completed by the end of 2015.

Until the new station is fully open international routes are operating from one of several stations located around the city. Routes from western Austria and Germany arrive at the Westbahnhof, located to the west of the city, with connections to the U3 and U6 underground lines, the Schnellbahn and several tram and bus routes.

International routes from southern Europe arrive in Vienna at Bahnhof Meidling, which is conveniently situated on the U6 underground line in south Vienna. Routes from northern Europe terminate at Franz-Josefs-Bahnhof in the north of the city. The station is served by the Schnellbahn and the cross-city D tram that goes directly to the Ringstrasse. Trains from Neusiedl am See, Marchegg, Bratislava and Brno stop at the Wien Hauptbahnhof at Südtirolerplatz, within walking distance of the Belvedere Palace. The Wien Hauptbahnhof has connections to the Schnellbahn and D and O tramlines. As soon as the

Eurolines coach connecting Vienna with the rest of Europe

new Hauptbahnhof is fully operational, the Westbahnhof will then serve domestic routes only. Check online at www.oebb.at or www.hauptbahnhof-wien.at for more information on how the works affect your travel plans.

All the stations have taxi ranks and a range of facilities that include shops, luggage storage, food outlets and cash points. The travel agency *(Reisebüro)* at Wien Mitte station is open from 9am to 7pm Monday to Friday and can provide travel information as well as assistance with booking hotel rooms. Once in Vienna, visitors can find rail information in English by calling the **Öbb Call Centre**.

Ticket offices can be found in all larger railway stations. There are many types of tickets, such as group, family and tourist travel, with or without concessions. When buying a ticket, seek advice at the ticket office as to which one is best for you. You can also book tickets through the Öbb Call Center or online at the **Austrian Federal Railways** website. Austria's Railjet high-speed trains, which run between Austria, Germany, Hungary and

Switzerland, offer special fares on a limited number of seats. These need to be booked well ahead (up to 90 days in advance).

On overnight rail travel to Vienna it is possible, for a small fee, to reserve a seat or a bed up to two months before travelling. Snacks are sometimes sold on board and most overnight routes will include a Continental breakfast if you are booked on a sleeper or couchette. Expect to pay around €40 for a trip from Vienna to Budapest, a journey of 3½ hours.

Arriving by Coach

Vienna's main coach station, the Vienna International Bus Terminal (VIB), is located close to Erdberg U3 underground station. Services, run by **Eurolines**, arrive here from most major European cities including Budapest, London and Paris. Prices vary, but expect to pay around €75 from London to Vienna (senior discounts apply). **Postbus** runs routes throughout Austria and Slovakia. Coaches arrive in Vienna at the Wien Hauptbahnhof bus terminal.

Arriving by Car

Austrian roads are well constructed with good, clear signage and ample lighting for travelling after dark. Carrying your driver's licence is mandatory in Austria. You must also have car registration documents and insurance papers at hand. Visitors need an overseas extension of their annual insurance, such as a Green Card. An international driver's licence is required for anyone using a language written in a script other than Roman. Seatbelts must be worn at all times. Note that children

A train near Ollersbach, en route to Vienna

up to the age of 12 or under 1.5 m (5 ft) must be seated in suitable child-safety seats.

Tolls are compulsory on all motorways in Austria and a *vignette* sticker, should be purchased and attached to the inside of the windscreen before travel on motorways. *Vignettes* are available for 10 days (€8.50), two months (€24.80) or one year (€82.70) and can be purchased at fuel stations and newsagents. All hire cars should have a *vignette* provided. Drivers without a valid *vignette* can be fined up to €3,000.

There are four main routes into Vienna by road. The Südautobahn is made up of the A2 and A23 motorways, it provides access into the city from the south. The Donau-uferautobahn (A22) is the main northen motorway. The A1 (Westautobahn) and the A4 (Ostautobahn) enter Vienna from the west and east respectively. Motorways

converge on the outer ring road (Gürtel). The city centre is marked *Zentrum*. The **Austrian Automobile Club (ÖAMTC)** provides daily reports on road conditions.

Arriving by Boat

From April to October you can arrive in Vienna by boat along the Danube from Bratislava, the Wachau and the Budapest. Companies such as **Viking River Cruises** also run cruises into Vienna from Budapest. Boats dock at the **DDSG–Blue Danube** landing station at the Reichsbrücke bridge. The landing station is close to the Vorgartenstrasse U-Bahn station on the U1 line. An information counter at the dock sells tickets and provides city maps and schedule information. A seasonal hydrofoil links Vienna, Visegrad, Budapest and Bratislava. Discounts apply for children (2–14) and students (ID required).

DIRECTORY

Arriving by Rail

Austrian Federal Railways
W oebb.at

Öbb Call Centre
Tel 051717 (rail information).

Arriving by Coach

Eurolines
W eurolines.com

Postbus
W postbus.at

Arriving by Car

Austrian Automobile Club
W oeamtc.at

Arriving by Boat

DDSG–Blue Danube
W ddsg-blue-danube.at

Viking River Cruises
W vikingrivercruises.co.uk

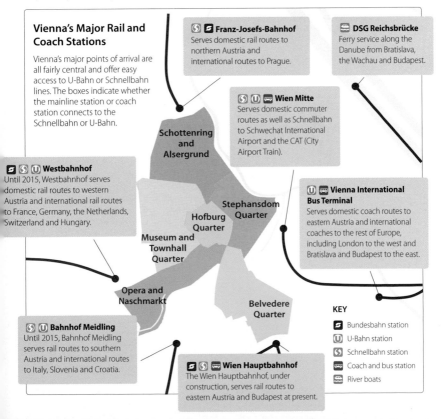

Vienna's Major Rail and Coach Stations

Vienna's major points of arrival are all fairly central and offer easy access to U-Bahn or Schnellbahn lines. The boxes indicate whether the mainline station or coach station connects to the Schnellbahn or U-Bahn.

Franz-Josefs-Bahnhof
Serves domestic rail routes to northern Austria and international routes to Prague.

DSG Reichsbrücke
Ferry service along the Danube from Bratislava, the Wachau and Budapest.

Wien Mitte
Serves domestic commuter routes as well as Schnellbahn to Schwechat International Airport and the CAT (City Airport Train).

Westbahnhof
Until 2015, Westbahnhof serves domestic rail routes to western Austria and international rail routes to France, Germany, the Netherlands, Switzerland and Hungary.

Vienna International Bus Terminal
Serves domestic coach routes to eastern Austria and international coaches to the rest of Europe, including London to the west and Bratislava and Budapest to the east.

Schottenring and Alsergrund

Stephansdom Quarter

Hofburg Quarter

Museum and Townhall Quarter

Opera and Naschmarkt

Belvedere Quarter

Bahnhof Meidling
Until 2015, Bahnhof Meidling serves rail routes to southern Austria and international routes to Italy, Slovenia and Croatia.

Wien Hauptbahnhof
The Wien Hauptbahnhof, under construction, serves rail routes to eastern Austria and Budapest at present.

KEY
🚆 Bundesbahn station
Ⓤ U-Bahn station
Ⓢ Schnellbahn station
🚌 Coach and bus station
⛴ River boats

GETTING AROUND VIENNA

With so much to see, compact central Vienna is best explored on foot. Paths are well maintained with adequate signage marking major sights and attractions. Traffic-free areas offer pedestrians the opportunity to shop and sightsee away from tooting horns and congestion. Numerous cobblestone plazas, gardens, parks and cafés offer plenty of places to stop, draw breath, check the map and enjoy a cup of coffee. Viennese drivers are dissuaded from driving through the city centre by a complicated and frustrating one-way system and sky-high parking tariffs. However, if the legwork gets too much, Vienna's network of buses comprehensively crisscross the city centre. The underground system is also clean, efficient and easy to use. As part of the City of Vienna Transport Authority's interconnecting public transport system, it is supplemented by a coordinated tram and bus network. Services operate from 5am to 12:30am to a highly reliable timetable.

Tourists walking in the gardens at Belvedere Palace

Green Travel

As one of the greenest cities in Europe, Vienna has invested heavily in an impressive array of environmentally-friendly transport initiatives. A highly efficient public transport system and 1,500 km (900 miles) of bicycle paths offer viable eco-friendly alternatives to driving through the city. Over 1,000 rechargeable electrically-powered bicycles (an environmentally sound rental scheme) are available for hire at very affordable rates from nearly 100 strategically positioned stations throughout the city *(see Cycling)*. Almost every part of the metropolis is accessible by public transport and timetables for trams, buses, underground and trains neatly dovetail each other. Inexpensive tickets and discounted fares for combined use of all modes of transport ensure the public network is very popular for locals and tourists alike.

The ultimate green transportation in Vienna are the pedicab taxis known as **Faxi Taxi** *(see p252)*, which operate in the city centre around major sights and attractions. Powered solely by a cycle mechanism, the Faxi Taxi is also cheaper than a motorized taxi. The only drawback is that Faxis accommodate just two passengers with light hand luggage.

Parking, a rare and expensive option in Vienna, also serves as a deterrent to drivers. Indeed, an entire vehicle-free housing development has been built in the capital. "Bike City" focuses on the needs of cyclists with the whole complex benefitting from easy access bicycle paths and excellent direct links to public transportation.

Walking

There is no better way to see the city than to walk around Vienna at your own pace. Major sights and attractions are conveniently clustered together in close proximity and attractive streets are peppered with inviting cafés and cake shops. The area around Kärntner Strasse, Stock-im-Eisen-Platz and Graben is entirely traffic free. Numerous tour companies offer multi-lingual guided walks with a wide variety of fascinating cultural themes and intriguing historical topics. Contact the *Wiener Tourismusverband (see p238)* for more information.

Exploring Vienna on foot is not without its hazards; traffic rarely stops at pedestrian crossings, so it is wise to be cautious when crossing the road. British and Australian visitors should remember that motorists drive on the right. In addition, keep an eye out for cyclists; they often share the pavement with pedestrians and, if they are travelling at some speed, may not have time to stop if you stray onto their section of the pavement. At all times, pedestrians should take care not to walk along bike paths and tramlines, as this is prohibited. On the Ringstrasse, trams run against the traffic, so looking both ways is essential. Jaywalking is illegal in Vienna, and this law is enforced by police – even if the roads are quiet. To avoid a hefty fine, it is important to abide by the signals at the pedestrian crossings; do not cross a road when a red figure is showing.

Cycling in the Prater

By Fiaker

Traditional horse-drawn open carriages or Fiakers, many driven by a bowler-hatted and whiskered coachman, are a novel and relaxing way to get around. Remember that part of the route is on the busy Ringstrasse. You can hire a Fiaker at Stephansplatz, Heldenplatz or Albertinaplatz, but to avoid an unpleasant surprise, agree the price and length of the trip with the driver before you set off. Even a short trip can be costly.

Cycling

With its plethora of bike paths, Vienna is a great city for cyclists, as long as the main roads and tramlines are avoided. A 7-km (4-mile) cycle path round the Ringstrasse takes you past many historic sights, and there are also bike paths to the Prater *(see pp164–5)* and to the Hundertwasserhaus *(see p166)*. If you are a keen cyclist, a booklet called *Radkarte* illustrates all of Vienna's cycle routes and is available from a number of bookshops. Bicycles can be rented at some train stations and discounts are given with a train ticket, or from any of the 100 or so **Citybike** stations. To use a Citybike, you need to register first with a debit or credit card, either online or at the station's terminal, for a one-off fee of €1; when the bike is returned, the charge (maximum €4 per hour) is calculated automatically and debited from your account.

City cycle tours take place during summer *(see below)*. Pedal Power's 3-hour city tours leave from Schillerplatz/ Elisabethstrasse at 09:45am every day.

Guided Tours

Vienna Sightseeing and **Cityrama** are two of the city's largest tour operators, and their buses and coaches are a common sight – especially during the summer months.

Trams are a good way of seeing the 19th-century buildings in the Ringstrasse because you can choose where to get on and off. Organized tours are run by the **Tram Museum** in a 1920s tram from a meeting point at Otto Wagner's Karlsplatz Pavilions *(see pp150–51)*. Private groups may also hire a vintage tram to go to the Prater or a *Heuriger* (tavern) or simply to tour the city.

DDSG–Blue Danube organizes tours on the Danube River and the Danube Canal to sights such as Otto Wagner's Nussdorf locks. From April to October the **Twin City Liner**, a high-speed catamaran, makes a round trip to Bratislava three times a day.

In the summer there are guided walking tours, in English, French or Italian, with a variety of themes. From May to September, cycling enthusiasts can book tours through Pedal Power *(see Cycling)*. Tours are available in German or English, but Italian or French can be arranged. **Segway public tours** run from April to October, and the 3-hour excursion includes a brief lesson on how to ride the Segway personal transport.

Driving

As in many European cities, drivers in Vienna are aggressive and single-minded. Vehicles swap lanes at speed, lose patience easily and show little regard for other road users. Drivers need to be alert at all times.

Priority is always given to the right unless a "yellow diamond" indicates otherwise. Trams, buses, police cars, fire engines and ambulances all have right of way. Vienna's speed limit is 50 km (30 miles) per hour. Police carry out checks with infra-red guns and can issue fines on the spot. The limit for alcohol is 0.5 mg per ml of blood (about 1/3 litre [11 fl oz] of beer or 1–2 glasses of wine). Spot checks are common and anyone exceeding the limit is likely to face a hefty fine and the loss of their licence.

Drivers who belong to an internationally affiliated automobile association can make use of breakdown services provided by ÖAMTC (the Austrian Automobile Club). Radio station FM4 has traffic news in English.

Parking

Apart from Sundays, when shops are closed, finding a parking spot in Vienna is a very frustrating and time-consuming exercise. *Anfang* (beginning) and *Ende* (end) signs are posted everywhere, and it is prohibited to park between them. You'll need to

Car park sign

go to the police or telephone the pound (76043) if your car is clamped or towed. The City of Vienna operates a park and pay scheme in districts 1–9 and 20 from 9am–10pm Mondays to Fridays *(see p252)*. Parking disks are sold at newsagents (*Tabak Trafiken*), some banks and petrol stations. Usually, a maximum stay of 2 hours is allowed in any space. In other districts, a blue line by the kerb indicates a pay and display scheme. Note that car parks are expensive.

Faxi Taxis lined up on a Vienna street

Taxis

Taxis in Vienna are instantly recognizable by a TAXI sign on the roof. If available for hire, the sign will be illuminated. Taxis can be found at ranks across the city but they cannot be hailed in the street. Alternatively, one can be summoned by phone – there are three numbers: 313000, 40100 or 60160. For a short trip, expect to pay from €7 to €10 with additional charges for extra passengers, luggage, and late-night and weekend journeys. Tipping about 10 per cent of the fare is customary, rounding up to the nearest euro. A trip to the airport costs around €32.

Vienna's Faxi Taxi pedicab is a quick way to get around the centre of the city *(see p250)*. Find them at taxi stands or flag one down in the street. Journeys up to 2 km (1 mile) cost €5. One-way journeys more than 2 km cost €10.

Public Transport

Vienna's transport network is made up of trams *(Strassen-bahn)*, buses *(Autobus)*, underground (U-Bahn) and trains (S-Bahn). The city's transport system, **Wiener Linien**, works largely on an honesty system. There are no ticket barriers at stations, allowing passengers to hop on and off. Formal checks by transport authority staff do take place – you'll be asked for your *Fahrschein* (ticket) by a uniformed guard. Anyone caught without a valid ticket is fined €103 and charged. Smoking is banned in stations and on public transport. Children under 6 travel for free year-round while those aged under 15 travel free of charge on Sundays and holidays. The latter also qualify for half-price single tickets. Rush hour runs weekdays from about 7am to 9:30am, then again from about 4:30pm to 6:30pm.

Tickets and Travel Cards

Vienna's public transport ticketing system is less confusing than it appears at first glance. Buying a ticket in advance is the easiest option. Tickets are sold at newsagents *(Tabak Trafiken)*, from ticket machines at stations or over the counter at U-Bahn and S-Bahn offices. Vienna city is zone 100 of the regional fare system; a standard ticket covers all areas of the city and allows passengers to change trains and lines and switch from the underground to a tram or a bus, as long as they take the most direct route and don't break their journey. A single ticket costs €2.10 bought in advance or €2.20 on board.

Weekly season tickets (€15.80) are valid from 12am Monday to 9am the next Monday. These are good value for anyone using public transport for more than four days. The *8-Tage-Karte* (€35.80) is best for groups of travellers and consists of eight strips which, when stamped, are valid for a day. Up to eight people may stamp the same ticket; start with strip one or you will invalidate the other seven. Also available are 24-, 48- and 72-hour tickets costing €7.10, €12.40, and €15.40 respectively. The Vienna Card (€19.90) is a 72-hour ticket valid on all transport. It comes with additional discounts and benefits and only needs punching once.

DIRECTORY

Green Travel

Faxi Taxi
Tel 0699/12005624.
W **faxi.at**

Cycling

Citybike
Tel 0810/500 500.
W **citybikewien.at**

Pedal Power
Tel 7297234.
W **pedalpower.at**

Royal Tours
Herrengasse 1–3. **Tel** 710 4606. W **royaltours.at**

Guided Tours

Cityrama
Börsegasse 1. **Map** 2 D4 & 5 B1. Opernpassage, Top 3. **Map** 5 C5
Tel 5047500.

DDSG–Blue Danube
Handelskai 265.
Tel 58880. W **ddsg-blue-danube.at**

Segway tours
Elisabethstrasse 13.
Tel 7297234.
W **segway-vienna.at**

Tram Museum
Tel 790946803.

Twin City Liner

Schiffsstation Wien City, Schwedenplatz, between Marienbrücke and Schwedenbrücke bridges.
Map 6 E2. **Tel** 72710137.

Vienna Sightseeing Tours
Stelzhamergasse 4–11.
Map 4 F1 & 6 F3.
Weyringergasse 28A–30, entrance Goldeggasse 29.
Map 4 E4. **Tel** 7124683.

Driving

ÖAMTC
W **oamtc.at**

Parking

Am Hof. **Map** 2 D5 & 5 C2. Börsegasse.
Map 2 D4 & 5 C1. Universitätsring.
Map 1 C5 & 5 A2. Morzinplatz.
Map 2 E4 & 6 D. Stephansplatz 6.
Map 2 E5 & 6 D3.
Other car parks are shown on the Street Finder map *(see pp262–7)*.

Public Transport

Wiener Linien
W **wienerlinien.at**

Travelling by Underground

Vienna's underground system (U-Bahn) is one of Europe's most modern networks and is a clean, fast and reliable way of crossing the city. Construction commenced in the late 1960s, with the inaugural journey taking place in the mid-1970s. It has since undergone expansion and refurbishment in phases to a total length of 75 km (50 miles). The U-Bahn now has 105 stations with ongoing development plans into 2019.

The Underground System

The U-Bahn is generally safe (see p240), but in case of emergencies there are help points on most platforms. Smoking is prohibited on U-Bahn platforms and on the trains themselves. Displays above the train doors show stations and connections, and a recorded voice announces stops and also connections to trams and buses. Signs indicate where prams can be stored by the doors. Bicycles are allowed on a few carriages, although not before 9am and between 3 and 6:30pm Mon–Fri. Be aware that doors are opened manually and can be stiff and heavy. The U-Bahn operates seven days a week from around 5pm to 12:30am. During the day, trains depart every 5 minutes or so, less frequently after about 8pm. A 24-hour service runs at weekends and public holidays. Outside these hours, the U-Bahn service is replaced by Vienna NightLine buses (see pp254–5). The U-Bahn's five colour-coded lines are U1, U2, U3, U4 & U6. Confusingly, there is no U5 line. The Vienna U-Bahn has been earmarked for extension as part of an ongoing city transport expansion project that is expected to run until 2019. This will involve constructing additional stations and new stretches of track – check the Wiener Linien website for updates (see p252).

Making a Journey by Underground

1 Look for your destination on a U-Bahn map. The five lines are distinguished by colour and number. Make a note of whether and where you need to change lines. Connections to other forms of transport are also shown.

2 Insert your ticket into the ticket-stamping machine in the direction of the arrow. Wait for the ping indicating that it is validated, and pass through the barrier. Follow the signs (with the number and colour of the line) to your platform.

3 On the platform, check the indicator boards for the direction and destination of the trains.

4 Stops along the line are shown on a plan in the train.

5 At your destination, follow *Ausgang* signs to reach street level.

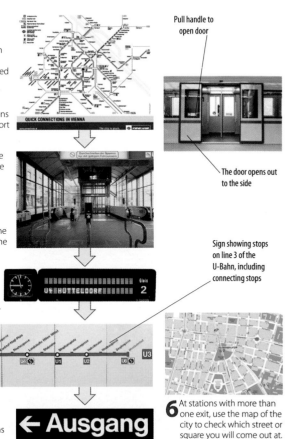

Pull handle to open door

The door opens out to the side

Sign showing stops on line 3 of the U-Bahn, including connecting stops

6 At stations with more than one exit, use the map of the city to check which street or square you will come out at.

Travelling by Tram, Bus and Train

Travelling on the tram, bus and train is a pleasant and easy way to get around Vienna. Trams are instantly recognizable with their red and white livery, and no visit to the city is complete without a nostalgic tram ride. Little hopper buses serve the city centre, while larger buses run from the inner suburbs, Ringstrasse and Prater to the outer suburbs. Popular with commuters, the Schnellbahn (S-Bahn) runs beyond the city limits to outer suburbs and further afield.

Trams

Vienna's tram network is one of the largest in the world, with over 28 routes. Known locally as "Bim" for its distinctive bell sound, it is a delightful way to get around the city. For the ultimate experience, seek out one of the old, traditional models with their wooden seats and vintage interiors.

Most of the main sights in Vienna's historic centre, such as the State Opera House, Imperial Palace, Parliament and Vienna City Hall, are located on the popular Ring Tram route. Passengers will need to purchase a Round-the-Ring ticket (€7) for a complete unbroken journey or a 24-hour Ring Tram ticket (€9) for a hop-on-hop-off service. On-board services include audio-visual information about highlights along the route, delivered via a multi-lingual multimedia system. Trams depart every 30 minutes all year round, from 10am–6pm.

All trams are equipped with seats for disabled travellers. However, the modern low-riding trams are a more wheelchair-friendly option. Look for vehicles with the ULF (Ultra Low Floor) sign.

Buses

Buses are comfortable, air-conditioned and equipped with CCTV. Bus stops are marked by a green "H" for *haltestelle* or stop. All stops display bus numbers, destinations, timetables and route maps. Buses should stop automatically on main routes but if you are in any doubt, flag it down. Tickets purchased from the driver will be valid for one bus journey only. If you have already purchased a ticket from a newsagent or ticket machine, you will need to validate it in the blue ticket-stamping machine on the bus. If you have already made part of your journey by tram or U-Bahn, there is no need to stamp your ticket again. Limited services run on holidays and Christmas Day. On New Year's Eve, buses and other forms of public transport run all night. All buses in Vienna are wheelchair-accessible.

Night Buses

Vienna's night bus service operates every night of the week starting at 12:30am and then at 30-minute intervals until 4am in the morning. There is some variation between the services operating on weekday nights (Sunday to Thursday) and those at weekends and on public holidays. Night buses are marked by the letter "N". All night buses in Vienna start from Schwedenplatz, the Opera and Schottentor, and run out to

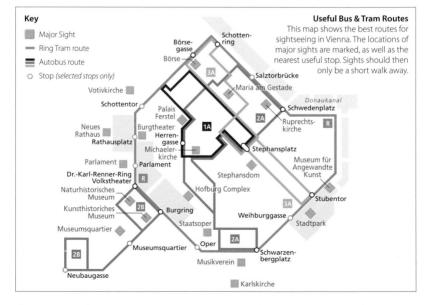

Key

- ◾ Major Sight
- ▬ Ring Tram route
- ▬ Autobus route
- ○ Stop *(selected stops only)*

Useful Bus & Tram Routes

This map shows the best routes for sightseeing in Vienna. The locations of major sights are marked, as well as the nearest useful stop. Sights should then only be a short walk away.

A typical Vienna city bus at Leopoldau bus station

most suburbs. Tickets can be purchased from the driver and all other pre-bought tickets and passes are valid. Passengers can pre-arrange a taxi to wait at the destination stop if they are staying some distance from a night bus route. A number for a local taxi firm can be obtained from the Transport Office in Schwedenplatz or from the Wiener Linien hotline (7909100).

Trains

Known colloquially as the S-Bahn, the Schnellbahn (Fast Train) is recognizable by its blue and white logo and is primarily a commuter service. A metropolitan route has stops in the centre of Vienna interconnecting with mainline stations *(see p249)* but is generally used as a means of getting farther afield. The local Bundesbahn is also a commuter service and is sometimes called the Regionalbahn on maps and timetables to distinguish it from national routes. Timetable information is available from station information offices and is displayed on departures/arrivals boards. When travelling within the city limits all public transport tickets and passes are valid on the Schnellbahn. For Schnellbahn journeys outside of Vienna a ticket must be purchased in advance. See the **Austrian Federal Railways** website for more information and a useful journey planner.

DIRECTORY

Austrian Federal Railways
W oebb.at

Wiener Linien
W wienerlinien.at

Travelling Beyond Vienna

Vienna is a great base from which to discover other parts of Austria as well as neighbouring European destinations. The historic cities of Salzburg, Innsbruck, Graz and Linz are well-served by public transport from the city, and car hire is a viable option to reach more rural areas.

Domestic Flights

Frequent domestic flights with **Austrian Airlines** link Vienna with Graz, Klagenfurt, Salzburg, Innsbruck and Linz. Air travel in Austria is expensive, however, and with the extra time needed for checking in, getting to and from the airport, and for retrieving your luggage, it is not always the fastest and most convenient way of getting to another destination within Austria.

Trains

Trains to the west and north of Austria depart from Westbahnhof, including hourly services to Salzburg. Routes from Franz-Josefs-Bahnhof station connect Vienna with Tulln, Krems an der Donau, and the Wachau region.

Hertz logo

Car Hire and Road Travel

Car rental is an option for excursions; expect to pay about €170 for a 3-day rental. The minimum age for hiring a car is 21 years. You'll need a driver's licence, a credit or debit card, passport and third-party insurance.

Boats

Boat trips regularly set off from Vienna along the Wachau Valley. Alternative trips in the other direction head to Bratislava (1 hour) and Budapest (4 hours). All ships have restaurants and sundecks.

A hydrofoil service (www.tragfluegelboot.at) runs from the DDSG–Blue Danube landing station at the Reichsbrücke bridge, connecting Vienna with Visegrad, Budapest and Bratislava. Return fares cost €38 for Vienna to Bratislava and €125 for Vienna to Budapest.

DIRECTORY

Domestic Flights

Austrian Airlines
W austrian.com

Car Hire

Avis City
Airport **Tel** 7007 32700.
W avis.at

Budget City
Airport **Tel** 7007 32700.
W budget.at

Europcar
Tel 7146717.
Airport **Tel** 7007 32812.
W europcar.at

Hertz City
Tel 5128677.
Airport **Tel** 7007 32661.
W hertz.at

STREET FINDER

The map references for all the sights, hotels, restaurants, bars, shops and entertainment venues described in this book refer to the maps in this section. A complete index of street names and all the places of interest marked on the maps can be found on the following pages. The key map *(right)* shows the area of Vienna covered by the *Street Finder*. This map includes sightseeing areas as well as districts for hotels, restaurants and entertainment venues.

All the street names in the index and on the *Street Finder* are in German – *Strasse* translating as street and *Gasse* meaning lane. *Platz* or *Hof* indicate squares or courtyards. Throughout this guide, the numbers of the houses follow the street names, in the same way that you will find them in Vienna.

View of Vienna's roof tops
from Am Hof *(see p89)*

Key to Street Finder

- ■ Major sight
- ■ Places of interest
- ■ Other building
- **U** U-Bahn station
- **S** Bundesbahn station
- **Ⓑ** Badner Bahn stop
- **Ⓢ** Schnellbahn station
- **𝒊** Tourist information office
- **✚** Hospital with casualty unit
- **🏛** Police station
- **✝** Church
- **✡** Synagogue
- — Railway line
- ▬ Pedestrian street

**Scale of Maps 1–4 &
5–6 respectively**

0 metres	250	
0 yards	250	1:14,000

0 metres	125	
0 yards	125	1:9,000

Section of the Austria fountain
(1846) by Schwanthaler (left)
and side view of the
Schottenkirche *(see p112)*

0 kilometres	1
0 miles	0.5

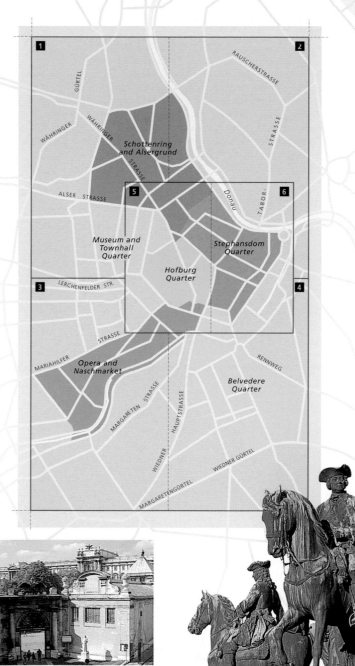

Gateway leading to the Burggarten from Albertinaplatz in the Hofburg Quarter

Generals on horseback guard the statue of Maria Theresa (1888) in Maria-Theresia-Platz, Museum and Townhall Quarter

Street Finder Index

Vienna's street and place names are generally spelt as one word; -platz, -strasse or -kirche are put at the end of the name, as in Essiggasse for example. Occasionally they are treated as separate words, for instance Alser Strasse. Abbreviations used in this index are Dr as in Doctor-Ignaz-Seipel-Platz, and St as in Sankt Josef Kirche. Some entries have two map references. The first refers to the smaller scale map that covers the whole of central Vienna, the second refers to the large-scale inset map that covers the Stephansdom and Hofburg Quarters.

Useful Words

Gasse	lane, alley
Strasse	road, street
Platz	square
Hof	court
Kirche	church
Kapelle	chapel
Dom	cathedral
Denkmal	monument
Markt	market
(often the sight of an old market)	
Brücke	bridge

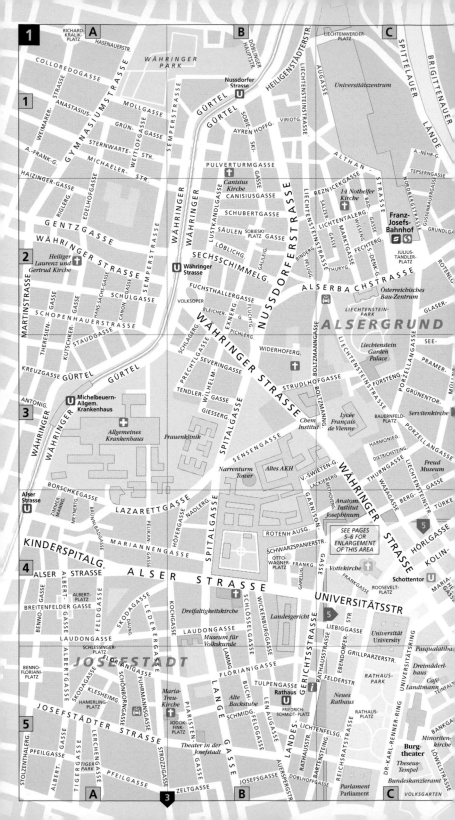

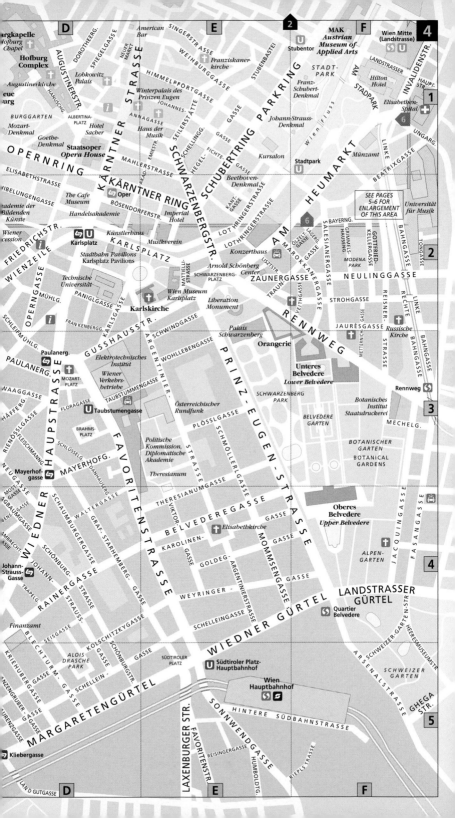

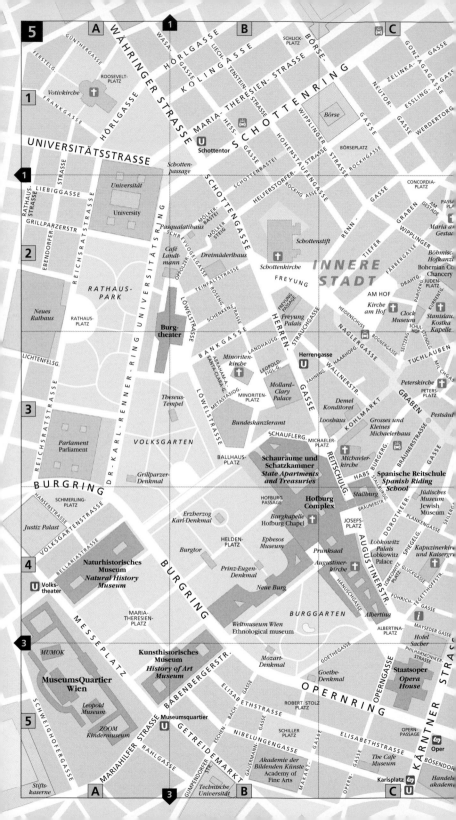

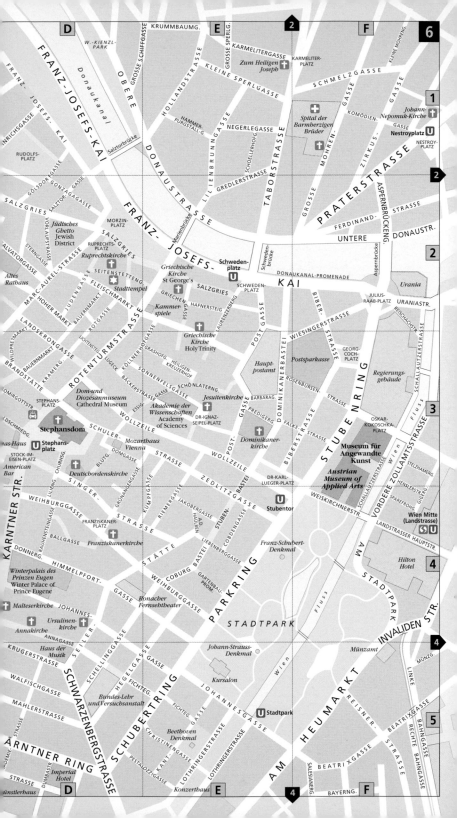

General Index

Acknowledgments

Dorling Kindersley wishes to thank the following people who contributed to the preparation of this book.

Main Contributor
Stephen Brook was born in London and educated at Cambridge. After working as an editor in Boston and London, he became a full-time writer in 1982. Among his books are *New York Days, New York Nights; The Double Eagle; Prague, L.A. Lore* and books on wine. He also writes articles on wine and travel for many newspapers and periodicals.

Additional Contributors
Gretel Beer, Rosemary Bircz, Caroline Bugler, Dierdre Coffey, Fred Mawer, Nicholas Parsons, Christian Williams, Sarah Woods.

Proof Reader
Diana Vowles.

Design and Editorial
Managing Editor Carolyn Ryden
Managing Art Editor Steve Knowlden
Senior Editor Georgina Matthews
Senior Art Editor Vanessa Courtier
Editorial Director David Lamb
Art Director Anne-Marie Bulat
Consultant Robert Avery
Language Consultant Barbara Eichberger

DTP
Vinod Harish, Vincent Kurian, Azeem Siddiqui.

Revisions Team
Louise Abbott, Ashwin Adimari, Emma Anacootee, Ros Angus, Claire Baranowski, Marta Bescos, Tessa Bindloss, Jane Edmonds, Gadi Farfour, Emer FitzGerald, Fay Franklin, Rhiannon Furbear, Camilla Gersh, Sally Gordon, Emily Green, Alistair Gunn, Swati Gupta, Elaine Harries, Melanie Hartzell, Mohammed Hassan, Paul Hines, Laura Jones, Priya Kukadia, Joanne Lenney, Carly Madden, Hayley Maher, Ella Milroy, Deepak Mittal, Sonal Modha, Kate Molan, Melanie Nicholson-Hartzell, Catherine Palmi, Helen Partington, Sangita Patel, Alice Peebles, Marianne Petrou, Robert Purnell, Rada Radojicic, Nicki Rawson, Sadie Smith, Sands Publishing Solutions, Simon Ryder, Andrew Szudek, Samia Tadros, Lynda Warrington, Susannah Wolley Dod, Johanna Wurm.

Additional Illustrations
Kevin Jones, Gilly Newman, John Woodcock, Martin Woodward.

Cartography
Uma Bhattacharya, Mohammad Hassan, Jasneet Kaur, Peter Winfield, James Mills-Hicks (Dorling Kindersley Cartography) Colourmap Scanning Limited, Contour Publishing, Cosmographics, European Map Graphics, Street Finder maps: ERA Maptec Ltd (Dublin).
Map Co-ordinators: Simon Farbrother, David Pugh
Cartographic Research: Jan Clark, Caroline Bowie, Claudine Zante.

Additional Photography
DK Studio/Steve Gorton, Ian O'Leary, Poppy, Rough Guides/ Natascha Sturny, Steve Shott, Clive Streeter, Daniel Wurm.

Fact Checkers
Dieter Löffler, Melanie Nicholson-Hartzell.

Special Assistance
Marion Telsnig and Ingrid Pollheimer-Stadtlober at the Austrian Tourist Board, London; Frau Preller at the Heeresgeschichtliches Museum; Frau Wegscheider at the Kunsthistorisches Museum; Frau Stillfried and Mag Czap at the Hofburg; Herr Fehli-nger at the Museen der Stadt Wien; Mag Schmid at the Natural History Museum; Mag Dvorak at the Österreischicher Bundestheaterverband; Dr Michael Krapf and Mag Grabner at the Österreichische Galerie; Robert Tidmarsh and Mag Weber-Kainz at Schloss Schönbrunn; Frau Zonschits at the Tourismusverband.

Photography Permissions
Dorling Kindersley would like to thank the following for their kind permission to photograph at their establishments:

Alte Backstube, Bestattungsmuseum, Schloss Belvedere, Bundesbaudirektion, Deutschordenskirche and Treasury, Dom und Diözesanmuseum, Sigmund Freud Gesellschaft, Josephinum Institut für Geschichte der Medzin der Universität Wien, Kapuzinerkirche, Pfarramt St. Karl, Stift Klosterneuburg, Wiener Kriminalmuseum, Niederösterreichisches Landesmuseum, Österreichischer Bundestheaterverband, Österreichische Postsparkasse (P. S. K.), Dombausekretariat Sankt Stephan, Spanische Reitschule and Museum für Volkskunde. Dorling Kindersley would also like to thank all the shops, restaurants, cafés, hotels, churches and public services who aided us with photography. These are too numerous to thank individually.

Picture Credits
a = above; b = below/bottom; c = centre; f = far;
l = left; r = right; t = top.

Works of art have been reproduced with the permission of the following copyright holders: *Brunnenhaus* Ernst Fuchs © DACS, London 2011; *The Tiger Lion* 1926 Oskar Kokoschka © DACS, London 2011 157t; © **The Henry Moore Foundation:** 146bl.

The Publishers are grateful to the following individuals, companies and picture libraries for permission to reproduce their photographs:

4corners Images: Damm Stefan 11br; **Alamy Images:** David Coleman 238cra; Christopher Gannon 250cla; imagebroker/ Christian Handl 205tl; INSADCO: Photography/ Martin Bobrovsky 205c; John Kellerman 108; Art Kowalsky 10cla; John Lens 178cr; LOOK Die Bildagentur der Fotografen GmbH 12tr; Barry Mason 207c; mediacolor's 178 cla, 206cla; David Noble 207tl; Robert Harding Picture Library Ltd/ Richard Nebesky 204cla; Jack Sullivan 241cla; vario images/ Stefan Kiefer 245tr, 251crb; vario images/ Thomas Jantzen 245bc; Ken Welsh 10bc; **Graphic Sammlung Albertina,** Wien: 28–9; **Ancient Art and Architecture Collection:** 26b(d), 27tc, 31cra; **Akg-Images:** 18(d), 21tc(d), 21br(d), 23bc, 24–5, 26cla, 26–7, 27cb, 27bl, 28cla, 28br(d), 29tc, 30cl, 30br(d), 31tc, 30–31, 30cl, 31bl, 32cl, 34cl, 34br, 35bc, 36br, 38tl, 40bl, 57br(d), 89b(d), 100cl, 112br(d), 149cra, 154clb, 174bl, 237 inset; Erich Lessing 11tl, 40clb, 41crb; **Hotel Am Parkring:** 196bc; **Austrian Archives:** 37tl; **Austrian Telekom:** 244cla

Bank Austria. UniCredit Bank Austria AG: 242bl; **Hotel Beethoven GmbH & Co KG:** 198bc; **Belvedere, Vienna:** 158br;

Thomas Preiss 159cra; **Bildarchiv Preussischer Kulturbesitz**, Berlin: 25bl, 37cb, 94tr; **Casa Editrice Bonechi**, Firenze: 169cra; **Christian Brandstätter Verlag**, Wien: 22ca, 33crb(d), 35tl, 36bl, 85tc, 101c; **Bridgeman Art Library**, London: 135bl(d); Albertina, Wien 48br; Bonhams, London 26cl; British Library, London 4t(d), 21bl(d); Kunsthistorisches Museum, Wien 21tr(d), 48cl; Museum der Stadt Wien 35tr, 40cr(d), 40clb, 41cl; Österreichische Galerie 37tc; **Hotel Bristol**: 192cra, 217br; ©1999 Bundesgärten, Wien: 174cl; Bundesministerium Für Finanzen: 29cb(d); Burghauptmannschaft In Wien: 103ca, 103crb, 103br.

Courtesy Of **Café Museum**: 60br; **CaffèCouture**: 214bl; **Archäologischer Park Carnuntum**: 23tc; **Casinos Austria**: 227cra; **Cephas Picture Library**: Mick Rock 163br, 208tr; Wine Magazine 240br; **Citybike Wien**: 251tl; **Contrast Photo**: Milenko Badzic 67ca; Franz Hausner 170crb; Michael Himml/ Transglobe 154tr; Hinterleitner 227br; Peter Kurz 65b, 141tl, 233br; Boris Mizaikoff/Transglobe 65cra; Tappeiner/Transglobe 234c; H Valencak 180b; **Corbis**: 8-9; Rudy Sulgan 160. **DK Images**: Courtesy of Schloss Schonbrunn, Vienna 13br; **Do & Co Hotel**: 197tl, 212tl; **Dreamstime.com**: Amoklv 144; Andreykr 90; David Bailey 12bc; Goran Bogicevic 70; Gunold Brunbauer 182; Chaoss 2-3; Digitalpress 236-7; Ginasanders 114; Sergey Pushkarev 68-9; Tupungato 42; Yarchyk 190-1; Robert Zehetmayer 136; **Café-Restaurant Dunkelbunt**: 200cr; **Et Archive**, London: 40br; Museum für Gestaltung, Zurich 36cl; Museum der Stadt Wien 28bc, 33tl, 40ca; **Eurolines**: 248tr; **European Commission**: 243; **Mary Evans Picture Library**, London: 20cla, 20bl, 20crb, 21tl, 24c, 27br, 29br, 32ca, 32bl, 32br, 37br, 41t, 74tr, 177b.

F. A. Herbig Verlagsbuchhandlung GmbH, München: 100bl, 100br, 101bl, 101br. **FAXI Das Fahrradtaxi**: 252tl; **Robert Harding Picture Library**: Larsen Collinge International 44clb, 234tl; Adam Woolfitt 64cra, 139cra, 152tl, 180cla; **Heeresgeschichtliches Museum**, Wien: 49br, 168cla, 168bl, 169tc, 169br; **Hertz**: 255cb; **Historisches Museum Der Stadt Wien**: 19b, 23ca, 23crb, 30crb, 34cb, 34bl, 35cla, 35crb, 45tr, 49tl, 51cl, 141cra, 141tr, 147ca, 171tl; **Hollmann Beletage, Vienna**: 193t; **Hulton-Deutsch Collection**: 30bl, 38tr(d), 40br(d), 170cla; **The Hutchison Library**: 202tl; **The Image Bank, London**: Fotoworld 43bl; **Hotel Imperial**: 192br. **Josefstadt Theatre**: 226cl. **Wilhelm Klein**: 25tl, 28clb; **Kunsthaus Wien**: Peter Strobel 50tr; **Kunsthistorisches Museum**, Wien: 26cb, 43crb, 48tr, 50bl, 58cl, 97tc, 97bc, 101t, 102 all, 124–5 all, 126–7 all, 128–9 all, 177tc.

J & L Lobmeyr, Wien: 51tr; **Leopold Museum-Privatstiftung**: *Selbstbildnis*, 1910, by Egon Schiele 48bla, *Hockender Weiblicher Akt*, 1910, by Egon Schiele 122tr, *Self Portrait with Chinese Lantern*, 1912, by Egon Schiele 120tr, *Die Schnitter*, 1922 by Egger-Lienz 122t; **Lonely Planet Images**: Richard Nebesky 233tl; **Magnum Photos**: Erich Lessing 20tr, 22cl, 22bl, 22br, 23tl, 23clb, 24clb, 25ca, 28c, 31br, 32–3, 33b; **Restaurant Motto**: 203br, 219b; **Cafe Restaurant Mozart bei der Opera GsmbH**: 201t, 213br; **Museum Judenplatz**: Votava/PID 88tl;

Museumsquartier, Errichtungs-und Betriebsgesmbh: Lisi Gradnitzer 120br; Rupert Steiner MQ E+B GesmbH 43br, 121tl, Martin Gendt MQ E+B GesmbH 121bl; MUMOK, **Museum Of Modern Art Ludwig Foundation Vienna**: *Homme accroupi*, 1907, by André Derain, © ADAGP, Paris & DACS, London 2011, 121br; *The Red Horseman*, 1974 by Roy Lichtenstein, © Estate of Roy Lichtenstein/DACS, London 2011, 122bl. **Narodni Museum**, Praha: 20br; **Naturhistorisches Museum**, Wien: 48cla, 130–31 except 131br, 235c.

ÖBB-Personenverkehr AG: 248bl; Österreichische Galerie, Wien: 49crb, 156clb, 157 all, 158bl, 159br; Österreichisches Museum Für Angewandte Kunst, Wien: 30cla, 49cra, 58tr, 59clb, 84–5 all except 85t; Österreichische Nationalbibliothek, Wien: 22crb, 25crb, 38cb; Österreich Werbung: 5cl, 29cra, 33tc, 33cra, 36ca, 46bl, 100cbl, 103tc, 140br, 165cr, 165bl, 174t, 181cl, 232cra. Photolibrary: Merten Merten 159tl; Popperfoto: 39tc; Raiffeisenbank Wien: Gerald Zugman 36ca; Manya Rathmore 153br; Restaurant at Eight: 202b, 212br; Retrograph Archive, London: Martin Ranicar-Breese 193clb; Rex Features, London: Action Press 38bc, Adolfo Franzo 39tl, Sokol/Sipa Press 123crb; GEORG RIHA: 75t; Ronacher Variety Theatre/CMM: Velo Weger 226t.

Café Sacher: 201br, 216br; Hotel Sacher: 195tr, 199br; Hotel Sans Souci: 194tl, 198tl; Schloss Schönbrunn Kultur-und Betriebsges Mbh, Wien: Professor Gerhard Trumler 174cl, 175 all except 175b, 176 all, 177tr; Schloss Schönbrunn Kultur-und Betriebsges MBH 1999: Wolfgang Voglhuber 143br; Cafe Sperl: 216tc; SYGMA: Habans/ Orban 39tr, Viennareport 39ca; Surfland Internetcafe: 244crb; Travel Library: Philip Entiknapp 221tr. Restaurant Vestibül: 203tr, 215tl; Vienna Airport: 246cla, 247tl, 247bl; Vienna Police: 240bl, 241tl; Vienna Tourist Board: 238bl; Viennaslide: Harald A Jahn 232bc; Karl Luymair 232cla; Museum Für Völkerkunde, Wien: 51br, 235bc; Votava, Wien: 165tc; Werner Forman Archive: Museum der Stadt Wien 62c; St Stephens Cathedral Museum 25cr; Wiener Linien GmbH & Co KG: 25cr, 253c, 253c, 253cb, 253br, 255tl; Wien Museum: 88br, Longcase Clock c.1762-69 David A.S. Cajetano 88cb; Wiener Sängerknaben: 5cr, 41br, 66bl; Wiener Stadt- Und Landesbibliothek, Wien: 38ca, 38bl; Wigast AG: 194br. ZEFA: 155c; Anatol 100–1; G Gro-Bauer 181tr; Havlicek 179cr; Sibelberbauer 64bl; Streichan 39bl; V Wentzel 43cb. Zoom Kindermuseum: Alexandra Eizinger 120cla.

Front Endpaper- **Alamy Images**: John Kellerman Rtc; **Dreamstime.com**: Amoklv Rbr; Andreykr Rcr; Goran Bogicevic Rtr; Ginasanders Lcl; Robert Zehetmayer Lbl;

Map Cover - **Superstock**: Lucas Vallecillos/age fotostock.

Jacket: Front and spine - **Superstock**: Lucas Vallecillos/ age fotostock.

All other images © Dorling Kindersley. For further information see: www.dkimages.com

Phrase Book

In Emergency

Help!	**Hilfe!**	hilf-er
Stop!	**Halt!**	hult
Call a doctor	**Holen Sie einen Arzt**	hole'n zee ine'n artst
Call an ambulance	**Holen Sie einen Krankenwagen**	hole'n zee ine'n krank'n-varg'n
Call the police	**Holen Sie die Polizei**	hole'n zee dee pol-its-eye
Call the fire brigade	**Holen Sie die Feuerwehr**	hole'n zee dee foy-er-vair
Where is the nearest telephone?	**Wo finde ich ein Telefon in der Nähe?**	voh fin-der ish ine tel-e-fone in dair nay-er?
Where is the nearest hospital?	**Wo ist das nächstgelegene Krankenhaus?**	voh ist duss next-g'lay-g'ner krunk'n-hows?

Communication Essentials

Yes	**Ja**	yah
No	**Nein**	nine
Please	**Bitte**	bitt-er
Thank you	**Danke vielmals**	dunk-er feel-malse
Excuse me	**Gestatten**	g'shtatt'n
Hello	**Grüss Gott**	groos got
Goodbye	**Auf Wiedersehen**	owf veed-er-zay-ern
Goodnight	**Gute Nacht**	goot-er nukht
morning	**Vormittag**	for-mit-targ
afternoon	**Nachmittag**	nakh-mit-targ
evening	**Abend**	ah'b'nt
yesterday	**Gestern**	gest'n
today	**Heute**	hoyt-er
tomorrow	**Morgen**	morg'n
here	**hier**	hear
there	**dort**	dort
What?	**Was?**	vuss?
When?	**Wann?**	vunn?
Why?	**Warum?**	var-room?
Where?	**Wo/Wohin?**	voh/vo-hin?

Useful Phrases

How are you?	**Wie geht es Ihnen?**	vee gayt ess een'n?
Very well, thank you	**Sehr gut, danke**	zair goot, dunk-er
Pleased to meet you	**Es freut mich sehr, Sie kennenzulernen**	ess froyt mish zair, zee ken'n-tsoo-lairn'n
See you soon	**Bis bald/bis gleich**	bis bult/bis gleyesh
That's fine	**Sehr gut**	zair goot
Where is…?	**Wo befindet sich…?**	voe b'find't zish…?
Where are…?	**Wo befinden sich…?**	voe b'find'n zish…?
How far is it to…?	**Wie weit ist…?**	vee vite ist…?
Which way to…?	**Wie komme ich zu…?**	vee komma ish tsoo…?
Do you speak English?	**Sprechen Sie englisch?**	shpresh'n zee eng-glish?
I don't understand	**Ich verstehe nicht**	ish fair-shtay-er nisht
Could you please speak slowly?	**Bitte sprechen Sie etwas langsamer?**	bitt-er shpresh'n zee et-vuss lung-zam-er?
I'm sorry	**Es tut mir leid/ Verzeihung**	es toot meer lyte/ fair-tseye-oong

Useful Words

big	**gross**	grohss
small	**klein**	kline
hot	**heiss**	hyce
cold	**kalt**	kult
good	**gut**	goot
bad	**schlecht**	shlesht
enough	**genug**	g'nook
well	**gut**	goot
open	**auf/offen**	owf/off'n
closed	**zu/geschlossen**	tsoo/g'shloss'n
left	**links**	links
right	**rechts**	reshts
straight on	**geradeaus**	g'rah-der-owss
near	**in der Nähe**	in dair nay-er
far	**weit**	vyte
up	**auf, oben**	owf, obe'n
down	**ab, unten**	up, oont'n
early	**früh**	froo
late	**spät**	shpate

entrance	**Eingang/Einfahrt**	ine-gung/ine-fart
exit	**Ausgang/Ausfahrt**	ows-gung/ows-fart
toilet	**WC/Toilette**	vay-say/toy-lett-er
free/unoccupied	**frei**	fry
free/no charge	**frei/gratis**	fry/grah-tis

Making a Telephone Call

I'd like to place a long-distance call	**Ich möchte ein Ferngespräch machen**	ish mer-shter ine fairn-g'shpresh mukh'n
I'd like to call collect	**Ich möchte ein Rückgespräch (Collectgespräch) machen**	ish mer-shter ine rook-g'shpresh (coll-ect-g'shpresh) mukh'n
local call	**Ortsgespräch**	orts-g'shpresh
I'll try again later	**Ich versuche es noch einmal etwas später**	ish fair-zookh-er ess nokh ine-mull ett-vuss shpay-ter
Can I leave a message?	**Kann ich etwas ausrichten?**	kunn ish ett-vuss ows-rikht'n?
Hold on	**Haben Sie etwas Geduld**	harb'n zee ett-vuss g'doolt
Could you speak up a little please?	**Bitte sprechen Sie etwas lauter?**	bitt-er shpresh'n zee ett-vuss lowt-er?

Staying in a Hotel

Do you have a vacant room?	**Haben Sie ein Zimmer frei?**	harb'n zee ine tsimm-er fry?
double room with double bed	**ein Doppelzimmer mit Doppelbett**	ine dopp'l-tsimm-er mitt dopp'l-bet
twin room	**ein Doppelzimmer**	ine dopp'l-tsimm-er
single room	**ein Einzelzimmer**	ine ine-ts'l-tsimm-er
room with a bath/shower	**Zimmer mit Bad/Dusche**	tsimm-er mitt bart boosh-er
porter	**Gepäckträger/ Concierge**	g'peck-tray-ger/ kon-see-airsh
key	**Schlüssel**	shloss'l
I have a reservation	**Ich habe ein Zimmer reserviert**	ish harb-er ine tsimm-er rezz-er-veert

Sightseeing

bus	**der Bus**	dair booss
tram	**die Strassenbahn**	dee stra-sen-barn
train	**der Zug**	dair tsoog
art gallery	**Galerie**	gall-er-ee
bus station	**Busbahnhof**	booss-barn-hofe
bus (tram) stop	**die Haltestelle**	dee hal-te-shtel-er
castle	**Schloss, Burg**	shloss, boorg
palace	**Schloss, Palais**	shloss, pall-ay
post office	**das Postamt**	dee pohs-taamt
cathedral	**Dom**	dome
church	**Kirche**	keersh-er
garden	**Garten, Park**	gart'n, park
library	**Bibliothek**	bib-leo-tek
museum	**Museum**	moo-zay-oom
information (office)	**Information (-sbüro)**	in-for-mut-see-on (-zboo-roe)
closed for public holiday	**Feiertags geschlossen**	fire-targz g'shloss'n

Shopping

How much does this cost?	**Wieviel kostet das?**	vee-feel kost't duss?
I would like…	**Ich hätte gern…**	ish hett-er gairn…
Do you have…?	**Haben Sie…?**	harb'n zee…?
I'm just looking	**Ich schaue nur an**	ish shau-er noor un
Do you take credit cards?	**Kann ich mit einer Kreditkarte bezahlen?**	kunn ish mitt ine-er kred-it-kar-ter b'tsahl'n?
What time do you open?	**Wann machen Sie auf?**	vunn mukh'n zee owf?
What time do you close?	**Wann schliessen Sie?**	vunn shlees'n zee?
This one	**dieses**	deez'z
expensive	**teuer**	toy-er
cheap	**billig**	bill-igg
size	**Grösse**	grers-er
white	**weiss**	vyce
black	**schwarz**	shvarts
red	**rot**	roht
yellow	**gelb**	gelp
green	**grün**	groon
blue	**blau**	blau

Types of Shop

antique shop	Antiquitäten-geschäft	un-tick-vi-**tayt'**n-g'sheft
bakery	Bäckerei	beck-er-**eye**
bank	Bank	bunk
book shop	Buchladen/Buchhandlung	bookh-lard/n/ bookh-hant-loong
butcher	Fleischerei	fly-sher-**eye**
cake shop	Konditorei	kon-ditt-or-**eye**
chemist		
(for prescriptions)	Apotheke	App-o-**tay**-ker
(for cosmetics)	Drogerie	droog-er-**ree**
department store	Warenhaus, Warengeschäft	vahr'n-hows, vahr'n-g'sheft
delicatessen	Feinkost (geschäft)	fine-kost (g'sheft)
fishmonger	Fischgeschäft	fish-g'sheft
gift shop	Geschenke(laden)	g'shenk-er(lahd'n)
greengrocer	Obst und Gemüse	ohbst oont g'moo-zer
grocery	Lebensmittel-geschäft	layb'nz-mitt'l-g'sheft
hairdresser	Friseur/Frisör	freezz-**er**/freezz-**er**
market	Markt	markt
newsagent/tobacconist	Tabak Trafik	tab-**ack** tra-feek
travel agent	Reisebüro	rye-**z**er-boo-roe
café	Cafe, Kaffeehaus	kaff-**ay**, kaff-**ay**-hows

Eating Out

Have you got a table for… people?	Haben Sie einen Tisch für… Personen?	harb'n zee ine'n tish foor… pair-**sohn**'n?
I want to reserve a table	Ich möchte einen Tisch bestellen	ish **mer**-shter ine'n tish b'**shtell**'n
The bill please	Zahlen, bitte	tsarl'n **bitt**-er
I am a vegetarian	Ich bin Vegetarier	ish bin vegg-er-**tah**-ree-er
Waitress/waiter	Fräulein/Herr Ober	froy-line/hair**oh**-bare
menu	die Speisekarte	dee **shpize**-er-kart-er
fixed price menu	das Menü	duss men-**oo**
cover charge	Couvert/Gedeck	koo-**vair**/g'**deck**
wine list	Weinkarte	**vine**-kart-er
glass	Glas	glars
bottle	Flasche	flush-er
knife	Messer	mess-er
fork	Gabel	garb'l
spoon	Löffel	lerff'l
breakfast	Frühstück	froo-shtook
lunch	Mittagessen	mit-targ-ess'n
dinner	Abendessen/Dinner	arb'nt-ess'n/ dee-**nay**
main course	Hauptspeise	howpt-shpize-er
starter, first course	Vorspeise	for-shpize-er
dish of the day	Tageskarte	targ-erz-kart-er
wine garden(s)	Heuriger (Heurige)	hoy-rigg-er (-e)
rare	englisch	eng-glish
medium	medium	may-dee-oom
well done	durch	doorsh

Menu Decoder

See also pp 202–9

Apfel	upf'l	apple
Almdudler	ahlm-dood-ler	herbal lemonade
Banane	bar-nar-ner	banana
Ei	eye	egg
Eis	ice	ice cream
Fisch	fish	fish
Fisolen	fee-soul'n	green beans (haricot)
Fleisch	flysh	meat
Garnelen	gar-nayl'n	prawns
gebacken	g'buck'n	baked/fried
gebraten	g'brart'n	roast
gekocht	g'kokht	boiled
Gemüse	g'mooz-er	vegetables
vom Grill	fom grill	grilled
Gulasch	goo-lush	stew
Hendl/Hahn/Huhn	hend'l/harn/hoon	chicken
Kaffee	kaf-fay	coffee
Kartoffel/Erdäpfel	kar-toff'l/air-dupf'l	potatoes
Käse	kayz-er	cheese
Knoblauch	k'nob-lowkh	garlic
Knödel	k'nerd'l	dumpling
Kotelett	kot-lett	chop
Lamm	lumm	lamb
Marillen	mah-ril'n	apricot
Meeresfrüchte	mair-erz-froosh-ter	seafood

Mehlspeise	mayl-shpize-er	dessert
Milch	milhk	milk
Mineralwasser	minn-er-**arl**-vuss-er	mineral water
Obst	ohbst	fresh fruit
Öl	erl	oil
Oliven	o-**leev**'n	olives
Orange	o-ronsh-er	orange
frischgepresster Orangensaft	frish-g'press-ter o-ronsh'n-zuft	fresh orange juice
Paradeissalat	pa-ra-**dice**-sa-lahd	tomato salad
Pfeffer	pfeff-er	pepper
pochiert	posh-eert	poached
Pommes frites	pomm-**fritt**	chips
Reis	rice	rice
Rind	rint	beef
Rostbraten	rohst-**brart**'n	steak
Rotwein	roht-vine	red wine
Salz	zults	salt
Sauce/Saft	zohss-er/zuft	sauce
Schalentiere	sharl'n-tee-rer	shellfish
Schinken/Speck	shink'n/shpeck	ham
Schlag	shlahgg	cream
Schnecken	shnek'n	snails
Schokolade	shock-o-**lard**-er	chocolate
Schwein	shvine	pork
Semmel	zem'l	roll
Senf	zenf	mustard
Serviettenknödel	ser-vee-**ert**'n-k'nerd'l	sliced dumpling
Sulz	zoolts	brawn
Suppe	**zoop**-er	soup
Tee	tay	tea
Topfenkuchen	topf'n-**kookh**'n	cheesecake
Torte	tort-er	cake
Wasser	**vuss**-er	water
Weinessig	vine-ess-igg	vinegar
Weisswein	vyce-vine	white wine
Wurst	voorst	sausage (fresh)
Zucker	tsook-er	sugar
Zwetschge	tsvertsh-ger	plum
Zwiebel	tsveeb'l	onions

Numbers

0	null	nool
1	eins	eye'ns
2	zwei	tsvy
3	drei	dry
4	vier	feer
5	fünf	foonf
6	sechs	zex
7	sieben	zeeb'n
8	acht	uhkht
9	neun	noyn
10	zehn	tsayn
11	elf	elf
12	zwölf	tsverlf
13	dreizehn	dry-tsayn
14	vierzehn	feer-tsayn
15	fünfzehn	foonf-tsayn
16	sechszehn	zex-tsayn
17	siebzehn	zeep-tsayn
18	achtzehn	uhkht-tsayn
19	neunzehn	noyn-tsayn
20	zwanzig	tsvunn-tsig
21	einundzwanzig	ine-oont-tsvunn-tsig
22	zweiundzwanzig	tsvy-oont-tsvunn-tsig
30	dreissig	dry-sig
40	vierzig	feer-tsig
50	fünfzig	foonf-tsig
60	sechzig	zesh-tsig
70	siebzig	zeep-tsig
80	achtzig	uhkht-tsig
90	neunzig	noyn-tsig
100	einhundert	ine **hoond**'t
1000	eintausend	ine **towz**'nt

Time

one minute	eine Minute	ine-er min-**oot**-er
one hour	eine Stunde	ine-er shtoond-er
half an hour	eine halbe Stunde	ine-er hull-ber shtoond-er
Monday	Montag	mone-targ
Tuesday	Dienstag	deen-starg
Wednesday	Mittwoch	mitt-vokh
Thursday	Donnerstag	donn-er-starg
Friday	Freitag	fry-targ
Saturday	Samstag	zum-starg
Sunday	Sonntag	zon-targ

Vienna transport network

There are five U-Bahn lines running across the city, each identified by a number. The Schnellbahn is essentially a commuter service. Bundesbahn trains to the rest of Austria and Europe run from Vienna's mainline stations. The Badner Bahn operates between its terminal opposite the Opera, and Baden. For more details, see *Getting Around Vienna* on pages 250–55.

Key

- U1
- U2
- U3
- U4
- U6
- Schnellbahn line
- Badner Bahn line
- ○ Interchange
- Bundesbahn station
- CAT (City Aiport Train)
- Schnellbahn terminus
- Bus station
- Major sight

Oberdöbling

Krottenbachstrasse

WÄHRING

Nussdorfe Strass

Gersthof

WÄHRINGER STRASSE

Währinger Strasse Volksoper

Hernals

HERNALSER HAUPTSTRASSE

Michelbeuern Allgem. Krankenhaus

WATGASSE

Alser Strasse

JOSEFST

Ottakring

OTTAKRING

Josefstädter Strasse

WIENER GÜRTEL BUNDESSTRASSE

Thaliastrasse

Kendlerstrasse

KOPPSTRASSE

NEUBAU

Burggasse - Stadthalle

FLÖTZERSTEIG STRASSE

S45

MARIAHIL

Hüttledorfer Strasse

Neubau-gasse

Johnstrasse

Westbahnhof

S50

MARIAHILER

Breitensee

Schweglerstrasse

Ziegler-gasse

HÜTTELDORFER STRASSE

S45, S50, S60

S45, S50

S50

Penzing

U4 Hütteldorf

Unter Sankt Veit

Gumpendorfer Strasse

Pilg

Braunschweiggasse

WIENER BUNDESSTRASSE

Margareten-gürtel

Hietzing

WIENER BUNDESSTRASSE

Schönbrunn

MA

Längenfeldgasse

Eichenstras

S60

LAINZER STRASSE

Schloss Schönbrunn

Meidling Hauptstrasse

Niederhofstrasse

Wolfganggasse

BRUNNER-BUNDESSTRASSE

S1, S2

SCHÖNBRUNNER SCHLOSSPARK

Speising

MEIDLING

Meidling/ Philadelphiabrücke

S1, S2, S3

S80

Hetzendorf

S60

U6 Siebenhirten